BETWEEN SYSTEM AND POETICS

This is the first book-length examination of the work of an important contemporary thinker in the continental tradition, William Desmond. His thought is a new, post-modern way of articulating what he calls the 'between'. Rooted in Plato and Augustine, and advancing through a confrontation with Hegel and Nietzsche, Desmond rejects facile scepticism and wins through to a strikingly original and powerfully searching articulation of the human. The present volume contains essays on Desmond's work both by emerging scholars and by well-established thinkers. It also contains a specially written essay on the practices of philosophy by Desmond himself.

William Desmond

Between System and Poetics

William Desmond and Philosophy after Dialectic

Edited by
THOMAS A.F. KELLY
National University of Ireland, Maynooth

ASHGATE

Published by
Ashgate Publishing Limited
Gower House
Croft Road
Aldershot
Hants GU11 3HR
England

Ashgate Publishing Company
Suite 420
101 Cherry Street
Burlington, VT 05401-4405
USA

Ashgate website: http://www.ashgate.com

British Library Cataloguing in Publication Data
Between system and poetics: William Desmond and philosophy after dialectic
    1. Desmond, William, 1951–
    I. Kelly, Thomas A.F. (Thomas Augustine Francis)
    192

Library of Congress Cataloging-in-Publication Data
Between system and poetics: William Desmond and philosophy after dialectic / Thomas A.F. Kelly, editor.
        p. cm.
    Includes bibliographical references and index.
    ISBN 0–7546–5206–8 (hardcover: alk. paper)
    1. Desmond, William, 1951– I. Kelly, Thomas A.F. (Thomas Augustine Francis)

    B1626.D47B48 2005
    192—dc22

                                                                2005000661

ISBN-13: 978-0-7546-5206-9

Typeset by Express Typesetters, Farnham, Surrey.
Printed and bound in Great Britain by MPG Books Ltd, Bodmin, Cornwall.

Contents

Notes on Contributors

Garrett Barden was born in Dublin in 1939, and has taught in France, Iceland, Ireland, Slovakia and the US before retiring to Tallow, a village in County Waterford, Ireland, where he now lives and writes on the philosophy of law and religion. His *After Principles* was published by Notre Dame, and *Essays in a Philosophical Theory of Justice: the Virtue of Justice* by Mellen.

Jason J. Howard is an Assistant Professor of Philosophy at Viterbo University, Wisconsin. He has published on Kant and Hegel, and was a doctoral student of William Desmond. His major areas of expertise are German Idealism and ethics.

John Hymers earned his doctorate at the Catholic University of Leuven, on the Ontological Argument, under William Desmond, for whom he was also an assistant. He has published on Just War theory, St. Anselm, Hegel, Feuerbach, P. Singer and P. Sloterdijk, among others. He is an academic translator and has worked on architectural publications. He is currently completing the translation of a book on Schopenhauer's aesthetics.

Richard Kearney holds the Charles B. Seelig Chair of Philosophy at Boston College and has served as a Visiting Professor at University College Dublin, the University of Paris (Sorbonne) and the University of Nice. He is the author of over 20 books on European philosophy and literature (as well as two novels and a volume of poetry) and has edited or co-edited 15 more. His most recent work in philosophy comprises a trilogy entitled *Philosophy at the Limit*. The three volumes are *On Stories, The God Who May Be* and *Strangers, Gods and Monsters*.

Thomas A.F. Kelly is Senior Lecturer in the Faculty of Philosophy of the National University of Ireland, Maynooth. He is a native of Dublin and was educated at University College Dublin, Trinity College Dublin and the University of Fribourg, Switzerland, from which he holds a doctorate, *summa cum laude*. His research interests include ontology, philosophical theology and anthropology. Among his publications are the books, *Language and Transcendence: A Study in the Philosophy of Martin Heidegger and Karl-Otto Apel* and *Language, World and God: An Essay in Ontology*.

Ian Leask is a lecturer in philosophy at the Mater Dei Institute, Dublin. He is the author of *Questions of Platonism* and of numerous articles on ancient philosophy and contemporary continental philosophy. He is also joint editor of the collection, *Givenness and God: Questions of Jean-Luc Marion*.

James McGuirk is a graduate of the National University of Ireland, Maynooth and the Catholic University of Leuven, Belgium. Having completed Bachelor's and Master's degrees at NUIM, he enrolled in the doctoral programme at the Catholic University of Leuven, where he defended a doctoral thesis entitled 'Eros and the Indictment of Philosphy' in December 2004. He taught at the Faculty of Philosophy at NUIM between 2001 and 2003, and is the author of several journal articles on the philosophy of Plato. His current research interests include hermeneutics, aesthetics, Greek philosophy and phenomenology – particularly Heidegger and Lévinas. He is currently living in Norway.

James L. Marsh is a Professor of Philosophy at Fordham, and teaches and writes in the areas of phenomonology, hermeneutics, Marx and critical theory. He has published seven books, including *Process, Praxis and Transcendence* and *Unjust Legality: A Critique of Habermas's Philosophy of Law*.

John Milbank is Research Professor of Religion, Politics and Ethics at the University of Nottingham. He previously taught at the universities of Lancaster, Cambridge and Virginia and is the author of *Theology and Social Theory* and *The Suspended Middle* amongst other titles.

Duston Moore completed his doctoral dissertation under the direction of William Desmond at the Institute of Philosophy of the Catholic University of Leuven, where he also earned his Bachelor's and Master's in philosophy, as well as a Bachelor's degree in theology. Currently he is Assistant Professor of Philosophy at Indiana University-Purdue University Fort Wayne (IPFW). He is also the Associate Director of the IPFW Institute for Human Rights, and has published on Whitehead, Marcuse and Plato.

Cyril O'Regan is Huisking Professor of Theology at the University of Notre Dame. He works in systematic theology, continental philosophy and their intersection. He is the author of *The Heterodox Hegel, Gnostic Return in Modernity* and *Gnostic Apocalypse: Jacob Boehme's Haunted Narrative*. He is currently working on a multi-volume project on Gnostic trends in modern discourse, and also on a two-volume work on the theologian, Hans Urs von Balthasar.

Catherine J.C. Pickstock is a Senior Lecturer in Philosophy of Religion at Cambridge University, and Fellow and Tutor at Emmanuel College, Cambridge. She is author of *After Writing: on the Liturgical Consummation of Philosophy* and co-author, with John Milbank, of *Truth in Aquinas*.

Renée Ryan is currently a PhD candidate, working under the supervision of William Desmond at the Institute of Philosophy of the Catholic University of Leuven. Her dissertation, in which Saint Augustine plays a pivotal role, is an exploration of the nature of sacred space. She is an academic assistant at the Institute of Philosophy, and an adjunct instructor at the Rome campus of the Thomas More College of Liberal Arts.

Peter Scheers holds graduate degrees in philosophy (Leuven), international politics (Antwerp) and values and the environment (Lancaster). He obtained a PhD in philosophy from the Free University, Amsterdam. He is predominantly concerned with the issues of perfective axiology and environmental perfectionism. Main publication: *Towards a Complex Perfectionism*.

Christopher Ben Simpson is currently finishing his studies at the University of Iowa where he is writing on Desmond's thought, particularly in relation to the question of God and postmodernity. He studied with Desmond in Leuven as a US Fulbright Scholar in 2003–4.

Miles Smit earned his PhD in Philosophy from the Catholic University of Leuven, on the topic of 'Symbol and Community'. He has served as managing editor of the journal *Ethical Perspectives*, and works on a variety of issues pertaining to ethics and policy.

Jere O'Neill Surber completed his doctoral studies at Pennsylvania State University and the Rheinische Universität/Bonn, and is currently Professor of Philosophy and Cultural Theory at the University of Denver. He has published widely in nineteenth- and twentieth-century European philosophy, and is best known for his work on the linguistic thought of the German Idealist philosophers, especially Fichte and Hegel. He has counted himself a friend of William Desmond since graduate school and has taught and collaborated with William on numerous occasions, particularly as a Visiting Professor at the Catholic University of Leuven.

List of Abbreviations of the Frequently Cited Works of William Desmond

AO	*Art, Origins, Otherness*
BB	*Being and the Between*
BH	*Beyond Hegel and Dialectic*
DD	*Desire, Dialectic and Otherness*
EB	*Ethics and the Between*
PO	*Philosophy and its Others*
PU	*Perplexity and Ultimacy*

Details are given in the Bibliography of William Desmond's Works at the end of this volume.

Chapter 1

Introduction

Thomas A.F. Kelly

William Desmond is Ireland's most distinguished living philosopher. Although he is an original thinker, rather than merely an interpreter, writing in the 'continental' or 'European' style of philosophy, he is an English speaker, and one who has been formed by, and still carries the imprint of, Irish culture in general and Irish philosophical culture in particular.

Desmond was born in Cork city in the south of Ireland in the 1950s. His background, upbringing and education were very typical of the time. He was born into a more simple, more pious, more aproblematically Catholic family and, indeed, country, than would be likely or possible today. As he himself put it, 'I grew up in the Middle Ages'. God and the Catholic Church, and all the values and perspectives which belong with and to that Church, were part of his daily experience both at home and beyond it. There was a sense of tolerance and acceptance where all were 'in it together' in a parochial and not very economically prosperous Ireland. Yet there was humour and song and poetry, and that quality which in Irish is called, almost untranslatably, *muintearas*, a kind of homeliness and general hosptiality which very much takes people as it finds them. People that are today categorized as marginal were then called *daoine le Dia*, 'people for God', and for whom God was believed to have a special care. There were no other philosophers in Desmond's family.

Desmond grew up loving poetry. His boyhood literary passion was for the Romantics, especially Wordsworth, whose sensuous and pagan appreciation of nature resonated with a delight in the world of nature that Desmond imbibed from his native *milieu*. Desmond was never any kind of dualist, and he has never been willing to countenance the resolution of such artificial scissions in a peremptory 'either/or' for the good of one artificially isolated element over the other. So it was never a case of 'God or the world', or indeed of 'matter or mind'. Desmond's thought, though keen and critical, is often an attempt to do justice to both, where possible to reconcile, but always, where there is a tension, to dwell in the between which it generates.

The study of Shakespeare, and in particular of *Hamlet* was to be a formative influence. But he was also gifted in mathematics, and the clash between its univocal clarity and the systematic ambiguity and denseness of poetry – and Desmond's intellectual being in this between – was to bear fruit later. At age ten Desmond was awarded a County Council Scholarship, much to his own surprise, since the general expectation regarding such a scholarship was that it was almost too difficult to get. He had already been chosen by the Christian Brothers, who ran the school, to be in an elite scholarship class, containing about twelve boys, whom the Brothers considered intellectually gifted and likely to succeed: the 'schol' class. It is perhaps typical of Desmond that he preferred to be in the general class and made his way back there, but he was unceremoniously 'hauled back' to the schol class.

Like many young Irish men of his generation, Desmond spent a year at age seventeen exploring the possibility of a religious vocation with the Dominicans, the Order of Aquinas. This, however, was not to last, and after a friendly parting with the Dominicans he enroled in University College Cork, one of the universities which compose the National University of Ireland. His original enrolment was to study engineering, a course on which he had been advised to embark on the basis of his exceptional performance in mathematics and science. But Desmond's love of poetry ensured that this flirtation with engineering was only of a few weeks' duration, after which he began to read for a degree in English and Philosophy. This does not mean that he gave up on science. Desmond's thought is one which stretches between what he himself calls 'philosophy and its others'. To use a metaphor which he himself does not use, instead of simple harmony or mere cacophony, Desmond seeks to establish a polyphony between many really differing, but somehow related, voices.

Desmond took to philosophy fervently, as though to a religious vocation, and throughout his life he has lived his philosophy in this way, with high seriousness and a total moral and personal commitment. For Desmond, being a philosopher is not reducible to being an academic employed in a prestigious university. Rather he finds the Socratic imperative of thinking to be essential in his moral as well as his intellectual life. To do philosophy for him is to obey this moral imperative which comes from the deepest constitutive level of his person.

But the philosophical vocation dawned only gradually, growing out of his engagement with poetry. An essential part of his love for poetry was his engagement with it *as* thinking, although the literary theory fashionable at the time neglected this dimension. It was in poetry that Desmond found himself engaged with the questions that arise inescapably with human being, questions of fate and origin, questions regarding action and human identity.

It is for this reason that the vocation to thinking was never, for Desmond, a concern with the merely abstract. As with a poet, Desmond's whole thrust is towards the concrete, the dense individuality of things and people. For that reason his thought is global, seeking to be adequate to the diversity which being individual imposes, seeking to be adequate to the many dimensions of the person, not amputating, as penalty for its inconvenience, the spirituality and affectivity which he sees as proper to it and inalienable. Desmond's thought never fails to be in this sense through and through existential.

Irish philosophy tends towards polyphony: there are voices, not *a* voice, of Irish philosophy. Probably there is rather more interaction between the voices now than then, for then it was more a case of diverse voices in different rooms. The voices which compose the polyphony, or composed it then, are perhaps predictable in the light of Irish history and culture. As Anglophone – though it is to be noted that

Desmond himself is a lover of the Irish language – Ireland finds itself between Britain and America, and there are in Ireland institutional and individual commitments to the Analytic tradition. But history scattered many of the Irish in Europe, and so there are affiliations to what is called Continental or European philosophy. And there is, or was then, a vigorous Thomism, and many Irish philosophy departments, even if not avowedly Thomist, held Thomas in the highest regard, placing his thought on the curriculum alongside Aristotle and Plato. Desmond was exposed to all these currents in his undergraduate years, and read assiduously and systematically in all three, and was powerfully marked by all three. Though he was drawn into European philosophy, he retains a well-read interest in, and influence from, those others to the path he has chosen. Here too Desmond maintains a between: an English speaker who works within the Continental tradition. It is these tensions in his work which make it both fertile and unique.

In 1972, Desmond began studies for the MA. His director, whose first graduate student Desmond was, was Professor Garrett Barden, an essay by whom is included in this volume. The two became friends, and their philosophical conversation has gone on, as at this writing, for more than thirty years. Desmond's thesis was on the imagination in Collingwood, but the work of Collingwood proved to be, for Desmond, a propaedeutic to Hegel, whom he was to discover when he travelled to Penn State University, where he wrote his doctoral dissertation entitled 'The World as Image and Original', under Carl Vaught.

From Hegel and also from Plato, Desmond learned of dialectic. Yet Hegel's version was closed and totalizing, seeking to embrace, even subdue, everything within a self-enclosed and self-justifying system. While Desmond admitted the necessity of dialectic alongside, or as culmination of, the analogical, of which he had learned through his Thomistic education, he transforms dialectic along the lines of a balanced tension with genuine alterity, an open dialectic of true difference, the working of a difference-in-community that transcends that of analogy, and is the very antithesis of a univocity in which difference is either ignored or sacrificed for the sake of a simple unity. Desmond may be a thinker of the One, but his One is gifted and giving, and not riven by the many.

Here Desmond had found his philosophical voice, best suited to his preoccupations which have always been irreducibly metaphysical: Desmond sees it as his task to find an adequate place for genuine alterity, the other which is nevertheless not alien, to revitalize the transcendent and to show its ineluctability for the ontological constitution of the human and of any understanding of the human which can lay claim to adequacy. Yet this path brings Desmond into conflict with many entrenched (though nonetheless not well-founded) opinions, fashions and ideologies. But then, Desmond sees no difficulty in the idea of the philosopher as a disrupter of cosy familiarities, precisely in performing the sensitive task of uncovering and evaluating the tacit and assumed, of exposing distortions for what they are. It is perhaps not without interest to remark that the two world-class philosophers whom Ireland has produced, Scottus Eriugena and George Berkely, though very diverse in time and in thought-content, were nevertheless both metaphysicians who took a path contrary to majority opinion. It is Desmond's notion of transcendence which offers the key to the understanding of his work.

Desmond understands transcendence in more than one way. The word, in its origin *trans scandere*, bespeaks a stepping over a limit. That which transcends can do so either as stepping over a limit or as being beyond the limit, and these are conjoined. Desmond takes 'transcendence', stepping-beyond, to be an ontological designation of the kind of entity we are. To be human is to transcend, and to cease to transcend is to cease to be. In the Introduction to his book *Hegel's God*, Desmond distinguishes three senses of transcendence. He is most concerned with the third sense he discerns in it, namely transcendence as other to human self-transcendence, but which does not diminish that self-transcendence.

This is not to say that all previous philosophical thought has been adequate to describe the constitutive going-beyond which we both are and have to be. The Cartesian self is the first image from modern philosophy in which this going-beyond one's limits begins to be lost. Though in the *Meditations* Descartes tries to vindicate our real attainment of a world outside the self, this attempt is vitiated, and what emerges is a self, discarnate and solipsistic, removed from the world and even from its own body, and knowing nothing, at least directly, except its own contents, which are meant to be guaranteed as adequate to the world by what turns out to be an unattainable divine veracity.

In subsequent modern thinking this loss becomes ever greater. It becomes the phenomenalism of Hume in which both world and self dissolve into an irretrievable confusion of what would later be called 'sense data', and via Hume it takes the form of the divorce in Kant between an unattainable and contradictorily asserted *noumenon*, and the phenomenon which is formed and articulated in and by the synthesizing 'I think', where the condition of the possibility of knowing the object dovetails with its condition of possibility *tout court*.

The inconsistency of Kant who affirms the *noumenon* as both existing and as incapable of being thought or spoken is resolved in nineteenth century German philosophy in favour of the proximal pole of the *noumenon/phenomenon* distinction, and in Hegel there emerges a self-thinking thought which is hostile to any real other and to all real distinction.

Even Heidegger, at least in his earlier period, a thinker of Dasein as being with others in the world, allows his ontological project to be derailed by the unresolved but active residues of previous thought in his own, and attempts a monochromatic view of Dasein which eschews any real attempt to articulate the other and, consequently, the good.

Desmond's thinking is therefore a retrieval or, better, an original rethinking, of what has been lost, and from this it derives much of its power. Seeing the unjustifiable and polymorphous constriction of the self in modern thought for what it is, he articulates, not a new picture of the 'self' or the 'world', but a relational and communal account of what it is for the human to be. The human is that which always transcends and must transcend, and towards a genuine other, which is at the same time not alien. Every thinker creates characteristic images, and it is this which defines that thinker's style. This is one figure which, in polymorphous fashion, ramifies throughout Desmond's work.

In this work of retrieval, in this thinking-back, Desmond can avail himself of all the richness of premodern thought; he is also able to transform and rework the more ambiguous heritage of the modern and contemporary. Desmond's thinking, therefore, is no simple-minded antiquarianism which overleaps the modern and, with endearing or annoying eccentricity, takes medieval or ancient dress for its costume. Desmond is our contemporary. His horizon is that of our world, and what he reaches out to beyond that horizon is transformed by being uttered here. Desmond's thinking is subtle, inventive, poetic, respectful of difference and of the mystery of being. Desmond *struggles* to think, to bring into view what has been hitherto concealed or distorted. He is well aware of the limits of an explanatory project. He evokes as much as he explains. He allows what is mysterious to be as mysterious, and always from an original point of view and with sensitivity. He always practises a courtesy of thought.

This courtesy most obviously takes the form of a respect for what Desmond, perhaps disconcertingly, calls 'the idiotic'. What Desmond is concerned to highlight here is the *idios*, the private, the intimate, what is radically most one's own, and which as such cannot therefore be shared. But the idiotic in this sense cannot be mapped or evoked or pictured in a neutrally descriptive way. What it requires for its disclosure is an essentially benevolent regard. But such a universal, existential and attitudinal benevolence is the root-meaning of a much overworked word, namely love, and love in its various forms can be seen as an outgrowth or as the evolved forms of such benevolence. Through and through, then, Desmond's philosophy is a philosophy of love, where this is to be taken as a subjective and an objective genitive: a loving thought which is a thinking of what love is. And two forms of love dominate Desmond's thinking, in a tension which is fecund for all his thought: agape and eros.

Desmond's thinking, then, is not only metaphysical as a thinking of transcendence and 'of love', it is so first in a Platonic way, which owes much especially to the *Symposium*. His way of thinking the transcendent in the human is by way of Plato's eros, which is at once particular and universal. Eros is 'lack of'. It is therefore intentional, intending an object, often it knows not what, which it must use its cunning to discern and win. But this energy which is eros is itself polymorphic, as burning desire for the truth, for the other, for the ultimate, for God, and supremely idiotic, for it is no 'relation' or 'property' of an already formed 'self', but an openness or relation in which first and in which alone, anything like a human self is possible. Without access to its end, eros would be pure lack, and as eros precisely it energizes its bearer as painfully incomplete, as longing, at every ontological level. A far cry indeed, from the self-enclosed self-sufficient Cartesian self, which needs nothing other than itself either to know or to be (besides being and knowing there is nothing else), and far also even from the sexless, otherless Dasein of Heidegger: otherless because the other is an *a priori* feature of the being-in-the-world which is always *mine* to be. Where, one might ask, is Heidegger's treatment of friendship and love? Where his treatment of the good is, one might reply.

The presence of agape in Desmond's thought is witness to Desmond's conscious and deliberate inheriting of the Christian tradition, though his thinking of agape is far from being meant to disinherit those who are not Christian. Desmond is unashamedly God-centred, one might even say God-haunted. God is the ultimate other for whom eros exists, the supreme good which eros yearns for, the good in whose goodness all participate by existing. Agape is divine love, and it is not merely a gentlemanly respect for the lesser goods of creation, a letting things have their way. Rather it is self-sacrificial and kenotic, gentle, courtly and persuasive. It is intertwined with eros, yet it is a check on eros, for it is coterminous with the very being of things. It would be no exaggeration to say, in Thomistic terms, that love for Desmond is a new transcendental property of being. Where eros is exclusive and particular by its nature, agape is inclusive and salvific. Agape wills the salvation of the world, and as such it is both origin and goal: it is what God is. It therefore well represents the complementary fullness to the essentially directed lack which is eros.

These considerations allow us to grasp something of the dimension of that most characteristic concept deployed by Desmond, that of the between, which figures in the titles of his most important books, the still incomplete trilogy, *Being and the Between*, *Ethics and the Between* and *God and the Between*, the last of which remains to appear. These titles are significant. The 'between' is Desmond's most radical and original ontological characterization of what it is for us to be. Of Platonic origin, it is the *metaxu*, between being and non-being, an ontological state which is fitting for something which is receptive of being, and in no sense, therefore, masters (its own) being, but which remains always a being for being, an erotic intentional lack, a vector towards being and the good with which being is coterminous.

Ethics, Being and God are the terms with which the between is conjoined in these titles, a fact revelatory of the direction of Desmond's thought. Between them, these three terms create the geography which the between inhabits and without which anything like our kind of being would be impossible. The three interpenetrate one another. Being bespeaks, not stasis, but a dynamic one-in-many and many-in-one, where the One is God, the term which evokes the mystery that something, that anything, is, and more: that something is, is not mere given, but gift. The One *is* giving, is what Desmond calls agapeic origin. Moreover, for Desmond, unity is essentially plurivocal, and the giving One gifts the creation in and with its irreducible pluralism. Thus Desmond has hesitations about how the One is thought by many philosophers.

Being presents itself not as neutral plain or 'geometrical space' but as geography, as interactive pathway. If being is not static, neither is it neutral or impersonal. What we are is revelatory of what being is, so that to read the human is to create an onto-logy, and also a theo-logy. Moreover an englobing name for our ineluctable negotiation of this path is ethics.

In this way, the Desmondian themes are thickly interwoven and mutually impacted. For Desmond this interweave is the given which it is the task of philosophy to untie and to trace, not so that the ultimately mysterious nature of this given shall be dispelled, but so that the mystery may be seen the clearer, and so that the task which being human is may be more apparent. For Desmond, we cultivate philosophy in order to be good, in order to be more human. It is precisely for this reason that philosophy can exercise a moral imperative over our minds.

For Desmond, human life is dwelling in being, but progression also inward towards the truth of what we are, and upward towards that which being is, which is the truth of what we are. Ironically Desmond's own life has also been one of motion, of change, of travelling and settling elsewhere, of exile – which is perhaps not too strong a word; such, indeed, has been the experience of about half the Irish population throughout the twentieth century. Desmond has lived very little in Ireland since his mid-twenties, though there have been summer visits almost every year. There have been long sojourns in the United States, teaching and researching at various universities, and currently he holds a professorship at the Catholic University of Leuven, Belgium, where he directs the English-language programme in philosophy. These long sojourns abroad have been creative and happy times for Desmond, but he is still very much an Irishman abroad, his accent is still that of Cork. Desmond is very much an Irish philosopher; the accent of his thought, as much as that of his speech, remains recognizably Irish.

These remarks are not meant to be exhaustive. They are more in the way of whetting the reader's appetite for what is to come. What follows is an attempt by various scholars who know Desmond's work to trace and explore some of its themes. Some of these scholars are already well established, others are at the beginning of their careers. Their work bears witness to the richness and fertility of Desmond's, and they show how his concerns transcend the limits of philosophy to enrich other areas. To be a disciple is to be one who is taught; to be a disciple of Desmond is, under the guidance of a highly sensitive and original mind, to discover the wealth of being and of being human, the manifold ways in which it is possible to be alive. It is to discover the depth and extent of the good. It is to encounter ideas that can be fruitful in the arts and sciences as well as in philosophy. Like any great teacher in philosophy or art, Desmond teaches us to look again.

The Structure of this Book

This book is divided as follows: Part I, 'William Desmond on Philosophy', contains an essay by Desmond, written for this volume, on what he takes the practice of philosophy to be, and what it means for him to follow the vocation of philosophy.

Part II, 'Desmond and Irish Philosophy', contains an essay by Desmond's teacher at University College Cork, Garrett Barden. As well as being a contribution to a philosophical dialogue of many years' duration between Barden and Desmond, this essay represents the philosophical *milieu* which was the seed-bed of Desmond's thought.

Part III, 'Reading Desmond' contains two essays. Jere O'Neill Surber discusses the far from neutral topic of philosophical style, and in particular in relation to the 'who' of Desmond in his writings. Cyril O'Regan discusses the possibility of reading Desmond's philosophical enterprise as a refiguration of Platonic themes with the work of Vico as template.

Part IV, 'Desmond and Metaphysics', examines a foundational issue in the thought of Desmond, namely the attempt to retrieve the metaphysical and thereby to win for metaphysics a viable and radical redefinition. James Marsh shows how Desmond transcends the so-called 'overcoming of metaphysics' in a manner which is no mere repetition of the past, while Catherine Pickstock offers a (re)thinking of metaxological metaphysics, the metaphysics of the between, as metaphysics of light.

Part V, 'Desmond, Love and the Good', also examines an issue at the very heart of Desmond's thinking, namely the good, and the love from which the good is inseparable. Renée Ryan explores the Augustinian sources and parallels in Desmond's thinking of what he calls the agapeic origin, while Jason Howard studies Desmond's conception of freedom in its necessary, and necessarily mutual, relation to the good. Miles Smit explores the geography formed by the good and the *metaxu* by means of a seminal model derived from geometry.

Desmond's work on love and the good is inextricably interwoven with his thought on eros: 'Desmond on Eros' therefore forms the theme of Part VI. Here James McGuirk investigates the relations between the triad formed by eros, power and justice in the context of the fruitful antagonism between Desmond's thought and Nietzsche's. Duston Moore offers a Desmondian reading of the text which is cardinal for Desmond's thought in this area, namely Plato's *Symposium*.

Desmond's thinking of the question of God forms a necessary third element in the unitary but plurivocal ensemble formed by the themes of love, as eros and agape, and the good. In Part VII, 'Desmond and God', Richard Kearney offers a contribution to a conversation with Desmond on Kearney's conception of a God Who May Be.

Part VIII, 'Reading with Desmond' is an attempt to explore the fertility of Desmond's ideas for areas beyond the immediate horizon of his own thinking. Although other essays in this volume could be used to show what it is to read texts of Plato, Augustine or Nietzsche under the guidance of Desmond's thought, this part is dedicated to this theme, and contains an example of a Desmond-inspired reading, undertaken by Ian Leask, namely of a passage in Plato's *Phaedrus*.

Finally, Part IX, 'Desmond, Science, the Arts and the Environment', takes us beyond the confines of the discipline of philosophy, though not beyond the possible influence of Desmond's thought, and shows how powerful, and stimulating to new insight and vision, that thought can be in such contexts. In a very rich essay, and by way of what he calls a 'tributary *mimesis*', John Milbank shows what it is to *think* science in a Desmondian fashion. He also shows how this thinking overflows the limits of physical science into literature, music and theology. Christopher Simpson's essay represents an application of Desmond's thought within the arts by offering a reading of Terrence Malick's 1998 film *The Thin Red Line* as a metaxological document. John Hymers shows how Desmond's thought could transform architecture, while Peter Scheers shows how Desmond's thought could more deeply humanize our relationship with the natural world of plants and animals.

Acknowledgments

I would like to thank various people without whom this enterprise would never have been possible. I wish above all to thank William Desmond, not only for his characteristic courtesy, generosity and encouragement throughout the gestation period of the book, but also for the unique and uniquely excellent gift of philosophy which, over many years, he has given us. I wish also to thank all the contributors for their patience and understanding. I would like to thank Sarah Lloyd and Barbara Pretty at Ashgate Publishing for all their help and encouragement, and last but not least, as they say, I would like to thank two people who made the task of editing very much easier than it otherwise would have been: Caroline O'Kelly, the indefatigable proofreader and friend of many years' standing, and Ann Gleeson, the Senior Executive Assistant of the Philosophy Department at NUI Maynooth, and also a good friend; you both have my heartfelt thanks – I couldn't have done it without you.

Thomas A.F. Kelly
October 2006

I
WILLIAM DESMOND ON PHILOSOPHY

Chapter 2

Between System and Poetics: On the Practices of Philosophy

William Desmond

Vocation

There are many practices of philosophy. The plurality is remarkable. There is no Platonic form of philosophy reserved in heaven. Moses, stumbling down from Mount Sinai, did not forget an eleventh commandment that would charge us, on pain of sin against reason, to philosophize thus and thus only. Further, the practice of philosophy is not the same as the job of a professor. I get paid to be a professor, no-one pays me to be a philosopher.

No-one ever asked me to be or become a philosopher. From where then does a call to philosophy come? Is it a calling? I think it is. I know we are more likely than not these days to squirm with such language of calling. We uneasily suspect something of the religious behind it. And maybe our suspicions are not entirely wrong.

What does it mean to be? What does it mean to be good? To know? To be truthful? To create? To speak? To communicate? To be a thing? To be intelligible? To be a human being? What does it mean to be God? There is no speciality of being, of life, of mindfulness that would exhaust such questions. Professionals get paid for their expertise, and hence scholars, technicians and scientists can be rewarded for what they produce or contribute. The scholar, technician, scientist, poet, priest, revolutionary, hero and sage were the significant others, diversely defining the self-image of the philosopher that I portrayed in the first chapter of *Philosophy and its Others*. The practices of philosophy are not solely self-defined but come to shape in the interplay between it and its significant others. The poet may get his grant, the technician his patent, the scientist his Nobel prize, the scholar his honourary degree, the priest his dues, the revolutionary his Mercedes when he comes down from the hills, the hero may now ascend to the exalted status of the celebrity intellectual, and where, oh where, is the sage, except perhaps in California or some points eastwards of it. What are the rewards of philosophy? All said, it is a practice of mindfulness for free.

Professionalization is excellent, but it can be the death of philosophy as the practice of a certain kind of mindfulness. There is no speciality of the whole of life, no specialization of porosity, no technique of ultimacy. Finesse is needed for a way of life. Philosophy is a way of life, in which thoughtfulness about first and last things shapes one's relation to the between of being at all. There is a theoretical side to it, but this is less the modern sense of theory as an instrumental hypothesis than the earlier sense of theory as delight in seeing what is. There is a practical side to it, since it is the enigmatic charge of what it means to be good that perplexes the thinker. What does it mean to be? What does it mean to be good? These questions have a bearing on how one is to be, and how mindfulness enters into our own being between ignorance and wise humanness. The practice of philosophy is as much in the living of the thought, as in the life of thought. The life of the mind is inseparable from a mindful life.

Betweens

Between system and poetics: here the word 'between' can have different meanings. It could signify something like 'versus'. Consult, for instance, the old quarrel between philosophy and poetry. I will come back to this, since this quarrel is by no means univocal, and its meaning for philosophy is still in question – philosophically. In any case, one implication here seems to be that this 'between' as 'versus' faces us with a choice: one or the other, but not both together: either system or poetics but not both.

Other meanings of 'between' are less overt. Thus it might mean less a tension or agon between these two, as more an opening to something *beyond* system. One might say: into that space between system and something beyond, the poetic inserts itself. Thus there are philosophical occasions when system no longer seems relevant and appropriate and something beyond systematic encapsulation calls forth a different response at the limit. Instance: think of how in Plato when discursive reason reaches a certain limit, there is a resort to more poetic and, crucially, more mythic ways of speaking. This space of the beyond of system requires a different voice, and this is not necessarily an abjuration of philosophical reason but a response called forth from philosophical reason at the limit, or at the utmost reach of its explicitly discursive powers. This too is an important sense of 'between' to which I will return.

Another meaning of 'between' points in the following direction, and here we are perhaps on more familiar ground. I mean there is a space between poetics and system, but that space refers us to *origins* rather than to what is aimed at 'beyond' system. I am thinking here of the view that the more original sources of articulation are poetic rather than conceptual, imaginative rather than intellectual, and hence there is a *beyond in the root of articulation*, in relation to which the poetic is initially more intimate. Poetry first, philosophy later. So the view of Vico, to mention an important instance.

Again different postures to this are possible. One is the response of the philosopher who looks at this original space as something primarily the source of *equivocation*: something to be overcome by an articulation more intellectually univocal. That is to say, poetics is enmeshed in the equivocity of origins, philosophy transcends this equivocity and replaces it with univocal *ratio*. Not myth beyond philosophy, but myth prior to philosophy, but myth now that inevitably must be demythologized, that is, displaced, surpassed and replaced. The space between poetics and system is one between the equivocal and the univocal, but for philosophers the former poses a problem, the latter alone the promise of its solution. Interestingly in Socratic practice you find something of this in the *elenchus*: investigate, search, interrogate, put to the test the insinuations of the equivocal and replace it with the intelligible constancies of univocal definitions.

Then again we must consider this further different view. Suppose the space of the origins to which poetics is intimate is less an indigence of intelligibility than a *reserve of importance* to which every intelligibility is indebted, but which no univocal or dialectical intelligibility can exhaust. Then the equivocal is deeply fertile, and without it there would be no living intelligibility. It is a matrix, but a matrix that is never exhausted by its more univocal offspring. If religion and poetry are the first born of this matrix, philosophy is second born. To continue to be (re)born and to thrive, philosophy must find its way to honour its mother – and keep alive its familial bond with religion and poetry.

Two responses would seem to be precluded by this rebirth: first, that *dualism* of poetry and philosophy, in which opposition defines the exclusion of the putatively more primitive partner, that is, the poetic, or the religious; second, that *dialectical sublation* that grants provisional rights to the poetics, or the religious, only to go on to claim that everything essential will be preserved in the conceptual overtaking of the image or the religious story. When philosophy thus overtakes the poetic, or the religious, there will be no more need of image or story: perhaps not for the conceptually unsophisticated, but certainly for the philosopher. This second response is obviously closer to Hegel's *Aufhebung* than to either a Platonic exclusion or the Platonic transcendence.

Metaxology

I think a *metaxological* response can make sense of all these responses, but it need not, cannot, endorse them simply. It can accept some more readily than others, and with appropriate qualification. As the between here is plurally possibilized, so also a plurivocal dwelling with the between may be needed, issuing into mindful expression that asks for a more plurivocal practice of philosophizing. The stress in this practice would be sympathetic to acknowledging that the poetic, or the religious, does show a certain intimacy with the original sources of articulation, intimacy in both a non-reductive and a non-sublatable sense. There would be a philosophical willingness also for the transcending character of the between in which the utmost reach of system *finds itself 'overtaken'* or exceeded by non-systematic considerations that nevertheless ask for some articulate and thoughtful response. With this too, the reserves of the poetic, or the religious, must again come into play.

That said, I think we have to attend to yet another sense of the 'between' in which we always are: not so much at the limit of origin or verging on the 'beyond' of given immanence, but *constitutively* in that given immanence, relative to our daily being just so in the midst of things. We find ourselves *in medias res*, and often so seemingly without our faces turned to any extremity of origin or beyond. I say 'seemingly', since the everyday is the milieu of 'seems' where what seems so is not always so. In a word: this everyday between is a *milieu of the equivocal*.

How do we address this equivocity? Obviously in many ways. I will later say something about the mind of *finesse*. The question comes: does the everyday itself harbour reserves of importance? Would not being in the midst of things, in the givenness of the ordinary and its reserves, ask for both a systematic and a poetic response – and this in *philosophy* itself? The answer must be yes, if all knowing at some point must turn to what shows itself, must turn to the phantasm, as Aristotle and Aquinas aver. Perhaps too what we mean by 'phantasm' now must have a sense more surplus and saturated than it always seems to have with these two thinkers: excess there in midst of things in their givenness and its intimate reserves? Equivocal excess, since the showing too is inseparable from seeming?

And are not we too a middle in that midst? Are we not ourselves a 'between', insofar as we are as intermediating with that reserved givenness? More, do we not also have to mediate (with) *our own* reserved givenness – our own originality and transcendence, at once both intimate to us and strange? Are we too not a concretion of fertile equivocity and a sign? Can we be the absolute measure of seeming, since we ourselves are a seeming show? Can we be the full measure of equivocity, if we too are constitutively equivocal? A perplexing question for systematics, a provocation for poetics.

It is also a perplexity for our being religious. Let the human being be the measure of all finite things other to itself; is the human being the measure of itself – of its own fertile equivocity? Is there an other originality and transcendence, in the dimension of the hyperbolic, more than the human measure, or more than any human measure? In the deepest intimacy of being religious, there is an elemental porosity to the hyperbolic. There is no finite measure, no human measure of this porosity, ultimately.

System

I will come back to this, but let me backtrack a little and say something about system. 'System' indicates an organized whole composed of many parts; and there can be many such organized wholes, material or bodily, musical, intellectual, social and political, and so on. '*Sustema*', deriving from *sunistanai*, refers us to a togetherness (*sun*) that is brought to stand (*histanai*). That *sustema* brings a togetherness to stand suggests less a block unity than a 'being with' – a between of relation. The question is the character of this between of relation, the how of the togetherness, the openness of it, or how closed it is or must be on itself. Thinking in terms of this between, what is to preclude the thought of an open system?

In modern philosophy one associates the systematic impulse with Kant's *desideratum* of categorical completion, and with the impetus of his successors to develop or deduce such a categorical completion from one principle, culminating in a totality of thought determinations which constitutes one absolute whole. The term 'system' now evokes distaste, if not abuse. I think of Nietzsche to this effect: the will to system evidences a lack of integrity. One can sympathize: I think of those systematizers who (mis)behave like the ugly sisters of Cinderella: the glass slipper will fit the foot, must fit the foot, never mind the blood on the carpet! I often imagine how things were among academic philosophers in Germany, in the wake of Kant's transcendental turn, and then Hegel's idealism: for a while, all bewitched, besotted with system. Such were the times when Hegel 'came on the scene'. Let us not be too snide. It is easy to mock those Hegelians, since they are all dead. Idealistic reason is not alone in being susceptible to bewitchment. Think of, in our day, the scholastic Heideggerian, indeed the scholastic deconstructionist, and the most grotesque of all, the scholastic Nietzschean.

To be fair to the earlier systematizers, there is something disingenuous in Nietzsche's denunciation of the will to system. The dazzling surface of his own rhetoric often dissimulates the systematic recurrences of certain basic themes in his way of thinking, recurrences that honesty would prefer were sometimes set forth by Nietzsche more forthrightly. Many of these recurrences have a family relation to idealism, and the blood of Schopenhauer always circulated in Nietzsche, even granted it nourished another body and helped grow a different flesh. Schopenhauer is often the 'system' recessed in the unsystematic Nietzsche. In that respect, to know the more systematic Schopenhauer is to be able to detect more clearly an ensemble of certain basic ideas with which Nietzsche plays: plays, as he plays with us a game of poetic peek-a-boo – now you see it, now you don't. Some readers are not always blessed with memory long enough to recall what you then saw, and now don't, hence to see that one and the other don't always easily go with each other. And Nietzsche's rhetoric sometimes keeps such things from us, since it always ushers us on, relentlessly keeps us on the move.

System, for many today, is identified with a certain closed arrangement of concepts or ideas, themselves tending to highlight the sameness of things and lowlight the differences. We live reactively in the wake of system, in which previously recessed differences are brought forth to parade, sometimes in very showy or gaudy garments. Of course, we identify system most strongly with Hegel and idealism. But one can argue that the desire for system takes on a particular character in modernity, not entirely unrelated to the upsurge of a more radical univocalizing trend in *all spheres of human life*, but especially in science, and strongly reflected in philosophy itself.

I refer, for instance, to the powerful univocalizing mathematical tools developed in modernity to transform the notion of science, in terms of method and strict standards of coherence and exactness. In previous times, there seems nothing quite like the limits to which this now is driven. One can see this as a response to the seeming of the equivocal. One thinks of mathematics in terms of exact univocity and a rigorous internal coherence of connections. One thinks of a system of relational implications, implicit in the beginning but needing proper methodical development to be laid out in its fullest and most explicit rational intelligibility. The implications extend beyond pure mathematics itself. For some such ideal of system is also pervasive in the reconfiguration of everyday life in the last centuries. Coming from some enigmatic source not at all mathematically univocal, one hears the relentless urging: make it systematic! Make science systematic, make medicine, make transport, make economics, make education, make politics systematic, the list could be continued. The culmination comes in talk of THE SYSTEM. This is the word used simply for that *pervasive configuration of everyday life* under the dominion of variants of scientific–technical rationality, variants themselves particular offspring of Enlightenment reason.

Anti-system

Not surprisingly, there arose the *rebels* against THE SYSTEM. And then too the rebellions they led were themselves made possible by the system, and the conveniences of life that it produced, not least the material reserves it offered. Not unexpectedly also, the rebels, grown a little older, I won't say wiser, often become mainstays of the system. One sees this expressed in the swing between Enlightenment and Romanticism, variations of which swing are still with us to this day. See the loopy flowers of hippy counterculture versus the straights and squares of the system (1960s) as a variant of Pascal's contrast of finesse and geometry. Today we have made our peace with a more or less (self-)satisfied collusion of the two: cybernetic systems of information processing effectively produce comfortable cocoons for consuming subjectivities. The two go hand in glove: technology and our comforts; the computer and pornography on the web; hard reason, the mushy mess of eros. The collusive 'dialectic' of Enlightenment and Romanticism, of modernity and postmodernity, of (calculative) cybernetics and (recreational) sex expresses something of the late modern reconfiguration (if not the corruption) of the fertile space between system and poetics.

To consider something of the philosophical expression of this, think of the turn to self in Descartes, the *cogito* as the one principle. One thinks of this more radically in Kant's transcendental unity of apperception. Then 'come on the scene' his more extreme sons among the idealists. And we hear the loud complaint of these first rebel sons at father Kant's failure to deduce all the categories from one principle. These rebels were also dutiful sons as well, and there is an almost lethal earnestness in their working out of the ideal of system in terms of systematic coherence and completeness with reference to an absolute unity. Consult Fichte, consult Hegel, but not him alone. We find a post-transcendental offspring of the homogenous unity of original Eleaticism, now become a self-differentiating One which develops itself and contains all the essential differences in itself. We find a post-Kantian Spinozism in this sense: not Spinozism as geometrical univocity; more a transgeometrical univocity, defined by the self-development of the absolute subject, not substance (Hegel: Substance become Subject). All of this is oriented towards totality, or an absolute holistic unity to which all differences are immanent, or self-differences.

There are admirers of Kant who breathe a sigh of relief with the cautions of a

Kant versus the extravagances of a Hegel, but it was the canny Kant who raised the stakes about completeness and unity with respect to system. For that matter, there are claims Kant makes on behalf of his own work which are pretty close, in their hyperbole of self-congratulation, to claims such as Hegel made to turn philosophy from love of wisdom into accomplished *Wissenschaft*. And in all of this there is the issue of radical immanence, and the opening of the between to ultimate transcendence.

It is important to remind ourselves that these post-Kantian idealisms are philosophies of *radical immanence*: radical immanence under the *sign of unity* and totality. Kant is not quite so radical a philosopher of immanence, though he made possible and influenced the genesis of such a philosophy. His 'postulatory deism', itself a kind of philosophy of finitude, inspired and ceded to a kind of 'sublationary infinitism' in which the absolute, self-determining subject of idealism comes ultimately to include all otherness within itself. The immanent whole knows only *its own otherness*. From first to last there is the absolute One and this is the immanent whole beyond which there is no other.

There are later philosophies of radical immanence under the *sign of difference*. These are philosophies of 'postulatory finitism', philosophies no less hostile to radical transcendence (consider here God's irreducible otherness) than, say, Hegel's 'sublationary infinitism'. I think of Nietzsche and Deleuze. The post-modern Spinozism of Deleuze is evident: Spinoza, he says, is the 'Christ of the philosophers'. Something analogous holds for Nietzsche, the anti-Christ of the post-philosophers. While the idealist philosophies of totality and the anti-idealist philosophies of difference are ostensibly opposed, in fact, they are deeply at one in this stress on radical immanence; and even though the latter stress the poetics rather than the systematics, as do the former.

As a philosophy of immanence, 'postulatory finitism' complements, even while deconstructing, 'sublationary infinitism'. The metaxological way of being between system and poetics is other than both, since the between cannot be closed into radical immanence, either under the sign of unity as with speculative dialectic, or under the sign of difference as with equivocal (anti-)dialectic. The conjunction of Spinozistic holism and (post-)Kantian transcendental autonomy generates a new configuration of immanence closed off from radical transcendence. The metaxological practice of philosophy, systematically without being the system, dissents from this. On this point, it is as much anti-Nietzschean as anti-Hegelian.[1]

It is fair to say that much of the negative reaction to system is conditioned by a long and complex development in modern philosophy. The hyperinflation of the systematic claims of reason generates a variety of seditious deflations of all claims made by reason. Many of these negative reactions are defined by exploiting one part of the ensemble of ideas developed previously in a systematic context and using these ideas as weapons against the claims of completeness made on behalf of the system. Call it deconstructed, or discomposed Hegelianism, if you will. Or, for that matter, rebellious Kantianism: the good will of rationality has recessive genes that are later born in some black sheep of the idealist family, most evidently in that bad boy Nietzsche and his unruly will to power.

And, interestingly for our theme, it is in bad boy Nietzsche that the urge for poetics *against* system is most powerfully expressed in post-idealistic thinking. At one level, this is a *return* to the ancient quarrel of poetry and philosophy; at another level, it is a *turn away* from system, in that it seeks to resolve the quarrel with a different stress on the poet than the one held in the rationalist and idealist lines of inheritance. Not: poetry to the exclusion of philosophy. But: a redefinition of the range and ambitions of philosophy in terms of a far more sympathetic and symbiotic relation to the poetic.

Being Systematic

I have much sympathy with this last as a *desideratum*. I have less sympathy with the way the *desideratum* is pursued. Why? Because it is too unselfconsciously *heir* to many of the views it claims to be deconstructing. It is too totalizing, in its own way, of the longer tradition of philosophy, where I find a more plurivocal practice of philosophy. It is somewhat sleeping to the other senses of 'between' that I more 'systematically' outlined above, and especially to those senses bearing on the excess of origin and the 'beyond'. It is too negligent of the issues of origin and transcendence in the favour it gives to a certain radical immanence or 'postulatory finitism'.

We need to think through the hyperboles of being in the between. Hyperboles of being: happenings in immanence which yet exceed the terms of immanence. We need to pay attention to the different senses of 'between', and to do so more 'systematically', in order to clarify for ourselves that there is an issue here that is not a local one for late modernity, but a deeper one that is elemental and constitutive of our ontological endowment; and this particularly with respect to the between defining our relation to the origin, and our relation to the 'beyond', and how both these enter our passing sojourn in the middle of a given life.

For one can reflect systematically without necessarily claiming possession of the system in the closed and totalizing sense. Let such a being systematic be called 'systematics', by contrast with 'the system'. The practice of philosophy necessarily requires some sense of systematics, again by contrast with the system, if one's ultimate sense of being and mindfulness is metaxological. Such metaxological systematics is not fixed by the univocal sense of being and by unmediated unity; not totalized by self-mediating dialectic and its inclusions of difference within one comprehensive unity; and not just cast abroad on unrelated diversity by equivocal heterogeneity, or deconstructive difference that holds itself in suspension over the promise of a certain togetherness of and in the between. There is a complex and rich togetherness in the nature of things, a community of being, reaching all the way to ethical and religious community; a community impossible without irreducible otherness, but also defined by constant identities, themselves not beyond the processes of passage that constitute our ambiguous emplacement in creation as the universal impermanence. We need systematics in the sense of a disciplined understanding of connections;

connections stabilized but not frozen by samenesses; connections defined and developed by dynamic differences; connections not enclosed in one immanent whole; and all in all, connections enabling complex interplays between samenesses and differences, interplays exceeding the closure of every whole on itself.

I would also say: without poetics, no systematics. And: without a more original porosity of being, and our given *passio essendi*, no poetics either, and hence also no systematics. This means that there is a more original sense of being religious prior to being artistic and being philosophical. Poetics and systematics are ultimately less original than the porosity of being that opens us up as a being between, or as being a between. We human beings are a medium of passage – a middle capable of becoming mindful of what has passed, what is passing, and what is coming to pass. It is being religious that lives this porosity in the form of the finesse of prophetic mindfulness. Ultimately this is gifted and perhaps is one of the ultimate gifts. I will come back to this.

To the present point: without the poetics of coming to be, for us there is no systematics of being at all. Poetics deals with a bringing or coming to be; systematics finds interconnections in what has come to be. Poetics deals with creative overdetermination; systematics with created determinations and self-determinations. Poetics reveals the more original coming to be, or showing; systematics articulates forms of interconnection that issue from the more original forming. Poetics concerns the forming power(s), prior to and in excess of determinate form, for it is intimate with the overdetermination of the original source(s). Thus, in truth, systematics makes no intelligible sense without presupposing the poetics, poetics often forgotten when more formed intelligibilities have arrived and when what they bring has come to occupy us.

Modernity after Descartes has often been infatuated with the systematics to the neglect of the poetics. This neglect verges too often on a betrayal of finesse; though, in fact, the best moves of systematics are themselves in debt to what overtly they seem to slight. Differently put: first and last, finesse is more original than geometry. You have to discern differences, see differences as differences, and thus discriminate them as identities, before you can analyse their forms of interconnection. Finesse is even more the first requisite, if the form we seek to comprehend is not static but a dynamic forming. Even in the (static) form that has come to a stand there is hidden the memory of a dynamism of coming to be formed. Recall remarks above about '*sustema*' as deriving from *sunistanai*: *sustema* brings a togetherness (*sun*) to stand (*histanai*). Finesse does not so much fix the form as move intelligently with the dynamically forming – in coming to be itself activated mindfulness. Poetics is alive to this energy of coming to be. Poetics itself, in its finessed mindfulness, is alive with this energy.

There have been practices of philosophy that are systematic, without being obsessed with the system, and in search of interconnection out of resources seeded in the poetic. Such thinking seeks out connection; knows that to think of one thing means to think of another, and vice versa; knows that there are articulations already at work to which we must be faithful; knows that we construct connections in a field of being that is open to further determinations; knows also that the universal impermanence will dissolve in time these finite constructions.[2]

We think from the midst, and work our way out, so to say, from where we find ourselves there. And we do not say: there *must* be a unity whose circumference must be laid around the totality of things, and which we can project from our place in the midst. A thinking in the midst, while systematic, can be much more open to the ruptures that define difference and sameness there; can be much more diffident about extrapolation to a putative Whole of wholes from its middle condition; can be porous to the hyperboles of being, happenings of finitude that exceed finite determination.

Hegel was not unaware of some sense of the middle condition, but his approach to and understanding of it are not fully metaxological. Hegel has a dialectical feel for the dynamics of forming, prior to and beyond the fixations of form. But with him the system overreaches the poetics and the systematics. The overdetermination of poetics becomes an indeterminacy lacking intelligibility until it is given determinacy and form by the systematics; while systematics itself is overtaken by the absoluteness of the system as the apotheosis of self-determination. Absolute self-determination comes to itself absolutely through its own otherness. This is the one form of (self-)mediation in all interconnections, within which fall all determinations, through which is overcome all indetermination, and because of which the overdeterminate is neither recognized nor minded. System overtakes poetics, and closes down the porosity of systematics to what is beyond system.

Hegel highlights important considerations in our being the midst, most particularly connected with the power of (inter)subjectivity to be in relation to itself, while being in relation to what is other. The recurrence of this structure of relation he 'projects' onto the whole, or perhaps projects a whole, in claiming this to be the dynamic of structuring of the whole. This claim about the whole is built upon a certain understanding of otherness and sameness, which puts into recess forms of otherness that cannot be contained in the dialectic as he understood it; that is, as too under the influence of the modern turn to the one and the self. Hegel is, in that regard, another ugly sister of Cinderella in his practice of philosophy. I cannot detail here the small horrors of what little toe is here and there cut off, nor stay to mop the blood on the ground. I will only say that the amputations and squeeze affect how he thinks the between, relevantly to our current theme, in the interplay between art and philosophy, and between religion and philosophy.

Finesse

Being systematic in one's philosophizing is not the same as having THE SYSTEM. Yet there are ways of being systematic that are truer to what is at play in the milieu of being, and that develop modes of mindfulness that are more finessed for the fuller subtleties of what is there at play. When I mention finesse I inevitably bring Pascal to mind with his marvellous distinction between *l'esprit de finesse* and *l'esprit de géométrie*.

I am no enemy of geometry, but its great helpfulness with univocal exactness is not always the most helpful. This is particularly true when we are dealing with the equivocities of the human condition. Pascal is a great exemplar of the tremendous advances in the modern scientific univocalizing wrought by empirical and mathematical science. Unlike Descartes and Spinoza, Pascal was not bewitched by its power, or seduced into making it the one and only way to truth. Spinoza is not without his own finesse, but in his ethics *more geometrico* I can find no appropriate name for its generous acknowledgment. Quite the opposite, geometry seems to be usurping the role of finesse.

Spinoza makes an astonishing statement to the effect that the human race would have lain for ever in darkness were it not for the development of mathematics. 'Truth would be eternally hidden (*in aeternam lateret*) from the human race had not mathematics, which does not deal with ends but with the nature and properties of figures, shown to humankind another norm of truth' (*Ethics*, Part I, Appendix). If I read this right, a (quasi-)soteriological power is being claimed for mathematics. Prior to the geometrical sages of modernity, humanity seems to have been lost in the caves of night. After the new mathematics, rational salvation offers humankind the possibility of release into light, into blessedness. What release? What blessedness? If mathematics saves us from purposes and ends (*fines*), its knowing would be a purposeless knowing in a purposeless universe. If this is an advance beyond darkness, it is also an advance into a different darkness, darker in its intelligibility than the unintelligible darkness we have now supposedly left behind. This to me seems like a geometrical counterfeit of saving knowing.

Finesse is more a readiness for saving knowing, bearing on what is prior to and beyond geometry. I would say that finesse bears on a mindfulness that can read the signs of the equivocal, and not simply by the conversion of these signs into a univocal or dialectical–speculative system. It is here that the powers of the poetic come into their own. To the extent that philosophy itself requires finesse, it must go to school with the poets. If it wants to approach saving knowing, it may need finesse further again. I mean finesse that is the sister of religious porosity.

Finesse is by its nature an excellence of mindfulness that is singularly embodied. It cannot be rendered without remainder in terms of neutral and general characteristics. It cannot be geometricized. We come first to know of it, know it, by witnessing its exemplary incarnation in living human beings of evident finesse. There is no geometrical 'theory' that could render it in an absolutely precise univocal definition. It refers us to the concrete suppleness of living intelligence that is open, attentive, mindful, attuned to the occasion in all its elusiveness and subtlety. We take our first steps in finesse by a kind of creative mimesis, by trying to liken ourselves to those who exemplify it, or show something of it. This creative likening renews the promise of finesse, but it also is itself new, since it is openness to the subtlety of the occasion in its unrepeatable singularity.

Singularity here does not betoken a kind of autism of being, nor does it mean that any communication of its significance to others is impossible. Rather this singularity is rich with a promise, perhaps initially not fully communicated, and yet available for, making itself available for, communicability. Communicability itself cannot be confined to articulation in neutral generality, or homogeneous universality. Finesse is in attendance on what is elusive in the intimacy of being, but that intimacy is at the heart of living communicability.

The poetics of a metaxological philosophy must seek to be true to this intimacy. Its very efforts at systematics must show themselves to be open to this promise. That is, the systematics must be born of an intimacy of being that the more determinate systematic articulations of thought never completely exhaust. It must be open beyond itself to what transcends itself, just as systematics. Earlier I drew attention to a sense of 'between' as at the origin, and as at a boundary pointing to the 'beyond' of the immanent middle. This 'beyond' (as well as this 'before') cannot be uprooted from the intimacy of being and hence requires more than 'theory'.

The occasional nature of the happening of being turns us to the poets, turns us into poets. *Being as occasion* also brings us into neighbourhood with religion. And this, in our attendance on the amazingness of the everyday, the mystery of our being in the midst. A genuine occasion has something of the momentous about it. Systematics may not always avoid the seductions of the neutral universal, but it can at least be ready to confess its sins and grant there is *more* than *that* neutral universal. The practice of philosophy can be a reminder of this 'more'. Finesse may require a love before and beyond purposeless 'theory'.

Poetics

Given this singularity, perhaps I can say, must say, something about my own itinerary in finesse, or lack of it, and some occasions of its evocation. I recall as a young person my attractions to the ordered thought of mathematics. This was balanced by being disturbed, imbalanced, by the darker perplexities induced by, for instance, the study of *Hamlet*. On the one hand, the consolations of coherence and systematic univocity; on the other, the slippery ambiguities of the human being awakening to itself as a question to itself, a question that nothing definite can determinately answer, univocally. What is geometry to this quintessence of dust? Nothing. To itself this creature, the human being, though it fears it is nothing, is something – something in question to itself. This creature of dust is a creature of finesse, hence more than a quintessence of dust.

Then there were, there are, the extreme claims made in being religious. I mean not first doctrines whose claim to be revealed mysteries cast all pretensions to univocity into disarray, but also the extreme claims made on the practice of a life, if this first claim has any truth: to be as truthful, in accord with a certain trust in God. This reflected something of the ethos of Irish culture at the time. Religion, Roman Catholicism, provided the hegemonic overarching, overreaching horizon within which questions of the meaning and practice of life were to be answered. A between opens up for a philosopher who is perplexed by these claims. Thinking is here double edged: it can be critical in a destructive way; it need not be so destructive, may be moved by its own proper reverence. There is a practice of philosophy that ultimately is seeded in reverence as religious, but grown into thoughtfulness about religion by the press of ambiguous life itself. If there was a single tradition of philosophy in Ireland while I was growing up, it was a form of scholasticism, newer forms influenced by teachers trained at Leuven: ancient and medieval philosophy, combined with phenomenology and existentialism – a not unfertile mix. But to go to school with some questions means there are no schools that will do. One may find oneself outside the guilds, be they analytic or continental.

The poets: there was always a very long line of respect for these in Ireland. When I first studied at University College Cork, a few of my friends were budding poets. I do not think I entirely lack poetic powers but I went my own way, though that philosophical way does call upon early affinities with the poetic. I think I came to poetry from religion, and came to philosophy perhaps directly from poetry, but certainly religion stood over this transition as the elder sister. One could make a cultural claim in Ireland if one were a poet, but of course in Ireland, as Patrick Kavanagh said, the standing army of poets never falls below three thousand. I did not join the army, nor was I recruited or dragooned. I went my way. I do not think I have been unfaithful to a certain muse whom I have not ceased to woo, or scatter tokens of affection for throughout my writing. It is not quite, in Eliot's words, a matter of making 'raids on the inarticulate', for there is articulating and thinking that is not thievery. And with all due respect, among the poets I did not always find enough of the kind of thought I instinctively sought, often not quite knowing what it was.

In the practices of my own philosophizing, one can find some extremes of abstract dialectic – I can do that – leaving some readers exasperated or gasping for more familiar concreteness – and then, by contrast, the eruption of another language – poetic – seemingly entirely other, imagistically concrete, too concrete for some abstract thinkers. Some of my readers are discomfited by this doubleness. Others, I am happy to report, approve of it in some way. Perhaps the mixture of being discomfited and being moved has something right about it. We can be lulled into a false sense of philosophy with respect to abstract dialectic; as if that, and only that, were philosophy; and not the emergence of thinking from an ambiguous ethos; not also the reinsertion of thought in the flow of life itself. For me, the thinking must address the *movement between*: up from the ambiguous matrix, above the flat wastes of thoughtless life; down again from the dry, oxygen-less ether into the red bloods of life, feet contacting once more the rougher ground. True, in the movement up, we may suffer from altitude sickness, we cannot breathe and our minds become dizzy; in the movement down, the glut of life may be too much for us to digest, and we settle on a vanishing diet of anorexic abstractions.

The movement between: a process of transcending in being mindful, that emerges from roots often lost to thought in darkness before articulation; that points above univocal articulations; that puts pressure on the reassuring forms of domesticated life; that also paradoxically returns us to these daily forms but now

with some shift in seeing, or some hidden access of light allowing one to see things differently, or see not quite straight anymore. For this turn back down may require of one a kind of *night vision*, and initially all one can make out are dull shapes shifting in a gloaming. There is nothing simple about this at all. Even with one's feet back on the rough ground, one may stumble on the trivial thing. Falling over the everyday: 'falling over' is a being off balance; it is also one of our ways of describing love. Not only, only connect; but also making one's peace with the many farewells of life. And there may be portents that there is an under-ground to the firm earth, as before there appeared a sky above one. Being willing to enter the under-ground might have much to do with communicating with the more intimate sources of thinking and speaking and creating. Going into those sources is to risk a kind of dying, for this under-ground is as much tomb as womb, and it is the death of false selving that is terrifying for those singers who must spend a season in Hades.

The poetics of my own practice of philosophy: this is not a matter of giving to thought a kind of 'feel'; not simply a kind of evocation, though it can be both; not just a rhetorical embellishment that otherwise puts drapery over the sturdy drab furniture of thinking. It has more to do with *enactment*: the very concreteness of thinking itself as performed in fitting words. The words are not just a matter of 'talk about' a something, but are uttered or written somehow to bring to pass a happening, to enact it mindfully. Performance is a (per)forming, a coming to be of significant form, through (*per*) a passing from silence to speaking. The saying is as important as the said; and sometimes the saying says more than the said. The faithful thought finds fruits in its fitting word.

The mindful enactment, the performance of thinking, has something to do with a wedding of form and content. The form is the forming of the content, a bringing to form, not the superimposition of a form on a matter or content already fixed. Thinking, in this regard, is like a *poiesis*: a coming or bringing to be; an emergence as if from a kind of nothing, but then also a becoming in terms of a forming. There is something prior to form: intimate, originally idiotic sources of thinking. The form that *has* become is not the end of the matter since it points back to these, its own hidden original sources. Yet formed thought also points beyond itself, either in terms of its own dissolution, or self-surpassing, or in terms of another exigence emergent with it at the extremity of its own self-becoming. Then something other than the self-becoming of thinking is communicated: the other beyond the self-determination of thought. This other calls further the self in self-becoming beyond self. It also calls for thinking what is other to thought thinking itself.

So images, metaphors and suchlike are not mere rhetorical adornments in my practice of philosophy. There is a rhetoric, yes, but this can aim at a fidelity to coming to be and the forming of the content: the thinking itself in its own singular forming. I would say that there is always the taste of singularity to fresh thought, even if it repeats thoughts that are the same as those that have already been thought by others, or that can be thought again. The freshness comes from a dipping of mindfulness into the original sources of articulation. This is impossible without imagination, whether poetic or philosophical or religious.

This for me is not an optional thing. It is a fidelity to what is communicating itself or being communicated. The fact that some professional philosophers might not recognize themselves in this does not settle the question between us. We all tend to be initiated into a practice of philosophy, but no practice is entirely immune from question. A thinking that seeks immunity for itself, while accusing or judging everything other, immediately makes itself suspect. By claiming to be above suspicion, it straightaway arouses suspicion. Some pretensions to the system can claim a kind of immunity from incompleteness. Who or what grants the immunity? Can philosophy grant immunity to itself, and still remain a creditable witness to thought? Essential to *any* practice of philosophy is its willingness to call itself into question. Professional, professorial philosophers ought to remember this and not feel self-satisfied that they are safe insiders of a professional guild. A different nakedness and exposure to the outside is needed in philosophy: this is also a 'being between'.

Singing Thought

This recalls the theme of different betweens earlier laid out. There is clearly a 'between' that yields to more systematic treatment: an interconnected web of thoughts, or happenings, each related to others; and a systematic thinking can follow along the lines of articulation defined by the web of such interrelations and interconnections. Hegel exploits this, and makes a certain claim to complete the explications of the web of interrelations of thought and being. But this sense of between is one which is primarily *immanent*. My question is whether this immanent between gives witness to another sense of between that is at the boundary of immanence, or itself between immanence and transcendence. I do not want to put the point too dualistically, for I think that signs of this other between emerge in immanence itself. These signs are signally given in what I called the 'hyperboles of being': happenings in immanent finitude that yet cannot be determined completely on the terms of immanent finitude. They point beyond, and again in no dualistic manner, but rather in terms of the excesses given to showing in the immanent between itself. The immanent between is porous to something other to it.

How then to be in this *other* between? And how to address it? This is not an easy question. I am not sure one can give a direct answer. I am not sure what an 'answer' might mean. Addressing this other between, or letting oneself be addressed by what is communicated in and across it, is, I think, inseparable from the religious. But there is a poetic side to this address and openness, that asks for the allowance of attention to the hyperboles of being in the immanent middle: hyperboles, however, *occasionally communicated*, and not simply in terms of neutral generalities.

The poetic and the religious are familially intimate, as I suggested. I would speak of what it means to be in the between beyond system; which is again both a pointing beyond, and yet a return to something very elemental. *If the pointing beyond is recognizably religious, in a more usually accepted sense, the return to the elemental is poetic.* I would say however, that the poetic is also pointed beyond in the elemental, just as the religious, in its transcendence, brings us back into intimacy with the elemental. Poetry is exposure; religion is nakedness; both are ultimate porosities. But how to remain true to the occasion? Can philosophical thought ever find the fitting words?

I have written some more systematic works, and hope to bring a trilogy of systematic works to some completion with *God and the Between*. One would be deceived to think of this as 'system building' in a more traditional sense, where things are put in their place and then it is done. Not at all: I see systematic thinking is a *working through* of fundamental possibilities of minding and being, which having been done might *release one* to be again, to be mindful again, otherwise. If and when I finish that trilogy, I have a desire that would bring me back to notions such as I had when I spoke in *Philosophy and its Others* of thought singing its other. Not thought thinking itself, nor quite thought thinking its other, but mindfulness as thought singing its other. What would singing thought be? I speak metaphorically. I speak in a way that an admirer of Vico might understand when he says that song is the source of speech. But there are songs also beyond first speech, the songs of a second spring beyond the self-becoming of the middle of life. There are songs proper to a before, to a middle, to a beyond. Perhaps, *apropos* the latter, these are the songs of age, the songs of time. If, on one side, we are directed to the *poetic immanent*, on the other, we are solicited by the *religious beyond*.

This dream of singing thought might be expressed, for instance, in mindfulness of the processes of selving, the selvings of a life, the communicabilities of living. Could one do that philosophically, and do it in terms of thought singing its others? This would be very difficult. One knows of artists who have told the stories of various selvings, and without loss of either the intimacy of occasions or of communicability beyond oneself. For example, the beginning of James Joyce's *Portrait of the Artist as a Young Man* seems to enter immanently into being in the between as a baby, whose later selvings are said by some commentators to be modelled on Aristotle's *De Anima*. In Charles Dickens's *David Copperfield*, early chapters are written from the view of a child, more or less; there are touches that sketch the occasion of being small, as in David Copperfield's being struck by Mr Barkis swallowing the pie whole, like an elephant; or the child enduring the impenetrability of adults, in the heavy woman descending from the mail carriage, like a *haystack*; there is a later episode when David gets drunk for the first time, and Dickens marvellously enters into the skewed self-intoxication of a first getting sloshed.

Other artists could be mentioned, but one might say that great art tries to remain imaginatively true to the occasion of being. (For instance, consider Joyce's *Ulysses* as an extended fidelity to the occasion of 16 June 1904, now artistically immortalized as Bloomsday.) But how to *think*, in the middle, of the *surplus of the occasion*? For there is, in the between, a surplus immediacy. But when we think, do we not distance ourselves, mediate this surplus, and so seem to deal with something other to the surplus? We seem to have to choose either the surplus occasion or the thought. How then is possible a singing thought, faithful to both the surplus and the thought? This would ask a mindful fidelity to the surplus occasion, as much affirming the occasion as articulating its surplus. But can that be done by philosophical thought? Is it only the poetic image or the religious story that is both surplus and articulate, and each in its own way faithful to the occasion? If we desire fidelity to the surplus occasion, must we be confined to the intimate only, the intimate as the 'merely' private? Or is there an intimacy of being not private? Is there an *intimate universal*? Is it only in being religious that we enter into the intimate universal: an enabling middle between the human and the divine; a between that neither betrays our intimate singularity of being nor abdicates responsibility for a more unconditional communicability? Would one not need something like *agapeic mindfulness* to be true to it? Who has that mindfulness? Perhaps nobody except God: mindfulness as knowing love of the singular, communicated as care for the mortal creature.[3]

The artist has poetic licence, we say, and the story. But what kind of licence does philosophy have? What licenses philosophy? The language is still used (in Belgium, where I teach) of earning the degree of a *licentiate* in philosophy. A college of professors confers that licence, but is there a deeper authorization of philosophy? Is a storied philosophy possible and who or what would authorize it? I do not mean a philosophy of stories but a storied philosophy – enacting something of the occasion of being – not just reflecting on it. This is a point I put above about a certain poetic practice of philosophizing: participating in the occasion, not just talking about it, and yet both participating and speaking in a philosophical register.

This point might be said to be consistent with a metaxological practice of philosophy, if we connect the *metaxu* with a reformulation of the idea of philosophy as a 'meta' discipline. Philosophy as a 'meta' discipline is often thought of as a second-order discipline, reflective of and on a first-order activity, but I would stress the doubleness of the meaning of 'meta'. 'Meta' can mean 'in the midst', as well as 'over and above, beyond'. If 'meta' as 'in the midst' refers us to a first-order activity or performance, 'meta' as 'over and above' refers us to reflection on this first-order activity. A metaxological practice of philosophy could not endorse any sharp division of these two. This practice would seek to be at once first and second-order: not one, not the other simply, but both, and the movement between the two, in which the intimacy of the one to the other is shown both as 'in the midst' and 'over and above'. This would also have implications for the movement between immanence and transcendence.

I can envisage a storyline that would bear on the poetic, religious, philosophical significance of human selvings, or our being in communities. How to relate the story or stories, and to do so philosophically, and yet not to betray the poetic and the religious, and to relate it from within out, as well as to be true to what we have received? Inevitably we think of life being lived forward and understood backwards. How then to think the promiscuity of the forwards and the backwards, doing justice to something of the systematics and the poetics? Would one perhaps have to invent a new genre of writing in the process? Not the philosophical novel, but storied philosophizing, where the stories are not mere illustrations of concepts. I don't know if it can be done, I don't know if I can do it. It might mean that one must simply turn into a poet, a religious poet perhaps. Even if so, could philosophy still be carried (over) in hidden reserves, offering accesses to what more often than not is closed to poets and perhaps religious thinkers? (Is Kierkegaard someone here to think of as showing a way?)

Whatever one might think of these suggestions, important for all of this will be to come anew into the *elemental porosity of being*. This is first dependent on a kind of *metanoia* of selving, and a renewed release into the space of communicability. Only later do the imaginative or reflective articulations come. I know, of course, the turn about, the renewed release, and the new saying cannot be separated into detachable phases; though there are those who have been in the turn about and release and who do not have the resources to articulate what is occasioned there; just as there are the loquacious who talk too much and do not know what they are talking about, for they have not undergone the *metanoia*, and their loquaciousness counterfeits the passage of the true word.

Religious Porosity

Mention of this porosity of being makes me turn from the poets to the *priests*. I was myself attracted to the priesthood. The complications here for the philosopher, for the thinker between religion and philosophy, are multiple. There can be religious cultures that are inhospitable to philosophical thought. Perhaps earlier in the Ireland in which I grew up, there was a certain conservative bent that either looked askance at the asking of questions or else gave its permission as long as the pursuit kept clearly to the sanctioned pathways. Rural people are often sceptical about fancy talk, while bourgeois city dwellers may have justified pretensions to education but often hesitate before taking directions too disturbing to more settled pieties. I once published some articles on Marx in the *Cork Examiner*, and my granny immediately pronounced I was finished. She was not entirely wrong. Among some, my own studies of Hegel, against whom I have struggled, led to my being deemed guilty by circuitous association: Hegel – Marx – Lenin – Stalin, and now we are being shot.

While the circumstances that occasioned these associations do not now quite press home on us, yet in every occasion genuine philosophy requires a different amplitude of mind. Arrogance *vis-à-vis* the others is not called for or justified. Nevertheless it well may be that the pursuit of thought puts a person on an edge relative to others, and sometimes pits them against each other. That said, there is now a culture of severe criticism, if not undisguised hostility, towards the religious orientation of that earlier time. One understands this, in part, because of the sometimes heavy-handed use of hegemonic power by ecclesiastical institutions. Nevertheless the hostility is not justified if we take the viewpoint of that ampler horizon of mind and consider the human being as *homo religiosus*, and without excessive fixation on the putative hang-ups of (Irish) Catholicism. Being religious is immensely plurivocal, and yet at the centre of it all is the most elemental of all elemental relations: the human in relation to the divine, the divine in relation to the human – let the divine be interpreted how you will.

And then too there is the tunnel vision of retrospective score settling that often descends on 'enlightened' discussions of religion. I tend to think that human generosity has a certain fundamental constancy, as do malice and small-mindedness. To think there was nothing of generosity in former times smacks of the ultimate in self-righteous arrogance on our part. In any case, my own experience of being religious in Ireland was on the whole something that deeply impressed me: impressed itself on me, and in a manner that I think was indelible. Images: neighbourly generosity; some individuals marked by a sense of marvel and gratitude for life; the immense delight – not exclusive of a mockery, itself a kind of delight – in the stunning mystery of human beings, coming and passing in all shapes and sizes; guilty sympathy for those less fortunate than oneself in a time when the material resources to help them were far less than is now the case; unself-conscious enactment of the urge to pray, and so to place oneself in a space where the presence of the divine offers itself to us; rituals with their own majestic aesthetics, and indeed a magnificent sensuousness by comparison with which the stripped-down efficiencies of recent years strikes one as dull and devoid of any sacred flamboyance. For there was more unself-conscious excess in that direction. But then the human being is excess; and if the exceeding will not be given its out in the religious direction, it will find other, less wholesome, even vicious, sinister, malignant expressions. Vice too can be in the dimension of the hyperbole. (Had Hitler succeeded as an artist, who knows what would have followed. A dark, dark instance of Cleopatra's nose?)

My point: there is an urgency of ultimacy about being religious which can be the familial, intimate other to a similar searching for ultimacy that can consume the philosophical quest. True, in modernity the search for system has put strain on this familial relation. In more scientistically oriented systems, religion becomes utterly subjective and privatized: in a bad subjectivity more often than not, and the intimacy of being is betrayed. In more idealistic systems, there is the betrayal of the intimate universal of being religious and its substitution by a putative higher, impersonal rational universal. The question has still to be posed as to whether this way of thinking is a systematic undercutting or violation of the sense of mystery and transcendence which, one might argue, is intimate to religion, and, not least, religions coming from Biblical inspirations. I have given much thought to this space between philosophy and religion, as well as between philosophy and art. I mention my continuing quarrel with the Hegelian sublation of art and religion in this regard, but I will not go into it here.[4]

I think this between asks philosophy to be open to the religious, as perhaps a more intimate and ultimate between: in the sense of having intimacy with the primal between, the porosity of being between the human and the divine. More and more I think that being religious is dedicated to keeping unclogged this porosity which is at the well-spring of life itself. Indeed, without that porosity being kept unclogged, the deeper sources of philosophical thinking would themselves wither. It is no wonder that, in our time, the end of one of the triad, art, religion, philosophy, is often accompanied by the putative end of one or more of the others. The so-called 'end of art', the so-called 'death of God', the so-called 'end of philosophy' together make us wonder if these three are Siamese triplets whose lives rise and fall, die or are wasted, by the death or sickness of the others.

The issue is not exclusively with one or the other, though it is more deeply religious than anything else: it bears on that primal porosity in which the seeds of reverence, of inspiration, and the grounding confidence in truth and thought either grow or perish. We live in an ethos of autonomous humanity in which we have reconfigured the space of porosity in terms of our own self-determining powers, sometimes blocking the space of communication between us and transcendence as other. The reverence at issue suggests the thought of something strange: not seeds growing in a fixed ground, but, since the ground is a porosity, we must think seeds growing in a kind of openness or a seeming nothing. We are asked to think an energy of passing, or passage in which we are first opened before we open ourselves. We are a *passio essendi* before we are a *conatus essendi*: first given to be, before we endeavour to be. The issue is one of gratitude for this being given to be, and reverence for its source.

What I am here calling the primal porosity is connected with the between (discussed before) relative to the origin, and relative to the 'beyond'. But this porosity is always configured one way or another in the daily, more domestic middle. A great task for the practice of life itself in the daily middle is to keep this porosity unclogged. Being aesthetic, religious and philosophical are our great helpers here. I do not forget being ethical: this is our willing care for the good in the ethos of being. A deeper understanding of this ethos brings us back to the *passio essendi* and to the porosity, and transforms being ethical in a more agapeic direction, that is, in the direction of the service of the other that has been recommended to us by the great religious traditions. Neither a culture of autonomous art, nor ethics, nor philosophy is best suited to dwelling thus in the between, or the ethos or the porosity.

Beyond the hegemonies of past sacred univocities in which worldly and spiritual will to power too often colluded equivocally with each other, we need a new or renewed way of being religious. But without gratitude for what has been given, it is hard to see how we could find our way to the renewed reverence.

Beyond the Solitudes of Immanence

That reverence has come under attack in modernity, for reasons complex enough to require an exploration of their own, but among them is the extremely strong drive in modernity to univocalize all being.[5] In postmodernity there are assaults on that univocity, and celebrations of equivocity, assaults and celebrations that arouse in us our own equivocal assessment. By contrast with both the drive and the counter-drive, one could argue that the longer tradition(s) of philosophy testify to something of the plurivocity of philosophy itself. This plurivocity betokens a rich sense of the space between poetics and system, and asks finesse for its fertile equivocity. On occasion that finesse might have to confront wrong-headed univocalizings, as well as celebrate, with postmodernity, the richness of the equivocal. But there are other occasions when it must allow the fitting univocity its proper place, as well as demurring about any apotheosis of equivocity that reneges on mindful intermediation and communicability. Flinging in our faces absurdities that repress intelligibility is no response to false clarities oppressing honest mindfulness.

Still one might press the objection that in all these past practices of philosophies there is a central quest for an understanding as univocal and systematic as possible. Certainly philosophers often do show a strong predilection for univocity. Yet even if proper univocity is one of philosophy's *desiderata*, the practices of philosophizing extend beyond that. Thus there is the search itself – this cannot be univocalized, even if it searches for univocity. There is the origin of the search – in a radical astonishment that may give rise to the search for univocal cognition but that itself cannot be univocalized completely. Even if we begin in the negative of astonishment, namely doubt, doubt itself cannot be completely univocalized, even when its secret desire is for a certainty that gives absolutely univocal knowing. There is the eros of the search: eros for univocity cannot be itself univocalized. Thus, for instance, the passion for scientific and mathematical truth is not itself scientific or mathematical; it exceeds what it seeks; were this not so, there would be no seeking at all. The passion for objective knowing is not itself fully objectifiable.

There is also the fact that the practice of philosophy can never be absolutely solitary. There are solitudes, and philosophy drives one into many,[6] but these are finally always qualified by communicative intermediations with others, whether overt or *incognito*. This is evident in the dialogical practice of philosophy – if we go back to the beginning of dialectic (*dia-legein*) in conversation. The '*dia*' is always a double, even as it is also a porous medium (as when we say something is diaphanous: the '*dia*' names a middle, via which a light passes). There is always a pluralization at work.

The communicative practice of philosophizing is more than the said: in the communal saying, and in the being truthful of the speakers, something of the true comes to be communicated. This saying and this being truthful cannot be univocalized or systematized. You could not have a conversation at all, if all speaking were reduced, or reducible, to complete univocity. Even more evidently so, there would be no eros; nor could our conversation be marked by irony or laughter or mockery and suchlike. Nor could you have a conversation if all speech could be systematized. You might have a monologue of thought alone with itself. I do know Aristotle and Hegel named their god as thought thinking itself, but this to me smacks of a return on the speculative heights of a certain acme of univocity. One might call it the 'religious poetry' of speculative univocity, but even then it is not enough. That it is religious poetry shows that there is more than univocity at the highest acme of speculative univocity.

Religious poetry has not been to the tastes of modern philosophers whose practices of philosophy have especially been influenced by a scientific and mathematical self-image. Sometimes one finds in the not distant past philosophy denounced as 'secretly theology'. But is not *all* philosophy, in a way, a secret something or other, or in open or screened relation to its own significant others? Otherwise the limit of such solitary self-containment of philosophy would be a kind of autism of being and mind. In truth, an interplay with significant others, expressed or reserved, always influences the self-understanding of the philosopher. And this even when philosophy lays claim to complete autonomy. To grant this interplay, of course, is immediately to undercut the claim to complete autonomy: what autonomy is claimed is itself dependent on something received. In *Philosophy and its Others* (as I mentioned at the outset) I speak of the plurivocal practices of philosophy in terms of the following significant others: the scholar, the technician, the scientist, the poet, the priest, the revolutionary, the hero, the sage. Being in relation to an other or others is always important, indeed constitutive. Depending on the significant other(s), the self-understanding and practice of the philosopher will differ. The scientist, technician, scholar and, perhaps, revolutionary have been important in modernity, but all these influences are qualified by a belief in system as autonomous knowing.

What is wrong with that? The disingenuousness of the claim to autonomous knowing; and the occlusion of the between, that is here, of philosophy's own being in relation to an other or others, that shape the self-image and practice of the philosopher. This is so willy-nilly, let the overt rhetoric say the opposite as much as it please. We neglect the fact that the practices of philosophy are between philosophy itself and these others. We lose sight of the fact that it is perhaps philosophy's special vocation just to attend to that space 'between', as it attends to both itself and its others. This is more than a simplistic emulation of the other held significant. It is being in relation in a double sense: *defined as self by being defined in relation to what is other*: inhabiting the space of thought in a metaxological manner. The modern ideal of self-determining or autonomous knowing has put this into recess, while, in fact, it is always parasitical on that which it has recessed. The autonomy of philosophy is not univocally self-produced. What freedom philosophy gains comes from the manner in which it inhabits the *metaxu*. There is always indebtedness to the other, and indeed the possibility of gratitude for what is given to it, and not simply produced through itself alone.

This stress on autonomous knowing, coupled with the turn to self, with the increased demands made on univocity in modernity, and with decreased patiences for the sometimes intractable equivocities of being – all these feed into a formation of the systematic impulse that itself makes more and more demands on the desire for absolute unity and completeness, culminating in its conceptual hyperbole in Hegel's system. It is entirely just from that point of view that many of the discontented thinkers of modernity since Hegel would find some bone to pick with him. Latent in his ambitions and claims to achievement are many of these questionable assumptions. Admittedly they are given their own form by Hegel and, as we might also grant, in his own way he did struggle against some of their deficiencies, even while being their victim, also in his own way.

Do the anti-idealist deconstructors of totality offer us enough? I think neither Hegelian system nor the detotalizing practices of such critics open for thinking the porosity of the needed reverence that releases us beyond the solitudes of immanence. Hegel offers a 'sublationary infinitism': the finite is sublated in the infinite, and the results are a self-circling immanence. The detotalizing practices of the critics of 'sublationary infinitism' are often marked by 'postulatory finitism'. And it is by virtue of opposition to such 'sublationary infinitism' as untrue to finitude, or not true enough, that 'postulatory finitism' borrows much of its contemporary persuasiveness. But 'postulatory finitism' is also given over to self-circling immanence, though the self-circling is tortured rather than reconciled. In truth, 'sublationary infinitism' and 'postulatory finitism' share the fact that they are philosophies of *unremitting immanence*.

If and when these two come to the boundary between immanence and transcendence, they swerve off that boundary, back to immanence; swerve differently certainly, whether in dialectical–speculative or in detotalizing form, but both offer us at most an immanent self-transcendence. Neither robustly addresses the ultimate between where in intimate immanence all solitudes are surprised, or overtaken by, or shocked into an unexpected porosity to transcendence as irreducibly other. This is not a transcendence defined by immanence, but a transcendence that gives immanence itself to be, and endows the immanent between with the plurivocal promise of immanent self-transcending beings.

A philosophy of this ultimate between requires something other: a philosophy of finitude not postulatory; a philosophy of infinitude not sublationary; a philosophy in which we are not closed off from rethinking transcendence in a sense other than either of these positions can, or will, contemplate. Perhaps some deconstructions of Hegelian system seem to look for something reminiscent of metaxological philosophy, but do they have the resources needed for thinking in the space *between* system and poetics? If their reaction to positions like Hegel's are bewitched by the notion that he has the monopoly on 'system', the temptation will be strong to turn that between into a 'versus', undervaluing the systematic, even while granting the poetic a new respect.

As I suggested at the outset, this 'versus' is not the most fruitful for us, in addressing the different betweens that call for thought. A post-dialectical practice of philosophy must enact something of metaxological mindfulness that, while not claiming to be the system, does justice to both the systematic and the poetic – and the religious. If I am not mistaken this means for philosophy a return to the plurivocal condition of the *metaxu*, to permeability to the others, and to the porosity of being in the between. This porosity looks like a return to zero and yet is not an empty nothing. In and through it, we are offered, so to say, a fertile poverty that, in a new interface with creation, and in dialogue with the others, especially the poetic and religious, occasions the release of philosophizing from the solitudes of self-circling immanence.

Notes

1 See, *inter alia*, my *Hegel's God: A Counterfeit Double?*; on 'postulatory finitism', 'sublationary infinitism' and related issues, see my *Is There a Sabbath for Thought? Between Religion and Philosophy*, New York: Fordham University Press, 2005, especially Chapter 1.

2 See, for example, Plato's *Philebus*, where an ensemble of supple systematic resources – one and many, like and unlike, same and other, and the fourfold of limit and unlimited, mixture and the cause – are deployed to fruitful effect.

3 On some of the themes mentioned above see my 'Surplus Immediacy and the Defect(ion) of Hegel's Concept', in Glenn Alexander Magee (ed.), *Philosophy and Culture: Essays in Honour of Donald Phillip Verene*, Charlottesville, Virginia: Philosophy Documentation Centre, 2002, pp.107–27; for agapeic mindfulness, see chapters 4 and 6 of *Perplexity and Ultimacy*; on the intimate universal, see *Is There a Sabbath for Thought?*

4 See *Hegel's God* and *Is There a Sabbath for Thought?* This matter is also a concern of *Art, Origins, Otherness*. These last two books try to give some indication of what a metaxological dialogue between art, religion and philosophy might look like. I am suggesting a kind of metaxological rethinking of Hegel's absolute spirit and the triad of art, philosophy and religion, though perhaps we must make that a quaternity, since the ethical cannot be excluded, in that the good of the 'to be' is at stake. With these others, philosophy is one of the essential ways of being true to the between, though not the only one. Metaxological philosophy does not crow on the conceptual apex, for in the porosity of the between there is no such apex, though there are songs of passage.

5 See 'On the Betrayals of Reverence', *Is There a Sabbath for Thought?*, Chapter 8.

6 See 'The Solitudes of Philosophy', in Lee Rouner (ed.), *Loneliness*, Notre Dame, Indiana: University of Notre Dame Press, 1998, pp.63–78.

II
DESMOND AND IRISH
PHILOSOPHY

Chapter 3
Transcendence and Intelligibility

Garrett Barden

The following essay is offered as part of a dialogue with William Desmond that began in 1972 when he was my first graduate student.[1] Our friendship began then and has continued. Philosophers, no less than imaginative writers, attempt to find a way of writing that, in their attempt to find, may bring them, slowly and tentatively, to the discovery of what they want to think; to what is given.

It is easier to write of the human as simply rational than to take desire, sentiment and sympathy into account. In many discussions with William Desmond over more than thirty years, what I have learnt from him is the enduring insistence on the incorporation of these and of love in the discovery of transcendence, in the realization, in both senses of that word, of what is beyond. Neither interpretation, nor commentary, this essay is a response to, and within, a conversation, both spoken and written, for which I am grateful.

1.00   The question as to whether or not we transcend ourselves and, if in fact we do, how we do so, cannot be answered otherwise than by showing an act or acts that we engage in and that are properly understood as acts in and by which we transcend ourselves. In the course of the investigation how these transcending acts are related to intelligibility will become clear.

1.01   'Transcendence', 'transcendent', 'transcendental' are not used in the same way in different philosophies: contrast the uses of 'transcendental' in Kant and Schelling. In the same philosophy it can happen that, for example, the relation between 'transcendent', 'transcendence' and 'transcendental' is not at once clear: see Bernard Lonergan or Wittgenstein. In the *Tractatus*, is *tranzendental* used in 6.13 ('*Die Logik ist tranzendental*') precisely as it is used in 6.421 ('*Die Ethik ist tranzendental*')? I think not; nor is it a flaw that the uses are different. So it will not at once be evident how I use the term 'transcendence'. However, rather than attempt a definition, I shall let its meaning appear in its use. Enough to say now that 'to transcend' is 'to go beyond' and in that ordinary use there is the notion of limit or boundary.

2.00   Humans dream, imagine, ask questions, suggest answers, confirm or refute suggested answers, decide.

2.01   Consider conscious dreaming, that is dreaming when the dreamer is aware in their dream and can say, when they waken, that they dreamt and sometimes can recall the dream. In that activity the person does not go beyond, does not transcend, themselves. They are *extended* in the dream as we are extended in all our actions. Had they not dreamt, or had they dreamt differently, they would have been extended differently and they, or what Leibniz called their 'notion', would have been, very slightly, other than it is.

2.011   When we imagine, we extend but do not transcend ourselves. When we read a novel, listen to a piece of music, dance, paint or look at a picture we extend ourselves, sometimes greatly, but we do not yet seem to go beyond ourselves. As ordinary readers concerned only with reading we take for granted that reader, book and author are distinct; I presume that I am the reader, and that the text that I am reading and I are not the same thing. If, in fact, text and reader are distinct, readers do, in fact, go beyond themselves. But the presumption, to which we shall return, is taken for granted, not focused upon.

2.012   When we read, we read; we do not ask what we are doing, what is happening. The written text, which we know so well how to decipher that often it no longer feels like deciphering, persuades us to use our own language in a particular way. When we read a sentence, we understand it as if we had written it. When we hear a sentence, we understand it as if we had spoken it. The written or spoken text presents us with an image, and we ask what we would have meant had *we* produced that image. In that understanding we extend ourselves sometimes with ease, sometimes with great difficulty; we understand as we had not understood before but we do not yet go beyond ourselves. To understand a text is to be able to speak or write it oneself.[2]

2.0121   Sometimes we read a text that we ourselves have written without recognizing at once, or perhaps at all, that we wrote it.

2.013   We may imagine a circle and an ellipse with equal perimeters. Are their areas necessarily equal?

2.0131   We try to understand what we have imagined. The distinction between the image and the one who imagines is not a distinction between two separate things.

2.1   Here geometric figures are not significant for their own sake. The point is to show how the text, written or spoken, guides the competent reader or listener (in this case, readers or listeners who know English and some geometry) to ask the questions. How they have come upon those questions is, in some respects, unimportant.

2.2   We take for granted that I have suggested the questions and that you have or have not taken them up: we take for granted that you and I are distinct; but we do not focus on this.

3.00   Here is how far there is truth in solipsism. In a strict and fully worked out solipsism there is one subject in my world; the limits of what I can know are the limits of my world. I do not know *ipso facto* what these limits are, but I may try to give a structural account of them. My world is the extension of myself as my dreams are extensions of myself.

3.01   An account of solipsism attributed to F.H. Bradley runs: I cannot transcend experience, and experience is *my* experience. From this it follows that nothing beyond myself exists; for what is experienced is its (the self's) states. This is logically flawed. What follows is that I cannot *know* whether or not anything beyond myself exists. Solipsism goes beyond this to the judgment that nothing but I (*solus ipse*) exist. For the solipsist, text and reader are identical.

3.011   The solipsist's world is a set of images to be correctly understood. The solipsist, as well as another, judges correctly that a square and a rectangle of the same area do not necessarily have perimeters of the same length.

3.012   Solipsism is not relativism. It is incompatible with relativism. To be a relativist, the solipsist would have to think that mutually contradictory propositions, p and $-p$, were true. Relativism requires more than one subject.[3]

3.1   Were the solipsist correct, the unique subject could extend but could not transcend itself. The limits of what it can know are the limits of its world. It and its world coincide. Beyond those limits there is nothing. Within the solipsistic world, transcendence is an illusion.

3.11   The limits of my language are the limits of my world. I know myself as limited. To know a limit is to imagine a beyond-the-limit. The solipsist's claim is that there is nothing beyond-the-limit. If there is nothing beyond a limit, what does a limit become?[4]

3.111   If beyond that which was thought to be a limit, there is nothing, what was thought to be a limit is not one. Fully developed solipsism excludes the idea of limit. Limit is an illusion.

3.2   Solipsism coincides with realism – that is, with a realism that asserts the existence of things other than the person knowing – except at a single point: the point at which these questions arise: can I or do I know X? does X exist independently of me? do I exist independently of X?

3.21   To these questions the solipsist answer is 'yes' to the first, and 'no' to the second and third. The realist answer may be 'yes' to all three. The realist answer is nuanced; it may be 'yes' to all three but this depends on what X is; a dream is not independent of the dreamer, nor an image independent of the person imagining, nor an understanding independent of the person understanding, nor a judgment independent of the person judging.

3.22   For the realist X may exist independently, be known to exist, yet not be otherwise knowable.

4.00   Normally we take for granted that others (other things, other people) exist. If I judge that only I exist, I deny what until then I had taken for granted. What I had taken for granted is judged to be an illusion.

4.1   In our judgments we state what we hold to be the case. The dispute between solipsism and realism is about the context; about what is 'taken for granted'. What is taken for granted is realist. We take for granted that we live in a world with other things.

4.11   So is reached the first question of transcendence. Is the world that I know composed of a knower that is myself and a known or to-be-known that is not myself? When I know myself, knower and known are identical. What I – as solipsist – know, is myself.

4.2   There is no prior self-evident set of premises from which follows the conclusion that knower and known are distinct.

4.21   That there are things distinct from me and independent of me is not an internal presupposition of knowing; it is a reasonable judgment of fact, not a rational conclusion from unavoidable premises.

4.22   When two people talk to each other, which is the more reasonable judgment: 'The "other person" is simply an extension of myself' or 'The other person is indeed other than me'? Either I am everything that is, or I am one of the many things that are. If I am the whole of being – everything that is – then the judgment that I am everything that is, is correct and solipsism is correct. If I am one of the many things that are, then the corresponding judgment is correct and realism is correct.[5] To ask which is the more reasonable judgment is to ask which hypothesis makes better sense of the data, which intelligibility is to be accepted.

5.00   What is 'taken for granted' is that other things, other people, are other than me. What is taken for granted is what this set of judgments asserts: 'I exist', 'X exists', 'I am not X'. That this is 'taken for granted' is not sufficient evidence for the truth of the judgment that the object of enquiry may be other, and so sufficient evidence for the refutation of solipsism. Simply put, what is taken for granted in living is realist.

5.01   If I know what as a matter of fact is distinct from me, then I have gone beyond myself. If I take for granted that the thing I know is independent of me, and if what I take for granted is so, then I take for granted that I have transcended myself. If I as solipsist know what is as a matter of fact distinct from myself, but think that it is not, then I have transcended myself but think that I have not. If I have examined what I have taken for granted and judge that what I have taken for granted is so, then I have transcended myself and know – philosophically, reflectively – that I have done so.

5.011   We transcend ourselves as a matter of fact.

5.1   The possibility of transcendence is that there *are* other things and that we can know them. Transcendence is realized when we know other things. Knowing the possibility of transcendence is knowing that there are other things and that we can know them. What is 'taken for granted' is, then, the possibility of transcendence.

5.11   To 'know' something that is other than myself, but to judge that it is not other than myself, is not to know it.

5.12   The realist lives among other things. The realist is a being with other beings. This is taken for granted.[6]

5.13   We are with other beings as knowers. We ask what they are. We ask what other beings there are. We ask how we can discover what other beings there are.

6.00   We are with other beings as ethical subjects, as lovers, parents, children, friends, colleagues, enemies, antagonists. We are with others as ethical subjects before we know, philosophically, what it is to be an ethical subject.[7]

6.01   Not only can we choose: we must. We must ask what we are to do. We must economize our scarce resources to attain what seems good to us, but we do so with others. And so there is a second or ethical transcendence.

6.02   As there is a fundamental intellectual question between solipsism and realism, so there is a fundamental ethical question. The ethical question arises only within realism.

6.021   The ethical question emerges within the realist world, a world that includes other beings with interests other than mine. The fundamental ethical question is this: will I define the good as that which answers my interests irrespective of the interests of others or will I take others' interests into account? This question looks to a decision.[8]

6.022   Within the solipsistic world this question cannot arise.[9]

6.1   As with intellectual transcendence, there is here a 'taken for granted'. In knowing others, we know of interests other than our own. We know of others' interests in concert with, or in contrast or opposition to, our own.

6.11   In loving, we discover ourselves to have taken another's interests as our own. Conflicting interests may remain, since the fact that people love each other does not ensure that their immediate interests will always coincide; what is significant is that, when there is conflict, the other's interests are accepted as relevant to the effort to discover what is to be done. This acceptance of the other's interest is 'taken for granted'. It is not added on to loving. It is not argued for. It is intrinsic.

6.111   It is not a commandment. (Yet it is said to be.[10] What is a commandment? Is obeying a commandment like obeying an order? Are the words used in the same way?) Is the Samaritan in the parable obeying a commandment?

6.112   Moral education in every human culture is largely the customary expression of taking others' interests, others' freedom into account. We are taught that we should not lie. Lying tends to destroy the fabric of human communication and so human living. Lying is commonly the promotion of one's own interest *against* that of others.

6.2   What is taken for granted can become the focus of attention, and the question arises as to why we should consider others' interests. To attend to the contrast between solipsism and realism is rare; it clarifies what is taken for granted but rarely disturbs what is already taken for granted. How will the solipsist bring up (illusory) children?

6.21   Attention to the contrast between considering and not considering others is more common and looks not to a judgment merely but to a decision. What is often but not always taken for granted is less secure. Reflection on what is taken for granted may easily lead not so much to a great change of practice in the shorter period but to a profound change in attitude. And a profound change in the world.[11]

6.211   To take account of others may be seen as merely useful in some circumstances: *if you wish to advance, take into account the interests of those who may be able to assist you.* 'The good man rests content with goodness; he that is merely wise pursues goodness in the belief that it pays to do so.'[12]

6.212   The basic ethical question – whether we should take account of others' interests or only of our own – may be dealt with in a vacuum, as if those who ask it were not already ethical subjects, as if they were neutral beings.

6.22   We *are* ethical before we ask about what is taken for granted in our practice and before philosophical questions about ethics arise.[13]

6.3   What is taken for granted, what is an intrinsic part, in loving another is a disinterested acceptance of the importance of others' interests, others' freedom. The honourable person who makes a contract does so because it seems at the time in his own interest, but once the contract is made he takes the other's interest as his own and will fulfil the contract, even if, when the time comes for it to be honoured, it is no longer convenient.

6.31   Tzvetan Todorov writing of Bartolomeo de Las Casas (*Historia de las Indias*, 1561): *La supériorité du Christianisme est en ce qu'il déclare tous les hommes égaux et qu'il met l'amour au sommet des vertus. Si les chrétiens décide* [sic] *à la place des autres ce qui leur convient, il* [sic] *les traite* [sic] *en êtres inférieurs; s'ils imposent ce 'bon choix'* [conversion to Christianity] *par la force, ils font l'éloge du glaive, non de l'amour (Le Monde, 8 November, 2002.)* 'The superiority of Christianity is that it holds all men equal and that it places love at the summit of the virtues. If Christians decide for others what is suitable for them, they treat them as inferiors; if they impose this "good choice" [conversion to Christianity] on them, they honour the sword, not love.'

6.32   Why take others' freedom, others' interests into account? There is no compelling reason. But in choosing to do so in principle (however in practice in the course of living one may fall from principle) one transcends oneself. We choose to do so because that is the way we want to be. We are brought to the moment of choice not through logical argument or even an accumulation of reasons but more through an accumulation of images in which the other appears as one who puts a demand on us; or as one to whose demand upon us we have already responded. The parable of the good Samaritan is such an image.

6.321   We may see others as putting a demand on us; we may see them as those whose interests we have already in principle acknowledged: the ethical *aspect* of the world.

6.33   Ethical transcendence is realized in personal choice and emerges from a demand in which we recognize an absolute, a value which is its own reason.

6.331   There is no premise from which ethical transcendence follows. The ethical subject is the principle from which it emerges, or does not.

6.332   Nothing logically follows from ethical transcendence alone. When I decide to take others' interests into account, I do not yet know what to do, how to act. Nonetheless I see the world differently.

6.333   The other puts a demand on me.[14] But I recognize or do not recognize it.

7.00   In both intellectual and ethical transcendence *existence* is taken for granted. What is taken for granted may become the focus of attention. In intellectual transcendence I go beyond solipsism, but that the world exists I take for granted; to say that I and other things exist is to say that the world *is*. In ethical transcendence I take others' interests into account but *that* we exist is taken for granted.

7.1   The question of existence is answered in human religions. It is answered obscurely. It is answered more clearly than it is asked. The story of creation in Genesis appears to be, and is, an account of how the world developed in seven phases. It is not a scientific account as it is not an answer to a scientific question. More obscurely, it is an answer to the question as to why the world is. Superficially, the Genesis story is about how the world exists or – and this is a distinct question – why it is as it is; profoundly it attends to the fact *that it exists*. God (Elohim in the first chapter of Genesis; Yahweh in the second) functions in the stories as the answer to the question of existence. But as the answer is a symbol, so the attitude of wonder that gave rise to it is a symbol; it is not a philosophical answer as it was not a philosophical question. In European Christianity, owing to its philosophical and theological tradition, the answer is communicated in philosophico-theological language before the question to which that kind of answer would be appropriate is asked, and some will never ask it, nor do they need to, for the religious attitude is not a preparation for philosophy.

7.11   God may become in a philosophy the name of the answer to a question that has not been asked.

7.12   For when we speak of God all our terms and actions seem to be part of a great and elaborate allegory. But this allegory also describes the experience which I have just referred to, namely, the experience that is best described by saying that 'when I have it, *I wonder at the existence of the world*'.[15]

7.2   The question here is not Descartes's question as to whether or not I and others exist, but what existence is.

7.21   Unless the world exists, the question as to why it exists does not arise. The judgment that the world exists is true. That the world exists is a fact. When Wittgenstein writes, *Nicht wie die Welt ist, ist das Mystische, sondern dass sie ist*,[16] he turns the fact into a questionable fact. When I wonder at the existence of the world, then that the world exists is, for me, puzzling.

7.211   If I do not wonder at the existence of the world, then that it exists is not, for me, puzzling.

7.22   I may address the question as to why the world exists. I may simply ignore it. It may never occur to me. Sometimes we are aware of the mysteriousness of the existence of the world; sometimes the question presses upon us; sometimes we wonder; sometimes we do not.

7.221   Actual wonder about this, as about anything, cannot be forced. Philosophy is autobiographical.[17]

7.2211   I may examine not the question itself but its emergence. Why does the question arise in me? There are cultural, psychological and autobiographical reasons. There are philosophical reasons, or rather there are intellectual presuppositions at work that philosophical analysis may disclose. There is what has been given various names in different traditions that in Christianity is called grace.

7.222   I do not stand outside the world but am part of it.[18] Why the world exists includes the question as to why I am. The sciences seek the intelligibility of the world, to understand *how* the world is. *That* the world is, the sciences take for granted. That what science investigates is intelligible is the operative presupposition of science.

7.2221   What is taken for granted is not – cannot be – a scientific conclusion.

7.2222   What is taken for granted may become the object of wonder because the only limit to our questioning is that a question does not properly arise. This is mind's unavoidable presupposition.

7.3   A question that does not properly arise is one that looks for an intelligibility where there is none. If the question of existence does not properly arise and therefore has no answer, the intended intelligibility does not exist and that the world exists is unintelligible, absurd.

7.31   That a question does not properly arise must be discovered. Absurdity is not to be simply asserted.

7.32   The question as to why the world exists does sometimes, as a matter of autobiographical fact, arise. (Equally, sometimes, as a matter of autobiographical fact, it simply does not arise.) It does so for the reason that any and every question arises: we discover that we do not understand. Were someone to say that the question does not properly arise, he must say why it does not, that is, he must show that here the natural movement of intellect stops. He can show this only by showing that what we want to understand is unintelligible, that is, absurd.

7.33   Sometimes the question is refused. With those who refuse the question, apparent answers cannot be discussed.

7.331   From those who do not ask the question, the absurdity of the unintelligible is hidden.

7.34   To say that something is unintelligible is not to say that we cannot understand; it is to say that there is nothing to be understood.

7.4   If that the world is, is mysterious, not absurd, still one may be able to say nothing more than that the existence of the world is mysterious, but I do not understand it. This, I think, is why Wittgenstein speaks of this matter as 'the mystical' in the *Tractatus* and as 'the miraculous' in 'A Lecture on Ethics'.

7.41   A comment on two short passages; the first from the *Tractatus*; the second from 'A Lecture on Ethics'.

7.411   *Tractatus* 6.432: *Wie die Welt ist, ist für das Hohere vollkommen gleichgultig. Gott offenbart sich nicht in der Welt.* ('How the World is, is for the Higher wholly irrelevant. God does not reveal himself in the World.') The first of these propositions states that, with reference to the question of the existence of the world, the question as to how it exists, the manner in which it is, which is the object of the sciences, is immaterial. See *Tractatus* 4.1122. The question as to why the world exists is not a scientific question. The second sentence, apparently very different, expresses the same proposition, that is, states the same thing: God, the name of the answer to the question as to why the world exists, is not discovered in the sciences because it is not the answer to a scientific question. God does not manifest himself *in* the world; the answer to the question of existence does not emerge in the sciences *of* the world because the question *cannot* be asked *within* the sciences of the world. Were God to manifest himself in the world, the world would hold the explanation of its existence, the existence of the world would be the object of science. Here 'God' is the name for the unknown explanation of what does not explain itself.

7.412   'A Lecture on Ethics', p.11: 'I now see that these nonsensical expressions were not nonsensical because I had not yet found the correct expressions, but that their nonsensicality was their very essence. For all I wanted to do with them was just to go beyond the world and that is to say beyond significant language. My whole tendency, and I believe the whole tendency of all men who ever tried to write or talk Ethics or Religion, was to run against the boundaries of language.' The recurrent temptation is to think of the question of existence as like any other question; this is what Wittgenstein would avoid. Because it is, significantly yet not utterly, unlike any other question, because it has been taken as simply another question, this must be concentrated on: does it properly arise? The boundaries of (scientific) language are not the boundaries of wonder.

8.00   Religion is never merely the acknowledgment that the intelligibility of the existence of the world is not in the world. Religion is a response to that intelligibility, however it has shown itself and whatever its name. The prayers, buildings, images, music, liturgies of the religions imaginatively articulate the appropriate response.[19] In Judaism, Christianity and Islam, the names of the intelligibility are Yahweh, Father, Son and Holy Spirit, and Allah. Religion intends transcendence.

8.01   If the philosopher accepts that the question as to the existence of the world properly arises and that therefore it has an answer,[20] then further questions arise, for the intelligibility of existence, including my existence, is no longer merely a fact: for the existence of what is merely a fact is unintelligible. The relationship between my factual existence and its exogenous intelligibility cannot be genuinely avoided.

8.011   The living of the relationship between me and ultimate intelligibility is religion. The study of it is the philosophy of religion.[21]

8.012   What in the Christian tradition has been called the 'presence of God' (it has different names and different symbols in other traditions) is simply that the world, intelligibly, exists. *To acknowledge* the presence of God is to find existence mysterious *and* to accept its intelligibility.

8.0121   What is thought to exist intelligibly is thought to exist differently from unintelligible existence. What in fact exists intelligibly exists differently from unintelligible existence.

9.00   There is no given proposition whence follows the proposition that existence is intelligible.

Notes

1   An earlier version of this paper was read at a meeting of the Irish Philosophical Society in Cork (29–30 November 2002).

2   We misunderstand often because we have not previously used words as they are used in the text and squeeze them into the ill-fitting moulds already available to us.

3   These points were expanded on by Barden in a letter to the editor. Barden writes as follows: 'I did not mean that the solipsist had to reject the principle of contradiction, but that, in order to be a relativist, he would have to. The relativist holds that A holds p, and B holds $-p$, and that both A and B may be correct to hold what they hold; that is, p is true for A and $-p$ is true for B. The relativist does not hold that p and $-p$ are true for himself; the relativist does not, or not usually, want to hold that the principle of contradiction is unsound for one person. Neither does the solipsist hold that the principle of contradiction is unsound. (Were one to hold that, one would also hold, or be able to hold, that the principle of contradiction was sound. This is the core of Gaston

Isaye's argument. [See note 6.]) Now, if *C* is both a solipsist and a relativist, *C* would hold that he is equally correct in holding *p* or −*p*; that is, *p* is true for *C* and −*p* is true for *C*; for *C* is the only existent for whom *p* and −*p* can be true.'

4 Wittgenstein, *Tractatus Logico-Philosophicus: The German Text of Ludwig Wittgenstein's* Logisch-philosophische Abhandlung, with a new translation by D.F. Pears and B.F. McGuinness, London: Routledge and Kegan Paul (1969), 4th impression; 5.6: *Die Grenzen meiner Sprache bedeuten die Grenzen meiner Welt*; 5.62: *Was der Solipsismus nämlich meint, ist ganz richtig; nur lässt es sich nicht sagen, sondern es zeigt sich. Dass meine Welt* meine *ist, das zeigt sich darin, dass die Grenzen der Sprache (der Sprache, die allein ich verstehe) die Grenzen* meiner *Welt bedeuten.* This must be understood in the light of 6.47.

5 'Realism' is not unquestionably the most illuminating name for *this* anti-solipsism. There are 'realists' for whom the taken for granted is obvious and unquestionable.

6 See Gaston Isaye, 'La Métaphysique des Simples', *Nouvelle Revue Théologique*, **LXXXII** (7), 1960.

7 See Garrett Barden (2001), 'Ethics and the Discernment of Spirits', *Ethical Perspectives*, **8** (4), pp.254–67.

8 See Gilles Bernheim, *Le Souci des Autres au Fondement de la Loi Juive*, Paris: Calman-Lévy, 2002; Esther Benbassa and Jean-Christophe Attias, *Le Juif et l'Autre*, Paris: Le Relie, 2002.

9 The term 'solipsism' is sometimes used to refer to egoism. As it is used here, the solipsist cannot be an egoist as there is no other interest for him to ignore.

10 Deuteronomy 6: 5; Matthew 22: 34–40; Luke 10: 25–28. However they are to be understood, the first and greatest commandment and the second that is like unto it (Thou shalt love thy neighbour as thyself) are not pure conventions.

11 See *Tractatus*, 6.43.

12 Confucius, *The Analects*, IV.2; Waley's translation.

13 That we do not choose to become, but rather discover ourselves to be, ethical beings is, incidentally, the foundation of 'natural law' as understood by St Thomas Aquinas: *Sum. Theol.* la, llae, Q.90 ss. See also Garrett Barden, *After Principles*, Indiana: Notre Dame University Press, 1990.

14 For Buber and Lévinas, mutual demand is the way in which we appear to each other.

15 Wittgenstein, 'A Lecture on Ethics', pp.8–10, published in *The Philosophical Review*, London, January 1965, pp.3–12.

16 *Tractatus*, 6.44.

17 Cyril Barrett (1998), 'The Usefulness of God', *Milltown Studies*, **41** (Summer), 33: 'wonderment [about existence] is not something that can be injected or inculcated. But nor can it be rejected in the name of science as unscientific. It is neither scientific nor unscientific: it is non-scientific.'

18 But I do not know myself *as subject*. I am myself as subject. See Bernard Lonergan (1967), 'Cognitional Structure', in F.E. Crowe (ed.), *Collection: Papers by Bernard Lonergan, S.J.*, London: Darton, Longman & Todd. See also Wittgenstein, *Tractatus*, 5.6–5.641.

19 For example, in the repetitive prayers, *dhikr* ('recollection of God'), written of by Al-Ghazali in the *Ihyâ' 'ulum al-Dîn*: 'There is no god but God alone. There is none like him. To him belongs Royalty and praise. He gives death and life. He is living and immortal. Goodness is in his hand and his Power is over all things.'

20 To say that a question has no answer is to say that it is not properly a question.

21 I have argued in William Desmond's seminar in Leuven (1998) that only the religious person can properly be a philosopher of religion. The essay appears in Babette Babich (ed.), *Hermeneutic Philosophy of Science. Van Gogh's Eyes and God: Essays in Honor of Patrick A. Heelan, SJ*, Boston Studies in the Philosophy of Science 225, Dordrecht: Kluwer Academic Publishers, 2002, pp.385–92.

III
READING DESMOND

Chapter 4

Metaxological Metaphysics and Idiotic Style: The 'Conceptual Persona' of William Desmond

Jere O'Neill Surber

I shall begin by confessing that this essay had its origins in my own sort of 'idiocy', in something quite anecdotal. Over the course of my career, it has been my decidedly good fortune to have worked and been friends with three fine thinkers, all of whom would certainly qualify as 'metaxological philosophers': Gottfried Martin, my sponsor and dissertation director at the University of Bonn; Paul Weiss, with whom I briefly studied and who was a colleague of mine for a time; and, of course, William Desmond. While such a complaint never appears in their published work, I have heard all, at one time or another, wistfully lament that, despite all their best efforts to remain true to the calling of philosophy, they did not feel that their work had been given the attention in the broader philosophical community that they had hoped. I have always thought, in all three cases, that this sense of neglect was completely justified. After all, each of them, in his own 'idiotic' way, persistently engaged the entire tradition of philosophy and its fundamental issues; each had as his aim nothing less than the articulation of a comprehensive viewpoint that could accommodate the most valuable aspects of other views, while maintaining a critical stance toward their deficiencies and excesses; each insisted that philosophy not merely be a sterile categorical construction but must also be driven by, and connect with, fundamental features of human life and experience; each lavished a great deal of attention on locating the discourse of philosophy among those of competitors such as art, science, religion and culture; and each attempted, carefully, generously, and in detail, to respond to other contemporary viewpoints. What more could one ask of a philosopher? And yet, when one observes the great number of seminars, journal articles and issues, and conferences devoted to a Kripke, a Putnam, a Davidson, a Rorty, or, yes, a Derrida, authors to whom, in my mind at least, the same term 'philosopher' could hardly be applied in the same sense as to those whom I have just mentioned, then one begins to wonder what is amiss here, what accounts for the relative neglect of thinkers who are so clearly exemplary for this enterprise.

Of course many explanations, most of them by now well canvassed, immediately come to mind. For instance, there is the frequently heard observation that it is just the *Zeitgeist,* that we simply live in an 'anti-metaphysical' or even 'anti-philosophical' era. Or perhaps it is that these 'metaxological metaphysicians' simply did not get one of the messages clearly delivered by their philosophical predecessors two hundred years ago: either that of Kant, that metaphysics of any but a very restricted sort is no longer a viable project, or that of Hegel, that the work of metaphysics has already been accomplished and anything further will simply be some permutation of what went before (if it is not a repetition of some part of Hegel's own system). Or perhaps these present-day metaxologists simply have not realized that we now live in a postmodern, post-metaphysical world, that the combined forces of science and technology have brought to concrete historical fulfilment the systematic dreams of the great system builders of the seventeenth and eighteenth centuries and that our task now is to awaken from the 'dream' and get on with the 'real work', either of realizing that the only philosophical task left to accomplish is one of 'clearing away the metaphysical rubble obstructing the path of scientific progress', or of 'thinking beyond the limits of the tradition' within the new 'opening' provided by the 'postmodern condition'. While some, or even all, of these views may possess a grain of truth, they tend, in one way or another, not to be very convincing with respect to the case at hand, since all the philosophers whom I have mentioned have explicitly confronted these very issues; indeed it is, I think, fair to say that they have all commenced their projects with such objections very much in mind, and have proceeded in ways designed, at least in part, to respond constructively to them.

Of course this in turn raises the further point of why their 'anti-metaphysical' opponents have usually not seen fit to offer a rebuttal, but have simply ignored their carefully crafted responses. On this score, I think it likely that their minds had already been made up, and that the only explanation must be sought in the realm of, perhaps, the social psychology (or perhaps pathology) of academic disciplines. More to the point, however, is the relative neglect of the modern 'metaxologists'' views on the part of others, those who have remained open-minded about the continuing possibility for philosophy; who are sceptical about the sweeping claims of those, whether on Kantian, Hegelian, Nietzschean or Heideggerian grounds, who would aver that the metaphysical (or even 'Western') tradition at some point reached its *telos* or culmination or, even worse, that the entire project was one massive historical error; and who remain sympathetic with the affirmative stance taken by the 'metaxologists', even as they elect neither to adopt some form of these views as their own nor to take on parallel projects that would directly engage them.

In what follows, I wish to suggest a different line to those mentioned above for understanding this phenomenon, one which, I hope, more directly and specifically engages such views, and which helps to specify more exactly where the root of this lies. As will become clear, my own view is that the problem is endemic to post-Hegelian 'metaxological' approaches themselves (of which Desmond's work is a particularly apt and explicitly articulated example). My sketch of this approach will involve two parts. First, making use of Desmond's own schema for defining his project, I will suggest that the 'metaxological approach' that he develops raises unique and critical questions concerning the 'style' of philosophical presentation, questions relevant to, but not nearly so decisive for, the other approaches that he discusses. In particular, I will suggest that the 'styles' of presentation of the 'metaxologists' are inseparable from the cogency of the particular conceptual frameworks that they are concerned to develop. Second, I will attempt to specify more precisely the connection between their 'idiotic styles' and their conceptual constructions, and propose a rather different alternative by borrowing some ideas from the remarkable last work of Gilles Deleuze and Felix Guattari, *What is Philosophy?*[1]: in particular, their notion of a 'conceptual persona'.

Desmond's 'Fourfold Stances' and the Question of Style

Desmond's major work, *Being and the Between*, opens by laying out a 'plane' (already to borrow a term from Deleuze and Guattari) upon which various broad types of philosophical views can be located along two major axes: the first axis concerns the sort of fundamental assumptions that are made about the nature of being (a sort of classification of possible 'ontologies'), and the second a discussion of the basic 'prereflective' or 'preconceptual' experiences or attitudes out of which discourses about being arise or, alternatively, which provoke and fuel such discourse. While a more complete and nuanced account of Desmond's views and procedures would trace the various ways in which these two axes intersect, and thus permit him to locate various philosophical discourses upon this plane, I will, for the purposes of this essay, restrict myself to a more general discussion of the four 'ontological stances' in relation to the question of philosophical style.

Before I begin, however, a few comments about Desmond's 'fourfold typology' are in order since, despite his own efforts, the gravamen of his discussion could be easily misconstrued. First, his distinctions among the 'univocal', 'equivocal', 'dialectical' and 'metaxological' should be read, I think, as at once demarcating a set of general ontological stances or attitudes towards being, and also specifying a general typology of ways that being can be (and has been) spoken about, and the methodologies, implicit or explicit, governing them. Second, it should not be thought that these four represent completely mutually exclusive cases, since not only is it possible for various hybrids to occur (as Desmond seems to suggest in the cases of Plato and the Neoplatonists, and of Aristotle and Aquinas, for instance), but individual figures may, at various points, even in a single text, adopt apparently different views. In fact Desmond seems to suggest that, in actual philosophical discourses, one (almost?) never encounters 'pure' cases of any one of these stances or attitudes. Most importantly, however, Desmond seems to maintain that there is an 'order of precedence' among them. As he himself puts it most succinctly, 'a dialectic tries to redeem the promise of univocity beyond equivocity, so the metaxological tries to redeem the promise of equivocity beyond univocity and dialectic' (BB, 178).

This suggests the important points that, while both the dialectical and metaxological stances will always at least contain traces of the univocal and equivocal (and the metaxological of the dialectical as well), there are also some important asymmetries and relations of exclusion obtaining among them. In a sense, then, Desmond's 'plane,' even on these grounds and excluding the other axis, is somewhat irregular, and not to be understood as some exhaustive whole or continuum (a result which should not be surprising, given Desmond's frequent insistence on the intrinsically incompletable and plurivocal nature of the task of philosophy).

Keeping these points in mind as warnings against taking any of the following discussion as harder-edged than its schematic character might otherwise suggest, I offer the following general overview of the relations between each ontological stance and the nature of the respective 'philosophical style' appropriate to it.

Univocal

Already with the first general ontological stance, the plot becomes complex, since what would seem to be the most straightforward view already harbours within itself a radical dichotomy when confronted with the question of style. If being is indeed one or, alternatively, if 'being' is predicated in a univocal sense, then at least two diametrically opposed styles of articulation present themselves. On the one hand, we might say that the only style appropriate to the univocal view of being is one that comes as closely as possible to employing discourse that is equally univocal in its meaning and signification. As Desmond himself notes, the 'ideal language' of the sciences so hotly pursued by the logical positivists might serve as one example, another being the never fully developed *mathesis universalis* proposed by Leibniz. Perhaps the closest example of such a style in the tradition that still maintained some connection with 'natural language' would be the *Ethics* of Spinoza. But, on the other hand, and especially in light of the discursive paradoxes presented in such Platonic dialogues as the *Parmenides* and the *Sophist,* not to mention the later thought of Heidegger, we might also claim that, if being itself is univocal, then *only* poetic language would constitute a suitable style, on the grounds that, while poetic language is able to 'disclose' being without opposing itself to it, all univocal attempts to make statements *about* being from a stance, as it were, 'outside being' would violate the assumption of univocity in their very utterance. That is, such univocal statements would succeed only in dividing Being into 'being' and 'discourse about it', in creating a 'two' (at least) rather than disclosing a fundamental 'one'. My main point here, however, is not the late Platonic one, but simply that the question of style in the context of univocal views is a relatively straightforward one that may call for a decision, but possess no genuine philosophical issue in its own terms. That positivists and mystics can live together under the rubric of univocity seems paradoxical, but it is an uninteresting paradox, one that, in the end, raises no open questions for further philosophical reflection (*pace* Heidegger) and that is, consequently, entirely external to the ontological view underlying it.

Equivocal

By contrast, if one's underlying ontological conviction is that 'being is many' or is 'said in many ways', then, in the most extreme case, there is no stylistic choice to be made; rather, any and every style, from rigorous *apophansis* to the most experimental poetry, will succeed in saying or disclosing something or other about the nature of being. Of course, in practice, most thinkers of equivocity (at least pre-Nietzschean ones) have tended to restrict the 'play of signification' to a more limited set of cases (as Aristotle or Kant do in their theories of categories, or as Hume does, at least implicitly, in his account of ideas coupled with passions). In such (one is almost tempted to say 'non-Nietzschean' or 'non-Derridean') cases, questions of philosophical style are, for the most part, predetermined by the specific categorical or psychological framework being endorsed. Typically, then, questions of style are, if posed at all, formulated on the assumption of some difference between 'philosophical style' (which is regarded as neutral and transparent, somewhat like Kant's 'transcendental idiom') and other occurrences of style in the context of 'ordinary language', aesthetics and the like. There is an appearance of paradox here as well, since the most extreme cases (like some parts of Nietzsche or the early Derrida) can scarcely be called equivocal in Desmond's sense, since they arguably lack any 'ontology' to begin with, while other more limited and 'impure' cases, like that of Aristotle or Kant, tend to smuggle in more univocal tendencies by which the specific question of philosophical style can be marginalized or neutralized in the manner indicated above. As a result, from a stance of equivocity, either there is no distinctly philosophical problem of style ('anything goes in the bacchanalian revel') or style is a matter for other modes of discourse, but not that of philosophy, where it is a neutral issue.

Dialectical

Viewed from the present perspective, Hegel turns out to be, as in so many other ways, a pivotal figure for the entire discussion (and how one reads Hegel will turn out, as Desmond often insists, to be a crucial matter, though I will not take up such issues as I have with his reading of Hegel here). For my purposes, one can interpret Desmond's claim that Hegel 'redeems univocity beyond equivocity' (BB, 178 ff.) as suggesting, among other things, that part of Hegel's task was to demonstrate, beginning with the myriad accounts of being constituting the tradition, that they could be read developmentally (or 'dialectically') in such a way that they could be understood as culminating in a comprehensive, internally complex and mediated, but nonetheless finally single philosophical standpoint, in other words, a higher order, dynamic, and multivalent type of univocity (what Hegel called 'the Concept', *der Begriff*).

Such a project naturally posed new and rather different questions about philosophical style than the preceding views. On the one hand, the dialectical approach, by acknowledging the plurivocity of the tradition, created a philosophical space in which, perhaps for the first time, questions of philosophical style could appear as significant and relevant, not, as before, more or less predetermined by, or directly fitted to, a philosopher's ontological starting-point.[2] On the other hand, however, Hegel seems, by his own procedures, to take back what he has offered when it comes to his own system. On his view, the diversity of philosophical styles turns out to be an effect or result of the fact that, prior to his system, the 'content' of philosophy has not yet come to coincide with its proper systematic 'form'. Pre-Hegelian philosophies, on this account, present a variety of styles and approaches that are, in an important sense, external to the 'content' (that is, the 'Truth' in Hegel's special sense of this term) that they are attempting, though inadequately, to articulate. As such, a philosopher's style of articulation is philosophically significant only as an index of its relative 'dialectical immaturity' in relation to Hegel's own view. Once the fully developed dialectical standpoint has been reached (one version of which is presented as the culmination of the Jena *Phenomenology of Spirit*), then 'pure thinking' (as pursued in the *Science of Logic*) can commence, relieved of any need to consider the merely 'external' stylistic issues arising in the preceding tradition.

Once more, although the dialectical standpoint does allow questions of style to emerge as philosophically relevant, their significance ends with the commencement of Hegel's own dialectical project. While the dialectical standpoint does place the question of style on the table in the case of other philosophical views, it then disappears as an issue from Hegel's own systematic project. I would add, as an aside, that the self-conscious and calculated stylistic devices employed by some of his immediate successors (Kierkegaard's pseudonyms and Nietzsche's various guises, tropes and aphorisms come immediately to mind) are not merely a product of idiosyncratic experimentation, but constitutive, in important ways, of their critical response to the neutralizing position of the dialectical standpoint with regard to philosophical style.

Metaxological

In contrast to the preceding standpoints, all of which, in one way or another, either fail to raise any serious issue regarding philosophical style, insulate it from the work of philosophy or neutralize it altogether, I want now to suggest that it becomes a fundamental, inextricable, even decisive issue for the metaxological standpoint. Recall Desmond's own characterization of this stance: 'the metaxological tries to redeem the promise of equivocity beyond univocity and dialectic'. Although a full unpacking of this formula would be (and certainly is throughout Desmond's own work) a highly complex and nuanced matter, I would offer the following as one characterization of Desmond's overall project. From his earliest works, in which Hegel serves as the central focus of the discussion, I think that Desmond makes three important concessions to Hegel. First, Hegel has decisively shown that there is an intrinsic and dynamic relationship between the stances of univocity and equivocity, such that neither can be articulated as an adequate philosophical standpoint without the employment, implicitly or explicitly, of the other. In other words, after Hegel, neither is available as the exclusive basis for philosophical thought. Second, he agrees with Hegel's insistence that such a demonstration is possible only within a systematic framework. That is, the first is not a point that can be made simply by random or 'external' argumentation. Finally, he affirms, with Hegel, that any systematic framework must be constituted by (perhaps among other things) a complex set of interrelations and mediations among concepts, that is, that concepts do play an important role in the articulation of any viable philosophical position.

Clearly, however, Desmond also wishes to distinguish his own metaxological view from that of Hegel on the grounds that Hegel himself ultimately accorded far too much weight to univocity, that, to use Hegelian terms, every relation between 'identity and difference' must be understood in terms of a 'higher identity'. For Desmond, the move from a dialectical to a metaxological stance is accomplished by the recognition that Hegel's own 'dialectical identification of identity and difference' opens a space, suppressed by Hegel's own procedures, for considering, as well, the 'differences between identity and difference'. Translated into Desmond's terms, the dialectical attempt to mediate univocity and equivocity at once suppresses equivocity in favour of a 'higher order univocity' and, at the same time, opens the possibility for a recovery of suppressed equivocity in the form of a metaxological project.

To return to Desmond's concessions to Hegel, this move from the dialectical to the metaxological requires that each of his concessions undergoes an important qualification or reformulation. First, while univocity and equivocity remain, from the metaxological viewpoint, complexly interrelated, the true complexity and nuance of their interrelations cannot be adequately described in terms of some dialectical synthesis or 'higher univocity'. They are simply more complex and, in a way, more unruly and asymmetrical than the dialectical account suggests. Second, although a systematic framework for exploring this complex web of interrelations is indispensable, it cannot constitute the sort of 'closed system' that the dialectical stance implies. While metaxological philosophy is, in its way, systematic, it is an 'open system' at least in the sense that new relationships, new and different ways in which univocity and equivocity engage one another, are always possible. Finally, while a metaxological perspective is not opposed to concepts, and indeed must employ them for the articulation of its basic framework, its concepts must continually maintain their connection with concrete experience, which lends to them a sort of openness and 'jaggedness' or 'irregularity of contour' suppressed in the dialectical approach, where all concepts neatly take their place and fold into the final, mediated univocity of *der Begriff*.

While I certainly do not regard this as a complete or adequate account of Desmond's views, I think the preceding discussion is sufficient to allow us to indicate more exactly the decisive role that style plays for the metaxological stance. If a (higher?) equivocity is to be redeemed from the 'higher univocity' of the dialectical, and if, as I have argued, it at the same time continues to maintain the importance of employing concepts ordered within a broader systematic framework, then the question arises: what serves as the underlying connective tissue of the metaxological standpoint, replacing the dialectical progression towards 'higher univocity' of the dialectical stance? I suggest that it can only be the philosophical style of the author that stands 'between', mediates and fleshes out fundamental concepts with the 'idiotic' particularities of experience (especially those wellsprings of philosophical discourse presented by Desmond as 'astonishment' and 'perplexity'). But this, of course, means in turn that a great deal of freight is carried by the metaxological philosopher's style itself, thus posing style as a question lying at the heart of this mode of philosophy. For metaxology, there is finally no escape from the question of style, since to ignore or marginalize it would be to signal the very cessation of the particular and 'idiotic' element that is required for the move beyond the 'stylistic neutrality' of Hegel's 'higher univocity'.

To return for a moment to my 'idiotic' opening discussion, I think this goes a long way towards explaining my own response, and perhaps that of others, to all the 'metaxologists' whom I mentioned. While their styles (understood in a broader sense than the merely literary) are quite different from one another, I have always had similar feelings in reading their texts. While I can always find in their texts many powerful insights, illuminating discussions and suggestive directions for my own thinking, the overall 'systems' which they develop and within which they locate themselves only come to life for me by virtue of their own idiotic styles. For instance, Weiss's *Modes of Being*[3] is certainly a robust and comprehensive philosophical construction, but somehow it took hearing Weiss explicate and work within it in his teaching (and, to a lesser degree, in his accompanying 'philosophical journals' called *Philosophy in Process*[4]) for me to appreciate its real cogency and power. Without Weiss 'at the controls', his system struck me as something of a great machine that required an equally great pilot to get it off the ground. Martin was, as well, a powerful teacher, but his meticulous scholarship, especially on Plato, Aristotle, Leibniz and Kant, provided the substructure for his major systematic work, *General Metaphysics*,[5] which seemed to me somehow flat without it. To his credit, Desmond has, for me, been the most successful of the 'metaxologists' because his own 'idiotic style', which I think of as a sort of philosophical poetry, or perhaps poetic philosophy, requires neither his actual presence as a teacher nor the production of other texts supplementary to his more systematic works. Rather his own seductive, eloquent and often inspiring 'idiocy' is a continual presence on every page of his texts.

But here is the crux of the issue. It reminds me of the story of George Gershwin, who, at the very height of his international fame as a composer, decided he had reached his own limits and went to Paris to seek out Maurice Ravel, then perhaps the most renowned living composer in Europe, for instruction in composition. On their first meeting, it was reported that Ravel declined Gershwin's request to become his student, saying, 'Ah, Mr. Gershwin, I am a great admirer of your own work; you do Gershwin so very well, but I do not think that your trying to do Ravel would be so impressive.' My point is that if, as I have argued, philosophical style is decisive for the cogency and power of a metaxological project, and if style is a radically particular, personal and 'idiotic' matter, then one can only admire any metaxological philosophy, perhaps gain some illumination from it, but one will always find it difficult to adopt as one's own stance. And, if this is the case, then even the most admiring and sympathetic reader is, at some, perhaps premature, point, likely to say, 'I realize that there is no benefit in my trying to do this; perhaps I should cultivate my own style and philosophy, and leave the metaxologist to do the same ... or, perhaps return to Hegel and see whether the "metaxological move" was even necessary in the first place.' Of course it may well be that this is, and always has been, the true mark of strong and innovative philosophers: that they provoke their readers to return to the wellsprings of their own discourse and articulate, in their own idiom, what it means to 'be between'. If this is the case, then the seeming neglect of the 'metaxologists' may well be a sign of their true worth as philosophers. Perhaps ceasing to read may, in the end, be the condition for starting to think for oneself, metaxologically.

Another Alternative: The Idea of the 'Conceptual Persona'

Having said all this, 'idiotic' as it surely is, I confess that I am not yet quite prepared to abandon the metaxological project entirely, nor am I quite ready to return, like a prodigal son, to Hegel. In this much briefer section, I would like to make one proposal as to how one might proceed in light of the issues I have raised. In doing so, I will poach some of the ideas developed by Gilles Deleuze and Felix Guattari in their quite remarkable final work together, *What is Philosophy?*, without, by any means, wishing to endorse either their overall viewpoint or other more particular aspects of their works, either written together or separately.

In this work, Deleuze and Guattari characterize philosophy as a distinctive type of enterprise, differing from, but intersecting with, those of art and science, whose fundamental and distinctive task is to 'construct strong concepts' on a 'plane of immanence' out of the 'chaos' of experience. In so doing, they wish to insist that philosophy emerges as a bidirectional and dynamic process of, at once, constructing concepts around which a plane of discourse coalesces and becomes organized, and determining the contours of this plane so that the 'strong concepts' can be seen to possess their own specific location or place with respect to the plane. In the course of their discussion, they make the further points that both concepts and their plane are, for numerous reasons, necessarily irregular and asymmetrical. From this point, the task of philosophy is to explore the network of complex interrelations formed by these always irregular concepts interacting with one another over a plane which, consequently, becomes itself 'warped' by the conceptual 'force fields' playing across it. Admittedly much of this account is metaphorical, but it does serve to suggest that we should never expect either complete consistency or rigorous predictability of the directions and turnings that a philosophy may take in the process of its elaboration. Further, viewed in this way, philosophy itself, and not just its style of articulation, will always be, to some extent, 'idiotic' (interestingly, the very same term used so often by Desmond).

Whether such a view of philosophy should be regarded as metaxological is difficult to say, but it does share certain important points with Desmond's description of this standpoint. Among them, Deleuze and Guattari agree with Desmond that philosophy must be conceived pluralistically, that any univocal view of 'properly philosophical' style, method or content must be rejected as untenable. While they are probably more critical of Hegel and the dialectical stance than is

Desmond, and hence more 'radically pluralistic' than he, they nonetheless share with him a desire to save equivocity from being extinguished in any 'higher univocal' framework, while insisting that this does not imply the wholesale abandonment of conceptual discourse in favour of the 'limitless play of signifiers', as some of the other postmodernists with whom they are often grouped have claimed. Finally their insistence that the real task of philosophy is the exploration of the 'network of connections' that make up the 'plane of immanence' is not far from Desmond's own characterization, especially in their mutual conviction that this process involves something of a risk and an adventure, not just a mechanical 'deduction' or methodological expansion of the starting-point of reflection. I think there are other similarities, although these commonalities should at least suffice to secure the plausibility of the suggestion I will make.

With regard to the issue of philosophical style that we have been pursuing, Deleuze and Guattari introduce a quite novel and striking idea: that of the 'conceptual persona'. Roughly, they suggest that the 'construction of strong concepts upon a plane of immanence' is performed by a 'conceptual persona' which, although it arises from the 'idiocy' (their word!) of the actual author, comes to possess a sort of life of its own as the 'thinker of concepts' and the occupant of their 'plane of immanence'. Perhaps this idea is most easily seen in some of the examples they offer: the Socrates of the Platonic dialogues, Descartes' 'hyperbolic doubter' in the *Meditations*, Kierkegaard's pseudononymous authors, and Nietzsche's Dionysus, Antichrist and, most of all, Zarathustra. Viewed as various 'conceptual personae', Deleuze and Guattari claim that these arise through a sort of 'schizoid process' on the part of the individual author, in which the author's radically particular 'idiocy' assumes the form of a sort of alter ego existing at the intersection where the 'plane of immanence' meets the 'chaos of experience' out of which it emerged. In the terms we have been employing, the function of such conceptual personae is clear: they serve to mediate between the radical 'idiocy' of the existing individual author and the level of conceptual generality that defines the 'plane of immanence' (or, as I would say, philosophical discourse). In particular, if I am right in my characterization of the crucial role played by style in the metaxological view, conceptual personae may be regarded as, to a significant extent, alleviating the burden and its attendant problems placed upon an individual author's own idiotic style. Perhaps, as Deleuze and Guattari claim, it is precisely the presence of such a device that accounts for the enduring character of some (if not all) important philosophical views, and that distinguishes them from the many others that have been relegated to the status of 'idiosyncratic footnotes' to intellectual history.

Of course, a metaxological thinker might well respond that the price to be paid for this solution to the problem of style is too high, that to ask a philosopher to begin with a 'schizoid process' or a masking, actually amounts to an act of intellectual dishonesty or inauthenticity that vitiates the very philosophical calling itself. But this cannot be entirely convincing when asserted by a metaxological thinker who otherwise affirms the inherent plurivocity of philosophy and has no hesitation in admitting that Shakespeare's plays, for instance, disclose a 'truth' of their own.

My tentative suggestion for reflecting further about the problem of philosophical style as I developed it in the first section, then, is this. While there has been a good deal of discussion (as evidenced by the title of this book) about the relation between systematic (and more particularly metaxological) philosophy and poetry, perhaps it might be more productive to approach these issues by focusing on 'dramaturgics' rather than 'poetics'. While 'poetics' tends immediately to mobilize assumptions and questions about the 'radically idiotic' nature of the poet and her 'genius', 'dramaturgics', I think, does not carry such baggage, and suggests the deployment of modes of expression that occupy a genuinely metaxological place, a location between 'individual idiocy' and systematic construction.

As a footnote to my suggestion, I would add the observation that, while poetry has stood at the centre both of Desmond's reflections on art and of his own chosen style, Deleuze has chosen to explore cinema as the art form closest to, and most revelatory for, his own view of philosophy. While 'cinematics' may also serve as one guideline for the direction in which I am pointing, I think, despite Deleuze's own preferences, that 'dramaturgics' may be closer to his own characterization of the nature of philosophy. Nonetheless, what a 'cinematic' approach to philosophy might look like remains an intriguing question, if one beyond the scope of my own discussion here.

Notes

1 Gilles Deleuze and Felix Guattari, *What is Philosophy?*, trans. H. Thomlinson and G. Burchell, New York: Columbia University Press, 1994. Originally appeared as *Qu'est-ce que la philosphie?*, Paris: Les Editions Minuit, 1991. The relevant pages for my discussion are 61–83 of the English translation.
2 In fact, it is instructive that in his lectures on the history of philosophy, Hegel occasionally injects remarks about the style of expression of various philosophers, and in the lectures on fine art he has a great deal to say about such matters.
3 Paul Weiss, *Modes of Being*, Carbondale: Southern Illinois Press, 1958.
4 Paul Weiss, *Philosophy in Process*, Carbondale: Southern Illinois Press, 1963 (multiple volumes).
5 Gottfried Martin, *General Metaphysics: Its Problems and its Methods*, London: Allen and Unwin, 1968.

Chapter 5

Repetition: Desmond's New Science

Cyril O'Regan

This essay represents the partial fulfilment of a promise made explicitly in an article on *Ethics and the Between*, in which I sketched the complex refiguration of Platonism that is a depth feature of Desmond's text.[1] There I wondered whether Desmond's refiguration repeated in some significant respects that refiguration of Platonism enacted by Giambattista Vico in the first half of the eighteenth century. If a good, promise keeping is a double-edged sword. On the one hand, thinking of a more historically proximate template for the basic commitments that drive Desmond's discourse than Plato or classical Neoplatonism better serves as a hermeneutic key for a discourse that articulates its constructive vision hand-in-hand with a searing critique of the reduction of discourse to science or its simulacrum. On the other hand, the risks are also obvious. First, in proposing Vico as a template, one might easily be taken to be arguing that there exist detailed substantive continuities between Desmond and Vico that can only be accounted for by the influence of the latter on the former. Second, in adducing Vico as a template, there is the real danger of mummifying Desmond's discourse, which is a thinking that is constitutionally explorative and open. Furthermore, when one recalls that Desmond is supposed to be repeating a thinker who himself is judged to represent a repetition of Platonism, the danger of mummification threatens to increase exponentially. The third difficulty is also non-trivial. Texts such as *Being and the Between* and *Ethics and the Between* are expansive, perhaps even encyclopaedic, while being multigenred, plurivocal and stylistically complex. Thus, relative to the modern canons of philosophical discourse, they are obscure. To avail oneself of Vico, whose discourse in *The New Science* and elsewhere has similar structural traits,[2] is to risk illuminating the obscure by the even more obscure (*obscurum per obscurius*).

These scruples, however, are not on a level with the real possibility that Vico's anti-Enlightenment intervention, and his articulation of a poetic and rhetorical philosophy as an alternative science, the 'new science' (*scienza nuova*), might illuminate both the content and linguistic performance of *Being and the Between* and *Ethics and the Between*. In these texts we witness an equally profound, but even more extensive, critique of the Enlightenment and its subsequent fallout, just as we find commitments to history, finitude, the erotic nature of philosophy, and community, without prejudice to the discourse of ultimate, as well as proximate, origins. Here too we discover and experience a style of philosophy that represents an alternative both to philosophy viewed as 'rigorous science' (*strenge Wissenschaft*) and an understanding of philosophy in which the disciplinary boundaries between philosophy and literature are completely blurred.

To get the conversation going, I will shortly provide a digest of those elements of Desmond's discourse that constitute it as a wisdom discourse to the side of philosophy, in either its foundational mode or its mode of reneging on truth. Before I proceed, however, I want to say that, while there exist very real difficulties in reading Desmond as a repetition of Vico, I should separate apparent from real difficulties. First, a Vichean reading of Desmond – which might also imply a Desmond(ian) reading of Vico – involves no claim that substantive positions found in *Being and the Between* and *Ethics and the Between* are actually influenced by Vico in the way that they, plausibly, are, for instance, by Plato, Neoplatonism and even Heidegger.[3] While, indeed, there are many substantive overlaps that merit attention, for example, Vico's and Desmond's critique of the Machiavellian and Hobbesian tradition of political thought, the repetition that is my focus here concerns the articulation of a fundamentally sapiential model of philosophy in a poetic, rhetorical and, one might even say, encyclopaedic, key. Second, it is apposite to recall that 'repetition' here bears the mark of Kierkegaard's conjugation, and implies his distinction between repetition and recollection. *Being and the Between* and *Ethics and the Between* do not re-collect, or collect again, what Vico has already collected. Precisely as repetition, Desmond's discourse represents the non-teleological future of Vico's 'new science', and is thus at once integral and novel. Third, even if one were to admit that Vico's discourse is far from transparent, this would not speak to its incapacity to illuminate Desmond's discourse, or suggest something flawed about it. The point would be that the non-transparency of Vico's discourse, with its commitment to the *chiaroscuro* matrix of all knowledge, and its elaboration of a poetic and rhetorical style, nonetheless tells us something important about the way Desmond understands the nature, task and limits of philosophy.

Key Elements of Desmond's New Science

Being and the Between and *Ethics and the Between* resist easy summary. The reasons are multiple and obvious: the range of subject-matter is so vast, the deployment of philosophical tradition so ample and subtle, the openness to other discourses (literature and religion) so transparently effective, the genre of the discourse so versatile, shifting easily from epic-like exposition to lyric riffs, and the style so richly textured, so irreducibly metaphorical and symbolical. Fortunately, my interest here is not so much a summing-up of the magisterial texts of his *œuvre*, but a sorting-out of that cluster or constellation of elements that mark Desmond's discourse off from other philosophical discourses in the modern and contemporary period, indeed that make it nothing less than a 'new science'. The cluster or constellation to which I refer has the following elements: (a) philosophy as reflective recognition and articulation of primal human response to a world sensuously, affectively and cognitively given, where this world is experienced as subtended and suffused by origin; (b) philosophy as a hermeneutic of the tradition, as even more specifically a hermeneutic of Plato and the Platonic tradition, in which the classical Platonic tradition is both emended and translated into a new key; (c) the ineluctable 'theological' dimension of philosophy; (d) philosophy as the commitment to a mapping of reality that is comprehensive, even encyclopaedic, in scope; (e) philosophy and its relation to, and limitation by, other discourses; (f) philosophy as a form of aesthetics and poetics; (g) philosophy as a form of rhetoric.

But before I proceed briefly to describe each of the elements of the constellation, it should be noted that there is nothing unselfconscious about Desmond's constructive proposal for philosophy in *Being and the Between* and *Ethics and the Between*. This proposal is asserted, in general, against a modernity in which philosophy has shrunk to a univocal discourse whereby the self, other selves, and particulars are successfully conceptually interned, and where contingency, individuality and community, as well as ambiguity, depth and height, are banished from discourse. It is asserted in particular against the backdrop of a rejection of the specifically modern turn to the subject, and the construction of science as a *mathesis universalis*, of a rejection of a material world whose *raison d'être* is to be exploited. As *Being and the Between* (BB, 56–8) in particular makes clear, Descartes is *primus inter pares* in setting the basic intellectual parameters of modernity.

Philosophy, Primal and Reflective

In *Being and the Between* and *Ethics and the Between*, as in many other texts,[4] Desmond conceives of philosophy as reflective recognition of experiences that are primitive, for example, that of others, evil or value, and of modes of experience that are primal, for example, wonder and perplexity. In declaring this, Desmond intends phenomenologically to redeem the classical tradition's sense of its mission of offering an explanation that is faithful to the given. The enterprise, therefore, is archaeological in the manner of Husserl and Heidegger, who quite clearly recognize that these responses are often buried in our quotidian life, in and through which we escape from exposure, and responsiveness, to reality.[5] Archaeology exposes a teeming and imbricated world of particulars that address us in their simple being-there, a world that differentiates into things, selves, relations and communities, that call for differential modes of response. Morever, if disciplined right, archaeology discovers and unfolds a world of height and depth granted by the origin that cannot be adequately cognized. In addition, as *Ethics and the Between* explores at great length, archaeology reveals the complex world of between as always already valorized, as provoking attraction or repulsion or reflection, owing to its surd character.

Desmond's texts proceed on the Whiteheadian and pragmatist assumption that a philosophy is valid to the degree to which it is adequate to experience, and invalid to the extent to which it is not.[6] The tradition of philosophical reflection throws up numerous examples of both fidelity to experience and infidelity. No particular moment in the history of philosophy is immune from infidelity. Desmond sees plenty of examples of infidelity in the classical and medieval, as well as in the modern traditions which bear the major brunt of his critique. For example, in *Ethics and the Between*, classical scepticism, Epicurianism (EB, 57–8), and even Stoicism (EB, 90, 341) are faulted for their stipulative bias that outruns, or even overruns, experience. Again, as *Being and the Between* makes clear, even if medieval Scholasticism does not represent a total derailment of the mission of philosophy, there is much that is vulnerable to a Heideggerian critique. It is possible, at the very least, that discursive reason is granted too much authority, and thus begins the contraction into a propositionalist and univocal form of discourse that constitutes the low-tide mark of modern philosophy. Moreover Desmond resists the easy options of making either Abelard (and Averoës), or Duns Scotus and Ockham, the scapegoats for what is wrong with medieval thought. There is weakness, *Being and the Between* suggests (EB, 212), in Thomas Aquinas, arguably medieval thought's most magisterial thinker. Indeed there is weakness precisely at what might be regarded as the strongest link in the Thomistic discursive chain, that is, the doctrine of analogy, often touted by Thomists as proof of Aquinas's successful resistance to philosophies which show either a univocist or equivocist bent. For Desmond, analogy at once runs the risk of bleeding the particular of its idiosyncrasy, what he calls its 'idiocy', and of compromising the transcendence and otherness of origin.

Still, infidelity is more than offset by the moments of fidelity. Leaving in parenthesis for the moment Desmond's real attraction to Plato, one can cite his approval of Augustine. Although Desmond's affirmation of Augustine can be justified on Platonic grounds, Augustine is at the same time an independent source or resource. It is Augustine who radicalizes our sense of the gratuitousness of ourselves and all that is given, who personalizes the good, who reveals human doubleness, and who probes into the nature and limits of human freedom and responsibility, and who is nothing if not a connoisseur of evil.[7]

Philosophy as a Hermeneutic of Tradition: The Particular Value of Platonic Tradition

At a fundamental level, it is clear that *Being and the Between* and *Ethics and the Between* recognize, with Husserl and Heidegger, that philosophy is always a beginning. Philosophy is destined to be a beginning, because it is not simply a language, it is the attempt to expose reality by being exposed to it.[8] The exposure is always new and the means for exposure are anything but invariant. To the extent to which philosophy really is the determined search for origin and what origin constitutes, that is, the complex world of the middle, philosophy quite literally is 'original'. To the extent to which the means are more than a mechanical repetition of previous deployments, then philosophical discourses enjoy the appearance of originality. Desmond's texts are obviously original in both the primary and secondary sense. Importantly, however, *Being and the Between* and *Ethics and the Between* authorize no cult of originality. However critical both texts are of major figures and movements in philosophy, the history of philosophy is given the benefit of the doubt. In its finest flowering, philosophy is the tradition of beginning, a tradition of its own perpetual renewal, what might be called, to use Marxist language for a non-Marxist purpose, the reproduction of its own newness. Desmond's texts, then, represent a reopening rather than the first opening. Moreover they do not simply mime the reopening executed by Husserl and Heidegger. *Being and the Between* and *Ethics and the Between* perform nothing less than a fundamental reopening of a philosophical discourse, which, from its first appearance in the Occidental tradition, intends the origin as the really real.

Precisely because of its mindfulness regarding origins, philosophy says and shows a hospitality and a reservation with respect to its past. At the same time, this past may cover over the origin and the field of between that it makes possible. As I have already indicated, *Being and the Between* and *Ethics and the Between* discuss examples of both. The pose towards the past, then, is double, because the complicated history of philosophy is ambiguous in its deliverances. In due course I will make the point that this doubleness is beautifully captured, not simply linguistically but substantively, by Vico's designation of 'generous vendetta'. Here it is more important to underscore the point that a systemic feature in Desmond's texts is to valorize in a special way the Platonic tradition. This tradition includes not only the historical Plato and his magisterial interpreters (Plotinus, Proclus), but arguably the entire spread of this philosophical tradition into the modern period, and also its Christianly-adapted strains in figures such as Pseudo-Dionysius, Eriugena and Nicholas of Cusa. It is plainly the case that Desmond's texts are pure retrievals neither of the historical Plato nor of his pagan or Christian successors. Nonetheless the discourses of Platonism provide a preliminary orientation for Desmond's discourse, and help to focus its aim. As I indicated, however, in an essay on *Ethics and the Between*,[9] this emphasis on the guidance provided Desmond by Platonism should be complemented by an equal emphasis on the way or ways in which Desmond's discourse amplifies the discourse of the Platonic tradition (experiential, theological), emends it by giving much greater privileges, for example, to contingency and particularity, and refigures it by rendering it in an aesthetic and poetic key.

The Theological Dimension to Philosophy

In an essay on *Being and the Between*, I commented briefly on the complex relation between Desmond's thought and that of Heidegger.[10] For Desmond, Heidegger is a genuine philosophical thinker who opens up being as phenomenon, and who succeeds in bringing from oblivion the eventness and giftedness of being, and the responsiveness of selves to gifting (see Heidegger's notion of *Ereignis*[11]) that constitutes their being-there (*Dasein*). Moreover Heidegger is a consummate thinker of the middle, to the extent to which the eventing of being opens up the space of transcendence, of depth as well as height, that constitutes world as such. The world is the milieu in which we experience the primal, just the contrary of what is second-hand. And Heidegger cements his status as a thinker of the middle to the extent to which he denies that this eventing can ever be conceptually mastered, can ever cease to be a disclosure or unconcealment, that has as its other side concealment (thus *lethe* is the backdrop of *a-letheia*). This point is negatively reinforced to the extent to which Heidegger engages in a radical and sustained critique of Hegel's middle, unveiling it as a spurious middle that issues in the *parousia* of being, and thus the infinitizing of a cognition commensurate to it.[12] There is, then, significant thinking along with Heidegger displayed in both of Desmond's texts, and especially in *Being and the Between*, a congeniality further illustrated in Desmond's critique of the rationalistic tendency of the Western philosophical tradition.

Desmond agrees with Heidegger that the basic problem of philosophy is that of seeking a foundation (*subiectum, hupokeimenon*) to which intellect can be adequate. Thus, while Desmond is not ennervated by Heidegger's (in)famous 'ontotheology' charge,[13] and questions whether Heidegger has the correct list of suspects, he is persuaded that modes of philosophy in the past and in the present do answer to Heidegger's description. If 'God' serves as nothing more than the guarantee of the intelligibility and integrity of modern science, that is, if 'God' is reduced to the God-function – as surely is the case from Descartes through Spinoza down to Kant and Hegel – then Desmond could not agree more. On a related issue, however, Desmond demurs. Desmond does not believe that, either historically or systemically, philosophy as such is subverted when the Christian God becomes involved in the Being-question.[14] In *Ethics and the Between*, as in *Being and the Between*, no excluding of God can be warranted on merely procedural grounds, just as there can be no procedural drawing of determinate boundaries between the discourses of philosophy and theology.[15] Whether God-talk is appropriate discourse with respect to origin must be decided solely on phenomenological grounds. The convertibility of God as origin and origin as God is, Desmond believes, validatable in experience, and has been so validated throughout the Western tradition of thought, superbly if not supremely, in Augustine, who is for Heidegger a profoundly ambiguous figure. If God is personal as origin, and origin as personal, then God is not a determinate object of experience. Thus the appeal to the Neoplatonic tradition of God beyond being. In his suggestion of God as superdeterminate rather than determinate reality (BB, 263, 268–9, 499–500; EB, 5, 7, 9, 11, 51), Desmond comes very close to the position of Marion in *God without Being*, where he attempts to justify the Dionysian–Bonaventurian view of God as Being beyond being.[16] At the same time, Desmond also comes close in *Ethics and the Between* to worrying, with Lévinas, that Heidegger's refusal of God-talk is predicated on a determined axiological refusal, the removal of all value from being. Being beings, time times, event events. The core is the neutral if not the neuter. The syphoning off of value, for Desmond, continues by other means, Nietzsche's nihilistic posture.[17]

Of course *Being and the Between* and *Ethics and the Between* do not argue in the strict sense for the identification of God and origin, any more than they attempt to secure a relation between origin and the middle regulated by grace rather than nature, by providence rather than necessity and chance, and joy and celebration rather than resignation. But these texts create the space for the redemption of such claims, which likely will be the topic of the crowning piece of Desmond's trilogy, *God and the Between*. It is important, however, to insist that, in his texts, Desmond continues to speak as a philosopher. He makes a plea as a philosopher that philosophical discourses should not *a priori* dismiss God-talk. Dismissal notices are incoherent, since the business of philosophy is to describe, rather than prescribe and proscribe. They are also impoverishing, since they make transcendence more difficult to maintain, and less resistant to the instrumental forms of discourse that dominate in modernity. Going back 'to the things themselves' will, Desmond feels, vouchsafe God-talk. Thus there is no disciplinary confusion. Desmond speaks of God, if not within bounds of reason alone, as Kant suggested, then within the bounds of philosophy alone. He makes no appeal to revelation; no appeal to the authority of Scripture or the authority of tradition. This does not mean, however, that appeal to biblical texts, or important texts of the theological tradition, is not a significant feature of Desmond's practice. Nevertheless, when Desmond avails himself of these texts, as he does importantly and with some regularity in *Ethics and the Between*, he exploits them as disclosive of phenomena that might be or could be disclosed in experience, or in and through other texts, but as a matter of fact are disclosed eminently, maybe even supereminently, in and through these texts.

Philosophy as Comprehensive and Encyclopaedic

The most cursory glance at *Being and the Between* and *Ethics and the Between* reveals a thinker who does not illustrate the Romantic love affair with the fragment. Rather these texts reveal a thinker who painstakingly and comprehensively articulates the dimensions of being and the good, and attempts to co-respond to the interconnectedness of phenomena. Thus, even if these texts express serious reservations with regard to method as the rule of philosophy, they are just as committed to system as philosophy has traditionally been, in both its classical and modern exemplifications. Moreover, given the exhaustive rehearsal of phenomena in both texts, one might think that these texts evince a commitment to the encyclopaedic. But, of course, what finally matters is not so much the commitment to comprehensiveness, as how the whole is understood. And what matters about the idea of the encyclopedia is not so much its putative range of subject-matter, as the understanding of the nature of encyclopaedic discourse that is thought to correspond to a complex between of reality. On both these counts Desmond's philosophy parts company with the modern philosophical views of the whole, and modern examples of the encyclopaedia.

For Desmond, the whole is not conjectural as it is for Bacon; it is real. Nor can it be reduced to the procrustean bed of objects verified in and through natural science, and exploited by the tools that science makes possible, and that make science possible. For Desmond, neither is the whole architectonic in Kant's sense,[18] thus merely regulative or heuristic. It is categorical. Nor does the whole in Desmond either inscribe or legitimate the Kantian dualisms of phenomenon and noumenon (EB, 35–6, 66–7), freedom and necessity (BB, 25–6; EB, 31, 35, 134, 318–19), duty and happiness (EB, 67, 119–20, 135–9, 142) or art and morality (EB, 68, 182–3). Again, not only in the two texts under discussion, and Desmond's upcoming book on Hegel, but in just about all Desmond's texts, the whole is self-consciously asserted against the dialectically mediated whole of Hegel. Desmond's whole is open rather than closed, fissured by transcendence rather than articulating immanence, and complexly intermediated rather than dialectically self-mediated.

Similarly *Being and the Between* and *Ethics and the Between* articulate a distinct genre of encyclopaedia. The encyclopaedia is not a Baconian figure of comprehensive knowledge, where knowledge quite literally is power over a universe reduced to manipulable facts. By contrast, the Desmondian encyclopaedia is a figure of humility, a comprehensive mapping of human responsiveness to the disclosure of being and the good, and human responsibility and stewardship of the between that being and the good ground and bring to light. Decidedly the encyclopaedism of Desmond differs *toto coelo* from that of Hegel, for whom the circular network of categorial determinations of thought renders reality transparent. By contrast, Desmond's encyclopaedism is simply the effect of the philosophical imperative to respond to the widest possible spectrum of phenomena of the between, with the keenest sense possible of the complex and heterogenous threads of relation that constitute the web of reality. The attempt to be adequate to the grounding gesture of philosophy issues in a labile discourse, which will always be liminal, since reality exceeds discourse, as it always precedes it. Thus, one could say Desmond's encyclopaedia is a *liminal encyclopaedia*, one that discloses rather than justifies. As total transparency with respect to phenomena and their interrelation is not available, neither is transparency reflexively available through the whole. The encyclopaedia is tormented by the Baroque figure of *chiaroscuro*.

Philosophy and its Relation to, and Limitation by, Other Discourses

Being and the Between and *Ethics and the Between* basically put a point to a position advanced as early as Desmond's first work, and asserted in numerous places thereafter.[19] Even if philosophy enjoys some special prerogatives, it is but one of the discourses of disclosure. Agreeing with Hegel that art and religion are also disclosive of the real, Desmond looks with something like Orwellian eyes on Hegel's strategy of reinscribing hierarchy: the three discourses are equal, except philosophy is more equal than the others. Consistently with earlier texts, philosophy cannot be claimed to disclose reality more adequately than the discourses of art and religion, but merely otherwise. Philosophy's approach to the real is obviously more self-consciously disciplined, and this will display itself in the discourse's favouring argument and the precision of concept, over other values. The more compact discourses of art and religion are irreducible, however, since they genuinely disclose being and the good in ways that philosophy is not able to repeat. Sophocles (EB, 112) and Shakespeare (EB, 82, 83, 111, 112, 393), unveil the drama and limits of the human situation in ways that are unsurpassable, just as the parables of Jesus and the Beatitudes unveil a mode of responsiveness that no philosophy before or after can match in terms of sheer explosiveness (EB, 112–13, 217, 508).

Philosophy therefore forgets itself to the degree to which it fails to recognize the ineluctability of these other discourses. But it is not simply that it deforms itself by being tempted into an imperialist or sovereign relation to other discourses, it also cuts itself off from resources that are constitutive of its own well-being. Desmond understands that, in addition to being a discourse that has its own way of disclosing the real, philosophy is inescapably a hermeneutic discourse, that is, a discourse that reflects on the less explanatory discourses of art and religion. As rendered in *Ethics and the Between* (EB, 101–3), philosophy is better rather than worse, to the degree to which it is open, for example, to Dostoyevski's depiction of the potential monstrousness of the self. To be open to art and religion, however, is to be continually challenged by a depth of disclosure that can be infinitely trawled. Properly understood, the hermeneutic activity of philosophy is a waiting on, and listening to, other more compact and symbolically dense discourses, that can be elucidated but not adequately translated.

Philosophical Aesthetics and Poetics: Aesthetic and Poetic Philosophy

That philosophy is necessarily aesthetic is a central feature of Desmond's alternative to the specifically Cartesian model of philosophy that denies the value of the primary qualities, fractures the embodied subject into what Ryle calls 'two collateral histories',[20] and denies the cultural embodiment of tradition and trope. Convinced no less than Whitehead regarding the disastrous consequences of the separation of primary from secondary qualities, unlike Whitehead, *Being and the Between* and *Ethics and the Between* go beyond the posture of mourning, and attempt to exhibit what fidelity to our primal aesthetic response to the real and the good would look like. In doing so, both books recall the ground-breaking phenomenological anti-Cartesianism of Merleau-Ponty.[21] Like the latter, Desmond insists on the primitiveness of the aesthetic layer to gain critical leverage on secondary constructions.

Throughout *Being and the Between* and *Ethics and the Between*, Desmond strives mightily to create a language of immediacy that remains faithful to the body, sensation and its inchoateness. Unlike Merleau-Ponty, however, in Desmond's archaeology a positive-teleological relation to higher-order, more linguistic and symbolic layers is not ruled out. In addition to 'the aesthetic', considered in its sensuous and perceptual aspect, both *Being and the Between* and *Ethics and the Between* want to underscore the primordial responsiveness that characterizes all experience of the between. Precisely in their embodiedness, selves are always already attracted by being and the good. This attunement and responsiveness names the second structural element of the aesthetic, which philosophy is under obligation not only to name, but to honour in a rich discourse that weaves together the multicoloured threads of responsiveness. The aesthetic must, however, be more than notionally approved by philosophy.

The aesthetic must be linguistically performed within a philosophy, if that philosophy is not to be a fabrication in which even the fabricator cannot live.

Honouring the aesthetic is, in *Being and the Between* and *Ethics and the Between*, a necessary, but not a sufficient, condition for honouring and performing the poetic. As a making, poetics has to do with configuration and style, as well as with language that would capture the immediacy of experience in image and metaphor. Although both *Being and the Between* and *Ethics and the Between* have a clear argument and cogent organization, their configuration cannot be described as linear. Phenomena treated in earlier parts of the text reappear later, to reveal new and different aspects. If there is a mimicking of Hegelian method here, the way travelled does not have as its destination a closure that facilitates the *parousia* of meaning. The Desmondian figure is the spiral rather than the circle.[22] But the poetic is not univocally defined by configuration; it also involves style or, better, styles, where style denotes position and point of view. It is at least an implication of *Being and the Between* and *Ethics and the Between* that zero style is ideological. Zero style suggests the possibility, even the actuality, of a view from nowhere (Nagel), which is indistinguishable from the absolute point of view. But no such perch is possible, according to Desmond, even if for some purposes philosophy can endorse a wide-angle perspective on things. This wide-angle perspective of a philosopher is, however, just one of the many perspectives adopted in Desmond's texts. Besides the quasi-objective wide-angle view, Desmond deploys a variety of narrower-angle viewpoints, for example the philosopher expressing the unique pitch of his or her own experience, or the philosopher addressing the reader whose experience is presumed not to replicate that of his interlocutor. There is, in addition, an in-between kind of perspective and thus style, and this is the philosophers' placing themselves within a tradition of similar perspectives, and thus recommending a community of perspective, as they advocate in some instances the perspective of a particular community (Platonic). Thus, in a sense, *Being and the Between* and *Ethics and the Between* endorse a plurality of styles as a necessity of philosophy, but do so without reducing philosophy to style, or without derogation of ontological and axiological seriousness.

Philosophy as a Form of Rhetoric

If *Being and the Between* and *Ethics and the Between* articulate reality in the aesthetic and poetic mode, their resistance to the reduction of philosophy to method, linguistic or otherwise, and to the model of philosophy as a rigorous science, suggests a commitment to the idea of philosophy as rhetorical. At the very least, they suggest the deconstruction of the ancient distinction between rhetoric and philosophy. Desmond understands well this ancient distinction, which pivots around the figure of Socrates, and affirms it in significant part (BB, 138–9; EB, 114–15). The distinction argued for and exhibited in the *dramatis personae* of texts such as *Gorgias* and the *Republic*, captures adequately the contrast between a mode of existence lived towards the truth, and a mode of existence lived for the consequences of persuasion: for example, reputation, influence, power or money

(BB, 38–9; EB, 85 n.3, 159). *Being and the Between* and *Ethics and the Between* think that this distinction was relevant, not only in the time of Socrates, but enduringly so. Desmond's texts resist, then, both Rorty's comfortable assimilation and Foucault's more tendentious adaptation of Nietzsche's view that philosophy is always a rhetoric in a degenerative sense, in that its real (as opposed to its apparent) aim is not so much truth as power. The *agon* between the philosopher's aim of truth and the Sophist's will to power is irredeemable and specifies the tragic situation of the philosopher, who may not have opinion on his side, who may be less capable of deploying moving figures of speech and thus be less pleasing or less plausible.

At the same time, both Desmond's reading of Socrates and the figures of his own discourse suggest that the relation between philosophy and rhetoric is not necessarily antithetical. As Desmond observes more than once (BB, 137–8, 217), Plato's texts are not constituted by the degree-zero of dialectic. They are moved subtly by narrative scene, threaded through with symbolic language, focused in myth which indicates the excess of desire over thought, and made plausible in and through the supple and fluent use of language that never jars. Thus, if Aristophanes' motive is questionable when he calls Socrates a rhetor or rhetorician (EB, 84), he is not, in the end, wrong. For if Socrates wishes to communicate the truth – and the myth of the cave suggests that this is constitutive of the vocation of the philosopher – then he too is involved in an act of persuasion. Persuasion is not the contrary to the aim for truth, in the way that uncritical acceptance of received opinion, and the will to manipulate and express one's sovereignty over others, are.[23] As acts of communication, *Being and the Between* and *Ethics and the Between* are attempts to incite recognition of the origin that grounds both our reality and the reality of the given, and to explore layers of responsiveness and agency that constitute selves and communities of selves. But incitement, for Desmond, demands all the resources of language and metaphor, both to push aside what covers over primal response and to serve as tools of excavation for what we have been given from the beginning, and for the excavation of where we have been from the beginning.

In deconstructing the binary opposition between philosophy and rhetoric, and thus in rehabilitating rhetoric, Desmond does not travel outside the Western tradition. For if the binary contrast of rhetoric and philosophy gets sanctioned in Greek philosophy, so also does *paideia*. And, as taken up in the Latin tradition, which interprets itself as being in continuation with Greek wisdom, *paideia* certainly involves rhetoric without compromise to its aim at truth, which is coextensive with its communication, for truth is for the good, not of the individual, but of society as a whole, and at a limit the *humanum*. The interpretation of the necessary complementarity of rhetoric and truth lasts into the modern period, and is illustrated well by a host of Renaissance thinkers, some not obviously Platonic (Erasmus) and others self-confesssed Platonists (Ficino, Mirandola). It is precisely this complementarity that is challenged in the modern period. Although Bacon has an appreciation of the value of the classical tradition of tropes not shared by Descartes among others, nonetheless even he tends to suggest the necessity of a decision between the moderns and the ancients that leaves rhetoric outside, because rhetorical discourses belong to the past. With Descartes, the distinction between philosophy and rhetoric becomes absolute. Beyond the application of a method aimed at certainty lies the continent or continents of sophistry and tropes. Moreover, while philosophical method is infinitely transferable, it is not communicable in the classical sense, since philosophical communication involved something like conversion, a *metanoia* that, more than giving one new information, gives one a new reality. *Being and the Between* and *Ethics and the Between* contest the separation made absolute in the modern period, and view it as a derailment from an important aspect of the classical tradition which, while it could for certain purposes valorize the distinction of rhetoric and philosophy, also pointed to their fundamental sympathy.

The Vichean Precedent

In offering a sketch of a constellation of elements that differentiate Desmond's constructive philosophical programmeme, I did so with a view to excavating a precedent that helps illuminate Desmond's idea of the nature and limits of philosophy. While Desmond may be closer to this or that thinker on particular points, I now want to suggest that it is Vico who provides by far the best model of what is going on in *Being and the Between* and *Ethics and the Between*. For it is precisely this constellation that constitutes the alternative sapiential model of philosophy that Vico proposes, against what he takes to be the specifically modern contraction of philosophy into method, and a foundationalism that despises – and thus excludes – the languages of poetry, rhetoric, history and tradition which were resources for philosophy before Bacon, and especially Descartes. No thinker in the modern period couples a critique of the discourses of modernity with the articulation of a rhetorical and poetic philosophy that bears comparison with Desmond's systematic breadth. For Vico, unlike Hamann and Herder,[24] is not simply a Romantic anti-modern, but a systematic thinker who rearticulates the very grounds of philosophy as a practice in the wake of its perceived destruction. Indeed, if we give in for a moment to the postmodern conceit of achronicity, Vico can become one of the more profound critics of Hegel: one who, while he appreciates Hegel's commitment to historicity, ethos, community and the necessity of the philosopher playing the role of archaeologist or philologist of culture, remains aghast at the denial in the Hegelian system of finitude, and our status as middle between the cosmos and the divine.

There can be little doubt that Vico's proposal of a poetic and rhetorical philosophy represents the other side of a critique of the Cartesian and empiricist lynchpins of modern philosophy. As *On the Most Ancient Wisdom of the Italians* shows in particular,[25] Vico's critique of Descartes is as substantively acute as it is concerted. Overlapping with other serious critiques of Descartes, for example, those of Mersenne, Gassendi, Arnauld, Leibniz and Malebranche, Vico argues that, in the claim to have the foundation of truth through the indubitable certainty of the *cogito*,

Descartes has confused a psychological experience with a principle of demonstrative knowledge. Similarly, Vico accuses Descartes of failing to articulate adequately the relation between extension, materiality and motion and, by way of a counter, articulates a metaphysics of *conatus* that bears a similarity to Desmond's painstaking effort in *Being and the Between* to articulate a dynamic metaphysics.[26] As is the case with his criticism of the *cogito*, while Vico is penetrating here, he is not necessarily original. Similar criticisms are made of Descartes by Spinoza and Leibniz, who essentially remain within the Cartesian fold.

Vico's most fundamental disagreement with Descartes concerns proper philosophical method. The disagreement has narrower and broader dimensions. Most narrowly, it has to do with the relative merits of synthetic, as opposed to analytic, geometry. This in turn involves Vico's dispute with Descartes concerning the relative activity versus the passivity of the mind.[27] More broadly, however, the disagreement touches differences concerning the *ratio studiorum*; whether the model of study that Descartes dispenses with should or could be replaced by a constructionist model that proceeds from indubitable foundations.[28] The worry is that such a reduction is at once overambitious in its aim – certitude – and too concessionary with respect to scepticism, in that it surrenders the subject-matter of the humanist, the tropes that concern the probable, which govern most of historical human life. Whatever the success of Cartesian method in the physical sciences, Vico does not think that it plausibly extends to society and history which, from his point of view, define the self, and not the reflexive affirmation of the unsituated *cogito*.

But it is not only Descartes and his followers who are resisted, it is also the empiricists. For Vico, the intellectual giant of the empiricist tradition is Bacon.[29] It is Bacon who, more than Locke and Hobbes, articulates the basic vision of enquiry that marks off the new from the old, and who outlines the encyclopaedic grasp of reality that would result. It is this 'new science' that Vico wishes to contest, to reverse, to displace with his 'new science', which is newer than the new, and definitely truer. Vico has considerably more sympathy for the logic of discovery articulated by Bacon than for Cartesian method, and Bacon's more sober view regarding the natural–pragmatic limits of human knowledge. He also appreciates Bacon's general eirenicism with respect to antiquity, the fact that tradition is not univocally banished from the brave new world that becomes possible with the new *organon* for the accumulation of knowledge. Nonetheless, in the final analysis, in Bacon's texts the battle is not only fought between the modern and the ancient, but the battle is won by the moderns.[30] At best, for Bacon, rhetorical modes of thought possess a merely contingent and relative grasp of the truth. From Vico's point of view, the superiority of the modern is presumed rather than successfully argued. He suggests once again that tropes adequately indicate the actual (as opposed to the putative) reach of human intellect. Human beings see enough to dispense with scepticism, and are blind enough to show up the ambition of demonstration with regard to human life as either conceit or *hubris*.

The above is the merest digest of Vico's complex critique of the two starting-points of a new dispensation in the understanding of the nature and task of knowledge, and the nature and task of philosophy. But it is sufficient to indicate what provokes his reconstrual of the nature and limits of philosophy which, if it calls on the models of the past, nonetheless is, strictly speaking, not identical with them. Whatever repetition there is therefore of early models, Vico self-consciously proposes that his is a 'new' science, or a new wisdom, by contrast with what the moderns produce, and by contrast with Bacon's *Novum Organum* in particular. It is 'new', not simply by default; that is, its *topos* is this side of the modern–ancient divide, and thus has lost its innocence. It is new also in that it represents a thorough vetting of the old, in which not only are some of the criticisms by the moderns maintained (for example, philosophy can ossify into an authoritarian discourse), but also there is a suggestion of the essential doubleness of philosophy: its promise to be faithful to the real is a promise that throughout the history of philosophy, and not simply in modernity, is betrayed as well as kept. What makes Vico so extraordinary as an anticipation of Desmond, of *Being and the Between* and *Ethics and the Between*, is that his constructive alternative to the moderns, his 'new science', essentially consists of the constellation of seven elements which, we have argued, are central to Desmond's proposal. It is to an articulation of these elements that we now turn.

Philosophy, Primal and Reflective

For Vico, the turn to method and epistemology in the narrow sense is as destructive of the philosophical subject as it is destructive to the subjects of philosophy; that is, its themes, topics and tropes. Not only is the subjective ground not indubitable, it is also an abstraction that fails to take account of the self that is imaginative and affective, as well as intellectual, and embodied not only physically, but also socially and historically. Against the authority of Descartes and Bacon, which mutes the classical sense that philosophy is the pursuit of wisdom by the whole person, and thus ultimately a form of life, Vico wishes to reassert the validity of the classical understanding or, better, revalidate it. In his situation, it is no longer trite to affirm that philosophy has its ground in 'wonder', or to attest to 'curiosity' as a secondary and attendant urge.[31] The reality of wonder and curiosity are archaeologically exposited, and are so in two ways. First, wonder and curiosity are taken to be more primitive than ratiocination and the instauration of methods of discovery. Second, wonder and curiosity are read off the testimonies and artifacts of human creation throughout history. Thus archaeology in the common sense can point to the most basic drives of human being, which a genuinely 'scientific' philosophy instances as well as acknowledges. Extraordinarily interesting in light of Desmond's reflection on the doubleness of 'perplexity', which matches up with Vico's 'curiosity', is the latter's underscoring of the double valence of *curiositas*. Curiosity may be degenerate, as it is in the modern turn to method that funds the attempt to acquire total knowledge, and thus absolute mastery of reality. Or curiosity may have as a key component of its comportment, *cura*,[32] that is, care and solicitude for the worlds of others, for the history that constitutes us as subjects, as well as the physical world.

In continuity with a host of Italian Renaissance thinkers (for example, Marsilio Ficino, Pico della Mirandola, Giordano Bruno) Vico has no compunction about offering an erotic reading of the self. It is eros that constitutes the human self as dynamic, and which indicates the transcendent horizon of the true and the good.[33] The difference between a philosopher and an ordinary human being is one of degree, in that eros is more intense and perduring, as well as reflectively embraced, in the philosopher. Thus, as with Desmond in *Ethics and the Between*, one witnesses in Vico the unembarrassed recovery of the Platonic notion of *daimon* as indicative of the ecstatic and maximally participatory form of life.[34]

The view of philosophy articulated by Vico is intended in the main to curb the overweening pretensions of modern species of philosophy, which commit erudition to the junk heap of history. At the same time, Vico is as anxious as Descartes and Bacon are to avoid the perils of destructive scepticism. He considers, however, that his erotic construal of philosophy represents a better, because more realistic, rejoinder to the sceptic, precisely because it does not countenance a foundation of certitude, and thus of truth, that bears the marks of a *petitio principii*, and an edifice of knowledge that is more promise than attainment. In a deservedly famous passage in *The Ancient Wisdom of the Italians*, Vico defines his philosophical ambition: 'a metaphysics compatible with human frailty, which neither allows all truth to men, nor yet denies him all, but only some'. Here Vico self-consciously tries to locate the philosopher as between dogmatism (even) and scepticism. In the background, however, is a more figural sense of middle defined in critical appropriation of Renaissance Neoplatonism's view of human being as a being of the middle.[35] Epistemology of the middle follows on an ontology of the between: human being is the middle between the cosmos and God. Human being is the place, the transit site of the ascending momentum of the one and the descending gift of the other.

Philosophy as a Hermeneutic of Tradition: The Particular Value of Platonic Tradition

The summary figure for Vico's view of the philosophical tradition is that of generous vendetta (*generosa vendetta*).[36] A philosopher is put in the situation of a vendetta because it may be necessary, for the sake of philosophy, to resist the tradition of philosophy that can prove oppressive and importunate. To adapt Joyce's famous adage, the philosophical tradition can prove to be the nightmare from which one should strive to wake. At the lower level of energy, dealing with the tradition demands sifting through it, for the tradition of philosophy is both plural and, in some instances, contradictory, so that, for example, to accept Epicurianism and Stoicism is not to accept Platonism, and vice versa.[37] But vendetta represents only one half of the requisite response, in fact, precisely that aspect of the appropriate complex response absolutized in the modern discursive regimes of Bacon and Descartes. There is the need for philosophy to be generous also. This, however, has more to do with the ability to receive than to give, and to recognize than to construct. To read the texts of the past is to get to the insights that animate them, and this is a genuinely philosophical skill. To put oneself and one's age in the position of debt, rather than peremptorily to declare oneself and one's age debt-free (for example, Bacon, Descartes), is a sign of maturity that makes the genuinely new possible.

For Vico, there is much in the philosophical tradition that is gift. There is approval of the discourses of Renaissance humanism, especially those of the Italian Renaissance. Augustine is a specially venerable authority, not only because he is a major purveyor of Platonism in the Christian tradition, but just as much because he corrects it. As *The New Science* shows with particular clarity, Augustine is a crucial resource for a philosopher concerned with history and its meaning.[38] Vico also validates juridical–political thinkers such as Cicero,[39] who are not only excluded by the moderns, but also marginalized in the premodern period, as belonging to the class of rhetoricians rather than the class of philosophers as such.

If there is a tradition within a tradition deserving of particular respect and retrieval, it is the Platonic tradition. Of course, this tradition goes well beyond the actual texts of Plato, and includes Plato's classical and Christian appropriations, and especially the texts of the Renaissance Platonists. This tradition is affirmed for a variety of reasons. First, it not only speaks of the eros at the base of all philosophy, it exemplifies it. It doing so, it demonstrates a profound sense of the limits of discursive knowledge, while at the same time underscoring the nobility of search. In the strict sense, philosophy is a heroic discipline. Second, Platonism is a form of piety.[40] It is so on its own ground. It is so also on Christian grounds, that Vico thinks are inalienable. Platonism's affirmation of transcendence and its uncognizability, and the reality of providence,[41] make its relation with Christianity non-accidental and harmonious.[42] Third, although there are strains to the contrary, on balance the Platonic tradition is more aesthetic than anti-aesthetic, in that it underwrites *mimesis* and participation, as it feels the lure of the transcendent. Again, while there are contrary strains, the Platonic tradition is more poetic than anti-poetic in its sense of the necessity for symbol and myth, and the need to incorporate these elements into a discourse that signals the limit of comprehensibility. Fourth, in a similar way, Vico does not oppose the tradition of Plato and the tradition of Cicero.[43] Sophistry may be Platonism's contrary, rhetoric is not. Platonism is a form of non-degenerate rhetoric.[44]

Nevertheless, following on the doubleness of a philosopher's relation to the tradition of philosophy, Vico's relationship to the Platonic tradition is not an instance of pure generosity. Critique, explicit as well as implicit, is involved. Vico's commitment to history, to contingency and particularity, goes well beyond that found in the texts of the historical Plato, and well beyond most philosophers in the Platonic tradition, if one excepts Augustine. As a servant of philosophy, Vico is precisely not the slave of Platonism, but a thinker who critically appropriates and recommends it.

The Theological Dimension to Philosophy

Vico clearly saw that modern philosophy's cleansing of the Augean stables involves not only putting transcendence into question, but also putting in parenthesis the *de facto* link in the Occidental tradition between transcendence and the transcendent.[45] From Vico's point of view, the result is a calamity that sins not only against the testimony of the *gentes* throughout history, but effects an impoverishment of philosophy by accelerating its decline into the empire of facts. Importantly, Vico's concern is not the consequences of this erasure for faith. While Vico is persuaded of the essential compatibility of faith and reason, and attests to the value of theology based on revelation, his interest is in the theological, precisely to the extent that it remains within the ambit of philosophy. The point bears remembering that, in the *New Science* (p.342) Vico claims that his thought is through and through theological, since, after *The City of God*, he is essentially offering an account of how divine providence works in history. Commentators need to recall the precise terms in which the *New Science* is theological. Exploiting Augustine's use of Varro's distinction between distinct kinds of theology (poetic, natural, civil),[46] Vico suggests that his theology is neither natural nor revealed theology, but what he calls a 'rational civil theology'. In claiming that philosophy can be – and is – a discourse about divine providence from a human point of view, Vico can be read as both anticipating Hegel's philosophy of history and critiquing it *avant la lettre*, since he refuses to confuse the appearance of providence with its reality, which is only in the mind of God.[47]

With its focus on providence, and thus on an ultimate horizon of action (ethics), Vico disagrees with those who would read history (for example, Machievelli, Hobbes) as reductively human, and therefore ultimately about power.[48] God secures value as well as transcendence,[49] for God is the shaper and organizer of human acts. At the same time, within the domain of philosophy, the divine that comes into play is a divine that is immanent in the world. Evocations of the Neoplatonic world-soul and the demiurge of the *Timaeus* are more than occasional. Moreover the recall of the demiurgic figure suggests that the world is a poetic and aesthetic whole, not necessarily reducible to the terms of discursive intellect.[50]

Philosophy as Comprehensive and Encyclopaedic

As an eminent commentator on Vico has brought to critical attention,[51] Vico's 'new science' is a variant of nothing less than the Renaissance fixed idea of supplying a map of the world, a *mappa mundi*, with specific reference to providing a map of the intellectual world that corresponds to the map of the physical world. This mapping, however, involves as much intellectual archaeology and philology as intellectual geography, since, for Vico, who we are as human beings is determined in significant part by the institutions, languages, myths and symbols of culture, as they develop and change over time. Successful mapping, in the case of either Vico or his Italian predecessors,[52] does not involve a reduction to a single principle of unity. To use the language of Charles Taylor, for Vico the sources of the self are too plural and heterogeneous for that.[53] Mapping involves a commitment to a complex form of unity, in which proximities and distances of discourses can be plotted, and stratigraphic layers of discourse exposed. It is clear, as the terrain of discourses is mapped, that ratiocination is by no means privileged. As Vico's investigations into the history of law reveal clearly to him, the ratiocinative intellect almost invariably follows customary law.[54] The logic of the legal system, the logic of custom, offer for Vico an alternative model of rationality to that proffered by Descartes and his deductivist minions.

To map the intellectual world is to produce an encyclopaedia of ideas, discourses and institutions as these have changed over time. The accent on genesis and change implies that the encyclopaedia cannot be closed. Vico's encyclopaedia is proposed as an alternative to Bacon's *novus orbis scientiarum*.[55] From Vico's perspective, the prescriptive nature of Bacon's 'new science' disqualifies it as science. It signals that the totality of knowledge attested belongs to the order of hope. In any event, the jettisoning of received wisdom represents an act of philosophical self-mutilation that makes impossible an adequate understanding of human being as incorrigibly social and historical, and as an always more than rational animal. Proleptically, Vico's encyclopaedia critiques both the French encyclopaedia of Diderot and d'Alembert, and the encyclopaedia of Hegel. While the French encyclopaedists, unlike Bacon, think institutions and customs worthy of discussion, nonetheless, the principle of assessment is that of reason. The contrast, as well as the positive relation, between Vico and Hegel have often been drawn. Vico's encyclopaedia is focused on what in Hegel would be called 'objective Spirit' rather than absolute spirit, even if Vico honours the discourses of art, religion and philosophy in a manner not dissimilar to Hegel. Most certainly there is no moment of return, or encircling (*en-kuklo*) that ties all expressions and modes of expression into a complete self-validating system.[56]

Philosophy and its Relation to, and Limitation by, Other Discourses

For Vico, modern thought evinced a total failure to understand that philosophy is but one discourse among others, and cannot claim to be a supreme discourse. The claim to superiority was hubristic. Not only did Cartesian rationalism and Baconian empiricism reveal that they were unable to redeem their claims to methodological sophistication and provide proof of the legitimacy of the expectation of comprehensive knowledge, they also seriously underestimated the intrinsic value of art (especially literary production) and religion, and failed to see how these discourses serve as both systematic and historical presuppositions for philosophy.

For Vico, in *The New Science* as well as elsewhere, as a mode of revealing truth, philosophy is not only limited by revealed religion, but in principle surpassed by it.[57] Vico devotes considerable space throughout his *œuvre* to the irreducibility of literature or poetry to philosophy. In Book Three of *The New Science*, the figure of Homer is at the centre of his argument.[58] Vico makes both narrow and broad points. The narrow point is that Homer's poetic language is untranslatable into a philosophical idiom.[59] Modes of interpretation, such as that practised by Plotinus, who provides an allegorical interpretation of the journey of Ulysses, are regarded as bankrupt.[60] The broader point made about Homer in *The New Science* is that the true contribution of Homer to culture, and thus a real understanding of the nature of poetic imagination, has remained obscured by the assumption that Homer is a proper name that refers to an individual author. From Vico's point of view, Homeric texts are more like anthologies and encyclopaedias than texts unified by a single authorial voice.[61] In proposing a shift in our understanding of authorship, Vico supposes that we will get a clearer idea of the general productive and imaginative capacity (*poiein*) of human beings, as they reflect and make a world of culture. While the reference to Homer is not intended to invalidate rational discourse, it is intended to humble it, for there is a power in Homer's discourse, despite or because of its crudity, that is ineluctable.

Philosophical Aesthetics and Poetics: Aesthetic and Poetic Philosophy

Against the assertion by the rationalist and empiricist traditions of the prerogatives of discursive intellect, Vico consistently asserts the value of image and imagination, and a view of human being as artificer and poet. It is interesting that it is the moderns who more or less exclusively bear Vico's wrath concerning the denigration of image and imagination, and human being's poetic capacity. For while the denigration is exacerbated in the modern turn to method and the love affair with clarity, nonetheless a negative attitude is a consistent feature of the philosophical tradition. Indeed suspicion of image and poetry is coincident with the very emergence of philosophical discourse in Plato. Even if Vico does not address this inconvenient aspect of the much-beloved Platonic tradition directly, it is clear that it is his recognition of this fact that provokes a rehabilitation, in which Plato's use of symbol and myth to render what is not available to the discursive intellect is cited as an indication of what is fundamental to Plato, and thus to the broader Platonic tradition.[62]

In Vico's texts in general, and especially in *The New Science*,[63] the affirmation of the poetic is closely related to the affirmation of the aesthetic. Here the accent falls on the mind's power to make and to construct. It is the poetic capacity of human being, rather than its genius for abstract notions, that strikes Vico as being more universal, because it is omnihistorical. The poetic capacity expresses itself in poetic figures and *fabulae* that are irreducible to rational intellect, being both broader and deeper. Poetic figures and *fabulae* are poetic universals that inchoately grasp the whole, and do so in a manner that involves all levels of the self, the affective, sensory, erotic and somatic as well as the cognitive level. Moreover the constructions of the poetic mind are more active than the conceptual schemes articulated by Bacon, and especially by Descartes. Vico therefore has little compunction about regarding poetic universals as being fundamentally, and not simply chronologically, prior to abstract or conceptual universals.

Importantly, Vico's conviction about the aesthetic and the poetic actually affects his philosophical practice and style. He realizes that he is on the other side of the irredeemable hiatus between the ancient and the modern, and thus that it would be spurious to affect a philosophical style that was not only naive, but blurred the boundaries totally between the philosophical and the poetic. Still, this notwithstanding, licence is given to image and imagination, just as the organization of the 'new science' displays anything but the linear logic recommended by the moderns. Organization in *The New Science* is serpentine, and the text is a compound of thematic treatment, historical enquiry, criticism of contemporary forms of thought, learned reference, purple passage and *aperçu*.[64] The organization is intentional: this complicated discourse is able to match the complication and co-implication of reality, in a way unmatched by a linear approach. Only this encyclopaedia, which is also a compendium of styles, can grasp or, better, receive reality.

Philosophy as a Form of Rhetoric

I have observed already that Vico is anxious to include Cicero and the rhetorical tradition in the positive hemisphere of the history of philosophy. This inclusion is not asserted simply in the interests of the self-justification of Vico's own profession, which is that of professor of rhetoric. Vico understands the rhetorical tradition as representing a healing of the break between rhetoric and philosophy, one that is coterminous with philosophy's very beginning, and as a riposte to the exclusion of rhetorical styles of thought from the commonwealth of reason that is executed by both Descartes and Bacon who, for Vico, are the twin founders of specifically modern discourse.

Vico acknowledges the double-headed character of rhetoric: it can be used for evil as well as good. Nonetheless, though double, rhetoric need not be duplicitous: it can persuade with respect to the good. Without explicitly asserting this, the interest in combating the Sophists being determinative, Plato's own language performs a denial of the absoluteness of the breach between philosophy and rhetoric, just as it performs a denial of the absoluteness of the breach between philosophy and poetry. For Vico, it is in Cicero and the rhetorical tradition that the split between rhetoric and philosophy is healed. Cicero understands well that eloquence is not a derogation from wisdom, but wisdom speaking copiously (*nihil enim est aliud eloquentia nisi copiose loquens sapientia*).[65] Copious or comprehensive speaking is intentional in that it has persuasion in mind, and multiperspectival in that it renders a phenomenon or truth from different angles, in order to effect persuasion in an audience that is various in starting-points, different in what they require by way of argumentation, and divided in terms of their affective and cognitive capacities. Copious speaking is also self-consciously stylistic and figural, for without a mode of communication that is interesting, even arresting, the truth remains stillborn in society.

Even more crucially, Vico's support of rhetoric is intended to challenge the discursive anorexia of modernity. Vico's most extended recommendation occurs in his *On the Study Methods of Our Time*. The turn to method has proved disastrous: 'Today, those branches of philosophical theory are taught by such a method as to dry up every font of convincing expression, of copious, penetrating, embellished, lucid, developed, psychologically effective, and impassionate utterance' (*Study Methods*, p.37).

The turn to method has authored a fundamental shift in priorities away from ethics towards natural science, in the naive hope that human affairs will admit of regulation in the way that phenomena of the natural world will. This hope, Vico believes, is illusory, since the complexity of human affairs will never admit of a logarithm:

> It is therefore impossible to assess human affairs by the inflexible standard of absolute right; we must rather gauge them by the pliant Lesbic rule, which does not conform bodies to itself, but adjusts itself to its contours.
>
> (*Study Methods*, p.34)

It is in the figure of the sage that eloquence and philosophy, as the search for truth, come together. For the sage, 'roundabout' communication may more effectively communicate the truth than bald enunciation, and thus, in paradoxical fashion, be the shortest distance between two points. Importantly, sages do not belong in the past. Vico does not wish to concede eloquence exclusively to the ancients, no more than he wishes to concede science exclusively to the moderns. The sage is not simply a figure, but a real possibility in modernity, to the extent to which it rows against the current of the methodological, and combats aspirations to knowledge that would disrespect the finitude of the human subject.

Conclusion

The persuasive force of the case that I am making that Desmond's philosophy operates essentially within a paradigm for philosophy set by Vico, depends upon seeing *Being and the Between* and *Ethics and the Between* as repeating, in unanticipated fashion, a constellation of substantive and discursive commitments found nowhere else in modern philosophy. At the very least, this involves binocular vision. Probably it involves much more, since I have hardly 'proved' my case. Nor could I have, given the relative abstractness of my sketch of Vico, and my lack of attention to the way the group of elements is integrated in Desmond as well as in Vico. This essay, then, suffers from an Anaxamanderian guilt of incompleteness. Yet if the essay, even as a fulfilment of a promise, is once again promise, it is for all that an enriched promise. For interpretively it opens rather than closes Desmond's texts. Vico is himself more, or less, than a proper name, even the name for a style. 'Vico' is, as Joyce recognized, himself an imaginative universal, that opens up dimensions of Western discourse and thought and their relation which, if buried, are too fertile to be lost. Joyce also recognized not only that adequately appropriating Vico's thought called for great ambition, extraordinary literacy and facility with thought and language, but also that appropriating Vico, like appropriating Homer, was never something merely antiquarian. Vico could only be revoiced; and as revoiced, he not only seemed different, he was different. In this lay his power and his claim.

Notes

1   See O'Regan (2001), 'The Poetics of Ethos: William Desmond's Poetic Refiguration of Plato', *Ethical Perspectives*, **8** (4), 272–302. See also William Desmond's response, ibid., pp.303–6.

2   See Vico, *The New Science of Giambattista Vico*, trans. Thomas Goddard Bergin and Max Harold Fisch, Ithaca, New York: Cornell University Press, 1983.

3   I make the point in 'Poetics of Ethos' that Desmond is influenced by Plato and the Neoplatonic tradition, without this tradition being constitutive of his work. A similar point could be made about Heidegger. Heidegger is important to Desmond for the ontological turn he makes in phenomenology, and for his powerful reading of the Western philosophical tradition. Here again, however, Heidegger is but an important interlocutor, indeed one whose fundamental philosophical direction and metahistory of philosophy have to be contested. See O'Regan (1997), 'Metaphysics and the Metaxological Space of the Tradition', in *Tijdschrift voor Filosofie*, **59** (3), September, pp.531–49, especially pp.537–41.

4   The concepts of perplexity and astonishment, which, with a de-emphasis on the noetic, correspond to Aristotle's 'wonder', are central to *Being and the Between*, and examples of their use can be found in just about every chapter. In *Ethics and the Between* these concepts are not quite so conspicuous. The reason is simple: they are presupposed. Still they are deployed, especially in Chapters 1 and 2, pp.1, 10, 17, 18, 19, 20, 40, 42, 52, 55, 76.

5   The commitment to 'unearthing' the primordial layers of experience unites Desmond to Husserl and thus to phenomenology in general. While it is clear that Desmond would sanction, with Husserl, the necessity of overcoming the 'natural attitude', there is nothing in his work redolent of eidetic or phenomenological reduction. While he does not make the point thematic, the latter in particular would worry him, since it represents a shift in a Cartesian direction that brings to fruition the very worst trait of modernity. At the same time, it is consistent with Desmond's overall philosophical tendency to suggest that Husserl's philosophy of the *Lebenswelt* might be regarded as an opening, for the self finds itself already implicated in a world of meaning and affect, indeed within a matrix from which it is impossible to extricate itself.

6   For a brief reflection on the relation between Desmond's thought and that of pragmatism, see 'Metaphysics and the Metaxological Space of the Tradition', pp.346–7. I recall Whitehead's declaration in *Science and the Modern World* that philosophy is valid and valuable only to the degree to which its discourse is regulated by the experiences and observations which gave rise to it in the first place.

7   Despite the fact that there is only an inconsiderable increase in the quantity of explicit citation, it could be argued that there is a shift in the Augustinian index between *Being and the Between* and *Ethics and the Between*. To the extent that this is so, the shift in subject-matter is in the main responsible. In *Being and the Between* Augustine's main role is to point to a self-transcending self, oriented towards its origin (pp.419, 496, 521). By contrast, the focus of *Ethics and the Between* is on the complexity of this self, the nature of the origin, and how Augustine in particular represents an answer to the nihilism of the modern age inaugurated by Nietzsche. It should also be said that Desmond's Augustinianism extends beyond the historical Augustine. In a very real sense, Desmond reads Dostoyevski as if he were Augustine. Moreover, what is abiding about Kant's contribution regarding the self lies latent in the Augustinian element.

8   For Desmond, while philosophy is a privileged site for this double exposure, it is not the only site. In stark contrast to Hegel's hierarchical stratification of the discourses of art, religion and philosophy, Desmond thinks that the languages of art and religion have equal claim to meaning, meaningfulness and truth.

9   See 'The Poetics of Ethos', pp.280–86.

10 See 'Metaphysics and the Metaxological Space of the Tradition', pp.537–41.

11 *Ereignis* is one of those words that mark off the later Heidegger from the earlier. Roughly translated as 'appropriation', it is availed of by Heidegger to indicate, among other things, the shift of focus from *Dasein* to *Sein*, while at the same time problematizing the language of Being itself. It also connotes an initiative to which Dasein responds, rather than *Dasein* having the initiative. It is availed of in a multitude of contexts, from Heidegger's exegesis of the poems of Hölderlin and commentary on Hegel to more systematic texts such as *On Time and Being* and *Contributions to Philosophy*. See especially Heidegger, *On Time and Being*, trans. Joan Stambaugh, New York: Harper & Row, 1977; also, *Contributions to Philosophy* ('From Enowning'), trans. Parvis Emad and Kenneth Maly, Bloomington and Indianapolis: Indiana University Press, 1999.

12 See Martin Heidegger, *Hegel's Concept of Experience*, trans. Glenn J. Gray, New York: Harper & Row, 1970; also *Hegel's Phenomenology of Spirit*, trans. Parvis Emad and Kenneth Maly, Bloomingon: Indiana University Press, 1988; also 'The Onto-theological Nature of Metaphysics', *Essays in Metaphysics: Identity and Difference*, trans. Kurt F. Leidecker, New York: Philosophical Library, 1960.

13 The classic essay is 'The Onto-theological Nature of Metaphysics'.

14 Heidegger makes the point both before and after the so-called *Kehre*, and in a variety of ways. Perhaps his best-known avowal of what amounts to a thesis of contamination is to be found in his *Introduction to Metaphysics*, trans. Ralph Mannheim, New Haven: Yale University Press, 1959, pp.6–7.

15 Of course a real issue in Heidegger's prohibition against the mixing of discourses, only one of which is defined by unlimited questioning (philosophy), is whether the ban is merely procedural, and Heidegger's atheism merely 'methodological'. This issue has been much debated in Heidegger commentary and criticism. I articulate my own view in an essay 'Answering back: Augustine's critique of Heidegger', published in *Collecteana Augustiniana* in 2004.

16 I elaborate this point in 'The Poetics of Ethos', pp.288–92.

17 For Desmond, it is Nietzsche who essentially sets the agenda for contemporary philosophy. Particularly in *Ethics and the Between*, Nietzsche is not just one voice among others (the voice of the equivocal). He has named the loss of confidence in foundations, and exposed the *libido dominandi* at the heart of philosophy. Not only he, but the situation he describes ('the death of God' as the destruction of all value) must be overcome. Heidegger is one example among many of an inability to overcome the Nietzschean legacy.

18 Kant explicitly elaborates his view of the 'architectonic of pure reason' in chapter 2 of 'The Transcendental Doctrine of Method' near the end of *The Critique of Pure Reason*. See pp.653–66 of Norman Kemp Smith's (1966) translation, London: Macmillan. He also lays it out in brief in the Preface. Desmond comments on Kant's architectonic ambitions in *BB*, pp.23–4.

19 See *Art and the Absolute: A Study of Hegel's Aesthetics*; see also *Philosophy and its Others*.

20 See Gilbert Ryle, *The Concept of Mind*, London: Hutchinson, 1949.

21   I drew attention to this aspect of Desmond's thought in 'Metaphysics and the
      Metaxological Space of the Tradition', p.542. I am thinking in particular of Merleau-
      Ponty, *The Phenomenology of Perception*, trans. Colin Smith, London: Routledge &
      Kegan Paul, 1962, but see also his *The Visible and the Invisible*, trans. Alphonso
      Lingis, Evanston: Northwestern University Press, 1968. It would also be interesting to
      explore the relation between Desmond and Bergson on this point.

22   Even 'spiral' is too simple a figure for the complexity of Desmond's style. Perhaps a
      more adequate figure might be Deleuze's rhizome.

23   For this point, see 'Poetics of Ethos', pp.278–81.

24   Isaiah Berlin at once ties Vico and Herder together, and dissociates them by making
      Vico and not Herder the father of modern historicism. See Berlin, *Vico and Herder:
      Two Studies in the History of Ideas*, London: Hogarth Press; New York: Viking Press,
      1976.

25   See Vico, *On the Most Ancient Wisdom of the Italians: Unearthed From the Origins of
      the Latin Language*, trans. and intro. L.M. Palmer, Ithaca, New York: Cornell
      University Press, 1988, pp.53–66. For a good account of Vico's anti-Cartesianism, see
      Palmer's introduction, pp.1–34. Another commentator who is excellent on this point is
      Mark Lilla, who explores Vico's critique of a host of modern thinkers, political and
      otherwise. See Lilla, *G.B. Vico: The Making of an Anti-Modern*, Cambridge, MA:
      Harvard University Press, 1993, pp.35–6, 47–52.

26   See *On the Most Ancient Wisdom of the Italians*, pp.67–84. Lilla has good things to say
      on the subject in *G.B. Vico*, pp.40–45.

27   In *On the Most Ancient Wisdom of the Italians*, originally published in 1710, Vico
      defends a principle that proves central to *The New Science*. This is the principle of
      verum esse ipsum factum, which can be translated as 'the true is the thing made'.

28   The text which makes the point clearest is the 1709 text, *De Nostri Temporis Studiorum
      Ratione*. See the English translation, *On the Study Methods of Our Time*, trans. and
      with an intro. by Elio Gianturco, with 'The Acadamies and the Relation between
      Philosophy and Eloquence', trans. Donald P. Verene, Ithaca, New York: Cornell
      University Press, 1990.

29   See *On the Study Methods of Our Time*, pp.3–5. See also Vico, *The Autobiography of
      Giambattista Vico*, trans. Max H. Fisch and Thomas G. Bergin, Ithaca, New York:
      Cornell University Press, 1944, p.139. See also Vico's *magnum opus*, *The New Science
      of Giambattista Vico*, trans. Max H. Fisch and Thomas G. Bergin, Ithaca, New York:
      Cornell University Press, 1948, p.359.

30   In *On the Study Methods of Our Time*, Vico famously complains: 'Thus Bacon acted
      in the intellectual field like the potentates of mighty empires, who having gained
      supremacy in human affairs, squandered immense wealth in attempts against the order
      of Nature herself, by paving the seas with stones, mastering mountains with sail, and
      other vain exploits forbidden by nature' (p.4).

31   The relation between 'wonder' (*maraviglia*) and curiosity, especially as these play a
      role in *The New Science*, is brilliantly commented on by Giuseppi Mazzota. *The New
      Map of the World: The Poetic Philosophy of Giambattista Vico*, Princeton: Princeton
      University Press, 1999, pp.108–10.

32   For this point, see *The New Map of the World*, p.110. The doubleness of curiosity goes
      back at least to Stoics such as Seneca, with whom Vico was quite familiar.
      Interestingly, in his elaboration of care (*Sorge*) in *Being and Time*, Heidegger appeals
      to the ambiguous nature of *cura* in the Stoics, which at least in part was taken over by
      Augustine.

33   See Oration 1 in Vico, *On Humanistic Education: Six Inaugural Orations, 1699–1707*, trans. Giorgio A. Pinton and Arthur W. Shipee, intro. by Donald P. Verene, Ithaca: Cornell University Press, 1993.

34   The text that is most assertive on this point is Vico, 'On the Heroic Mind', trans. Elizabeth Sewell and Anthony C. Sirignano, in G. Tagliacozzo, M. Mooney and Donald P. Verene (eds), *Vico and Contemporary Thought*, Atlantic Highlands, NJ: Humanities Press, 1979, pp.228–45. While doubtless Vico is here following on Pico della Mirandola and Gioradano Bruno, he is more broadly following in the Platonic tradition. See Nancy du Bois Marcus, *Vico and Plato*, New York: Peter Lang, 2001, pp.50–1, 54–5, 214–15, 218–19.

35   Of course, the view of man as a middle between cosmos and God was made famous by Pico in his famous 'Oration on the dignity of man'. See Pico, 'The Dignity of Man', in *On the Dignity of Man,* trans. Charles Glenn Wallis, Paul J.W. Miller and Douglas Carmichael, Indianapolis and New York: Bobbs-Merrill, 1940, pp.1–34.

36   For a reflection on this notion, see Mazzota, *The New Map of the World*, pp.36–7.

37   See *The New Science*, pp.130–31; also pp.335, 342, 345.

38   Vico's most sustained engagement with Augustine is in *The New Science*. As befits the topic, which is nothing less than a science of humanity as producer of culture, the text with which Vico is most in dialogue is *The City of God*. The importance of Augustine, and especially *The City of God,* has been recognized by most commentators on Vico. Two commentators who mark strongly the influence of Augustine, but who offer different readings of how the influence works, are John Milbank and Nancy du Bois Marcus. See Milbank, *The Religious Dimension of the Thought of Giambattista Vico 1668–1744. Part 2: Language, Law and History*, Lewiston: Edwin Mellen Press, 1992; du Bois Marcus, *Vico and Plato*, Part 2, pp.75–148.

39   In *On the Study Methods of Our Time*, Cicero is described as a sage (pp.35, 37). For a good account of the influence of Cicero on the thought of Vico in general, and his conviction that a rhetorical style of philosophy is a *sine qua non*, see Michael Mooney, *Vico and the Tradition of Rhetoric*, Princeton: Princeton University Press, 1984; also du Bois Marcus, *Vico and Plato*, Part 2, pp.59–74. Vico approves of Cicero's definition of eloquence as wisdom speaking copiously in the *Autobiography*, p.199. Cicero's definition was *nihil enim est aliud eloquentia nisi copiose loquens sapientia (de part. orat.* xxiii, 79).

40   This is a view made current in contemporary philosophy by John Milbank and Catherine Pickstock. This view is central to Pickstock, *After Writing*, Oxford: Blackwell, 1998, ch. 1.

41   *New Science*, p.131.

42   While this relation is harmonious, it does not mean that Vico perceives himself to be doing anything other than philosophy. This is a point at dispute between du Bois Marcus and Milbank. The advantage clearly goes to du Bois Marcus, who draws attention to Vico's expression of the limitations of his enterprise; that is, that it reflects on the patterns of history from the human and not the divine point of view. See, in particular, *The New Science*, p.131.

43   See *Autobiography*, p.199.

44   Here Vico is following a tradition of interpretation that goes back as far as Marsilio Ficino and Pico della Mirandola.

45   For Vico, this is certainly true of Descartes. It is also true of Hobbes and Machievelli, relatively indifferent between the Platonic and non-Platonic traditions.

46   *New Science*, p.366.

47   See *New Science*, p.949. For helpful comments on this point, see du Bois Marcus, *Vico and Plato*, pp.108–9, 126–7.

48   See Lilla, *Vico: The Making of an Anti-Modern*, pp.40–45.

49   *New Science*, p.343.

50   For the influence not only of the *Timaeus*, but the *Symposium* and the *Phaedrus* on Vico's justification of the aesthetic approach, see du Bois Marcus, *Vico and Plato*, pp.199–219. Again Vico is here continuing an Italian Renaissance tradition, exemplified above all by Ficino.

51   I am referring to Mazzota's fine book, *The New Map of the World*. See in particular the Introduction, pp.1–15, especially pp.1–3.

52   Predecessors include such luminaries as Campanella, Comenius and Giordano Bruno. See *The New Map of the World*, pp.5, 43, 45 *inter alia*.

53   Mazzota insists on the heterogeneity that resists the reduction to a single unifying principle, dialectical or otherwise. It is this that makes the Vichean encyclopaedia so different from that of Hegel. See *The New Map of the World*, p.95.

54   Mark Lilla, *The Making of an Anti-Modern*, is particularly good on this point. See also John Milbank, *The Religious Dimension in the Thought of Giambattista Vico 1668–1744*. Part 2.

55   See Mazzota, *The New Map of the World*, pp.102–4; also pp.32–3, 54–7, 92–3.

56   See ibid., pp.97, 102.

57   This is made particularly clear in Books 4 and 5 of *The New Science* which contain the essence of Vico's philosophy of history. Vico is persuaded, as Augustine is, that history is ruled by divine providence. The difference is that this can be seen by human eyes, and does not itself require something like a supernatural vision. See the helpful reflection of du Bois Marcus, *Vico and Plato*, ch. 5, pp.103–27.

58   The title of this book is 'The Discovery of Homer'.

59   *New Science*, p.780.

60   Ibid., p.403. See du Bois Marcus, *Vico and Plato*, pp.29–31, for a development of this point.

61   The general importance of Book 2 of *The New Science*, entitled 'Poetic wisdom', should be underscored. It sets the basic frame for the discussion of Homer in the next book. In addition, it has been one of the most discussed aspects of *The New Science*. Donald Verene has written especially well on this topic. See Verene, *Vico's Science of Imagination*, Ithaca: Cornell University Press, 1981. There Verene lucidly describes Vico's argument to the effect that imaginative or poetic universals are more basic than abstract universals. On the basis of Book 2, Vico argues that 'Homer' himself is a concrete or imaginative universal. One can see how the idea of a nation or a group as the author of fabulation would have appealed so much to Joyce, who relies so heavily on the basic *corso-recorsi* architectonic scheme in *Finnegans Wake*.

62   As du Bois Marcus points out, despite the wish to continue to distinguish between sophistry and authentic philosophy, the Italian Renaissance refigured Plato so that Plato is not so much the enemy of rhetoric as of its illicit use. See *Vico and Plato*, pp.7, 60–61, 67, 199, 203–4.

63   The focus on making the true is already present in *On the Most Ancient Wisdom of the Italians* and, as just about all commentators agree, is a crucial element of *The New Science*. For a good discussion of *verum-factum* see Milbank, *The Religious Dimension in the Thought of Giambattista Vico*, pp.77–116.

64   A long passage from Mazzota's *The New Map of the World* is worth citing in full. *The New Science* is 'an encyclopedia of disjointed parts – not as a rational scientific

method, but as a critical and poetic rethinking of history's memories and shadows. As a poetic encyclopedia, it is a model for what humans can make. More precisely, the *New Science* is in the mixed mode of brief philosophical essays, poetic fragments, maxims, fables, and sentences. Its aim is to give a representation of the modifications of the human mind. Because the way of writing is for Vico a way of knowing, Vico's many styles recall among other texts Eramus's *Adagia*, Pascal's *Pensées*, the *Maximes* of La Rochefoucauld, as well as the *Aphorisms* of Bacon. These styles constitute Vico as an author whose imagination ties together facts and fictions, philology and philosophy, and whose narrative needs readers to remake the movement of his thought. These many styles that resonate in his text constitute his poetic philosophy, a mixture of lapidary fulgurations, oracular obscurities, and rational criticism that together reach before a time when a new Homer, the true educator of Hellas and the blind seer of the past, will wage a mighty war against time and thereby reacquaint man with death's pageants' (p.112).

65   See note 39.

IV
DESMOND AND METAPHYSICS

Chapter 6

William Desmond's Overcoming of the Overcoming of Metaphysics

James L. Marsh

I am a relative newcomer to William Desmond's philosophy. As I was in the process of finishing up my own systematic venture in metaphysics and philosophy of religion, *Process, Praxis and Transcendence*, in 1998, I finally was able to take up the work of this thinker, whom people had been recommending to me for years: 'You must read Desmond'. *Being and the Between* had recently appeared, and I worked through that with pleasure and profit, and then all or most of his other volumes in the next year or so.

Needless to say, I was not disappointed. I found myself confirmed in my own efforts in philosophy to articulate a position that does justice to difference and otherness within metaphysics, and here I discovered a kindred spirit who had been working in the same vineyard for years. Moreover I was delighted and surprised to find someone who was as hard, if not harder, on the postmoderns as I am. Desmond, for example, is not afraid to refer to the French Nietzscheans as 'philosophers on show' (PO, 373, n.6). Nor is he afraid to ask the following kind of question: 'Is Professor Derrida a real shark? Or a postmodern Alexandrian? He seems to be an original (but of course deconstruction denies the possibility of originals) generating a thousand clones – strange epigonal champions of difference, an endlessly disseminated mimicry of Derrida' (PO, 316, n.10). Nor is he reluctant to claim that Heidegger, like Derrida, tends to 'totalize the tradition of philosophy as univocal logocentrism' (DD, 242–3, n.14). Nor is he afraid to take on Derrida with humour and irony and comedy. 'What would post-phallocentric thinking be like? Do we need a Derridean Pharmakon to make the organ of logos lie limp, no longer a weapon to dominate the Nietzschean feminine flux, impotent to bang becoming into monogamous categoreal submission?' (PO, 358, n.6) Here I discovered to my delight, is a marvellously unfashionable thinker, not afraid to tread on the toes of the right or the left, and this trait is most important in the United States, where postmodernism and deconstruction have become the fashion, the 'in thing', especially in continental philosophy. Such dominance even seduces those on the radical political left in the United States not to be too critical of postmodernism, to talk about us all, modernists and postmodernists, as political partners in the same political enterprise of opposing capitalism and imperialism, and to be too cautious about calling philosophical nonsense by its right name. 'Be reasonable, Marsh,' I am told. 'They are on your side.'

In response, I ask how bad philosophy can give rise to good social theory or practice, and I wonder about the inability to take legitimate philosophical offence at such bad philosophy. And in the spirit of Marx, who referred to similar philosophical efforts in his time as 'German ideology', I have begun to articulate, define and write about something called 'French ideology', apparently on the left, apparently with its heart in the right place, but ultimately more harmful than helpful to the ends of any legitimate, progressive politics.[1]

Desmond's argument with and against postmodernism is complex and many-levelled. The approach I will take here is to look first at how he moves to an evaluation of postmodern claims from the perspective of his own 'system', then consider the way he historically and critically reflects on postmodern thinkers in themselves, and finally conclude with a few reflections, questions and implications.

The Desmondian Fourfold and its Implications

Desmond's fourfold, in contrast to Heidegger's, is situated within metaphysics, and helps to constitute metaphysics. In his thought there is a movement from the univocal, as basic identity, to the equivocal, as fundamental difference, to dialectic, as a mediation of identity and difference, to the metaxological, as intermediation between identity and difference, self and other, from the point of view, and for the sake, of the other. The other can never be captured completely within the net of philosophical thought, but always retains an excess, motivating a subsequent wonder that deepens the original wonder with which philosophy begins (BB, 3–46).

This original and subsequent wonder reveals not simply a lack in the self and being, but a positive presence and fullness that is celebratory, reverential and even sacrificial. Heideggerian 'thinking as thanking' or 'questioning as the piety of thinking' Desmond is able to ground and do justice to inside metaphysics, not outside it, as Heidegger thinks necessary.[2] Only because Heidegger wrongly totalizes the tradition as univocal and logocentric does he think that one has to step outside it to wonder and question in a spirit of reverence for mystery. As Desmond puts it succinctly and pointedly, '*Denken* is old speculative vintage poured into the new bottles of post-philosophical philosophy' (BH, 51).

The authentic philosophical thinker, then, stands in the 'between' of the fourfold in wonder and reverence, and moves to understand and articulate reflectively the univocal, equivocal, dialectical and metaxological, but is under no illusion about total mastery. This is bad metaphysics. The 'between' is an on-going interplay between determinacy and indeterminacy, self and other, immanence and transcendence, and particular and universal. Metaphysical wonder consists in responding to this interplay in all its complexity and mystery. Metaphysical inadequacy lies in trying to absolutize one moment and stay fixed on that moment, reducing all else to it, and substituting the part for the whole or taking the part for the whole (BB, 3–46).

When we move to the univocal as a valid first moment in our approach to metaphysics, that identity breaks down and difference emerges if we are faithful to the movement of our thought. The duck–rabbit figure dear to Gestalt psychologists can be read more than one way, the bent stick in the water turns out to be straight, and the beautiful woman in the department store window turns out to be a dummy. There is a legitimate 'triumph of ambiguity', as I put it in my first book, that must be celebrated.[3] Celebrating such a triumph, however, is different from being stuck in it, or absolutizing it, or moving back and forth endlessly between univocal and equivocal in an 'either/or' manner.

All of these are moves made by postmodernism. It falsely, negatively totalizes the philosophical tradition and falsely, positively valorizes the moment of difference. The inadequacy of such a stance points to the necessity of identity mediating and accompanying all difference, and vice versa. People, for example, perceive themselves as different within the context of a common life-world and shared humanity (BB, 85–130).

Nietzsche, for example, simply exalts difference in a one-sided way. Moreover he privileges flux or change in such a way as to deny any determinate meaning. Yet, as so often is the case, there is a self-referential problem here. If all knowing is imposition, then there is no basis for critique itself. If all metaphysics is rooted in a perspectivally oriented will to power, then the deconstruction of metaphysics is no truer than metaphysics itself. Indeed the doing of metaphysics becomes as legitimate as its denial. Moreover, as is often the case, there is an experiential, phenomenological implausibility to such claims. For there clearly is an experienced difference between meanings imposed and meanings discovered. The duck–rabbit figure, for example, is easily seen as a duck or a rabbit, but less easily and more implausibly as a deer, bird or antelope. Postmodernism does violence not only to the philosophical tradition, but also to experience itself (BB, 342–6).

Rather than being thrown back and forth ceaselessly between univocal and equivocal, a thinking, faithful to the desire to know animating thought, moves to dialectical mediation between the contraries of identity and difference, permanence and change, self and other. We begin to see that identity and difference imply one another. A human child grows up into its identity as a mature human being, and its changing is meaningful in the light of such emerging identity. The idiot self becoming authentic is not cut off from the universal, but related to the universal in its own way (BB, 131–5).

Nor is dialectic simply to be understood as the expression of the will to power. Both Plato and Aristotle were aware of the danger of philosophical discussion sinking or degenerating into simply trying to win the argument. Hence they distinguished carefully between philosophy and sophistry, dialogue and eristic, arguing to discover the truth and trying to prevail over my opponent at all costs. Here Nietzsche and the 'French Derrideans' do violence to experience and tradition. 'And if the philosophers of difference cannot open themselves to the difference of speculative philosophy, one wonders what this says about such philosophies of difference. How different are they to the totalizing philosophies of the same they like to lash?' (BB, 226, n.l).

Dialectic is a distinct stage and aspect of metaphysics, and already it overcomes the sterile absoluteness of univocity and equivocity. Already being and philosophy are shown to be more complex and differentiated than postmodernism allows. Dialectic, however, is not enough either. It is an integration of self and other, identity and difference, from the perspective of the self and identity. But a further stage is desirable and necessary, in which thought relates to the other for the sake, and from the perspective, of the other. Thought and freedom move outside themselves centrifugally to affirm, choose, serve and love the other. I think the other, and give myself to the other, for the sake of the other (BB, 177–222).

In a way that reminds us of Heidegger, Desmond affirms that metaphysical thinking on this level is a kind of thanking. I value the gift of being enough, find being wonder-full enough, to think about it reverentially and patiently.

> We begin to make ourselves worthy by thanking: saying yes to being: it is good. We make thanks (*gratias agimus*). Thanking is a doing of being, a being agapeic, a saying yes to the other for its otherness. Making thanks is a making beyond self-mediation, a release towards the good of the other. (BB, 194)

Unlike Heidegger, however, Desmond finds no reason not to put thinking as thanking within metaphysics, not outside it. Only Heidegger's one-sided totalization of the philosophical makes him think he has to go outside the tradition to move into thinking as thanking.

Agapeic mindfulness is the metaphysical thinking of transcendence. The happening of the 'between' is a metaxological community with transcendence. There is a crossing of infinitudes here; my inner infinitude reveals itself as more than lack, and encounters an outer infinitude of transcendence that in its mystery is the fulfilment of thought, not its negation. The initial wonder that gets philosophy going is now deepened in a subsequent wonder that finds itself in the midst of a positive or constitutive ambiguity that is not equivocal lostness; rather it 'can offer the signs of finding, or of being found, even in erring; it can be a reminder of home in homelessness itself' (BB, 207).

This theorizing of the metaxological is one of Desmond's most profound and meaningful insights. More than anyone else I can think of, he has thematized the metaxological, shown how it is related to, and yet different from, the univocal, equivocal and dialectical, and yet he has put it within metaphysics as the crown and glory of metaphysics. In contrast to postmodernism, he has not rejected the univocal and dialectical, nor has he absolutized them either. Rather they have a meaningful role to play in any metaphysics, but must be situated in relation to difference and the other. These are not absolutized either, or pushed into some esoteric realm outside metaphysics, but are aspects of a more complex metaphysical whole. Thus, in answer to postmodernism's question about whether metaphysics can do justice to difference and the other, Desmond's own answer is a strong 'yes'. Is metaphysics possible? Even at this very early stage of systematic consideration, we see how plausible a 'yes' answer is. Desmond has not just asserted this 'yes', but has realized it in metaphysical performance. Fact proves possibility.

Historical Reflections: from the Negation of Metaphysics to its Possibility and Actuality

In the above, we see how Desmond moves toward a critique of postmodernism from the perspective of his systematic metaphysics. This gives him a strong, comprehensive, nuanced basis from which to evaluate the claims of the 'French Nietzcheans', as he describes them. Now we are going to move in the opposite direction from historical, critical reflections on postmodern thinkers themselves, back to the Desmondian fourfold. Historical, dialectical critique leads back to, and confirms, the 'system'; the 'system' grounds critique.

I am going to focus on two main texts here. One is Chapter One of *Beyond Hegel and Dialectic*, 'Speculation and Historicism: Between Hegel and Eternity', pp.43–55; and the second, in the same volume, Chapter Five, 'Comedy and the Failure of Logos: On Dialectic, Deconstruction, and the Mockery of Philosophy', pp.251–300. The first of these passages deals primarily with Heidegger in his relation to Hegel, and the second more with Derrida and his followers. Since these are the two main antagonists in Desmond's own encounter with postmodernism, we can gain a more comprehensive and detailed sense of how he interprets and criticizes it.

Desmond begins his discussion of Heidegger in *Beyond Hegel and Dialectic* by noting the tension between historicism and philosophy. Philosophy confronts the other of time in the rise and fall of figures in the history of philosophy, but thinkers as different as Hegel and Plato attempt to mediate between history and a non-historical dimension of transcendence. Heidegger, on the other hand, seems to give in to such historicism. The critique of historicist mind and instrumental reason is endangered by a one-sided reduction of speculative philosophy and its history to a univocal metaphysics of presence, which expresses itself finally in the twentieth century in technocracy. History in Heidegger's hands is thus ontologized, and time now does the work of eternity, which itself is identified with the rigid univocity of Plato's *eidos*. Yet how can being withdraw, even in its historical manifestations, if there is not an other of time, a non-reducibility of being to history, eternity to time (BH, 44–6)?

There are other ironies and contradictions. In tension with his critique of reason as instrumental is Heidegger's endorsement of philosophy as serving the state in work-service, military-service and science-service. Philosophy is totally instrumentalized from the right, which mirrors its corresponding instrumentalization from the left in Soviet Marxism (BH, 46). If the former is a lower historicism, there is a higher version in which there is acceptance of a certain sequence of philosophical positions as necessary or destined. Heidegger totalizes the Western tradition as an epoch of being leading to the global domination of cybernetic thought. In saying that all metaphysics, including its opponent, positivism, speaks Plato, Heidegger gives a simplified, totalized snapshot of the tradition in which all positions express the same ground. There is no discontinuity or radical rupture in this succession of positions. But, Desmond asks, how can one look down from the height if we are simply caught up in historical flux? How can he, Heidegger, say that all being is historical if it does not somehow transcend history? Is not such a claim self-deconstructing if it is made totalistically? In Heidegger, as well as in other postmoderns, self-referential problems arise in his critique of Western reason and metaphysics (BH, 47–8).

Other problems arise, in that instrumental mind is presented as the destiny of speculative mind without acknowledging that the latter is not reducible to the former, that the former is blind to the interests of the latter, and, if totalized, produces just the oblivion of being that Heidegger laments. The sickness is attributed to the cure (BH, 48).

Crucial philosophical differences are here ignored, such as that between speculative and instrumental reason, differences that Hegel begins to get at in his distinction between understanding and reason. Heidegger acquiesces or comes close to acquiescing in this reduction, especially in his bowing before the brute power of the winning cybernetic or Nazi side, a side that later lost. Any sense of an ethical critique of history is lost, and the higher historicism gives way to the lower (BH, 48).

Heidegger strategically blurs philosophical differences. There is a murder of the speculative other, analogous to the Nazi murder of the other. There is in modernity a reduction of speculative to instrumental mind that Heidegger rightly notes in Descartes' criticism of Plato and Aristotle as uselessly speculative. But Plato and Aristotle already knew that speculative mind was useless, and that this was its glory. Philosophy is that which milkmaids laugh at, and that is its glory.[4] Philosophy is useless, valuable in itself, thinking the other and celebrating the other for its own sake. Also Hegel and Husserl are two main figures often taken to be heirs to Descartes' legacy. Yet Husserl is a rigorous critic of historicism, and Hegel is not simply historicist. Both are Aristotelian in their emphasis on thought thinking itself. Such a description might be a basis for ascribing to them the metaphysics of presence, but this description does not exhaust either of these thinkers, or the tradition of philosophy (BH, 49).

Heidegger misses in Plato his sense of metaphysical otherness in the account of the good. Hegel certainly has a panlogist side to him, but Heidegger misses other aspects of Hegel, such as the openness of philosophy to religion and art, Hegel's positive evaluation of laughter in the comedy of Aristophanes, and Hegel's discussion of philosophy as bacchanalian revel. Heidegger accuses the tradition of being oblivious to the other of thought, but he himself is mute about the otherness of speculative thinking to instrumental reason. A final consequence is that Heidegger tries to recover some aspects of speculative thinking in his discussion of *Denken*, and questioning as the piety of thinking, but he puts these outside philosophy, a move made necessary by his own reductive totalization of philosophy. Any philosophy worthy of the name, Desmond suggests, will be animated by a questioning reverence for being, for the other, for mystery. In putting *Denken* outside philosophy, Heidegger is only responding to his own narrow caricature of metaphysics (BH, 50–51, 271–300).

The main question that runs through the treatment of Derrida in 'Comedy and the Failure of Logos' is this: can philosophy now laugh at itself, in a way that is even close to the laughter of Socrates, Plato, or even Hegel himself? We might say that the Thracian maid is revived in deconstruction, albeit more now in the form of a textual scholar rather than in that of a peasant girl. Laughter takes the form often of a heavy-handed, rhetorical 'overcoming of metaphysics', but the deconstructionist forgets that it is not Nietzsche, but Socrates, Plato's Socrates, who is the first philosopher to mock himself (BH, 257–8).

But, Desmond asks, if the deconstructionist can laugh at the philosopher, why cannot the philosopher laugh at the deconstructionist in a two-way conversation? But maybe the deconstructionist will pull a fast one at this point, and say to the philosopher that he is misrepresenting him. Like the woman in 'The Love Song of J. Alfred Prufrock', the deconstructionist says, 'that is not what I meant at all, that is not what I meant at all', as Derrida argued in his savage response to Searle.[5] I can debunk logocentrism, and say we are beyond representation, and that all readings are only misreadings, but when the philosopher tries to debunk logocentrism, he is told, 'Be logical. You are misrepresenting me.' It turns out that the deconstructionist knows too how to play the logocentric game. It turns out that the deconstructionist knows only too well how to have his cake and eat it too (BH, 259).

Philosophers have not always lived up to the truth that what is sauce for the goose is sauce for the gander. This ancient bit of Western lore, by the way, escapes the charge of phallogocentrism, because it transcends the dialectical opposition between male and female, and is the basis for a new deconstructionist feminism. If ontotheology and logocentrism are phallogocentric, what would overcoming phallogocentrism mean? What is being surmounted by the post-phallogocentric philosopher? What is sauce for the goose and the gander, and what could be saucy at all? Would ontotheologians have to imitate Origen, and become post-castrati, but without the justification of making themselves eunuchs for the Lord? Are there any more Lords or Ladies? Must one renounce logical uprightness, erectness, correctness, *adequatio* (in postmodern language, being up to it) and no longer be ontologically upstanding? And what does it mean to be with the truth? Must we cross out the copula (BH, 259–60)?

After this brilliant dialectic of the comical *vis-à-vis* deconstruction, Desmond goes on to consider its treatment of Hegel, who occupies a special place in its discourse. Derrida calls Hegel the last thinker of the book, and the first thinker of irreducible difference. He is the last ontotheologian who did not place the proper emphasis on the Heideggerian project of thinking difference *qua* difference. Hegel is presented as the dour panlogist who cannot laugh at himself, and who is indifferent or hostile to comedy. But are his claims true? Is there another Hegel who resists the postmodern reading (BH, 262–6)?

We need, if we are to be hermeneutically mindful, a hermeneutics of generosity in addition to a hermeneutics of suspicion. To such a hermeneutics, Hegel's resources of thought are extraordinarily rich, but did not and do not exhaust the possibilities of philosophy. Plato's notion of the good beyond being is an example of such tendencies in the tradition, and they are many. Armed with such hermeneutical generosity, we are properly suspicious when we hear Derrida say that a noun is proper when it has but one name and meaning, and univocity is the essence or *telos* of language, and that no philosophy has ever renounced this Aristotelian idea. Yet Hegel in his dialectic of identity and difference transcends such univocity, as do Aristotle and Aquinas in their doctrine of the analogy of being. Strictly speaking, Derrida's account does not do full justice even to Aristotle (BH, 267–8).

Derrida himself equivocates so much that it is hard to tell where he stands. He vacillates between a Lévinasian generosity and a Nietzschean suspicion, between finding an other within philosophy, and insisting that it is outside philosophy. Yet he says, 'I am not happy to be termed a philosopher.' I am interested in 'from what site or non-site (*non-lieu*) can philosophy as such appear to itself as other than itself … Such a non-site or alterity would be radically irreducible to philosophy. But the problem is that such a non-site cannot be defined or situated by means of philosophical language.' But such a stance already presumes a narrow caricature of philosophy as univocal and logocentric, and given over to the cult of presence, and what we need is plurivocal, agapeic thought, that is able to be within and outside of philosophy, intimate with itself and yet most strange to itself, and able to laugh at itself. Because deconstruction puts the question of the other, not from a point of view beyond dialectic, having understood dialectically the mediation between identity and difference, but from below dialectic, it runs the risk of being absorbed by Hegel as a non-question, or a one-sided, partial position. Thus deconstruction will turn out to have been, after all the clever pyrotechnics, in collusion with Hegelian philosophy. Its mockery of Hegel turns into Hegel's mockery of it (BH, 268–73, quotation from 268).

Being brought to nothing in laughter seems to be alien to Hegel, conceived as will to conquer all meaninglessness and all absurdity. And it is true that he resists the deconstructionist claim that nothing comes to nothing. 'Nothing' for Hegel is but a prelude to a higher stage of sublation. But is there only one kind of laughter and comedy? Are there plural possibilities here? Are deconstructionists univocal about comedy (BH, 273)?

One can laugh in different ways and different voices, and this possibility is rooted in a sense of otherness, doubleness and ambiguity, linked with the rich, metaxological community of being. Laughter can be rooted in an equivocal debunking that is nihilisitic in its own way, but can also emerge in dialectical and metaxological affirmation. Hegel's sense of the comic lies in the self-destruction of the finite in its contrast with, and contradiction to, the genuinely true, but in the self-destruction of the false, the self remains at home with itself. The merely laughable, on the other hand, in contrast with the comic, may indicate a not-being at home with being in which laughter takes the form of ontological aggression. In this distinction between the laughable and the comic, Hegel finds differences not apparently available to deconstruction. Even on this issue he is the truer friend of difference (BH, 273–4).

There is much else that is going on in this extremely rich discussion of Desmond's. Hegel's very method involves him in descriptive breakdowns and reversals. He describes an 'inverted world' which motivates laughter: the

Phenomenology is filled with images and posturings of the absolute that show themselves to be imposters; stiff univocal understanding is shown to be least at home with itself and laughable to the extreme. There is the use of humorous metaphors and images such as his description of the Schellingian *Indifferenzpunkt* as 'the night in which all cows are black', there is the deepest intimacy between the sacrifice of Christ and speculative thought, and Hegel's *Aesthetics* ends with the comic as he describes Aristophanes and Shakespeare. Derrida, while his own deconstruction is similar to Hegel's in its questioning of univocity, is caught in an equally stiff-necked and comic freezing and absolutizing of difference and equivocity and refusal to pass over to the dialectical and metaxological other (BH, 275–81).

I find Desmond's treatment of Derrida here, while it is clear that Derrida is not his favourite philosopher, very fair and respectful of Derrida's otherness and complexity, of positives as well as negatives in his thought. There is a negativity in deconstruction that is like dialectic in its unmasking of univocal sameness, but it is also very similar to Kant in his refusal to pass beyond that. In this respect, as Hegel is more comprehensive than Kant in his affirmation of a constitutive and not merely regulative dialectic, so is Desmond's thought more comprehensive than Derrida's. One more indication of Desmond's very fair but very critical reading of Derrida is the claim that 'Derrida is a kind of dialectical thinker who tries to use dialectic to confound dialectic' (BH, 268). But it is a dialectic whose results are equivocal in vacillating between Lévinasian generosity and Nietzschean suspicion. Derrida's laughter is the 'laughter of a thought that *stiffly insists* on being homeless' (BH, 290–91, emphasis in the original).

In summary, then, we note a variety of strands in Desmond's argument with Heidegger and Derrida: a dialectic of the comical, in which both positions, taken as absolute, deconstruct themselves; a hermeneutical testing of the adequacy of their accounts of the history of philosophy, and finding them wanting; a dialectical critique, in that the commitment to difference and otherness is contradicted by one-sided, univocal totalization of the philosophical tradition and individual thinkers within it; an experiential, phenomenological testing of their claims, and finding them wanting; and finding them guilty often of logical and performative inconsistency: recall, for instance, Heidegger's rejection of instrumental reason and his turning philosophy into a servant of the state.

Just as there is more than one kind of comedy, so also reason has more than one voice. Since the overcoming of metaphysics breaks down into comic, laughable failure, the way to metaphysics remains open. Indeed the postmodern overcoming of metaphysics amounts to a one-sided form of metaphysics that absolutizes difference. Since this bad or inadequate metaphysics breaks down, the way remains open to a more adequate form of metaphysics.

The above kind of argument in Desmond's work rarely appears apart from his systematic treatment of the fourfold, although at times, or most often, there is certainly a difference of emphasis, in that he is either dominantly making a systematic point about his own philosophy, or a historical point about someone else's position. Taken together, these two strands function as one argument for metaphysics and against its overcoming. This argument gives Desmond a basis in experience and reality for evaluating one-sided claims such as those made by Heidegger and Derrida. On the other hand, the historical consideration of these thinkers evaluates them more or less on their own terms. Perhaps Desmond's own distinction between dialectical self-mediation and metaxological intermediation applies to the distinction between his own systematic account and his account of the historical, postmodern other. In any event, both strands of Desmond's argument taken together reveal metaphysics to be a permanent vocation and call of the human mind and spirit, to which it can be open and accept, or refuse and fall into the contradiction of self-betrayal and inauthenticity.

Conclusion

Let us test these conclusions a bit. We might ask if any committed postmodernist fully open to the better argument would be likely to accept what I have presented here. Perhaps a fully open person would, but a more likely response is something like the following. 'What you have done, Desmond, or Marsh, or Desmond-Marsh, is to include difference and otherness inside metaphysics. In so doing, you have limited the two notions illegitimately to what would fit the parameters of a metaphysics, and have left out their wild, exciting aspects, which make them fully postmodern concepts.'

How could one respond to such an objection, one that is very common and almost predictable in such discussions? The way I have responded – and I suspect Desmond would sympathize with such a move – is to agree with the description of what we have done, but defend its validity. What is valid in the notion of difference and other can be included in a metaphysics. What cannot be included can be legitimately rejected.[6]

The motto here, in other words, is 'whatever you postmoderns do validly, we metaphysicians can do better, and whatever you do invalidly need not be accepted.' Here another relevant distinction between understanding and judgment is pertinent. On the level of understanding what the postmodern means, I understand the full meaning of difference and otherness in all their extremeness and wildness. On the level of sober, metaphysical judgment, I reject what is indefensible and unverifiable, and affirm what is metaphysically sensible and true. Consequently we have not been unfair to postmodern difference and otherness in any legitimate sense of 'unfair'. We have these concepts in all their full range and complexity. We just refuse, on the level of critical reflection, to accept them in their full postmodern meaning. To say that we are unfair in such a move is just to beg the question and be dogmatic.

Or so it seems to me. One recent instance of the 'unfairness' argument in the United States is that concerning Lévinasian alterity, which is the latest fashion in Continental circles, and has assumed the status of a veritable dogma. It is not enough, as Ricoeur and I try to do, to affirm the other phenomenologically as present to me in a conversation, as symmetrically present to me in a face-to-face relationship, and as asymmetrically present to me in a verifiable way in our many illegitimately marginalized poor, homeless and oppressed. No, we are commanded to move to the extremes of full, unverifiable Lévinasian alterity, present somehow noumenally or quasi-noumenally beyond intentionality, commanding us not to murder in an asymmetrical, non-dialogical manner, and so on. To which claim I am inclined to make the same response as I did above. A notion of alterity that cannot be verified phenomenologically, and that is somehow prior to the symmetrical presence of the other in the 'between' of a human community, is not worth the paper it is written on.[7]

There are many more aspects of Desmond's very rich thought that deserve mention. There is, for example, his inspiring, enlightening discussion of the philosophical hero, who chooses to break the bounds of mere finitude and reach for infinitude. I take it here that Desmond is describing the idiot self of the philosopher, as the philosopher confronts the false coin of postmodern heroism (PO, 23, 31, 54–5). Or I could be tempted to discuss his extremely interesting remarks about the relationship of the philosopher to revolution, and especially political revolution, a relationship which I have tried to build into my life and work. I am going to resist these temptations and end with his eloquent words from the last page of *Being and the Between*, with which I began.

> In ethical, religious, and philosophical service, beyond all determinate cognition, we live from agapeic astonishment, live in metaphysical perplexity before this mystery. In a mindfulness beyond determinate knowing, the Unequal comes toward us, offering over and over again the unearned gift of the agape of being, singing to our deafness the unbearable music of the ultimate amen. (BB, 546)

Notes

1   James L. Marsh, *Critique, Action, and Liberation*, Albany: SUNY Press, 1994, pp.291–312.
2   'Thinking as Thanking' appears in Martin Heidegger, *What is Called Thinking*, trans. J. Fred Wieck, New York: Harper & Row, 1968, p.143; 'Questioning as Piety of Thinking' appears in *The Question Concerning Technology and Other Essays*, trans. William Lovitt, New York: Harper and Row, 1977, p.35.
3   James L. Marsh, *Post-Cartesian Meditations*, New York: Fordham University Press, 1998, pp.23–39.
4   'Philosophy as That Which Milkmaids Laugh at' is in Martin Heidegger, *What is a Thing?*, trans. W.B. Barton, Jr. and Vera Deutsch, Chicago: Henry Regnery Company, 1967, p.3.
5   The quoted lines are from T.S. Eliot's 'The Love Song of J. Alfred Prufrock', in *T.S. Eliot: Collected Poems*, New York: Harcourt, Brace and Co., 1991, p.6.
6   James L. Marsh, Merold Westphal and John Caputo, *Modernity and Its Discontents*, New York: Fordham University Press, 1992, p.99.
7   I discuss these issues concerning Lévinas and the other in *Critique, Action, and Liberation*, pp.132–3, 172–6, 179–86; and in *Process, Praxis, and Transcendence*, Albany: SUNY Press, 1998, p.326, n.56.

Chapter 7

What Shines Between:
The *Metaxu* of Light

Catherine J.C. Pickstock

The work of William Desmond is remarkable and epoch-making. It is characterized at once by an extraordinary humility and an extraordinary daring. To read Desmond is akin to reading Dostoyevski: just as the latter makes you feel that almost all other novelists are superficial and less than honest, so Desmond makes you feel that most other philosophers are evasive and complex in a way that disguises the real issues. For Desmond is astonishingly direct and astonishingly clear. He points out to us the real choices, which assumed atheism tends to obfuscate. At the same time his work is full of subtle poetic hints, but this is entailed by the fundamental philosophical option which he favours.

There is modesty in the sense that Desmond rightly builds upon the modern greats; from Hegel he derives the need to recover mediation; from Heidegger the need to recover Being in its ontological difference from beings. In a sense, Desmond's stroke of genius is to put these two together in a way that returns us to the premodern classics: to Plato, Augustine and Aquinas. For if, on the one hand, as Desmond cogently concludes, dialectics actually suppresses mediation (since even its resolution collapses into the *agon* of same and different), then within the finite world it must lie rather in the never-resolved tension between Being and beings. On the other hand, if Heidegger's account of Being in the end suppresses the ontological difference (since it reduces Being to the ontic flow of time), then this difference must lie rather in analogical mediation. In the case of Hegel, there is something ignored which lies non-conflictually 'between' identity and difference; in the case of Heidegger, Being need not appear in the nullification of beings, nor need the latter be cancelled in the arrival of Being, since being participates in Being as such.

So we are returned to the premodern in its authentic form, of which Hegel and Heidegger (with half-innocence) did not really know, but not simply returned. Above all we are returned to Plato, who twice spoke of participation in terms of the daimonic *metaxu*, or between, which is the dynamic power of love. In Plato, then, analogy and participation have already an erotic, a temporal and a poetic dimension, because of the process of recollection, triggered by the active poetic response to love. By being true to Plato, Desmond also contrives to pay corrective tribute to Hegel and Heidegger: neither the former's attention to history nor the latter's poetry is neglected. For beyond Aquinas, Desmond stresses that analogy is dynamic: a likeness to the absolute is expressed, and one must advance further in the active and theoretical expression of this likeness, which is always specific as well as universal: always conceived poetically as well as philosophically.

In this way Desmond corrects the genealogy of the loss of being, seeing it as a modern, not as a Western, event as such, and rethinks the philosophical significance of the Western poetic legacy. Here his Wordsworthian, but also Irish, sense of the epiphanic departs from Heidegger's vision of an impersonal cosmic tension.

All this is one of the first genuine challenges to the reign of the postmodern, perhaps a more radical challenge even than that of Alain Badiou, who likewise has reinvoked Plato for our time. Desmond questions the assumption that the most fundamental discourse is differential, or 'equivocal' as he terms it, showing that this is only able, like positive univocal discourse, to capture a limited segment of that reality which normal existence acknowledges. In the end, it is the analogical, the 'metaxological', which best saves the appearance of this reality. Our fundamental experiences are of 'communion', of a mysterious sharing and bonding whose exact location eludes us. Without this, all dissolves into mechanical process without spontaneity (recognized now even by physics, as Desmond discusses at length), or else into a formal salute to the Other without eros, in the mode of Lévinas. A *dialectical* eros is indeed to be overcome, since this swallows the loved object or person into one's own egoistic projections or purposes; on the other hand, a metaxological *agape* can also be the Platonic erotic blending in an affinity that does not cancel a reserved otherness.

Yet Desmond resists a new academic imperialism: he will not say that there is only mediation, as for others there are only facts or there is only difference. Indeed he sees clearly that this would make no sense. If all were the between, there would be no between. So there must indeed be realms that are relatively univocal and equivocal and even dialectical, where there is a constitutive conflict and resolution. Desmond's own position entails generosity: A.J. Ayer and Hegel and Deleuze have indeed captured many real processes at work in nature, psychology and society, but not all of them and not the most fundamental.

Desmond has offered us a new metaphysic: one all the more convincing in not being too tightly defined. His work introduces a new era of the return of metaphysics, beyond both analytic and continental philosophy.

What follows is a small contribution to the metaphysics of the between. For Plato, one crucial figure of the between is light. Intellectual light mediates between the Forms and the soul, just as physical light mediates between the sun and the philosopher's sight, and the lover's sight of his beloved. But with light, the metaxological is doubled. For in Plato and then in the Western tradition up to at least the high Middle Ages, light is truly a middle stage between the spiritual and the material. Today we tend not to be able to mediate these two at all; they have seemed alien to each other ever since Descartes. We have physics and then we have psychology. But perhaps the medium of light still mediates for us between body and soul – could we but see this. This is what I will seek to demonstrate. I offer this attempt to William Desmond as a contribution to his endeavour to end the alienation of our spirit from the natural world, and the consequent abandonment of nature to a spiritual desolation, of which physical desolation is the inevitable consequence.

'At the beginning of creation, God said "Let there be light," and the light began.' In his gloss on these words from Genesis, Augustine introduces what might seem to us a rather peculiar theory of light. He insists that light became light not simply by suddenly existing, but by fixing its gaze upon God and clinging to God, the superlative Light which shone upon it.[1]

Why for Genesis was light the first thing created? And why for Augustine does this primary light seem to possess a half-cognitive function? It is as if, for the tradition, light is not merely a metaphor for knowledge, but a point of mediation between the material and the spiritual realms. This is exactly the kind of feature of the Western inheritance which it is easy to overlook, but perhaps there is a hidden truth to be explored here. Between a physics of light on the one hand, and a theory of knowledge on the other, which seems obliged to deploy a metaphoric dependence upon light, there lies a phenomenology of light which reveals that an *illumined* world is a world destined to be understood, while, inversely, human knowledge is grounded in natural light and is akin to an intensification of that light. In what follows, I am going to explore the importance of such a phenomenology and its bearings upon our understanding of the relation of knowledge to reality. To do so, I will consider two aspects of the traditional Western understanding of knowledge from Plato to Augustine, Aquinas and beyond. The first is the so-called *Meno*-problematic, or the question of how we set out to find the unknown in the first place. The second is the also problematic idea that the mind is a kind of inner light; problematic because one asks how is it that the invisible adds to reality a certain new visibility? In both cases, I hope to show how taking the metaphor of light in a strong sense – that is to say, as suggesting that physical light really does enact a certain mediation between matter and mind – helps us better to understand these two traditional conundrums.

Light was an important theological category for Augustine, for it provided a way of understanding the epiphany or showing forth of God Himself. Indeed Augustine only arrived at an affirmation of divine light once he had wrestled with the mystery of God's epiphany, of how it is that God is at once both wholly hidden and yet everywhere manifest. He expresses this mystery more precisely at the outset of the *Confessions*: how, on the one hand, if God is concealed, is one able to come to know Him at all? On the other hand, if God is disclosed, why are we nevertheless impelled to call upon God to reveal Himself to us in further ways in the future?[2]

This apparent contradiction relates to a fundamental problem: the conundrum of knowledge, or the *aporia* of learning which had puzzled antique philosophers as much as it did Augustine; if one is ignorant of something and knows one is ignorant of that thing, one must already know something of that of which one is ignorant in order to know that there is something of which one is ignorant. This problem, most famously set out in Plato's *Meno*, is one which we all experience to a degree, even on mundane levels. Nevertheless, it is such a fundamental problem that we tend silently to presuppose it, rather than bring this experience to our consciousness. It is seldom that one asks, 'How did I know to ask that question?' One just gets on and asks the question. But, on reflection, it is not clear at all how it is that we know to ask the question. It would appear that the very questions we seek to answer already, of themselves, half seem to know the direction in which to look; but if this is the case, then there must be an imperceptible but fundamental moment when the barrier of ignorance is pierced, but without our knowing it, so to speak. It is true that we are usually guided on where to look in the first instance by a teacher, but that merely pushes the problem back a further stage in time. Moreover there remain instances when people suddenly discover entirely new terrains of knowledge – like geometry, and then much later non-Euclidean geometry – which no-one ever suspected of existing prior to the discovery.

Augustine takes this problem of knowledge to the most difficult epistemological extreme by considering the question in relation to knowledge of God Himself. However, as we will see, it is at this extreme that the general problem can be resolved. It is only this most mysterious and difficult theological knowledge which finally offers us a clue to the mystery of knowledge in general.

If we have no knowledge of God, how can we know to call upon His Name? Inversely, if God is known to any degree, why do we continue to call upon His Name and ask Him to disclose Himself? It seems that, whenever one seeks to know something or call upon a person for the first time, some third principle must have been brought mysteriously into operation in order to carry our knowledge ahead of itself, and mediate between the person who seeks to know a thing and the thing that that person seeks to know. Yet, because the mind of the seeker is so intensely focused on the object or the person to be known, this third principle, or carriage for our thought, goes about its job unnoticed. As for the antique metaphysical tradition, including Augustine, this third principle can be spoken of in terms of light, since physical light is not something which can be seen in the manner of an ordinary object to which one can point, for it surrounds *us* and the things we desire to know. It is that *by which* we see things, and it is that which lets things radiate towards us and allows our eyes to operate. The sun, the source of light, is always playfully dodging us, to parry our observation. And it is precisely because light is so supremely present that we cannot see it; in fact, we scarcely notice it at all in the ordinary course of things. Without light, things would not be so radically disclosed to us and we would not be able to carry out such a detached consideration of things. Light seems to run everywhere, and yet at the same time to stand back. In these respects, it seems not only to prepare the ground for intellect, but to foreshadow the character of intellect. Similar things can be said of other sensory media, and they also have capacities which light does not possess. Yet light seems to be both the most disclosive and the most receptive and reserved medium. It is hard to know what human understanding would be without light; so much so that the world of visually impaired people is still given in the language of those who can see light. Perhaps, then, this analogue of light and its curious hyper-presence may be appealed to, to solve the conundrum of knowledge, and especially knowledge of God.

In his treatise *De Libero Arbitrio*, Augustine explored further the quality of light's hyper-presence. He compared different modes of human perception, noting that some, like tasting and inhaling, are appropriative of the object or odour being perceived.[3] For example, food, if it is to be eaten by one person cannot also be eaten by someone else, for the food which the person consumes will be forced to conform irrevocably to her own body.[4]

But there are some things which can be sensed in common by different people without becoming the private property of the sensing person, and the chief of these is light. The commonality of light arises in part because light is not an object in any ordinary sense, but is that by which we perceive objects.[5] And it is also due, according to Augustine, to the more diaphanous, more spiritual quality of light: like spiritual beings, light can be shared without diminution. Both these properties of light render it a suitable image for truth. Like light, truth is also disclosive, publicly available and inexhaustible. One cannot own truth because, if something is true, then other people by definition can also come to know it. And one might note here that modern science is built upon the premise that truth, like light, is democratic, or in principle evident to all.

But there is a further reason why light can be considered to reside at the apex of physical phenomena, to be the most spiritual of materials.[6] It is not merely that one can say that, unlike many other things, light remains unappropriated when it is perceived, in such a way that no beam of light is ever forced to conform to the eye which beholds it, like a morsel of food, irrevocably chewed and swallowed. To the contrary, it is rather that everything else in creation must abase itself before light, must in some way conform to light, for all created phenomena can only offer themselves – only be known to exist at all – insofar as they offer themselves to sensory disclosure, and supremely to the apprehension of the eye through the ministrations of light.[7] For how else can they be counted as phenomena, as things which show themselves? Augustine interpreted God's originary creation of light in Genesis as indicating that specifically spiritual light is the first element of the universe which God created (for Augustine, this was the literal meaning of 'Let there be light'). From this it was understood that everything is created in the light of wisdom, and in order to exist must present a manifest shape or form. All the successive acts of creation in some way mediate this archetypal creative act, so that all of creation is drawn into conformity with light's presence, and is created so as to let this light shine through it and reveal the divine glory.[8]

For this reason, according to Augustine, light is already said to be 'good' and not the mundane contrast of darkness, unlike the later creative dichotomy of day and night where the pair itself is said to be good, as with all subsequent structurations of the cosmos. Light is uniquely good as the formative source of all; but this makes clear that it is not good in the manner of a finished work, in contrast to the later achieved 'goods' of the structured universe. In Genesis, the later counterpoint to light that is said only to be good is 'man', who is not said to be good at all. Patristic and Renaissance commentators frequently read this as suggesting that the human being was uniquely an unfinished work which had to finish itself, and had a capacity for both good and evil. It seems appropriate to say that the ideal matter of the creation, namely light, resurfaces in its unfinished character, but now as self-willed and self-directing, in human existence.

A further and related aspect of light's mediation, often invoked in the metaphysical and theological tradition, is the way in which light travels with such infinite speed that there is never a time (for our observation) at which light has not yet reached the object upon which it shines. This seems only to confirm that light is the first principle of creation, and that all else in creation must obey light's dominion. Moreover light's apparently instantaneous diffusion appears to combine motion with rest, in this way resembling eternity, if one thinks of the latter as an infinitely realized act or motion. And just as eternity is always present, so it is true that, however fast we travel, light travels always ahead of us. It is always light which anticipates us. As the eighteenth-century poet Christopher Smart put it: 'Light is propagated at all distances in an instant because it is actuated by the divine conception.'[9]

How does one deploy these mediating properties of light as an analogue for an understanding of knowledge that can overcome the problem of the barrier of ignorance already mentioned? And how can one move from the idea of light as that which shines out of darkness to the light which shines in our heart, that inner light which Augustine invoked as the light of knowledge itself?[10]

It may be that the most extreme 'stretch' of human knowledge, knowledge of God, is able to point to the resolution of intractable problems concerning all human understanding. Augustine compared God to light by invoking the phrase of the Psalmist, 'In Thy Light shall we see light'. This implies that, when it comes to knowing abstract truths or spiritual realities, and especially when it comes to knowledge of God, there must be mediation, as in the case of things known by physical light. But in the case of knowledge of God, the principle which lets God be known to us is not a distinct or third variable; it is God Himself. For, unlike the ordinary objects which we seek to perceive, God is at once the thing we seek to know and His own mediation, for God is truth, goodness and knowledge itself. So much is this the case that to know God is to share God's own knowledge of Himself. However, if God's light is invisible and spiritual, how are we aware of it? Augustine here spoke of an 'internal Eternal'.[11] God's light is manifest to us in the lucidity of our mind which shines upon things, and enables us to discern mysterious measurements for which no simple rules can ever pertain. It is present to us, in other words, as our capacity for judgment.[12]

On the one hand, this inner capacity for illumination appears to arise in a very private way, within each individual in his series of unique circumstances. But, on the other hand, it seems that this discernment exceeds the merely arbitrary and subjective on account of its resemblance to the commonness and publicness of light and seeing. Our judgment or 'inner eye' shows us that which really is, although only under those particular aspects through which divine truth itself shines out to us through things in their specific bearings towards us. An epiphanic contagion of beams of light, mimicking the imperceptible rapidity of light's own diffusion, is suggested here: one's own judgement or inner illumination discloses something, but what it discloses is things of this world disclosing God. In this way, the Augustinian theme of illumination does not at all neglect the mediation of truth by sensibly perceived realities, nor does Augustine seek to remove us, during this corporeal life, from those realities.[13] In contrast to later medieval 'Augustinian' theories, much influenced by Avicenna, Augustine does not always see inner illumination as a citadel to which we must retreat to escape the delusive snares of the sensory world, but more often sees it as a light of judgment which must supplement the nonetheless necessary testimony of the senses. (This means that the contrast with Aquinas on this point is less acute than is often thought.)

How does the notion of an illumination by, or relay of, light help us to overcome the conundrum of knowledge? The answer at first seems simple: even before we try to know about something, a light inside us from beyond us starts to reveal the path towards knowledge. However the problem is still not resolved. The trouble is that we have so far thought of knowledge only in spatial terms, and ignored its temporal aspect. For it seems that all that inner light can illumine is a vague outline or glimmer of knowledge. But what we still cannot explain is why it is that one does not rest satisfied with the appearance of this outline. How are we to account for the fact that we know that the outline we perceive does not exhaust what there is to know? Why do we not simply assume that the outline is all there is? For example, if we see a vague silhouette of trees in the distance in the fading light of the sun, how do we instinctively know that there is a hidden wood to explore? One might say simply by past experience of what such outlines betoken, but that is not the point. Even when we see a strange outline, we are able to form some conjecture of what it might herald. Furthermore all we see – even the trees under the dazzling slants of sun-rays – is only ever a vague outline which has to be filled in if we are to see any specific thing at all. We never see the backs of trees and yet we see the trees as three-dimensionally round. Nor do we see the entire interior, nor the full life cycle, nor the inheritance, nor the metaphysical origin (as self-explaining form or as evolutionary accident) of trees. Yet if we do not always dimly and implicitly infer something like this, again we cannot see the trees at all. Indeed, if we were able to see the whole tree, or the whole of any object, would not the tree be swallowed up by our understanding? Would we not lose the sense of the tree as a real thing distinct from us? The impenetrability of a thing is actually central to our having understanding of a thing at all. Without it, our understanding would be like that of God who knows all the ideas of things simply in knowing Himself (according to Augustine and Aquinas). So how do we know that there is a hidden wood to explore? Once again, the conundrum of knowledge reasserts itself, but at a new level. One might note that Plato had already seen that this was the most acute mode of the problem. In the *Meno*, the question is not, as it is often taken to be, how can the slave boy interrogated by Socrates know the truths of geometry which he has not historically been taught, but rather, how can the slave boy have the sense that he will be able to find out new truths of geometry, even though he has reached a temporary impulse of perplexity, and is as one 'stunned'?[14] The problem is not that the boy seems to know certain things *a priori*, a problem which can be mythically resolved by appeal to the theory of the Forms, but would seem to be more rationally solved by a more Kantian theory of the *a priori* conditions of all human understanding.

Our first problem was to explain how knowledge arises in the first place, and this was resolved, following Augustine, by invoking a common spatial matrix: light embraces, and in some reciprocal way unites, the object to be known with the subjective knower. But now we face the further problem of how one knows that there is always more to be known of the thing one knows. The initial conundrum keeps arising again and again at every new stage of knowing a thing, and its first resolution via the idea of light as a common medium does not seem to be able to help us beyond the first barrier of ignorance. However, perhaps light still remains the answer, if we recall the further property of light as infinite speed.

The temporal or proleptic quality of light does indeed add something to our resolution of the conundrum of knowledge, for light does not merely reveal to us an object to be known, by means of a kind of static lighting-up. It does a great deal more than this: it discloses a passage for us to follow, or pathway of light or transparency, which suggests that light constantly enables us to draw nearer to the object of our knowledge, and does not merely reveal it once and for all. This quality of light seems to teach us that reality is arriving and complex, rather than given once and for all. This is bound up with its mutable, non-eternal character. Here mutability and temporal succession are the sign of the 'wound' of created dependency, and yet this wound is also its own salve; the need ever further to explore an arriving reality guarantees at once the reality of things external to our understanding and their signification of God, their origin. This property of light as passage, Augustine especially associated with Christianity. Platonism, he indicated, had already supplied us with the goal – light as source and ultimate reality in 'the land of peace' – but Christianity shows us the way to the goal: light as a guide and shining pathway.[15]

Even here, the way of grace, providing not only the vision but the means to see, is presented as a deepening of the Platonic resolution of the *aporia* of learning: the truth of the scriptures shows that 'he who from afar off is not able to see, may still walk in the way by which he may reach, behold and possess thee'.[16]

However, perhaps we are not so very much closer to resolving the conundrum, for even if it is always possible to approach more closely a known object, this might result in mere quantitative augmentation, and not any deeper grasp of the object's essence. Why should we assume that there is something essential still to be disclosed? At this point, a further temporal property of light can be invoked. Light not only travels ahead of us at an infinite speed; when it strikes the illumined object, it is reflected back to us in ever different refractions. The path of light which travels ahead of us also turns back upon itself and comes to meet us. This means that, while light enables us to advance towards an object, by its circular capacity of reflection, it also provokes the illumined object to proffer itself to us, so that the gaze of knowledge is not a matter of one-way illumination or singular command.[17]

Indeed, if knowing a thing were a one-way operation, we would never reach the thing to be known, for we would have to resign ourselves to the mere distant regard of knowledge hazily ahead of us. The rebound by which we achieve location of a thing just because we are ourselves located by the thing, guarantees an end, or rather, a relative end to the process of seeking to know. Light's reflective protocol seems to add a reciprocal aspect to knowledge which suggests that to know is not to wield sway over an object, but to be in some way regarded by it. Now it might here be claimed that this sounds rather like a form of animism, unless the object known-and-knowing is another person. For example, can such a known-object choose not to be known? Although they cannot do this in the way that a knowing subject might, there is a sense in which objects do elect to display themselves, else they would not be there at all: how can one separate a thing's existence from an impulse to make itself manifest? This, as Plato saw in the *Sophist*, is strictly unthinkable. Of course, this is to speak metaphorically, but nevertheless the object one looks at situates or forms one's gaze and perspective. Unless we submit to the object's way of being as appearing, we will not see it. And, indeed, one can also say that if objects are in a sense subjective so, inversely, subjects have an objective aspect: without an objective body, a person could not look at us; her eyes must be turned towards us, rendering her as the viewer also in principle viewable and vulnerable. Thus St Paul promises us that, in the ultimate knowledge of the beatific vision, we will come 'to know even as also we are known'.[18]

This reciprocity of knowledge is dramatized in the Book of Wisdom. Light is not just the impersonal sun of knowledge, but the personal hypostasis of wisdom who is the first emanation of God. Light or knowledge is now presented as coming to meet us, forestalling our journey: 'She hastens to make herself known to those who desire her, she goes about seeking those worthy of her, graciously appearing to them in their paths, and meeting them in every thought.'[19] One can note here that, despite Augustine's adding of the Christian way to the Platonic goal, it is not entirely clear that there is not something like a 'way' already anticipated within Plato's *Meno*. If the problem for that dialogue is not, as we have seen, simply one of *a priori* understanding, then its answer to the *aporia* of learning cannot simply be that we retain in the depth of our souls an obscure memory of what we saw in a pre-existent life. If it is possible for us to seek a forgotten knowledge, there must be a real ontological tie which allows us to recall another ontological dimension. It must be the case that the Forms in some way 'reach down' to us in the manner of light, showing us a path by way of participation (*methexis, mixis, sumploke*). In the case of Augustine, such participation is mediated by human teaching through time as well as by an interpersonal process. For this reason, part of his answer to the *aporia* is that we seek to know a thing because we have been told about it.[20] This is not the whole answer, because it is not always the case, and this answer alone only pushes the problem back to the collective human level. However, in Plato's *Meno*, we find a parallel situation. In a complicated conceptual knot, Socrates replies initially to Meno that he knows the answer to his conundrum (it will turn out to be the doctrine of recollection) because he has been taught it once in time by priests and priestesses.[21] So for Plato as well as for Augustine, part of the answer to the problematic is that illuminating light itself comes to meet us along the pathways of time. It is this which triggers recollection (Plato) or inner illumination (Augustine). However, perhaps the mere fact of knowledge's coming to meet us in our path is still not sufficient to explain how, when one is offered a glimpse of knowledge in advance, one supposes there is more to be known. This was, as we have seen, the mysterious situation of Meno's slave boy. Why, again, would one not remain content with a mere glimpse? What is it that drives us further?

Plato and Augustine both answer this question by invoking the category of desire which loves what it knows and therefore wills more to come.[22] For Plato, eros desires not only to seek more knowledge, but to 'bring to birth' more knowledge on the body of beauty.[23] But exactly what hope grounds this willing? It cannot simply be a matter of past experience of objects which turned out to yield more than was at first apparent, for this does not explain the *first occasion* when one looked beyond the merely apparent; and therefore why the search for knowledge should have arisen at all. Nor does it explain why things in their own specific nature seem to shine out towards us with an intrinsic promise of more to come. Nor can our willing be simply a matter of blind hope or haphazard trial and error, for we have already seen that the search for knowledge is in part provoked by light's prolepsis: the beautiful radiance of things which already exceeds the merely arbitrary. So what is the answer? It seems that desire is our being pulled forward ecstatically by something in the object itself, as if the object we seek to know in some way chooses to be known, or elects that it is to be known by a particular person. Plato conveys this circumstance in the *Symposium*: the beautiful object is potentially 'pregnant' with further truth.[24] For this reason, desire, as Augustine understands it, can objectively recognize truth, but this objectivity remains a very particular matter in which the truth is glimpsed from different perspectives.[25] In other words, if desire does disclose things really there, a thing will be disclosed in a diverse fashion according to the diversity of rightly directed desire; nevertheless these different aspects really do belong to the thing in question. (How very different this is from our tendency now to assign the role of desire to a more subjective realm.) It would seem that the desire issuing from us towards the object we seek to know is one and the same with wisdom coming towards us. Anticipation arrives as desire, but equally desire is the anticipation that wisdom allows us.

We have seen that the inner light is the power of judgment, and that this operates by means of anticipation, like a path of light travelling before us. Indeed Augustine invoked traditional medical theories of rays of light issuing from the eyes and showing us the path to follow.[26] But now we see that judgment is also a kind of higher eros, or desire, for our impulse to be united with what we know is the very moment of wisdom's hastening towards us to meet us on our path. Eros is the mediator, or as Plato put it, the 'between' (*metaxu*), since it is both the anticipation reaching down by participation of light coming towards us through time, and our own being drawn towards this advance.[27] For Plato, eros is the child of both lack (that which advances towards us) and of resource (our own creativity which causes us to desire what we can bring forth).[28] It follows, then, that if judgment only comes about through right desire, the truth which judgment recognizes is also the Good, meaning the genuinely desirable. In this way, knowledge of the truth and love of the Good are not in any way to be divided. We only recognize things truly when we love them. Augustine's image for this is a light that is also fire, like the burning bush and the fiery pillar, both figures of the divine presence in the scriptures. Just as the most intense light also burns, so the greatest intensity of knowledge involves a passionate, though miraculously non-consuming, love.[29]

This identification of knowledge and desire or love goes against any idea of knowledge as a cold, disinterested gaze. For this reason, like Augustine, one should disdain all claims to mere neutral inquiry as idle curiosity. Curiosity, or knowledge divorced from desire, is debased knowledge, since it seeks an exhaustive grasp of a thing in isolation, and not insofar as that thing might itself choose to be known by that particular person, or point beyond itself to further things. Thus, by seeking to know something only as an object, and to know it exhaustively, we miss its active relations with other things and its hidden links to the divine source, which are both aspects of its full reality.[30] One cannot know the full network of ratios which a thing is involved in, nor can we anticipate all that would become of it if it were to interact with other things. Some of these interactions could be spontaneous and not determined in advance (as modern physics has taught us). If this is true of 'things', then clearly it is even more true of persons.

Curiosity, in seeking to know objectively and completely, only succeeds in creating an object in the image of its own desire to master. By contrast, we more intensely adore the entirety of truth by remaining within the seeming limitations of the segment of reality shown to us, all the contingent influences upon us, habits and attachments we have formed, things and people for whom we have discovered an 'elective affinity'. But not only does an acceptance of this limitation let stand the entirety of truth invisible to us; it also renders something of this truth available to us via the mediation of a right desiring, whereas, if we seek merely to know, without love, we will find that we know nothing of the truth whatsoever. Following Augustine, we should resist the pious temptation to imagine that we will be closer to God and to the truth if we abstract ourselves from our own places, our gender, our specific biography, from our necessarily preferential and selective loves. The trouble is that to imagine this is to imagine that we can be God, who can indeed know and love everything through a superlative affinity for everything. But if we disdain our own peculiar affinities, we do not gain this closeness to everything, but rather a closeness to nothing, which is likely to be a disguise for the will-to-power. Moreover a specific path of light opened through time, traversing a series of local associations and particular bonds, is not a foreclosed path. To know and love anything finite aright, we must know and love it as yielding an inexhaustible depth which leads us back to God, its source. In this way alone, desire for the specific is exercised in due measure, as a rightly proportioned desire.

It seems that it is light as a probing desire, construed as divine grace in us, which offers a resolution of the conundrum of knowledge. And yet it resolves the conundrum by letting it stand as a conundrum. This is because we can now see that ultimate truth itself is characterized by a promise of always more to come. Truth arrives in the first and the last place in the mode of anticipation and desire. This is not the problem at all; it is rather the answer. Before we know, we desire to know as if we knew already, because what there is to be known is desire, is love, albeit a true love of the truly knowable. Nor is this an individual process. The contagion of beams of light as showing the way, and refracting towards us, and beaming forth from us as desire, does not for Augustine apply merely on a personal level; it applies also communally and historically. For, throughout history, just as God led the Israelites by the burning pillar of fire, God has shown us the way; but He has finally come towards us as wisdom incarnate in Christ, hastening to meet us on our path, and in Christ that reflex of light back to us coincides with a specific light. Augustine can say this because, in the Gospels, Christ is identified with the arrival of the eternal light in time which permits a renewed human recollection of God as the pure light of love, which is therefore nothing other than recollection of desire for the eschatological future when all will become apparent. It is because we are in time that we find the sharpest intensity of light in a specific human image of recollection, and the most acute instance of our being given what we seek to know in advance of replete knowledge.[31] But this specificity of light nevertheless reflects or rebounds upon other images, and is repeated in the lives of particular people who follow Christ under the prompting of His spirit.

This reciprocal aspect of the figures' dependency upon the light behind them, like depictions of saints in stained glass windows, and light's own invisibility without its mediation through the figures, reminds us that the manifestation of light in the diverse particularities of creation – consummated in Christ – co-belongs in equal measure with the source of light. For light's beams are as much light as light's own source: as the Book of Wisdom tells us, light is radiant and unfading. Where light is mediated, one finds no less a light than light's source, in the same way that Christ is co-equal with the Father in the Trinity. And where light rebounds from what it illuminates, the same equal light remains, just as Christ's truth rebounds upon his followers as the work of the Holy Spirit.

Augustine deciphers the conundrum of knowledge in terms of the idea of truth as the rightly ordered path of true desire shining through history like the path opened for the Israelites through the waters of the Red Sea. And this truth is divine truth, the truth of our salvation. But where does that leave ordinary knowledge and its mundane conundrum? If knowledge is inextricable from right desire, then even our ordinary everyday familiarity with things can only involve truth to the extent that we love things and people appropriately and in due measure. It might seem strange to suggest that knowledge and love are so entwined. But one cannot have a desire that does not also involve recognition. We have already suggested that one cannot have an entire knowledge of the truth of a thing, if it displays truly its essence and being, without judgment which involves also the orientation of the will to the rightly desirable (convertibility of the transcendentals). This desiring things rightly in turn requires the assumption that there is an inexhaustible depth within things which comes forward to meet us, recognizing us, as much as we recognize it. Without this depth and mutuality, there could be no reciprocity and no reliable longing in knowledge. Whenever we know anything at all, we already (whether we know it or not) recognize, know and love God. Indeed, since all human knowledge is mediated through the senses, whenever we see anything at all, we already see God. For light, we can now see, is literally, and not merely analogically, 'a glance of the glory of God'.[32]

Unlike Augustine, Descartes imagined that our thoughts could be as clear as if one were opening a shutter upon an underground cellar, and causing daylight to diffuse instantaneously into every corner.[33] But in elaborating the metaphorical basis for the notion of 'mental clarity', he seemed to forget that light itself and its propagation are no simple affair. For who can stand in daylight without being aware that the fundamental element of light nonetheless has a point of concentrated origin which we can neither gaze upon nor encompass, and which is in some ways a dark mystery? Moreover pure light would not illuminate at all. To be light, light requires the very things opposed to its nature that it illuminates: dense dark things which halt its passage, and at the same time make manifest the passage itself. And without manifestation, who can say that this passage would exist, since light is Being as manifestation? Light lies somewhere between an infinitely dark source and the immeasurable matrix of solidity. In this no-man's-land, light boasts its brightness, and yet this absolute condition of all truth itself dissembles (though without deceit, since it has no other side, no substance to deny) from the outset, since all it shows is what it is not.

Although light is the first source, it only begins to be when it leaves its unrevealed origin, and even these beams do not become visible until they have been reflected back from some quiddity. These aspects of light were neglected by Descartes: the sun's dark heart, its passage and its labyrinth of refractions. He neglected also to observe that, already, subjectivity is implicated in physical light, for light does not appear for insensate and mindless things, and when we say that light does not appear, how can we say that there is light? Or, indeed, that anything appears, or that anything is? Forgetting that physical light is subjective and complex, and that to see something one must turn one's attention in a certain direction, and reckon with obscurity, Descartes imagined that spiritual light is wholly subjective and yet simple and timeless, by analogy with flattened material light. By contrast, Plato and Augustine were more obeisant to physical reality. They realized both that the physical sun only illumines for the observing intellect, and that this intellect must closely track the paths of light at a higher level. In order to know, we must obscurely anticipate what there is to know, as if there were a beam streaming from us, which, like its solar counterpart, has no time to tarry in the darkness of its unrevealed source. Likewise we can only comprehend our own beams of illuminating reason when they fall upon things in such a fashion that these things themselves shape the idiom of our reasonings. There are never any such things as inert objects for our curiosity, nor autonomous gazes of the curious. Instead, if knowledge is an active seeking beam of love, it is equally true that the things we know elect to be known. Knowledge, like light, is a journey and a seeking, only enabled by the lure of what it seeks.

In the case of physical light, both the source of light and its refractions only arise as visible for a perceiving subject. Inversely, this subject's knowledge is always mediated by corporeal appearances. However, insofar as this subject sees a spiritual light through the physical, there occurs a kind of doubling of the perception of light. For in the spiritual realm also there is a source of truth, and a refraction of truth, which are both necessary for there to be truth. But what is it that holds together in us the arising of desire for truth and the relative satisfaction of knowledge in revealed phenomena? For Augustine, it was the divine light that shines within us from beyond us. However, since this light is only manifest insofar as it illuminates our desire, which is in turn only manifest insofar as it illuminates the realm of physical light, all the complex properties of physical light are to be found in an eminent sense, not only in our mind but in the divine Mind itself.

Augustine understood the divine light in Trinitarian terms: this light also encompasses a dark source, a transmitted rebound of reflection and a perceptive desire which mediates between these poles. But it is not simply the case that physical light is a necessary analogue for intellectual and divine light. They are not merely two parallel orders at different levels of a hierarchy, since physical light is incomprehensible outside manifestation. Since what is manifest is manifest to the mind, its dark source and beckoning path in some sense prefigure the psychic, and outside this prefiguring, we simply cannot make sense of physical light, or of other examples of physical–sensory disclosure. Inversely, if the mind as we know it involves a reference to phantasms, then the rebound of mental reflection retains always the imprint of a real physical rebound. To imagine a purely spiritual and intellectual light is really to imagine a supreme light beyond our perceived contrasts of the sun's radiance and the mind's clarification.

If these reflections contain any truth, then they suggest that the thought of the Christian past is valid in a particular respect, now infrequently considered, namely in terms of its elaboration of a 'fittingness' or *convenientia* between the physical world on the one hand and the world of knowing spirits on the other. If we are to overcome the legacy of Descartes, perhaps we need a discourse about the physical world which supplements that of physics with a speculative phenomenology, or, inversely, with an empirically attuned metaphysics. We need to attend more closely to the way we are able to be aware and to be conscious within a material world. On the other hand, we must supplement this attention with judicious speculation, because a careful gaze reveals that we must make surmises concerning the unseen if we are to see at all. Physical light appears to leave the gap for speculative metaphysical light. Even physical seeing requires a silent metaphysical operation. But the latter, the work of the mind, remains the rebound of the operation of physical light. Why should we be surprised when both light and mind are the work of one Creator, indeed are His first and last works, stretching from the radiating open good of light, to the equally open, but willed and deliberate good, brought about by human reflection?

Notes

1 Augustine, *Confessiones*: *Confessions*, trans. Henry Chadwick, Oxford: Oxford University Press, 1991, XIII, iii sq.; *De Genesi ad Litteram Imperfectus Liber*, trans. J.H. Taylor SJ, New York: Newman Press, 1982, I, 2–12.
2 Augustine, *Confessiones*, I, i, sq.
3 *De Libero Arbitrio, Corpus Scriptorum Ecclesiastorum Latinorum* (Vienna), 74, II, 7–8.
4 Ibid., 74, II, 7.
5 Ibid., 74, II, 7; II, 19. This commonality of light does not, however, mean that knowledge can be obtained via an instantaneous panoptic illumination; rather Augustine stresses the particularity of the path of light. See II,16, 19; III, 9; see also II, 2, 6–7. And see below in the main text.
6 *De Genesi*, I, 2, 4; I, 9, 17.
7 Unless a thing is itself illuminated, it is formless and hence unknowable: see *De Genesi*, I, 15, 30; 1, 16, 31.
8 *De Genesi*, I, 17, 32–4; *Confessiones*, XII, ix, 9.
9 Christopher Smart, *Jubilate Agno*, Cambridge, MA: Harvard University Press, 1954, Fragment B, 384. See also Fragment B, 325.
10 '… we are enlightened by thee, that we, who were sometimes darkness, may be light in thee'. *Confessiones*, IX, iv, 10, trans. J.G. Pilkington, *The Confessions of St Augustine*, New York: Livenight, 1943. See also *Confessiones*, X, vi, 8 and *De Genesi*, I, 17, 32.
11 *Confessiones*, IX, iv, 10. See also *De Libero Arbitrio*, II, 8; *De Genesi*, 3, 20, 31.
12 *De Libero Arbitrio*, II, 3–9, 12–13.
13 'These things was my inner man cognizant of by the ministry of the outer; I, the inner man, knew all this – I, the soul, through the senses of my body. I asked the vast bulk of the earth of my God, and it answered me, "I am not He, but he made me"': *Confessiones*, X, vi, 10 (trans. Pilkington, op. cit.).
14 Plato, *Meno*, trans. W.R.M. Lamb, Cambridge, MA: Harvard University Press, 1990, 80a–b, 84a–c.
15 *De Libero Arbitrio*, II,12. See also *De Genesi*, I, 1, 2 and I, 1, 3.
16 *Confessiones*, VIII, xxi.
17 *De Genesi*, I, 16, 31.
18 I Corinthians 13:12.
19 Wisdom of Solomon 6:16–17.
20 'But how shall they call on him in whom they have not believed? Or how shall they believe without a preacher?', *Confessiones*, I, 1.
21 *Meno*, 81a–b.
22 *Meno*, 84c, 86b–c.
23 Plato, *Symposium*, trans. W.R.M. Lamb, Cambridge, MA: Harvard University Press, 1991, 206e.
24 Ibid., 209b–c.
25 *De libero arbitrio*, II, 2, 6–7, 9, 16, 19, 27; III, 9.
26 *De Genesi*, I, 16, 31; 4, 34, 54; 7, 13, 20; 12, 16, 32; *De Trinitate*, 9, 3, 3 (*ML* 42, 962–3).
27 *Symposium*, 202a–e.
28 *Symposium*, 203c.

29   '*Hi enim non scintillantibus humanis ratiocinationibus, sed validissimo et flagrantissimo charitatis igne purgantur*': *De Musica, P.L.*, 32: VI, xvii, 59. In this passage, Augustine contrasts the *scintilla* of human reason to the infinitely more valid and most flagrant 'fire of charity'. The metaphor of increasing intensities of light stresses that reason and love are not opposed, and that love is an immeasurably more powerful enlightenment. Further, the metaphor implies that genuine knowledge and purification (or purging by flames) are commensurate.

30   *De Libero Arbitrio*, Book II and *passim*; *Confessiones*, VI, viii. See also the discussion of knowledge of perfect equality in *De Musica*, VI, xii, 34: we could not begin to activate our desire for perfect equality unless it were already known somewhere. Thus desire is already a kind of knowledge – or, could one say, desire is the way things are – desire is what is known. Whilst it might seem to us natural to link 'curiosity' with the discovery of truth and therefore with knowledge, for Augustine, curiosity is that which leads us away from the truth. He argues that *curiositas* is a quality concerned only with the discernment of proportionality for its own sake, that is, not in relation to other things. It does not, therefore, lead to genuine knowledge. This implies a second aspect of the *aporia* of learning, which is that one can only 'know' something in relation to everything else, which means that we must know the known in relation to the unknowable. This is because we only occupy a limited corner of the poem of the universe, as Augustine constantly reminds us. Thus the only hope for knowledge lies in desire. See further *De Musica*, VI, xiii, 39.

31   *Confessiones*, VII, xviii.

32   Smart, op. cit., Fragment B, 372.

33   René Descartes, *Discourse on the Method*, ed. and trans. John Cottingham, Robert Stoothoff and Dugald Murdoch, *The Philosophical Writings of Descartes*, vol. I, Cambridge: Cambridge University Press, 1985, Part VI, 71.

V
DESMOND, LOVE AND
THE GOOD

Chapter 8

An Archaeological Ethics: Augustine, Desmond and Digging back to the Agapeic Origin

Renée Ryan

This essay traces some Augustinian resonances within William Desmond's thought, particularly regarding the relation between the metaxological ethos and its agapeic origin.[1] Desmond is perhaps most explicit in his invocation of Augustine in his Introduction to *Desire, Dialectic and Otherness: An Essay on Origins*,[2] a work which he there describes as 'an Augustinian odyssey, embarked on in the wake of Hegel'. Like Augustine, he says, he wishes 'to do justice to the self-knowledge of desire and its openness to otherness, without falling into unacceptable dualism' (DD, 13–14). In effect this means that Desmond wants to steer away from a sense of the origin as static, as set apart both from us and the created order. This has many implications for his thought, which might perhaps come into bolder relief when seen in light of some aspects of Augustine's work. Both thinkers ground their movement in a sense of an origin to be sought throughout the created order, in an erotic striving toward the constantly issuing agapeic giver of being. This trajectory cannot be understood as strictly teleological, but rather as *archaeological*, as a quest for an origin that implicates within itself that *arche* from which the created order comes forth.

Such movement cannot, then, be imagined in strictly linear terms. Desmond often quotes Augustine's maxim, *ab exterioribus ad interioria; ab inferioribus ad superiora*.[3] His own understanding of the self's interiority, in relation both to creation and to the transcendent Creator, is very mindful of these words. Augustine himself couples this double progression with an advance from restlessness toward peace. 'Our hearts are restless until they rest in Thee,' he prays.[4] Yet, after his conversion, the saint is not in any kind of stasis. His sense of restlessness indicates the non-finite, unbounded nature of its ground. Before turning to God, his restlessness is characterized by an eroticism without nuance and devoid of real focus. Afterwards it is transformed and directed, but not toward any finite goal. He knows now that his desire is for something other than himself, and yet he is already suffused from within, and simultaneously outwardly surrounded, by its goodness. His source of peace is the overabundant answer to his inquietude. Here, then, we see two factors also very much at stake in Desmond's Augustinian odyssey. Firstly, our movement is such that our infinite inquietude can only be set to rest in an infinite source of peace, where the transcendent breaks through any naïve sense we might have of God as the finite end of our desires. Secondly, striving towards God does not demand a dualistic vision that precludes appreciation for creation. Instead our focus on the Creator intensifies our love for creatures.

These points are interrelated, because they hearken to the nature of the *agapeic origin*, as Desmond calls it throughout *Being and the Between* and *Ethics and the Between*, or *the absolute original*, as in *Desire, Dialectic and Otherness*. These works all stress the sense that being is good, and that it is good to be. That is, the ethos in which we live is charged with value, because the one who has given the gift of being is superabundant, and this excess flows into every one of his creatures. For humans, this means too a plenitude in the range of communication with and of the good, directed toward both creation and Creator. This over-abundance of possible meanings might be seen as infinite, but such infinitude must be qualified. Thus in *Desire, Dialectic and Otherness*, Desmond distinguishes among three forms of infinitude.[5] The more linear form of *infinite succession* refers to the constant becoming and multifariousness of creatures. According to this aspect, nature appears as progressing toward a not completely definable end. We can distinguish lines of similarity, in species of animals, for example, but variations in these lines seem to us limitless. Infinite succession can overwhelm us with its equivocity, with its constant emergence into such varied forms. If this were all we knew of infinitude, we would be scattered in our attempts to find meaning in our own infinite restlessness. *Intentional infinitude* changes such a perspective, setting us apart from this endless chain of progression. In Desmond's words, 'intentional infinitude specifically refers to the power of open dialectical self-mediation displayed in the articulation of human desire' (DD, 150). Human desire seeks unity, rather than dispersal. We want to mediate between ourselves and the world; but more, we want to communicate ourselves to ourselves. Desmond describes this potency as circular, though not in a closed way, and founded in the appreciation that humans seek to know themselves. In this search they strive for open wholeness, as the desired end to their infinite restlessness. As Augustine so well knew, however, no such integrity is possible through introspection alone. We must not only move inward; we must strive upward. This then brings us to *actual infinitude*, whereby we are opened up to 'the sense of something more' (DD, 151). That is, we become open to an intuitive knowledge of the transcendent, of something that so far exceeds our own possibilities of disclosure to ourselves and the world that we are in touch again with the surplus value of being itself. The transcendent breaks through our consciousness of the immanent, in such a way that our consciousness of the significance of creation is heightened rather than diminished, as it would be according to any dualistic signification. Actual infinitude brings us to the source of every other infinitude. It brings us to our absolute original, our agapeic origin. We are henceforth in a realm of paradox, where language can strive toward the expression of ultimate meaning, and yet must always fail.

Thus Desmond will speak in terms of 'the paradoxical coupling of wholeness and openness, completeness and infinity ... and overwholeness, as it were' (DD, 152). Our movement toward this actual infinitude as the open end of our quest is fundamentally Augustinian. Further indication of this is Augustine's own appreciation for the need of enigmatic language when speaking of his ultimate source of peace. Consequently, the *Confessions* in particular take the form of a prayer of praise, keeping the question in mind throughout, 'How can one pray to you unless he knows you?'[6] This desire for prayer becomes one with the desire for knowledge of the Creator, and together they form a more profound mindfulness toward the ultimate.

In fact, this movement of our inward desire toward our origin calls for a certain mindfulness toward both the world in which we live and the actual, infinite transcendence that suffuses this universe with value. These significations are for Desmond best expressed in his elaborations of the metaxological. So, when he asks at the beginning of Chapter Five of *Ethics and the Between*, 'Where are we?' (EB, 163), his question is more than rhetorical. It brings us to the core of his metaphysics. We are precisely here, in the between, in the overdetermined matrix of the metaxological, as it reminds us that it is good to be. The univocal, equivocal and dialectical modes of inquiry, taken separately, cannot bring us to ultimacy. Together, though, they anticipate a richer sense of what it is to be, so that they can be taken up into a full appreciation of the good with which we are at one, and yet which exceeds us. Here in the between, a dualistic vision is no real alternative. The dualist's stance separates us from our origin, whereas the origin calls us to participate in it. Interfused with goodness within the metaxological ethos, Desmond says, we are to become archaeologists of the good. We must dig to find our origin. Dwelling on the horizon, the intersection of earth and sky, we are grounded in a sense of the *elemental* that is both a part of us and beyond us.[7] For we ourselves are metaphysical, which for Desmond means that we can transcend ourselves while still being part of the between.

Furthermore, on this horizon we are at the meeting-point of two axes: the horizontal and the vertical. Surrounded on all sides by creatures and others in creation, if we are to find our origin, we must move along the vertical axis, thus transcending ourselves through ourselves.[8] Digging thus situates us vertically, and so our excavation toward the *arche* might seem to lead us downwards rather than upwards. In fact, though, this digging brings us toward the ground of being describable as *altus*, which as Desmond reminds us elsewhere can mean both *high* and *deep* (DD, 199). Our digging is so fundamentally elemental that it comprises participation with, rather than separation from, the world in which we live. Furthermore, its contact with the earth brings us not only to the profundity of our origin, but also to its loftiest heights. We may already be in contact with our ground, but we must penetrate its surface, in order both to explore its depths and to find its farthest reaching significance. If we see the origin as solely above, we risk cutting ourselves off from it, so that it becomes irrelevant to the way we experience the world and live our lives. However, in digging to find our roots, we allow ourselves to see that the origin is already ingrained within us, in our very marrow. Through our seeking to find it, it incorporates itself more and more fully into ourselves. In digging toward it, we can see it as the ground of all: not so much a distant goal as an ever-abundant source.

For Desmond, this archaeology stands in contrast to other images of earth, especially in *Ethics and the Between*, throughout his discussion of ethical ways. Our path to the good is already somewhat articulated, because it is our ground, but some ways of inquiry can disclose themselves as derivative and closed off when they resist moving deeper and deeper downward. For example, Desmond presents us with an alternative image of a cave in contrast to Plato's allegory. *Univocity* alone cannot give voice to the ultimately unfathomable depths of the metaxological ethos, and so, Desmond says, 'we must seek to build another ladder of thought in [the equivocal mud of the ethos], and up it climb; or [univocally] open a cave into the mud, a cavern into whose gloom we must climb down' (EB, 77). We should immediately note that here 'climbing down' is not to go back to the cave once we have seen the *Agathon*. Nor is it to be an archaeologist. The univocal man's cave puts the real quest for goodness at an end. He builds a dwelling-place in the darkness, so as to go no further. Thus he uses the gift of the ground as given to close himself off from the richness of the elementally giving source. The univocal way inward is not the way up. Rather it is a perversion of the Augustinian move from exterior to interior, for univocal interiority is claustrophobic. It closes off any access to the divine by giving its own univocal answers, and thus pulls in the ladder to the superior solely inwards, and upon itself.[9]

The univocal needs instead to be tempered by the *equivocal*, in order to escape from its ossified walls by mixing life-giving water with them, giving then a foundation for the equivocal. The equivocal is more akin to the metaxological, but is still not enough to allow us to appreciate what it is to transcend ourselves and thus relate back to the agapeic origin. Equivocity creeps in and clings to our boldest attempts to pin down the nature of the metaxological. As Desmond also says, God sows confusion (EB, 79–82) into the matrix of the world in which we live. Traditional attempts to give voice to the ethos can forget this confusion, *undermine* it in effect, so that ethical norms become sedimented, encrusted, incapable of breathing life into real appreciation of ethical values. Thus Plato must interrogate such univocal appraisals of norms through the questioning voice of Socrates. Says Desmond:

> Tradition supposedly shows the sedimented univocities of valuation, passed on thoughtlessly from the past. To say that these univocities ('values') must be desedimented means, in part, that they must be uprooted from the *sedes*, their seat, their sediment, their soil. Tradition, as the social context of generally accepted univocities, must be called into question. (EB, 80)

Equivocal Socratic questioning seeks to give back nurturing power to values all but lost, to breathe back into the earth its life-force. In a move unimaginable to Socrates himself, we might say that such breath derives its power from the very beginning of humanity as told in Genesis, where God breathed life into Adam, himself formed out of earth. This *humus*, inseparable from our humanity, can only speak to us in our metaphysical nature because of the life that sustains it. Again, we can think of this elementally, so that our incarnate nature offers a source of meaning, rich *because* of its double signification. The flesh alone cannot manifest ourselves to ourselves. It is rather the breath that makes this flesh live which opens us out toward the ultimate value of being.[10] Univocities of valuation sever value itself from the breath that gives it life: the breath of God, the origin. The strength of Socrates is that he moves beyond any implosive sense of traditional norms, any way of mindlessly accepting what is given. Plato's Socrates moves beyond the whole, but by first appreciating that seeing the *Agathon* necessitates going down to the Piraeus, into the darkness of Hades, and back into the cave. Similarly, in Desmond's Augustinian odyssey, we must go down, like the hero who visits the underworld, before we can appreciate the transformative words of Genesis, 'Let there be light.' Only in first approaching the mystery of our source can we see the elemental nature of an affirmation that itself is good.

The archaeologist, then, sees the real value of an equivocal mode of discovery, and digs beyond the space carved out by the univocal cave-dweller; but in his refusing to genuinely articulate this quest, the archaeologist's excavation is peril. Realizing this jeopardy, the archaeologist may be tempted to turn to a dialectical mode, but this too is inadequate to a proper archaeology of the good. While the *dialectical* approach may give a means to understand the workings of determinacy and indeterminacy, it comes to a dead end. Unable to do justice to erotic sovereignty, it cannot explain the goodness of the origin, and of being itself. Erotic sovereignty at its best is an affirmation of the self in interrelationships with others. Here the person progresses erotically, from lack toward fulfilment. Here too one is sovereign because with (and even through) others, one has found oneself. Emphasis on openness is essential if we are to live up to the infinitely open source that makes erotic sovereignty possible. Erotic sovereignty, according to the dialectical approach, is infinite desire that cannot mirror its source, and so is incapable of explaining that it is simply good to be. The dialectic cannot bring us to our agapeic source. It works toward an end, one of self-revelation and self-determination, but it can reconfigure, so as to effectively distort, the otherness of being as other, and most importantly the ultimate otherness of the source. Dialectic, especially in the hands of Hegel, works toward full disclosure, whereas in being metaxological we must be mindfully aware of mystery. The dialectical sense that the true is the whole, and that in the end we will see this whole, is opposed to the nature of the origin as agapeic. Its giving never ends, and so neither can our appreciation of it as gift. This means that we can never hold to the idea of a 'block creation' (EB, 164). The metaxological archaeologist cannot rest with such a bounded understanding. Instead, the archaeologist needs to communicate the ground in its dynamism.

This communication is possible because of the forms in which the ground communicates itself to us. For Desmond, this occurs in several ways,[11] but we are here concerned with how it takes place *elementally*, that is, through the *idiocy of being*,[12] whereby we are in immediate contact with others and the world. Without proving the surplus of the good, for this would be impossible, we dwell with it in 'an initially unarticulated intimacy' (EB, 170). The idiocy of being is *metaphysical*: it inscribes itself in us while still being beyond us, and does so best elementally, as our elemental, incarnate bodies manifest ourselves to ourselves as metaphysical, as being both here and beyond ourselves. Desmond's example of this is that of weeping in grief, whereby we are overcome, without being able to explain why, and this overcoming expresses itself physically, both by and through us. Weeping – and laughing too – express what Desmond refers to elsewhere[13] as our *passio essendi*. We are given to ourselves, our flesh communicating ourselves to ourselves, in manifesting values of being we cannot fully rationally understand.[14] Weeping again refers us back to the overabundance of our source, which allows us to love in ways beyond our understanding. Without love, there would be no grief. This love, issuing from the agapeic good, is further intimation to us that there is a good beyond anything we might see to be good or evil. Grief, in calling for us to affirm being even out of a sense of desolation, indicates the enigma that is our origin. This origin is intimately present and, whether communicated in joy or in despair, is primarily self-giving goodness. Thus, it is not distant from us, either as a far-off beginning point or as a distant finite end.

To reiterate, then; within Desmond's understanding of our movement toward the agapeic origin, which is our true and infinite end, there are two main Augustinian strains. Firstly, we see that the progression forms an erotic transformation of infinite restlessness into peace found in an actually infinite source. Secondly, our elemental worth issues from the valuable gift of being, and we experience this in a fundamentally life-affirming incarnational manner. To accentuate these points further, we turn now to the thought of Augustine himself, who anticipates and elaborates in particular upon a paradoxical and *non-linear* sense of origin, especially when he meditates on the origin of the universe as told in Genesis. For him, the original moment of creation resonates throughout the entirety of the universe, but most especially in the human heart.[15] Persons, unlike other creatures, have the unique opportunity to actually incarnate the Word – present at the beginning and still resonating throughout all that exists – within themselves. Thus, conversion becomes a new creation. In effect, it is through his moment of conversion that Augustine comes to understand the workings of God within creation. In throwing himself down on the ground of his garden, shedding tears in his anguish before conversion, he opens in himself the possibility for life in the wasteland he has become.[16] His grief is united with that of creation yearning to be redeemed. In terms of the saint's later explanations, Augustine longs to be *reformed*, or converted. For in the beginning, he later says in *The Literal Meaning of Genesis*,[17] whenever God uses the word *fiat*, or 'Let there be …', he actually allows for the freedom of possibility for everything created to turn back to him.

Thus a creature can tend toward nothingness or annihilation; or it can turn back to its origin and become truly formed, perfected in the light of divine love. Conversion for Augustine means fulfilment of being in a way that leaves no room for nihilism. As Desmond also holds, affirmation of the very goodness of creation is the essential response to nihilism. Like Augustine, he takes a metaphysical stance toward goodness. Thus, in *Being and the Between*,[18] he stresses that creation itself is of magnificent value, by virtue of its being good. This affirmation has ancient roots, but more is at stake here than tradition. When we say, as Desmond himself so often does throughout *Ethics and the Between*, 'it is good', we give personal testimony to the overabundant gift of being. With such transformation of the will, we can turn back to the very beginning of creation itself.

Yearning for this same conversion of will, Augustine in the garden is longing for perfection of salvation in his origin. He wants to turn back to the beginning, making it also his ending point. Again, though, he understands none of this in purely linear terms. Conversion is an ever new creation, so that he can exclaim later in the text, 'Late it was that I loved you, beauty so ancient and so new, late I loved you!'[19] Christ as the origin of the whole of creation is more ancient than the earth itself within whose domain Augustine seeks his maker; but he is new with the selfsame vitality present at the first moment of creation. This newness *reincarnates* itself within Augustine, when he willingly makes Christ's flesh his own.[20] For the saint, this incarnation of Christ within the self – the only true selving – is quite literal, grounded in a robust sense of the elemental. In fact Augustine's metaxological mindfulness constantly indicates his repulsion at a dualism that would separate him from the truths of the maker manifest in creation. Too often is it forgotten that Augustine's life after conversion to Christianity (and his corpus of written work expresses this) is actively opposed to any Manichaean tendency. He is essentially non-dualistic. While the Manichees hold that there is a radical split between goodness and creation, such that creation itself is the very incarnation of evil, Augustine sees such a continuity between Creator and Creation that no such dualism can be maintained. For him, instead, there is dynamic continuity between flesh and spirit, and this implicatedness of one into the other ultimately receives its own surplus value from the Incarnation of Christ.

Thus, while Augustine claims citizenship in the City of God, this does not mean that he ignores or neglects the created order. Instead, after his conversion, his vision is transformed. Previously everything in the world seemed hateful to him. He could find no place of proper rest within the world, no real solace in any finite earthly pleasure. Now, with newly opened eyes, he can see the beauty of a universe striving toward the one who formed it. When our love is properly ordered, so too will be our vision of the world. In fact, our love of God intensifies our love of Creation, by setting it in its proper order. This vision sees that our own end is united with that of Creation, as it *reforms* itself by turning back to the newness of its moment of origin. This moment is for Augustine an especially personal one, because it is in effect our meeting with the person of Christ. At that point, which we call the beginning, says Augustine, the Son of God was – or better said, is – present in two ways. He is 'the origin of created being, which exists through Him but still in an imperfect state'; and further,

> to him as the Word belongs the perfecting of created being, which is called back to Him to be formed by a union with its Creator and by an imitation, in its own way, of the Divine Exemplar, who, eternally and unchangeably united with the Father, is of necessity identical in nature with Him.[21]

Thus God the Son is the Creator of the possibility of the fullness of Creation, by means of a call which is inseparable from Himself, and which speaks the world into existence, while at the same time bidding its return. This turning back of creation is not simply the completion of a circle, so that as soon as beginning and end-point meet, a point of stasis is reached and a kind of closure attained that needs no further movement. This reformation is instead the recognition that the transcendent breaks into and through the world in which we live. The dynamics of desire, as Desmond describes them through the three forms of infinitude, point to this. Instead of closure, such that the ultimate is rejected for a form of immanent transcendence, motion, the life of the creature, is transformed and intensified. Augustine's maxim, 'love, but be careful what you love'[22] acknowledges that the objects of our love define us. The converted heart loves God, its will thus becoming more like that of the Creator. As agapeic, then, this love does not close off the possibility of loving Creation. Instead, in its all-embracing nature, it allows us to see Creation as it really is, in its beauty showing us vibrant and various images of the Creator's own mind. Thus Augustine says too,

> every creature has a special beauty proper to its nature, and when a man ponders the matter well, these creatures are a cause of intense admiration and enthusiastic praise of their all-powerful maker. For He has wrought them all in His wisdom, which, reaching from end to end, governs all graciously.[23]

In this new understanding of an economy of grace, of an interior rather than an exterior power, Augustine says that he finds 'deeper wonder at the agility of the mosquito on the wing than at the size of a beast of burden on the hoof, and ... more intense [admiration at] the works of the smallest ants than the burdens of the camels'.[24] Such attention to the details of the workings of the world were previously only important to Augustine as rhetorical devices. Now they are further evidences, intensifications, of his awareness of the elemental, made possible because love of something finite is no longer an end in itself. End is rather bound to end, not as a measure of extent, but as a unification of communicative power. Augustine's love strives now to be as infinite and self-giving as its source, so that in loving God he loves Creation both unabashedly and limitlessly.

How then are we to understand such love, which allows for no simple form of rest, but which rather is transformed by its new directedness into an outwardly embracing sense of the wholeness of Creation? We must turn primarily to Augustine's sense of the origin, which is at the centre of his own life, while underlying the whole of the universe. This origin is paradoxical, so it cannot be expressed in any, humanly speaking, temporal or spatial terms. In our own limited understanding, we form the places in which we live, and the time by which we calculate, from boundaries set and passed. Such cannot be the case for our origin, and this very paradox is indicated in the structure of Augustine's *Confessions*. The origin is at the beginning and the end of this text; but it is also at what is, spatially speaking, roughly its *centre*, the moment of the saint's conversion. Thus Augustine begins the work with a meditation on how we are to know God –

whether our praise or our knowledge of Him should come first. This temporal problem gives way to a meditation on the Creator's spatial relationship to the world. Augustine hence asks how God is in creation, in our lives, and yet beyond it and us. That is, he inquires into the metaphysical underpinnings of the created order, which in grounding us allows us to move beyond ourselves, back to ourselves, and thus to our true centre. The last paragraph of the work plays out again the Augustinian dynamics of rest. Where God sees everything, as he has made it, from eternity, we come late to the panorama of creation. Thus at first we do evil, but when our hearts conceive by the Spirit, we are able to do good. Augustine goes on,

> you, the one, the good God, have never ceased to do well. And we too have some good works, of your gift, but not eternal; after them we hope for rest in your great hallowing. But you, the Good which is in need of no other good, are always at rest, because you are your own rest.[25]

Thus in seeking God, in imitating him, we become increasingly aware that we can never find rest as mere stasis, because we can never achieve that rest which is God's own. Our rest comes from God, just as everything that we are comes from Him. Having converted, then, we may recognize our origin. To put on the flesh of Christ, however, means to know that within Creation our love imitates the self-giving surging power of the created order. This life came first through the Word, of whom all our finite words or actions are at least derivative, and at most imitative.

The beginning and the end of the *Confessions* are, of course, impossible for Augustine without its centre, which is the moment of conversion. Thus Christ, the Word, is at the centre of the work, which concentrates itself in Augustine's inner movements of the heart.[26] This movement is itself a *microcosmic* manifestation of the whole account of creation. It is a particular showing forth of the way that the origin grounds, so as to allow for the peacefulness that reveals itself in an almost overwhelming activity, in a constant showing of love of God in works. From this centre we can extend back toward the beginning, where Christ was too, as the Word through whom all receive life. The very start of the work asks how we can pray to God, if we do not know him. Is it through praising that we come to know him, he asks? The answer seems to be in the words of the *Confessions* themselves, which delve into the mysterious personal workings of the Creator in one particular human life. The *Confessions*, as exploration, as an archaeology of the good, are a work of memory. The fiery force of Augustine's conversion[27] sheds such light upon the whole of his thought that he can see how the Creator has always already prepared the way for him to come to know how Christ is within him. This light spreads too toward the end-limit of the work, as its final pages explore the initial moment of creation, delving into the meaning of the words of Genesis, which show *macrocosmically* the incarnation of Christ the Word in the works of Creation. The origin is then at the beginning and at the end for Augustine, only because Christ is at the centre, as limitless source.

If one might be so bold, then, as to speak of an Augustinian odyssey in the wake of Desmond, what we would have is a ground that continually reverberates throughout the whole of Creation, stable in its dynamism, constant in its eternally issuing agapeic love. Augustine's counter to infinite restlessness is not non-activity, but rather a sense of fulfilment that answers to its source in open-ended and constant selving. His sense in the *Confessions* is that the Word through whom all things were made continues to reverberate throughout Creation. Thus, he says, 'your Word is not speech in which each part comes to an end when it has been spoken, giving place to the next, so that finally the whole may be uttered. In your Word is all uttered at one and the same time, and yet eternally'.[28] Thus, the eternal speaking of the Word sustains everything in the created order. This does not mean that our own finite words are meaningless, but that we must strive to have them approach the richness of their source. In turning back toward the origin, we are transformed, and so are our words, which include not only verbal communication but also all of our various modes of communication with world, others, and ultimately with God. Thus, before conversion, the only possibility of true selving, we could do little better than to follow Augustine, falling on the ground to water it with our tears, for this elementally expressed need for our origin is a prayer for the grace of salvation. This plea once answered is not the end, but rather the beginning; of a life of digging back to the origin from which we were formed. It is fitting, then, that the first words of Genesis are *en arche*. As archaeologists, we do not look back to a fixed past, but to a moment of giving that does not end. This unendingness is what Desmond calls the *overdetermination* of the good. Thinking metaxologically, we come to know the good as *arche*, moving not toward complete disclosure, but toward an *open wholeness* (EB, 9). This open wholeness is the peace toward which we dig as archaeologists. It is the origin to which we come back, and our return finds its best articulation in prayer.[29] Prayer forms the ultimate *porosity* between persons and Creator, the greatest and most gracious communication between ourselves and God. Such porosity is necessary because of the openness of this exchange, and its experience as gift. In prayer, we can let rest our thinking, as He who is so greatly to be praised[30] communicates with us. He thus elevates us, beyond the farthest reaches of human thought. Prayer releases us, as our work is transformed through overabundant grace. In digging toward peace we return to our origin, so that we become more fully aware of the image and likeness in which we were originally formed.

Notes

1   I greatly appreciate William Desmond's comments on earlier drafts of the essay. I thank Jo Koehler too for his very constructive remarks.
2   Desmond has also written a paper on Saint Augustine, which discusses some of the same major elements focused on in the present essay: (1980), 'Augustine's *Confessions*: On Desire, Conversion and Reflection', *Irish Theological Quarterly*, **47** (1), pp.24–33.

3   Desmond quotes this in the Introduction to *Desire, Dialectic and Otherness*, p.13.

4   *Confessions*, I,1: *inquietum est cor nostrum donec requiescat in te*. The translation is
     that of Rex Warner, *The Confessions of Saint Augustine*, New York: Penguin Books,
     1963, p.17. R.S. Pine-Coffin translates the passage otherwise, as 'our hearts find no
     peace until they find rest in you': *Confessions*, London: Penguin Books, 1961, p.21.

5   See in particular DD, 149–54.

6   *Confessions*, I,1. Warner translation, p.17.

7   See, in particular, BB, 273–4 and PO, 273.

8   In this essay I concentrate mainly on the sense of the elemental as grounding. It should
     not be forgotten, however, that not only earth, but also water, fire and air speak to us,
     as we mindfully attend to the ways in which we experience ourselves as metaphysical.
     See Desmond's elaboration on this, in his discussion of what he calls 'rapturous
     univocity', in BB, 273–4.

9   It should be emphasized that the metaxological does not preclude the univocal (or for
     that matter, the equivocal and dialectical) expressions of our being in the world.
     Univocity here is characterized solely negatively, but Desmond speaks of a more open
     univocity, which is directly related to our present concerns, though not discussed in the
     body of the paper. Rapturous univocity 'corresponds to the lived immediacy of our
     being enveloped in the pure "stuff" of being' (EB, 273). This is not univocity as
     rational abstraction, but as lived harmony with the elemental world.

10   This refers in particular to the *passio essendi*, as described in *Ethics and the Between*.
     Here Desmond says, 'the ethical will must lie down again in itself, and see that it lies
     in the sty that is itself, and from the place of refuse come to itself as preparing for a
     different return to home. The divine is there in the muck ... Our suffering being, our
     temporariness, our ageing and dying bring us back to the earth, to the humus out of
     which our humanity is formed, and God is there in the humus, and this we come to
     know as His spirit is breathed in it, breathed in in the vital surge of growing life,
     breathed out as the spring tide ebbs, and the gift is taken back, perhaps given back'
     (EB, 367). This life-giving breath, then, allows us to know the value of being, and to
     undergo it metaphysically, that is, to know it elementally, but also by means of
     suffering, as personal experience of transcendence.

11   There are also the hyperboles, which remind us of the excess of being so we are
     'thrown above' ourselves. This is again the paradoxical meaning of metaphysical
     grounding as metaxological. Our ground makes us exceed ourselves, while still
     maintaining contact with our world. We are more fully ourselves when we transcend
     ourselves. For further discussion of the hyperboles, see BB, 217–22 and EB, 511–13.

12   For Desmond's discussion of the *idiocy of being*, see, for example, PO, 282–4 and
     303–11; BB, 379–84, 410–15; EB, 10–11, 170–78.

13   See in particular Chapter 12 of *Ethics and the Between*.

14   I would like to thank Professor Desmond for allowing me to read a paper as yet
     unpublished, 'The Body Beside Itself: On Weeping and Laughing'. For Desmond, both
     weeping and laughing show our metaphysical relationship to the body as it manifests
     our own transcending of purely rational modes of self-knowledge. For further
     reflection on what it means for the body to be beside itself, see also *Confessions*, VIII,
     7, where Augustine describes God turning Augustine around so that he can see himself
     in his depravity. This is just before Augustine's conversion, when Ponticianus is
     speaking to him of others who have already converted to Christ.

15   For the centrality of the heart in Augustine's philosophy of the person, see note 26
     below.

16   Weeping holds a place of real significance in Augustine's *Confessions*, as he seeks to
      understand his own heart. Early in the work, after the unnamed friend of his youth has
      died, he says that bitter tears replace his love for his friend. There follows a meditation
      on whether tears are by nature sweet or bitter, an expression of hope, a prayer, or else
      a reaction of revulsion, as expression of the realization that the object lost was never
      really properly loved (*Confessions*, IV, 4–5). When describing his conversion (VIII,
      12), Augustine reflects again upon the meaning of tears, which he describes as
      acceptabile sacrificium tuum, quoting Psalm 51:17, which refers to the broken heart
      and spirit as more acceptable to God than a holocaust. Monica's tears are also
      significant within the *Confessions*. In III, 11, Augustine speaks of Monica's tears as
      prayers for her son, watering the ground of every place she went. The next chapter
      recounts the story of Monica begging a bishop to reason with Augustine. The bishop is
      at first polite and tactful, not wanting to speak with Augustine, and yet trying to
      comfort his mother. Finally, in exasperation, he says to the weeping woman that the
      son of such tears will not perish. Here, then, Monica's tears are prayers for her son.
      When Augustine tells us of Monica's death and funeral, he again meditates upon
      weeping, in this instance his inability to weep immediately, or even during his mother's
      funeral (IX,12). He wants to weep, and yet feels that this would be inappropriate at the
      death of a woman of such faith. Even when the time would be fitting for him to shed
      tears in public, he cannot, and this also is a source of consternation. Finally he cries
      where only God can see and hear him, and refuses when writing of this to condemn
      himself. Monica had cried so many tears for him that this once he feels he can fittingly
      do the same in the face of her immediate loss.

17   Augustine, *The Literal Meaning of Genesis. Ancient Christian Writers*, trans. John
      Hammond Taylor SJ, New York: Newman Press, 1982, p.23.

18   For this discussion, see BB, 505–14. This theme is also very much present in
      Desmond's book, *Art, Origins, Otherness*, and again in Desmond, 'Hyperbolic
      Thoughts: On Creation and Nothing', in Santiago Sia and André Cloots (eds), *Framing
      a Vision of the World: Essays in Philosophy, Science and Religion*, Leuven: University
      Press Leuven, 1999, pp.23–43.

19   *Confessions*, X, 27: *Sero te amavi, pulchritudo tam antiqua et tam nova, sero te
      amavi!*; R.S. Pine-Coffin translates this as 'I have learnt to love you late, Beauty at
      once so ancient and so new! I have learnt to love you late!' (*Confessions*, p.231).

20   Augustine explicitly expresses this at the end of the *Confessions*, in a statement that
      refers back to his own conversion. Then, too, at VIII, 12, he quotes Romans 14:11, the
      passage he reads when a child's voice cries *tolle lege*, telling him to put on Christ
      (*induite Dominum Iesum Christum*). This means transformation of the flesh as a
      rejection of concupiscence. Later he says 'we see the things you have made, because
      they are, and they are, because you see them. Outwardly we see that they are; inwardly
      we see that they are good. But you saw them made when you saw that they were to be
      made. And we at a later time, after our heart had conceived by your Spirit (*posteaquam
      concepit de spiritu tuo cor nostrum*), were moved to do well' (XIII, 38, Warner
      translation, pp.349–50). This point is discussed further on in the present essay. I would
      like to emphasize here the fundamentally elemental sense in which, for Augustine,
      conversion refers back to the initial moment of Creation. It is a new creation, which
      means not the rejection of creation in its corporeality, but transformation of the
      physical. Augustine's flesh is changed because his spirit is renewed, and because of
      this he can begin to see the world as God first saw it, as good.

21   *The Literal Meaning of Genesis*, pp.23–4.

22 This is the translation given in Hannah Arendt, *Love and Saint Augustine*, trans. Joanna Vecchiarelli Scott and Judith Chelius Stark, Chicago and London: The University of Chicago Press, 1996. For the somewhat complicated history of the English translation of this text, see the Introduction, p.17. The Latin reads, *amate, sed quid ametis videte* (*Enarrationes in Psalmos*, 31.5), and thus asks us to be watchful over what we love. Augustine asks that we love with the open eyes of a visionary who sees the value of being because of the nature of his origin. The world is not loved solely for itself, which would be *cupiditas*. *Caritas* breaks free of such darkened understanding. God has made us to love, but to love Him first, and through Him the world. This new sight is again, therefore, a participation in Creation. Through Christ we are remade, just as through Him, in the beginning, the world was made.

23 *The Literal Meaning of Genesis*, p.90.

24 EB, 170.

25 *Confessions*, XIII, 35. Warner translation, p.350.

26 The heart is for Augustine that place where person and Creator communicate. It is the innermost room, which must be entered for conversion to be possible. Again, then, we see the Augustinian movement from the exterior to the interior and from the inferior to the superior.

27 This fire, it should be noted, is the fire of the weight of love for God. For Augustine, every created thing has its own proper weight. Human weight is not that of a stone, which sinks down to the ground. It is the weight of love, which rises like fire. *Pondus meum amor meus* (*Confessions*, XIII, 9); he says: 'my weight is my love'. God sets us on fire with his love so that we might move upward. This is the fire of *caritas*. *Cupiditas*, love for the things of the world, things which change and die, is characterized in the saint's words, *Veni Carthaginem, et circumstrepebat me undique sartago flagitiosorum amorum* (*Confessions*, III, 1). Warner translates this as, 'I came to Carthage, and all around me in my ears were the sizzling and frying of unholy loves' (Warner, p.52). These loves, intense as they are, are affiliated with death. In contrast, the fire of conversion refers to the dynamism of Creation, as it was in the beginning, and thus transcends any derivative fire of inferior love.

28 *Confessions*, XI, 7. Pine-Coffin translation, p.259. The Warner translation reads, 'it is not a case of first one thing being said and finished, then another thing so that all can be said: no, all things are said together and eternally' (Warner, pp.262–3).

29 These thoughts about prayer come from a paper, as yet unpublished, by William Desmond, 'Is There a Sabbath for Thought? On Peace – Between Religion and Philosophy'.

30 *Confessions*, I.1 (*Magnus es, Domine, et laudabilis valde*). Warner translation, p.17. This is the first line of the *Confessions*.

Chapter 9

The Equivocity of Freedom and the Suffering of Being: The Call of the Good and the Finesse of Other Forms

Jason J. Howard

The purpose of this essay is to explore the notion of freedom and its constitutive relationship to the goodness of being as developed in the work of William Desmond, especially his book, *Ethics and the Between*. I want to discuss this idea, because I believe it presents a compelling account of the intermediation between freedom and the good, which refuses to reduce the dynamics of this relationship to the language of self-interest or self-determination. For Desmond, freedom emerges in the 'overdeterminacy' of being, which he describes as an inexhaustible surplus of otherness. It is the very plenitude of otherness that frees the capacity for self-determination, enlivening human possibility from within a matrix of infinite determinability – 'the between' – which continually replenishes our powers of ontological determination. As the empowering locus of selfhood, Desmond sees the overdeterminacy of being as a fundamental expression of the goodness inherent to being, interspersing our capabilities in the indeterminate generosity of an otherness that exceeds all attempts to master it. Thus we do not first give ourselves freedom, traditionally seen as the reflective capacity to determine one's being, but are 'freed into being', coming to concreteness out of recesses that can never be entirely circumscribed.

More specifically, the goal of my reading is to describe this happening of liberty as it is experienced in the concretization of selfhood, in which the event of freedom erupts from the pathos of infinite desire. My account explores this dynamic interplay between freedom, desire and the good in three stages. First, I provide a very brief synopsis of Desmond's particular methodology, which he terms the 'metaxological', giving some indication as to how this sets the stage for his reflections on freedom. Second, I give an account of the initial emergence of freedom from the inchoate depths of desire, which Desmond terms 'adolescent freedom', and its constitutive connection with the goodness of being, specifying the equivocal beginnings of freedom in human agency. Third, I point out how the equivocal nature of freedom outlined in the second section also reveals the roots of freedom in the intractable suffering of being. Indeed, for Desmond, it is in our fidelity to this very contradiction, the happening of liberty in the intransigent anguish of being, that the reality of the good receives its fullest intimation, which is also why the porosity of the good cannot be entrusted to the work of philosophical reflection alone, but depends on the rejuvenating powers of other mediums – the talents of other forms, namely art and religion – to reveal the ubiquity of the good at work throughout the fragile depths of human becoming. I conclude my account by raising the issue as to what extent this surplus goodness of being (the overdeterminacy of being) can be said to be dependent on the mediums of philosophy, art and religion for its articulation, discerning the presence of the good *despite* its seeming absence in the trials and tribulations of selfhood in action.

The Method of the Metaxological

Desmond's particular methodology, which he terms the metaxological, can be seen as an attempt to extend the insights of Hegel's dialectic and its fidelity to the structure of lived experience, but without confining these insights to a teleology whose logic consists in continually overcoming the indeterminate nature of being.[1] In this sense, the metaxological is both an archaeology and a teleology, remaining faithful to the overdeterminacy of being in its constitutive depths through focusing on the concretization of this origin in the 'between', the becoming of human agency. Desmond claims his approach is able to remain truer to the 'ethos' of life through indicating the elemental ways in which the will is 'doubled' (inwardly and outwardly) in the indeterminacy of becoming. This doubled character refers to the distension between self-transcendence and the empowering capacity of what is not reducible to subjectivity, yet enlivens it, whereby the elemental powers of selfhood come into fruition as the promise of a more determinate coming-to-be, or 'selving'.

Moreover, akin to Hegel's dialectic, the metaxological is not concerned with directly refuting other methodological approaches, but with going beyond their limitations and one-sidedness, incorporating their insights by pushing them to the limits of their own intelligibility. Thus, it is a method which takes its lead from the rhythms of life in the 'between', accepting the ambiguity of these rhythms without either firstly, conceding to nihilism, secondly, dismissing these ambiguities in order to secure a standpoint of pure intelligibility, or thirdly, justifying such contingencies within a philosophy of immanence wherein ambiguity is acknowledged, yet only to the extent that it serves to clarify a larger teleological process, for example that of absolute knowing. By avoiding these extremes the metaxological perspective is more capable of discerning what Desmond calls 'the *incognito* of the good', intimating the manifold ways in which the 'hospitality of being' informs every manner of human potential and expression. This 'hospitality of being' is none other than the soliciting power of the good, which grants being the chance 'to be'. It is precisely this original granting or freeing of human possibility, an unleashing of will to move from the indeterminate to determinacy, that characterizes the 'good of being' and actualizes the infinite range of human expression. Understood along these lines, not even the principle of autonomy can be taken as the definitive truth of freedom, for autonomous self-determination can never secure for itself what it purports, but comes into being through a more primal happening, a fuller moment of release. The wisdom of the metaxological, then, lies in its recognition that it is only in coming to see our limits that the empowering efficacy of the good can be properly discerned, putting this wisdom to the test in its very analysis of experience. By focusing on the impenetrability of experience in terms of its final origin, ground and end, the metaxological seeks to rethink the issue of freedom in view of its ontological expanse, rather than approaching it solely in terms of an epistemology of first principles, as is especially evident with those positions that embrace autonomous self-determination as the definitive truth of being.[2] We now turn to Desmond's effort to clarify the origins of freedom in its fuller ontological depth, examining in more detail how selfhood is initially 'freed into being'.

The Equivocal Dawning of Freedom

Ethics and the Between employs the method of the metaxological with a view to unearthing other forms of freedom than autonomous self-determination, indicating how self-transcendence is already given by way of forces irreducible to self-mediation. For Desmond, freedom, far from being a clear-cut principle of rational self-determination, is perhaps the most equivocal conception of all, a conception whose fuller origins lie forever hidden in the oblique recesses of desire and transcendence. Freedom, then, is never a wholly univocal conception. Indeed freedom itself ages, just as the 'I' ages (EB, 269). This means that freedom is not just one idea, but bespeaks the multitudinous incarnation of transcendence itself, 'the creative power of the overdeterminacy of being' (EB, 270). As the singular will unfolds, it expresses itself through 'modalities' of willing, which are equally forms of freedom. Each of these modalities represents a way of mediating the otherness that defines us, which Desmond sees as a freeing of the will through otherness that is equally a way of embodying the good.[3] This freeing is the real enabling force of transcendence, transforming the will from its absorption in the indeterminate self-insistence of root desire to its more determinate configurations as purposive activity, moral autonomy and beyond. Now I want to look at the initial emergence of freedom in more detail, as it surfaces from the indeterminacy of desire. This entails reconstructing the awakening of freedom, along with the emergence of self-possession, in which the indefinite presence of the ethical is announced in the equivocal dawning of self-mastery. It is with this rise, the 'upsurge' of desire to extend itself, that the perplexity of ethical being comes to the forefront, as we struggle to enact the gift of our own powers as willing agents.

Our freedom overtakes us. Our very ability to fulfil our desires seems to give us the carnal right to satisfy them. Because we originally take up this freedom without reflection, which is to say we are first lived by it, we mistake the granting of freedom in the indeterminacy of desire for a straightforward givenness. The gift that I am becomes transformed into the preservation of my being. Here, whatever obstructs the imperative to self-satisfaction is removed, as we seek to lead a life 'free from' any external constraints (EB, 272). Desmond describes this initial happening of freedom as 'adolescent freedom', a savouring of one's possibilities that loses itself in the very wonder of the 'fact' that it is. We take this fact as licence to dictate the terms of being.

As Desmond emphasizes, this happening of freedom is already intermingled with the self-insistence of a root willing that affirms itself through flourishing in the openness that confronts it. Freedom rises to coalescence through encountering this openness and the will's attempts to preserve itself from within such openness. Try as we might, human ingenuity alone cannot account for this originary moment of releasing and the capabilities it bears; it is a fundamental expression of the goodness inherent to being. As Desmond remarks, freedom is lived 'in the inheritance of this contradiction', and we can only grasp the larger import of our freedom by returning to this primal happening of liberty, coming to terms with the living interdependence of self and its releasing moment (EB, 273).

What makes this happening of freedom all the more perplexing is that it proves almost impenetrable to clarification as it is being enacted. There is no stopping to reflect on this interweaving of transcendence – the movement beyond oneself – and the appropriation of what is other to the dictates of self. Our freedom is originally played out at a stage where the intentions of desire, and the will to fulfil them, lack any stability, refracting the light of conscious circumspection. Here one's purposes, just as much as one's sense of identity, have yet to coalesce into any stable constancy, lost in the interchange of determinacy and indeterminacy, wherein it becomes impossible to say where blind desire begins and conscious intellection ends. Within this confusion we strive for stability, for fulfilment, yet there is no sure way to differentiate what restricts us from what liberates us. In the midst of this confusion, the apparent limitlessness of desire's objects serves to fuel a sense of 'self-intoxication'. Indeed, desire entangles freedom from the very start, by insisting on its own elemental needs, forcing the form of 'self-willing' upon everything it encounters. It is within this elemental intermediation of desire and freedom that the suffering of being human comes to roost.

Through the restless impetus of desire, one is inevitably drawn into a world of others in which one's freedom is fulfilled through these others, by way of them. Thus it is equally the other that draws out the will's secret yearnings, but in doing so these others only serve as a pretext for what Desmond calls the 'bewitchment' of the singular will, the 'enchantment' of desire in the endless promise of the given and its self-satisfaction. Adolescent freedom is a confrontation with the other, and in this confrontation one tests the limits of one's freedom. The terms of this confrontation cannot be reduced to a simple choice between good or evil, between doing the right thing and avoiding the wrong, between manipulation and generosity. Good and evil, like the ubiquitous surge of freedom, are tangential to 'the immanent indeterminacy of our desire' (EB, 282). Just as our being is marked throughout by the restless surge of desire, so too, good and evil emerge in constant interplay, enticing the will to partake of the 'adventure' of existence.

Freedom begins its ascent in equivocity, unfolding in *confusion* over what one hopes 'to be'. Given the uncertainty of this ascent, what resists determination is taken back into the field of self-affirmation; in running up against the ambiguity of experience, we unconsciously react against our own confusion, and from out of this state of confusion arises an inner standard to mitigate the indeterminate. The inward depths of self materialize to meet the equivocal, yet this inwardness itself is indefinite, experiencing the openness of the 'between' as both 'lack' and 'exhilaration'.

Seen along these lines, adolescent freedom remains a way of flirting with the other that resists the other, yet in implicitly depending on the other the break beyond mere self-fulfilment is always present. Persisting in this reluctance of commitment towards anything definitive expresses a 'constraint' of desire and a 'betrayal' of further forms of freedom.[4] As Desmond explains, those that 'absolutize' this 'freedom from' subdue the pull of the other that emerges in adolescent freedom by fixating on the satisfaction of self-intoxication at the expense of everything else (EB, 289).

Freedom emerges, then, through the attempt to appropriate what resists any final incorporation, both inwardly in the openness of desire, and outwardly in the equivocal fulfilment of this desire in the world of others. In going beyond ourselves, in adventuring in the indeterminate, we both overlook our own equivocal beginnings and overreach our possibilities in attempting to overtake the endless array of otherness before us. As Desmond explains, desire thrives on its own indeterminacy, yet, as the will ages, so it inevitably 'must' become more determinate. This 'necessitation to determination' occasioned by the changing circumstances of one's life and experience – one's growing up – awakens the possible revolt of selfhood. The self finds its own sense of 'intoxication', its love of the '*undefined*', being forced into determination, that is, impelled to make a choice, choose a lifestyle. This 'pull' is not of its own sanction, and with this fact comes a diminution of the original freedom that was taken up as the inalienable right of selfhood.

As Desmond explains, we are born in the equivocity of freedom, and thus from the beginning in an inarticulate complicity with evil, just as much as we are stewards of the good. Evil does not first arise as a deliberate choice. We feel its grip in bearing the duplicitous weight of freedom. The limitations placed on our being, that we are bound to an indeterminate opening whose happening we cannot fully account for, stir up self-affirmation and self-insistence, which refuse to yield mastery of self. Because freedom arises in and throughout the promise of being, releasing the will into the indeterminate 'between', the pull of the other is always in danger of being met by the passion of base self-assertion. The logic here is carnal, the ground of freedom must be won back from the interdependence that transcribes the original empowerment of freedom. As self-grounded, the will must continually convert the inescapable fact of dependence upon the other into subjugation of the other, in order to distance itself from what it cannot fully mediate. Insofar as adolescent freedom refuses to concede its limitations, one's world becomes forged in the endless drive to confirm what cannot be wholly confirmed, to subdue what can never be fully subdued. When this happens, one has already moved away from the source of otherness as empowering, the goodness of being, and lives this otherness as a perennial threat to one's own ontological integrity.

To recapitulate, freedom surfaces in the equivocity of indeterminate desire. Its attempt to master this desire nourishes its own sense of self, yet in ways that remain unclear to the fuller light of rational agency. Out of this confusion we begin actively to differentiate self from other. Yet the adventure into otherness is tempted to preserve its own sense of identity, falling deeper and deeper into the inwardness of self, while mistakenly taking this fall as expressive of greater liberty 'to be': the enactment of adolescent freedom is lived in the attempts to disentangle ourselves from the otherness that continually empowers us.

For Desmond, freedom is the greatest gift of being, but the very awakening of freedom also carries inscribed in its possibilities the greatest betrayal of being as good, the effacement of otherness in light of self-assertion and self-preservation. Because the sources of this freeing are themselves indeterminate, the dynamic of freedom is always at risk of being bewitched by its own powers of self-determination.[5] There is no outrunning this equivocal dawning of freedom, given its origins in the overdeterminacy of being. This original freeing is the 'gift' of freedom, not simply a determination of being, for the issue of agency arises only at the moment of releasing, and not before. It is this interdependency and intermediation that shape the communicating surplus of the between as the happening of being.

Thus we must not forget that the granting of freedom also brings with it the confusion of being, for the promise of human 'selving' is not something we can simply determine for ourselves, regardless of how much we reflect on our own powers of ontological determination. And it is in this perpetual state of seeming uncertainty that suffering and anxiety disseminate themselves, for the happening of freedom is never without painful equivocations, burdening us with a world that has *too much meaning*; indeed we are inwardly tormented by this very overflow. In many ways, human experience is shaped in coming to terms with this plenitude, in which we also confront the intransigent reality of suffering. And it is to our experience of this suffering, which is elicited by the very overdeterminacy of being, that the goodness of being appears paradoxically both at its nadir and at its zenith, breaking down the self-sufficiency of knowing while soliciting the resiliency of hope. I now want to explore more closely this reflection of the good in the suffering of being by looking at the way the generosity of the good is able to reveal itself despite the recalcitrance of human fragility.

Suffering and the Intermediating Refrain of the Good

The dawning of freedom must inevitably bring with it the suffering of being. We are the passion of being, and as we unfold our own ontological integrity in the happening of the 'between', so too we cannot avoid suffering from the ambiguity that defines us. Suffering and freedom originally surface as indistinguishable from each other. Like the upsurge of freedom, the roots of our suffering could never be univocally pinned down and treated in such a way as to avoid entirely the possibility of suffering. Indeed the belief in the power to do so bespeaks a betrayal of the goodness inherent in being, since it presupposes that the depth of being can be mastered. This is obviously not to say that attempts should be abandoned which try to alleviate the prevalence of suffering in many of its guises, but that we also must acknowledge the inability to mediate this suffering fully in its more elemental forms: the frailty of age, the mourning over death, the pangs of love, or the impeding reality of one's own finitude. To live a life devoted to escaping the inevitability of suffering is to lead a life that remains indifferent to the gift of freedom and the origins of this freedom in the overdeterminacy of being. In the end, there are no therapies that could successfully elude the finitude of being, without at the same time distorting the meaning of this finitude. Moreover every attempt to do so only proceeds by way of negating the empowering multiplicity of otherness that underlies our drive 'to be'.

Traditionally, philosophy has had real difficulties acknowledging the inwardness of suffering and its ubiquitous character. More often than not, suffering becomes defined as a 'problem' that can be solved or, at the least, a state or situation that can be met by adaptation or adjustment of one kind or another (EB, 370). The drive to know overlooks the infinite inwardness of suffering, and thus misconstrues its own genesis in the pathos of freedom by devaluing whatever resists definitive incorporation and objectification in the projects of the human. Yet our freedom 'to be' in more determinate modes of 'selving' is inextricably intertwined with the passion of being human. Because many of the categories that define philosophy mitigate its exposure to the indeterminacy of being, the elemental character of being is quite often passed over at the expense of preserving the dignity of knowing. Where the resources of philosophical reflection often falter, however, other mediums take up their residence, emerging from the indeterminacy of being while readdressing this equivocity by remaining true to its perplexing depth. The recalcitrance of suffering to mediation is a central theme embraced by both the arts and religion; the continual portrayal of this pathos remains one of their lasting testaments, and is itself indicative of the equivocal bond between the creativity of freedom and its heritage in the suffering of being, liberating us from the indefiniteness of being through acknowledging limitation.

In saying this, my goal is not to define the rightful providence of philosophy, the arts or religion, but to point out certain constancies that arise in the naming of the happening of being, which is equally an expression of the way in which the gift of freedom is enacted in the promiscuity of discourse. Philosophy, the arts and religion distinguish themselves through their attempts to name the ground of their own milieu: the riddle that we are to ourselves. The very power to name, however, will always remain something enigmatic. It is in this very perplexity of play that the goodness *in-communiqué* throughout experience receives some intimation.

We thrive in an ontological condition of interdependence and intermediation, and this not only because we always find ourselves dependent on other beings, but also because this dependence itself resists any final formalization. *Ethics and the Between*, like many of Desmond's other works, wants to show us that the question of being is inseparable from the question of the good, and thus could never be exhausted in a 'metaphysics of presence', since being is nothing but the communication of the enabling force at work in transcendence itself, multiplying itself in endless configurations. Human beings are ethical through and through because we are always in communication with the good, indebted to otherness in ways that can never be fully determined, owing to the infinite character of our interdependence; it is the intimacy of this indeterminacy that equally brings with it the intractable reality of suffering (EB, 490). As Desmond points out in another work, *Perplexity and Ultimacy*, we live the 'ontology of loss' in the intimacy of our being.[6] This openness reveals what Desmond describes as an 'excess of exposure to an otherness that destroys every human self-sufficiency'; however it is equally this root exposure that draws us into the adventure of being and the gift 'to be' (PU, 28). Desmond explains this as follows:

> The elemental truth is that there is something radically unchosen about what one is, yet one can choose to accept, or not, this unchosen given. In this suffering of the unchosen, our choice can either institute a different suffering of self-discord, or a different freeing of self, flowing from consent to the given. (EB, 370)

Art, religion and philosophy are never self-sufficient, and for their own sake alone, but come to fruition from a more perplexing metaphysical happening (PU, 30). The difficulty of traditional philosophical discourse to articulate the elemental passion of being, its breakdown before the abyss of human suffering, points to the 'saying of art' and religion to illuminate what cannot be discerned in the clarity of logical concepts. This discernment is the work of practical wisdom, of what Pascal calls an *esprit de finesse* rather than an *esprit de géométrie*, and will always require the talents of other mediums, the intermediating voices of more patient forms than *gnosis*, to discern the diffuseness of the 'between', and bring it to light. Art and religion are living testimonies of the good in diffusion, taking us *through* appearance to the empowering multiplicity of being at the heart of appearance itself.

To summarize, the good distinguishes itself in its doubled character as fullness and lack, the abundance of transcendence as freeing and the determination of this original freeing through self-transcendence, which constantly strives to secure 'for itself' what resists incorporation. The overall point of Desmond's *Ethics and the Between* is to demonstrate that if the circle could be closed – if being could be determined in its totality – there would be no such thing as the good, and we would be left with simulacra, ideology and will to power.[7] The more we forget the truth of our ontological condition, of a goodness that empowers yet transcends human power and cognition – the origin as overdetermined in its vitality as opposed to underdetermined or simply meaningless – the more we are unable to discern the 'hospitality of being' incarnate in the world. This 'hospitality of being' intimates the original '*incognito* of the good', the promise of being as it subsists in the intermediating communication of otherness and its innumerable forms of empowerment, releasing the body, desire, the will and cognition into more determinate complexity, into fuller ways of being. Thus we live the good well before we could ever give an account of it, just as we are freed into being well before we could take responsibility for this freedom, and define what it means 'to be' free. If we want to be true to our ontological situation, then we must be mindful of the impenetrability of the beginning, of the origin, which is to say we must respect the intangibility of being free. The echoes of this truth resound in the profuseness of the between as the happening of experience in the determination of being. Art and religion, more so than philosophy, subsist in their choice to embrace this 'hyperbole' of being, pushing the boundaries of reflection beyond the categories of discursive reflexivity; yet the question remains whether the living dialogue of these modes or mediums of community and communication, like that of philosophy, does not also differentiate singularity from its beginnings, depicting the goodness of the origin only by soliciting singularity into the replenishing powers of communal reflection in teaching us how to *read* the engulfment of singularity in the world of experience.

Conclusion: Suffering, Mediation and the Spectre of Reflection

I now want to draw my discussion to a close by taking a brief look at the intermediating character of philosophy, art and religion in relation to the overdeterminacy of being. To have an experience is to have a determinate experience, even if this experience is indeterminate, because it is this indeterminacy itself, the ambiguous character of the encounter, which differentiates it from other kinds of experiences. Yet indeterminacy and overdeterminacy are not synonymous. If I am not mistaken, there are no experiences of overdetermination, of infinite surplus possibility directly intuited in a single phenomenal manifestation, but rather we have continual happenings, seemingly without end – slippages without number – in which we interact, intertwine and are implicated in being, at a myriad of levels and in a myriad of ways. From such plurality the overdeterminacy of being comes to intelligibility in the endless multiplicity of the experiences that we enact. If we experienced the world or ourselves as truly overdetermined, it seems there could be no moment to which we might give an account, no beginning to which a start could be made, nothing determinate in which being might become. Philosophy, art and religion, in their more authentic voices, attempt to see through this indeterminacy in order to point to the constitutive possibility of experience: experience as 'inexhaustible matrix of determinability', and thus of infinite ontological value. In creating a discourse about being human, they create a community that both expresses and lives the promise of the possible in the actual by reflecting on the infinite meanings of the given, yet this infinite character of the given remains something 'discovered' in the attempt to articulate the experience of being human.

It is in the releasing space of the 'between' that philosophy, art and religion come to be, while it is their fidelity to the 'between' that renews their possibilities as well as differentiates their possible voices, as each strives to re-enact the endless naming of transcendence itself, which is the original goodness of being. Yet does this not place the truth of ethical being, in all its complexity, at a remove from its own happening, as somehow dependent on the power of reflective activity to piece together, as it were, the ambiguity that lies outstanding? The goodness of being only becomes what it is in being articulated in a manner that allows us to see the fuller import of the beginning, which is itself a possibility that appears dependent on historical discourses, not so much to fulfil this promise, as to express what this promise could mean. The goodness of being in its overdeterminacy, then, comes to concreteness in the pathos of reflection on the suffering we embody as free beings; it is not fully synonymous with it, which is to suggest that, without the moment of reflection, the overdeterminacy of being must remain locked in indeterminacy until the dialogues of art, religion and philosophy discern the conceptual space in which the goodness of overdetermination can come to fuller manifestation. If my reading is correct, we seem justified in ending our account with the following query: does the very overdetermined character of experience mean the goodness of being is in some way dependent on reflection to obtain its truth, that the promise of being free cannot be discerned from the standpoint of singular being, but only in the discourses lived by this singularity? Otherwise put, is the spectre of Hegel's dialectic perhaps embedded deeper than the metaxological might lead us to believe, in that the goodness of being, and the continual event of reflection on this goodness, are inseparable?

Notes

1   As Desmond explains, 'we must both regather the energies of dialectic while reconnoitering its limits and extremities (a theme recurrent in many of my other works)', EB, 117. For an example of how this theme is explored in Desmond's other writings, see also *Desire, Dialectic and Otherness: An Essay on Origins*; *Philosophy and its Others: Ways of Being and Mind*; *Beyond Hegel and Dialectic: Speculation, Cult and Comedy*; and *Perplexity and Ultimacy: Metaphysical Thoughts from the Middle*. Desmond's latest two books, *Being and the Between* and *Ethics and the Between*, gather together the many insights that run throughout his previous works in order to present them in a systematic format.

2   For Desmond, Kant, Fichte and Hegel, as well as Nietzsche and Marx, all fall into this 'trap' of autonomy, although obviously to differing degrees, in which each recognizes only those limitations the subject gives to itself.

3   As Desmond explains, the unfolding of selfhood expresses different 'potencies of the ethical'. Each potency reveals a different intimation of the good, from the elemental experience of embodiment (aesthetic potency) to its further configurations in the dianoetic, transcendental, eudaemonistic, transcending and transcendent potencies.

4   Desmond explains that 'freedom from' changes into 'freedom to', which alludes to an even richer experience of freedom as 'freedom towards'. This final form acknowledges the fact that the other will never completely fall into determinate patterns of action and willing. 'Freedom towards' respects the limitless inwardness of the other and points to the 'agapeic relation' of human communities. See EB, 362.

5   EB, 286. As Desmond later clarifies: '*The divine gift of freedom takes itself as divine in its freedom*', p.332 (emphasis in the original). This tendency to idealize, or idolize as the

case may be, one form of being at the expense of all others is something shared by all communities, both the religious and the secular.

6   PU, 32. Desmond discusses the relation between tragedy, philosophy and the arts in more detail in Chapter Two of this work, 'Being at a Loss: On Philosophy and the Tragic', pp.27–55.

7   For Desmond, in the end, there is no final separation of the ethical from the religious; the one is inseparable from the other. In giving me the opportunity to become the promise of my own person, the communication of being is the original gift, the chance 'to be'. The only truly appropriate name for this elemental bestowing and enabling through otherness is God, and the fullest response to this givenness, our 'facticity' as beings of the good, would be reverence and respect for the wonder of being.

Chapter 10

A World of Values in Cones and Planes

Miles Smit

Although cosmology is not one of the main overt themes in the philosophy of William Desmond, his ethics has a robustly cosmic dimension because of his stated aim of challenging the drift in Modernity towards the denial of inherent value in being, and in the world. In considering the philosophy of Desmond on ethos and cosmos, I will concentrate on the last chapter of *Ethics and the Between*, 'The Community of Agapeic Service'. This chapter serves as a culmination of the multiple senses of 'ethos' which pervade the book. On the one hand, ethos is being as suffused elementally with value, and, on the other hand, this is expressed successively in different ways of being: forms and stages of character and conduct, aspects of selving, of community. I treat the community of agapeic service as a kind of simultaneous zenith and nadir. Many of the powers and capacities of the self and of the community have seeped away. This seepage is a feature of the porous character of existence, an incontinence of being which also allows us to receive, and to be in communion with, more than that of which we are *capable*. This quality of agapeic openness is an intimation of our community with God. We have here a moment of community, in a place of being where the porous openness or exposure of all in the community means that both vulnerability and the capacity to receive charity are at their extreme. Light and darkness, and the chiaroscuro of their contrast, are ineradicable faces of the value of being.

I also have recourse to some of Desmond's most reliable and true companions, including Pascal, Vico and Peirce, and – as he has often stressed that it is important for philosophers to 'do their work amongst the poets' – I turn to some of the poetic voices who can best help us to descry the landscape of the good that I wish to explore.

Implicit in the inarticulate strife over the nature and scope of cosmology which we all now face is the question of whether the characterization of the world, namely its being subject to an ethos, is really a matter of something like facts or truths *rather than* values, and indeed, whether these can really exist apart from one another. Are there indeed forms of knowledge and being in which values are not at play? Is there any kind of truth in which there is no fidelity or keeping faith? In the eye of the storm about the distinction of *is* and *ought* there is supposed to be a citadel of the mathematically true, both dependable and aloof in its exactitude. What is *ordine et more geometrico* is taken to be independent, absolute and indifferent to what is beyond its compass, not least because the former is nominal and unfettered even to the real. But does the geometric quality of the mathematical not have a value, if only it is discerned in the terror of the eternal silence of infinite spaces? In *Ethics and the Between*, Desmond parts ways in the last chapter with Pascal (who has been a true guide through much of the book) with the words, 'Pascal's finesse often extends primarily to the equivocations of the geometric mind' (EB, 478, footnote 21). But perhaps we may find in these equivocations a germ of the spirit which turns the geometric imagination to survey the landscape of the domain of good and evil.

This essay examines the intersection of the symbolic power of geometry and poetry in the conjoint philosophical consideration of cosmos and ethos. My twin foci will be cones and planes. Their meeting and mediation is the conic section. In the dispersed philosophy of Charles Sanders Peirce, there is a trichotomy, one of many, between *elliptical*, *parabolic* and *hyperbolic* cosmologies. These take their names from three different kinds of conic section, and are meant to characterize three different visions of the sweep, or arc, of a cosmic physics and metaphysics.[1] But I would like us to explore the rich imagery of the conic section in its mathematical vicissitudes, and as an image which occurs in the poetics of many literary and philosophical figures. Through an appreciation of the rapport between what Pascal distinguished as the *mores* or spirits of geometry and finesse, I hope to explore the saturation of nature with value.

I believe this approach dovetails with the preoccupation of philosophers with looking at what Weber called the 'disenchantment of the world', that is, the concern that nature or even being itself is devoid of value, and sundered from the good. Although William Desmond acknowledges that neither ethics nor metaphysics is merely cosmology – and vice versa – as stated above, he has taken an aggressive stance, and repeatedly voiced the concern that the overlap between being and the good has been eroded by the nihilist tendencies of Modernism. The problem of coming to nothing is exhaustively addressed in *Being and the Between*, but in much modern philosophy there is a convergence on the singularities or bare points of being in which difference cannot be discerned, and thereby in which value is greatly deflated.

The ethos of *Ethics and the Between* is characterized by the chiaroscuro or sharpness in the interplay of light and dark which is a major theme throughout Desmond's work. The interplay between light and dark is certainly a matter of finesse, but the sharpness in their contrast, and the way value and difference arise from that sharpness, is indebted to geometry. The distinction between the quantitative and qualitative senses of value is here becoming less clear. Both trade in differences or discrete states, but the extensive measure and intensive likeness of all sorts of value can slide into, and seize upon, one another. Are there values which do not admit of inflation or deflation, of appreciation, or what Kant called 'fancy price'? When a community of exchange comes to its extremity, it seems that all values are subject to inversion and slide.

Throughout the exploration of his ethics, Desmond treats difference as a robust element, but one which is dynamic as well as substantial: it is an engine for a ceaseless exchange between participants in community. Without difference, value subsides, deflates and ceases to oscillate. In some ways, all oscillations have an aspect of exchange and economy. The scope of the ethos includes the most worldly exchanges and communities, as well as the most intimate and most transcendent. For my money, Desmond's speculations on ethos and community reach a kind of apex in the treatment at the close of the book of the community of agapeic service as a *commons* (EB, 483). This community, which arises out of the ethos, is not only a character, but, as we have suggested, it is also a landscape. At the outset of the book, it is a nocturne, in which the last slivers of a waning moon are disappearing. In the darkness of the first chapter, on the brink of an 'ordeal of coming to nothing', we read that 'we are finished without confession' (EB, 47). There is darkness too in the last chapter, but, it is perhaps the waning darkness of a new moon, and the hope hidden in the light that seems about to break brings the promise of something outside the scope of simply being good. Desmond has said that the order of the book might well have been inverted and, while we wait in the 'vigil of another world' which it is not yet our turn to enter (EB, 514), we are not still at this periphery spiralling *into* the rigours of a dark passage of confession for the first time but, hopefully, spiralling outwards towards the light. This may well remind us of the epochal gyre of Yeats, inspired by Vico, which is derived from the image of a cone which is interpenetrated with, or stacked against, another. As one age comes to its broadest culmination, another germinates in its base, or at the end of its gyration. The tendency of the gyre in Desmond's ethos is to the good, to affirmation, but this is ultimately in the hands of the One who exceeds even the compass of the ethos.

If the commons of the community in the *extremis* of agapeic service is level or flat, just as other communities of exchange and usefulness tend towards a levelling out, this plain is, in its chiaroscuro also caught between cones of light and darkness. The plain is, in the poetry of the last two centuries, a place over which plays what Walt Whitman in '*Salut au Monde!*' called 'the curious rapid change of light and shade'. The strength of the chiaroscuro is such that, in the distillate of the poets, the whole world may appear as redeemed or damned. While the Welsh poet R.S. Thomas spoke in 'The Bright Field' of a pearl of great price, having 'seen the sun break through to illuminate a small field for a while', Matthew Arnold wrote more grimly of a 'darkling plain', 'where ignorant armies clash by night'. Light and dark are contending and strive for this field or plain, pitching between grace and purblind cruelty.

The one plain *is* the other, only under a different slant of light. We cannot get out, even if the hyperbolic tilt on which the chiaroscuro emerges covers an arc that exceeds any of our own motions. If we are trapped by community on an uneven plane, we might begin to think of the differentiation of high and low in terms of the steepness or slope of the contrast of light and dark. According to the mathematical definition, the 'cone' of a conic section is really two cones as we commonly know them, opposed and touching at the apexes. We are clearly making a distinctly adapted use of the Vichian gyre. The two intertwined cones might really be almost any sort of epochal opposition, and we are treating them as an interpenetration or interplay of light and dark values – as it were, positive and negative energies. And in honesty I confess that we are also in effect treating the cones of the gyre as a kind of shape of Creation within which, perchance by recreation in ethics, we come to know things in undergoing moral experience which cut against Vico's maxim. That is, they are things which we have not ourselves made.

The cone has been used as an image of creation by J.R.R. Tolkien in a way that addresses our present anxiety about value in the world in the face of the daunting scale of the heavenly spaces. The image which comes from Tolkien's *Silmarillion* is not very often cited, but it is striking:

> ... amid all the splendours of the World, its vast halls and spaces, and its wheeling fires, the Father of All chose a place for the habitation of his children in the Deeps of Time and in the midst of the innumerable stars. And this habitation might seem a little thing to those who consider only the majesty of the Holy Ones, and not their terrible sharpness; as who should take the whole field of the Realm for the foundation of a pillar and so raise it until the cone of its summit were more bitter than a needle; or who consider only the immeasurable vastness of the World, which still the Holy are shaping, and not the minute precision to which they shape all things therein.[2]

A cone also describes, not just sharp peaks and broad bases, and different slopes or scales, but also different oscillations, different arcs and curvatures (see Figure 1). These descriptions are in effect different tilts of a plane intersecting the cone. As a plane cutting through a cone is tilted up through circular and elliptical sections, the movement of the arc is one that returns to the point of departure in an orbit about either a single or a doubled focus. Tilting upwards, the plane matches exactly the slope or gravity of the cone, and at that tilt it describes a parabola, where the movement rises away from, and falls back towards, its centre of gravity. Tilt a little higher, past this tipping point, and the plane becomes hyperbolic. It cuts through *both* cones. The hyperbolic arc is 'overthrown': it escapes from gravity, but it always describes a double arc, one inflected upward, another downward. Alternatively it describes an arc seen two ways, from above and from below. Perhaps it is right to say that at any incline, our commons is like a coin, dark on the underside and lit on the topside, but in the hyperbolic openness of community *in extremis*, the flipsides are, as it were, both turned up at once. In Desmond's ethics, it is charity as much as anything which is both the gift and liability that binds light and dark together on a common plane. The commons of charity is coeval, a sort of simultaneity of the epochs of good and evil, light and dark.

This doubling in the hyperbolic of the gift touches on the chiaroscuro it convokes, of extreme suffering and grace. It is as if the plane of the community were cut between two cones, one of light, one of darkness. Laid bare and open, it is lit from above and darkened from below. What Desmond has sometimes discussed under the aegis of what is *altus*, both celestial and abyssal at once, appears on this flattened plane, in the form of its hyperbolic tilt, cutting sharply through the deepest, most absorptive darks, and the most blinding lights. There are dismal greys too, and sobering thoughts to be had in close proximity to true charity: after the bad news about despair and disillusion, for instance, we read that 'there is worse. In the gray of disillusion, a cold hatred can congeal' (EB, 509).

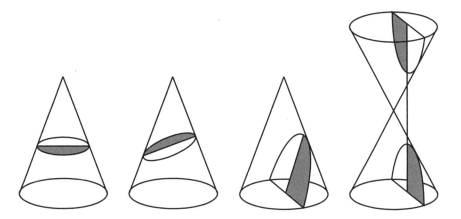

Figure 1   Illustrations of conic sections

There *is* good to match evil on this plane, and it has its poetry too, but it is a stark play of light and dark, battling for the upper hand in the gray. Just as the community of agapeic service is not a workers' paradise, it is also not an Arcadia or Elysium. It is in a way a place where we may forever be recreated and recreating, but also at a loss. The image of the plane is striking and resonant in terms of taking value as a matter of inclination or tilt. It certainly appeared this way to Nietzsche, who has been (as much as anyone) the bugbear to be tackled in confronting the philosophical aspect of coming to nothing, though he himself lamented the way the world has changed in our age, by way of images. He once confronted the vision that 'since Copernicus, man seems to have got himself on an inclined plane – now he is slipping faster and faster away from the centre into – what? into nothingness? into a *penetrating* sense of his own nothingness?'[3] We can fairly ask, what is mathematical in this image, and what revolts against the mathematical?

It is not entirely clear in the case of Nietzsche. But with Desmond, perhaps it is on this inclined plane that we are perched at the start of *Ethics and the Between*, on the cusp of confession. We come to nothing quickly enough on this plane. But as it crosses an agapeic commons of service, the plane is at a different tilt now, and it has certainly become more viscous. There are, in the course of Desmond's exploration of ethics, what he calls 'battles on the heights' and also excavations, and the descent into labyrinthine caves, and muddy subterranean bowels, but we are again out in the open – and often riveted to our spot – on a plain or commons which is exposed, even in its *penetralia*. If, through the leavening insistence of being, the ethos in some moments became turgid and swollen, reaching to the heights and the depths, it is rather unleavened now, even though it is caught in a highly fungible potency or gist which runs through it. Our being is not insistent here, but is uncannily persistent.

There is a chiaroscuro that stands in for high and low on this unleavened plain, but, unlike a chessboard, its boundaries of light and dark are not square and straight, but have become melted and irregular, which is how devils may pass for angels. To sharpen slightly the mindfulness of this community and its setting, we might explore a little the imagery which has been evoked. In speaking of dynamic processes, Desmond has said, 'consider the curvature'. Again, *different* arcs are described on the plane of a conic section as it gyres and wobbles, much as different cycles have been characterized throughout the book.

In his early work on conic sections, Pascal treated the different intersections a plane makes with cones. This treatise is mathematical in the univocal (some might say cool and objective) sense of the term most common to Desmond's usage. But the same Pascal who sensed the abyss two steps to his side was also touched by mathematical measure in another, more poetic and harrowing, way. Is his terror of eternally silent, infinite spaces not a specifically *mathematical* terror? Conversely, what kind of values do we need to shore up space for us and knit it away from the abyss? It is in this sense that I think the cone and the plane are also poetic images in the background to *Ethics and the Between*. They describe a place which is forever, like a blasted heath, being laid bare, bewildered, made strange and new and unfamiliar.

The utopianism of it (or its eutopian and dystopian characters, to use current parlance) lies in its forcefully paratactic quality. This community can connect and disconnect, quite apart from the sway of communities of familiarity, elective affinities, vocation, or time and place. It touches and puts pressure even on the integrity of the person or character who has followed the arcs of selving. The self is kept together by the religiosity, which is to say the trust or coherence of the community, as much as, or more than, by its own agency. This is a part of what distinguishes agape from eros.

As we dwell awhile here in this drift, and as our eyes adjust, we find that the light is surprisingly strong, stark even, in places. It is the *contrast* and play of light and dark, or their chiaroscuro, which is most striking. The sharpness of the contrast typifies the peculiar kind of value which drives the community of agapeic service. It is a matter of the most implicit trust and the most fearful threat of betrayal. Both light and dark are moving and alive in agapeic community as in the other phases of the ethos, so that more than one epoch or arc is in swing at every moment. The interplay of light and dark are not mere play or playfulness: they have a milling, grinding power to reduce the characters caught between them. We might here be reminded of Yeats's 'pestle of the moon'.

The rigour of this milling can be extreme. It grinds out to the periphery of the community of the living, and beyond. There is a sense in which the moment of the community of agapeic service is posthumous, and beyond the rigours of being: it is, so to speak, a drowned world, in which, like Ishmael in *Moby Dick*, we might well have expired, but yet we still abide, between two ages or between two worlds. While the wake or vigil is unbroken, the beatific vision of 'rebirth as prayer' has not yet been unveiled. This new moon, we might infer, will light the terrain of *Ethics and the Between*.

Throughout *Ethics and the Between* there is re-creation in cycles of four, and seven and six and three and nine that have marked the book. We have moved through trajectories that mark stages in a life, the arc of a whole life, and the ages which generations and wide communities pass through, and also elemental and cosmic cycles, both salvific and devastating. And yet, we do not really *move* in another sense, because the play of light and shade has been over the same moon. Cycles both intimate and grand are always in play together, so that the moments of the good of being are not totally sundered. They are also simultaneous and nested in one another, even if our mindfulness is not always on them. Perhaps, then, in this 'consummate' phase of the ethos and of ethical community, we may hope to glimpse not just the breaking of a new light, but, as it were, all at once to see the whole of the moon.

Where, then, are we? Both *passio essendi* and *conatus essendi* are intensive in the commons of charity, which thrives on a generous love, which acts but does not insist too much, and is forbearing. Materially, little or nothing differs from the other commonalities through which we have drifted to reach this point. Something as subtle as a different slant of light has changed in the way the good and goods of the commons are mediated. Charity is indeed perhaps the most thoroughgoing mediation we have yet encountered in Desmond's explorations of ethics. It is deeply metaxological, both in its riches and in its penury. One might characterize the ethos as a middle and a commons in which the metaxological emerges as that plain in which real alterity is at play. Charity emerges in a commons where all are on a level, neither assuredly sovereign nor servile. And yet if the commons is flat, it is also surpassingly steep, as it seems to sheer between Heaven and Hell.

A gyration or gimballing has brought the plane of the ethos around to where it is caught sharply between light and dark, and in such a way that both the utmost powerlessness and hope beyond hope touch us intimately. The plane is truly flat, in the measure that no one of us is on the heights lording it over others (any sovereigns there might be on the plane at this incline share the lot of the commons) and also because, in its terrific gravity, it is laid open and strafed from above and below by divine and satanic forces. Agapeic community opens the utmost trust, and so it is prone to the most diabolical betrayals. We were counselled earlier to be wary, given that 'monsters too come to visit – looking like angels' (EB, 456), and indeed both angels and devils circulate here in the coeval commons of an ethos *in extremis*. In the constant openness to good and evil is a kind of watchfulness. And in this vigil, there is a presence of the Others too. If the contractual civil society considered in previous chapters is partly constituted by what Burke called a partnership between the living, the dead and the unborn, then the permeable and haunted society of charity will be at the source of this. The abiding porosity of the ethos is hypertrophied now: just as the eyes dilate to discern the light, the irises of being are thrown quite open.

There is dignity in an agapeic community, just as there are goods and the good, but whereas we touch them and are touched too, the goods of charity, if abiding, are nonetheless not *durable* in a way that can be grasped. Just as the manna given to the Israelites in the desert mouldered if it was hoarded, and was given day after day, the good of charity which is given cannot be seized.

There is one aspect which, though subtle, deeply sunders the logic of agape;

from a dialectic of these elements of the ethos emerges a certain weakening of meaning insofar as it derives from opposition. There is a tension and a strife between passivity and activity, and between suffering and pleasure throughout the book. While wishing for an ethos in which the dark side of the good of being were abolished would be like asking for a one-sided coin, or a stick with only one end, in the agapeic community there is a dynamic of service which does not either have to deny, or quite admit, the sovereignty with which erotic communities culminate. If sovereignty is a 'being above', the level plain of the agapeic community is not quite abased in contrast, or rather it is, but this is not the point of the overthrow of pride. The sovereign or would-be sovereign says *non serviam*, but agapeic service is not a sentence imposed out of a care by some power to *force* the prideful to serve. That may be the sharpness of the particular chiaroscuro of agapeic community, but it is not, so to speak, its point. The quality of mercy is not strained in this sense: there is a kind of declenching of oppositions on this light and dark plain such that, while plenty and poverty, life and death and giving and taking are pressed into close quarters, they never quite intersect at a sharp point. Rather, light and dark, like the twin arcs of the hyperbola, are constantly darting over to one another and passing *over* the point at which they would cancel and come to nothing. This passage looks and behaves like an ineffably pliant meniscus.

Possibility as a trust fund for activity is overturned here. With cataclysms, such as the trials of Job, what happens was never *possible* before it happened, and this is true as well of the forgiveness afforded to the Prodigal Son. The son had exhausted his entitlements, but in the end he was saved because his pride did not prevent him from seeing that he was eligible for forgiveness. It is often tempting, and all too easy, to forgo the resourcefulness of friendship as it is all sources of charity. The pride that is a part of the erotic surges to sovereignty and can hardly accept any bliss that it does not win for itself. It may even cherish its defeats in a strange way, since these are in spite of its striving, and affirm at least the adversity which marks its vector of exertion.

A number of academics have concentrated on the forceful provocation of the question whether our dignity does not cut us off from charity, is not affronted by it. But the dignity (or worth, from the Latin *dignus*) we have here is not really our own. It is accorded to us, not by our insistence, but by the charitable acts of others. The body of the deceased, consecrated or preserved for burial, persists in dignity this way. In these extremities, we can talk of a severe *passio essendi*, or even, so to speak, of an *impassio essendi*, an intensity and valorization of being we live, but of which we are incapable. We said before that love as real charity does not overbear, and part of this is expressed in generosity of a kind that does not as such give anything except leeway, circumspection and a certain gracious delicacy.

The erotic subject, in its drive for sovereignty, thrives on its own activity and affirms itself by this recreation. It lives by choosing and electing but, in that state, it does not succeed in grasping the full meaning of eligibility, of being chosen. Those who are capable of *agapeic* sovereignty perhaps do grasp more fully what the dignity, both in felicity and burden, of being chosen implies. If the first is last, and the last first, could one seek to be first by insisting upon coming last?[4]

The onus or burden of eligibility is challenging because the good we are asked to give, and the service we are to render, is not fixed and has no set price. We cannot simply buy off or bribe away the needs of those who share the commons of the good with us, with bread or money, and if we have an insistence in agapeic communities, it is that we will not be bought off this way either. But the good which is more than a durable good cannot by our own guarantee be given and received by an exertion of will. The power of the heart to be disconsolate is vast, but the promise or trust of charity remains urgent and is not to be deterred, so we are caught in a web of liabilities that we might not be able to discharge.

Another complication is that the onus of service is leveraged against the responsibilities on which our erotic energies often feed most. One example of these is honesty, on which we can insist in a way that is not charitable, and which in a basic way is perhaps not truthful. Our honesty derives from our finite mindfulness of truth, but the operation of grace in agapeic service distends what is true and possible unpredictably. The good of this community is not estimable. Desmond himself consistently repudiates the notion of a 'Pollyanna' affirmation of life and being as a counterfeit of the primordial *yes*. But still we must retain something *blithe* in our hopefulness to succeed in giving and receiving agapeic service.

We may not fully grasp the good a small act of charity may give another, so, in strange ways, what might seem like a 'noble lie' to our honesty is in its service even more, and better, than that. Consolation has a power of which we are not the master. It is the good converse of the evil possibility of grave betrayal, which comes from the very rich promise and trust generated in the community of charity. William Desmond talks about those who may confront us bewildered or dumbfounded by adversity and loss. What do we crave when we are in such a state? This is what we could charitably give another. In the sort of direct imperative perhaps too rare in books on ethics, we read a short and helpful maxim: 'lessen their suffering' (EB, 506). If we succeed in carrying just this talisman through the rigours of our confession, we will have done well.

Notes

1 Elliptic or *Epicurean* philosophies believe that the universe does not evolve or progress, and is limited to what is measurable. Parabolic or *Nirvana* philosophies admit a 'drift in the course' of the universe, but believe that the principle of this development is a fixed formula. The hyperbolic philosophies, which are consonant with Peirce's own view, allow for a robust evolution in which 'the absolute consists of two distinct real points' such that 'the infinitely distant future' and the 'infinitely distant past' have a totally different 'general character'.

2 J.R.R. Tolkien, *The Silmarillion*, London: George Allen & Unwin, 1977, p.19; slightly adapted.

3 Friedrich Nietzsche, *The Genealogy of Morals*, III, par.25.

4 In a joke on this point, a Rabbi berates his Cantor: 'Look who thinks he's nothing!'

VI
DESMOND ON EROS

Chapter 11

Eros, Power and Justice: William Desmond and his Others

James McGuirk

General Reflections on the Connection between Ethics and Metaphysics

Though it is only in his most recent work, *Ethics and the Between*, that the notion of justice is discussed in any great detail, it is a notion that is central to the philosophical project of William Desmond taken in its entirety. That this is not always obviously the case owes much to his sense of the need of grounding ethics in metaphysics.

There are many who would argue that ethics requires no support from metaphysics, that it is a self-standing discipline which can be a subject for reflection independently of any consideration of more ultimate questions about the meaning of being as a whole. This kind of thinking is, in some respects, traceable to Aristotle's separation of the various disciplines according to which the cultivation of *phronesis*, or practical wisdom, does not of necessity require grounding in metaphysical or speculative thinking.[1] In other words, it is possible to be just and to act justly without cultivating an interest in metaphysics. To an extent, Aristotle's thinking on the matter can be understood in opposition to the 'all or nothing' approach of Plato.[2] For Plato, only the philosopher can be properly just or truly happy, since to be just entails understanding the form of justice as it is in itself. Such understanding provides a light by means of which 'earthly justice', if I may use that expression, can be assessed. Earthly justice, of course, can never do more than imperfectly approximate what is Ideal and, therefore, truly real. Understanding the Ideal provides a touchstone by means of which we can orient ourselves in ethical and political life. Without it, we are merely fumbling in the dark. Since contemplation of the hyperouranian ideas is the province of the speculative philosopher, it follows that only the philosopher can hope to live a properly integrated life. Thus ethics and politics are indebted to metaphysics in the most crucial of senses.

The preceding is something of a caricature! The situation is of course much more complex with regard to both Plato and Aristotle, whose insights I have dramatically undersold. It serves nevertheless to adumbrate my contention that there is far more of Plato than of Aristotle in the thought of the philosopher whose work we here acknowledge. I do not mean to say that William Desmond is a Platonist in any straightforward sense of that term, but simply that I find more of the spirit of Plato than of Aristotle in his work.

William Desmond on the Connection

His most recent work, *Ethics and the Between*, is the second part of a trilogy that began with *Being and the Between* and will be completed with the appearance of *God and the Between*. As such, it may be read as a continuation of the project of the first book and an anticipation of the third. Whereas *Being and the Between* dealt with the need to rethink the question of being in general, the second book deals with the implications of this in relation to the specific meaning of being good. Thus it is through and through a book about ethics, but at the same time a book that insists upon the need for a metaphysical grounding for ethics. Without that, ethics is condemned to be somewhat truncated insofar as it attempts to think about being good in the absence of any sense of the good of being. William Desmond attempts to show that these two questions are actually inseparable in that the first always entails some position regarding the second. In modernity, the 'overcoming of metaphysics' has made life easier insofar as we are no longer allowed or encouraged to think about 'big' questions, but it has also had the result of making ethical thinking problematic. How can we ground an ethics in a universe robbed of value? If the 'is' is barren, how can it generate an 'ought'? Certain thinkers, such as Hume and Schopenhauer, are honest enough to follow the implications of the devaluation to their logical conclusion. Such honesty is rare, however. Usually philosophers tend to try to resurrect the 'ought' otherwise, through social contract theories or maximization of pleasure or some such. In other words, they bow under the weight of Hume's well-known objection, and seek a new foundation for goodness.

William Desmond and the Thought of Justice

William Desmond's work, by contrast, rethinks and questions this kind of ethical nihilism in the light of a metaphysics that describes being as good, as the gift of an overdetermined source of goodness. In this light, the spuriousness of the fact/value dichotomy is suggested as the product of a metaphysical nihilism and an ethical reductivism which do justice neither to our lived experience of being nor to being itself.

   This brings me back to the main topic of this essay: justice. It is a notion that is rarely discussed in detail in Desmond's work, and yet it is a notion that colours his thinking almost from the start. Throughout *Being and the Between* and earlier, he speaks of philosophy as well as art and religion as ways of attempting to 'do justice to' what there is. His very attempt to reinvigorate metaphysical discourse is an attempt to 'do justice'. This notion of justice is therefore the perfect place to situate certain reflections concerning the relation between metaphysics and ethics. Detailed analysis of concrete ethical situations is beyond the scope of the present endeavour; what I intend to do, rather, is to offer some initial thoughts on the meaning of justice as 'doing justice' from the point of view of a phenomenology of experience.

If a major concern of William Desmond's is doing justice to what there is, it is legitimate to ask what this means. What does it mean to 'do justice to' something? In answering this question we will also surely indicate ways of doing injustice or ways of reneging on the possibility of justice. To do justice to something means to appreciate it properly or to be faithful to it. This, in turn, involves the notion of being true to the thing (be it situation or person) in question. Being true to something can be taken either in the sense of speaking the truth about it or of living the truth of it. Justice, then, is connected to truth. But now a further question is generated, namely, why is truth important or why should we be true? In the opening lines of Aristotle's *Metaphysics*,[3] there is the implication that this question is, in a sense, unanswerable. The desire for truth is written in our nature from the beginning to such an extent that it might be described as the very form of our mindfulness.[4] The implications of this fact are three. The first is the very general observation that now there appears to be some connection between desire and being true. Secondly, if we are seeking the truth we must lack it. Thirdly, the fact that it is written in our nature from the start means we must have an inchoate sense that the truth is good and that it is good that we seek it. The second of these opens the way for our various determinations of the desire, while the third allows us to give an after-the-fact affirmation of the unchosen way of being that is ours. In other words, we are already in the midst of certain ways of being, in advance of the emergence of any reflexive awareness of this fact. The desire to do justice as a desire to be truthful, then, is given us as a power that is not self-originating. It is not reducible to a point of view. To be sure, points of view can and must be taken with regard to the attempt to determine the meaning of desire, but the desire itself is prior to any of these. I will explain what this means presently.

Platonic Origins: Desire and Eros

This account of desire as suggesting both lack and fullness is Platonic in origin. In the *Symposium*, eros, as the form of the soul, is accounted for through the fanciful myth told by Diotima.[5] In this myth, eros is the product of the union of *Poros* and *Penia*, or Resource and Poverty. William Desmond frequently alludes to this myth in his treatment of the meaning of eros and desire. He points out, rightly, that this myth suggests a dimension of eros which makes nonsense of any attempt to discuss it in terms of pure lack. Pure lack is nothing, and eros is certainly not nothing. There is, to be sure, lack involved in eros. If there were not, it could hardly be described as seeking completion. For Plato, eros is often described as a desire for the Good. For Desmond, it is described as the desire to know determinately. In either case, it is a force that can be described as transcending. It moves us beyond ourselves towards that which we lack. So as much as there is lack at the core of eros, there is also power, the power to transcend. These factors combined constitute the essential openness of eros as both spiritual and physical. Eros is at work in us from the start so that we are always, in Desmond's sense, 'beings in the between'. Our openness in the world is fluid in a way that makes determining the meaning of our eros very difficult.

The Ambiguous Revelation of Eros

That eros is an ambivalent energy is already clear from the description of its double nature. But there is more to it than this. The ambivalence of eros is many-headed, for even its power is ambivalent with respect to its source and its meaning. I consider these two to be related and connected to Desmond's own discussions of the themes of origin and truth. Leaving aside the question of origin for the time being, we turn to the second problem, the relation of eros and truth. This may provide us with a context within which to reflect on the notion of 'doing justice'. The inarticulacy of eros is such that it knows neither whence it comes nor whither it goes. That it desires articulation is uncontroversial, but what does it articulate, and in what way can this articulation be said to stand in relation to the question of truth? In other words, the articulation of eros is a way of seeking to 'do justice', not only to 'what there is' but also to what *it* is. I mean to say that it seeks to do justice to what is revealed in its own power.

There are several possible responses to this problem, and I mean to look at two. The first can be described as Nietzschean, whilst the second is that of William Desmond.

Nietzschean Eros

Nietzsche tends to think of the desire to articulate in purely negative terms. For Nietzsche, there is nothing initially revealed in eros. This is an ontological 'nothing' that suggests that the foundation of self-being and being in general is meaninglessness. And yet this is not quite true, for there is something revealed in eros. It is power. This is power pure and simple, and as an end in itself. Put otherwise, power stands only for itself. This brute meaninglessness becomes the basis of Nietzsche's deification of power as merely neutral force. If this is what is revealed in eros, it follows that power and the discharge of power are the only authentic response to lack. The lack felt in eros is the lack of itself as articulate. Eros does not seek to articulate anything other than itself. Through this articulation, it is suggested, its longing will be sated. According to this view, eros is the answer to its own question insofar as lack is accounted for as the lack of self-articulation. Power is the means by which this articulation is achieved, so, in an important sense, what is affirmed is the power of eros itself. I am thinking here of Nietzsche's comment in *Beyond Good and Evil* that, in love, it is 'ultimately, the desire, not the desired, that we love'.[6] I take it that this is what Desmond means when he speaks of the closure of eros back on itself. If the lack in eros is felt as pure inarticulacy, then power, as the power of determining, is absolute. As absolute it is also neutral, and is thus reducible to force. It is *libido dominandi*. Its openness to what is other is aimed at an ultimate closure as completeness in which the void has been filled.

Whether or not this closure is possible is a debatable point, but our analysis seems correct at least in the sense that what Nietzsche's eros celebrates is simply power. He glories in the exhortation to be creative, and to forge oneself in the fire of one's own will.

If Nietzsche is correct, the universe must be described as simply an amalgam of power. It is a 'monster of energy'.[7] According to this view, to be true to the whole or to 'do justice to' means to articulate the power of my own desiring will. In this way, I make myself strong. This strength can and does involve a will to destruction; not self-destruction necessarily, though this is certainly involved, but destruction in the sense of violent appropriation, of what is other insofar as it threatens to curtail the exercise of my strength. In being strong in the exercise of power, I am being true to being, according to Nietzsche. In a certain sense, I am also being good. This is not good in the traditional sense: it is the good beyond good and evil.

So I repeat my central question: what does it mean to do justice? The answer for Nietzsche is to exercise my power, so that power and its articulation are the meaning of justice. Nietzsche is not the only thinker to express such a view. The identification of justice with power can also be found in the fictional views of two of Socrates' interlocutors (Callicles in *Gorgias* and Thrasymachus in *Republic* I) as well as in the thought of Machiavelli and the Marquis de Sade. I have intimated already that this involves a specific metaphysical viewpoint.[8] If justice can be identified with power, then the universe must be nothing more than indifferent power. The notion of being good *à la* Nietzsche must be beyond good and evil normally construed, since the traditional construal of these terms entails belief in a cosmic order of some sort.[9]

I said also at the beginning that any investigation into the notion of doing justice will also delineate what doing injustice means. So what can it mean for Nietzsche to do injustice to what there is? This is harder to discern, but it seems to mean reneging on one's power, since this amounts to a denial of what is true.[10] Powerlessness is not simply weakness for Nietzsche; it is also, in a sense, a metaphysical crime. It is for this reason that Nietzsche regards pity and compassion with such contempt. They are modes of inauthenticity nourished by adherence to a metaphysics that is untrue to what I am, and hence both false and unjust. The truest for Nietzsche are those who engage in 'the insatiable struggle for control'.[11] The greatest fear is the weak soul and its introduction of mistrust 'in life, in man, in ourselves',[12] with the result that 'the powerful and successful begin to doubt their right to happiness'.[13]

The injustice of the Christians and Socratics rests on the fact that they attempt to subordinate power to something more ultimate.[14] This something more is untrue and also pernicious insofar as it wishes to reduce all to a bland equality, in which the authenticity of the perspectival is undercut and condemned as sinful. But for Nietzsche power is the ultimate: there is nothing more. The perspectival is eminently true, since there is no outside of my power other than the universe itself,

as 'monster of energy' or the totality of power. In this respect the only thing that
limits my power is the power of the whole. The only thing I can know beyond the
perspectival is that all is power. And it is precisely in knowing this that a space for
affirmation opens up, in the sense that I can assent to the truth of this.

In being affirmative, Nietzsche wishes to overcome the pessimism of
Schopenhauer. And yet, in so doing, something strange happens, and his thought
becomes quasi-religious. By giving assent to the notion that 'all is power', he
acknowledges that my power is not its own source. It has been given to me from
outside. Given, not in any benevolent sense, but as the outpouring of sheer
explosive force. And yet there remain traces of gratitude in Nietzsche's thought,
and also an element of worship. Examples of this can be found in the *Birth of
Tragedy*, where Nietzsche speaks of the Bacchic frenzy that accompanies the
dismantling of the *principium individuationis*,[15] and in *Beyond Good and Evil*,
where he speaks of the noble man who 'reveres the power in himself'.[16] Insofar as
I create or destroy myself, I am giving thanks to the origin whence I came. I give
my assent to the monster and call it good.

According to our initial explication, doing justice means being faithful and
being truthful, both in the sense of telling the truth and of living the truth. The
opposite, injustice, entails unfaithfulness and the denial of the truth of what there
is. If we accept Nietzsche's account of the universe as a monster of energy, then
his understanding of what it means to do justice must also be accepted. The
implications of this view for thought are worth mentioning briefly here.

The connection between justice and truthfulness entails both living the truth and
telling the truth. If the second of these relates to philosophy, then its scope
becomes very narrow, simply because there is not very much truth to tell. There is
only one undifferentiated truth, that all is power, so we might say that philosophy,
as telling the truth, is not very important for Nietzsche. And yet it is crucial, since
this truth is the point around which the rest of his thought revolves, for it opens the
only possible space for affirmation insofar as being faithful and living the truth
amount to no more than the exercise of strength as will to power.

Thus the space for thought is both essential and also very narrow, and
philosophy, conceived as a never-ending quest for a deeper, more nuanced
understanding of the cosmic order in the Platonic sense, is rejected.

I would like to turn now to the question of the possibility of maintaining the
distinction between justice and injustice on the basis of Nietzschean philosophy.
We now have some sense of what it means to do injustice (to the whole) for
Nietzsche. But how does he respond to this injustice? He can and does complain.
In fact, a significant part of the Nietzschean corpus consists of an unflinching
polemic against the weak, and against ways of doing injustice to the whole, but to
whom is he appealing? Is it an appeal to the monster that cannot listen, or is it mere
self-exhortation? It seems he is addressing himself in an attempt to drive himself
forward so as to embrace his own power. If so, it seems that he wishes to be self-
affirming both because, and in spite, of the truth of the whole. *Because of*: because
he has already given his blessing to the philosophical truth that power is all there
is. But he also expresses a desire to be self-affirming *in spite of* this truth, insofar

as he wishes to differentiate in himself that which cannot ultimately be differentiated. Some of the ambivalence of this position can be seen in Nietzsche's oscillation in the *Birth of Tragedy* between affirmation of the Apollonian dream world, on the one hand, and the Dionysian frenzy that destroys the *principium individuationis*, on the other.

It is in this respect, I think, that Desmond highlights the impossibility of Nietzsche's proposed affirmation. What is meant is this: Nietzsche wants to affirm the reality of the universe as undifferentiated, neutral power. What there is and what happens are merely the expression of power, and power is justice. At the same time, Nietzsche rages about ways of being unfaithful to the truth and he therefore rages against the injustice of his philosophical enemies. But, if power is undifferentiated in this way, then these ways of being unjust (such as the Christian condemnation of strength) are just as much children of the ultimate as the ways of being just. Injustice is also 'what merely happens'. Am I being unfair to Nietzsche here? In a sense, yes, insofar as the notion of creativity is crucial to his distinction between the higher and lower forms of life, and it is precisely the lack of creativity that characterizes the weakness of the weak. But even so, creativity appears to involve embracing the will to power, or the 'truth about oneself'. While the weak seem to shun this truth, they do paradoxically live in will to power. Thus, in the *Genealogy,* Nietzsche claims that will to power is the source of the corruption of the 'ascetic priest'.[17] In this sense, justice and injustice are finally the same. This is insufficient as an answer, so we must look elsewhere and ask the question again, 'what does it mean to do justice to the whole?'

'Doing Justice' for Desmond

It is at this point that we turn to the thought of William Desmond. This is appropriate insofar as the discussion began with his notion of 'doing justice to'. I should mention that I am aware that this notion of 'doing justice to' is derivative of what we normally have in mind when we speak of justice: principles concerning moral conduct between people. The point is that, whilst this sense is derivative *qua* technical usage, it is, in a sense, philosophically prior. This is firstly because, in highlighting the relation between 'doing justice' and notions of faithfulness and truth, it tends to penetrate to the heart of what is actually at stake when we talk of justice.[18] Secondly, the idea of doing justice to what there is suggests a complexity beyond the temptation to treat justice on what Desmond might call a univocal paradigm.[19]

To be just, or to do justice, according to William Desmond, does not demand abnegation of power, so his thinking cannot be described as simply maintaining a negative relation to Nietzsche's ideas. He rejects Nietzsche's assimilation of justice and power, but he likewise rejects any simplistic dualism between the two that would present power as 'dominating force or of justice as some impotent ideal' (EB, 460). Rather, the exercise of power is essential to the meaning of justice. He also says that 'it makes no sense to abstract justice from power or power from justice' (EB, 459). The work of justice is, in an important sense, achieved in and through the exercise of power. We cannot of course take this to mean that, in rejecting Nietzsche, Desmond is embracing Hegel and offering a view of justice as achieved at the end of history through the process of the unfolding of Absolute Spirit. Desmond's is not a story of justice and truth *ex nihilo*. At the start we said that one meaning of the phrase 'to do justice' was 'to appreciate properly'. For Hegel this would make no sense. There is initially nothing to appreciate insofar as the origin is described in terms of the pre-dialectical identity of being and nothingness. For Desmond, power unfolds justice, if it can be said to do so, by making determinate what was there from the beginning in non-determinate form.[20] This is achieved in the thought of Desmond through a phenomenology of experience, which suggests fundamental experiences of the presence of goodness or the good of the 'to be' from the start. If this is correct, eros (as the eros of mind) alone, described in purely lacking terms, will not be enough, even if it is acknowledged that eros is fundamental to what we are. Furthermore Nietzsche's proposed equivalence of ultimacy and power will be shown to be a way of being forgetful, and therefore unfaithful to what there is.

So what are the essential features of Desmond's phenomenology of experience? At the most basic level, his thinking can be said to proceed through the analytic of the eros and agape of metaphysics. It is through these notions that he tries to speak the truth and therefore do justice to what there is. Eros and agape are treated as fundamental modes of being by means of which we can reflect on what it means to be. Here, as always, the challenge of faithfulness is the challenge to be attentive to what is revealed in the eros and agape of being, without being neglectful of either.

As to what these notions entail, we have already made some preliminary remarks about eros, and there is not much more to say here: it reveals a lack in our being and also entails the desire to overcome that lack. It is the desire to make determinate what is initially vague and indeterminate. In *Being and the Between* Desmond describes eros in terms of 'a movement of transcendence wherein mind mediates progressively with being's otherness to make its enigmatic face available to determinate intelligibility. It is driven to the ideal of comprehensive intelligibility and knowing' (BB, 7).

The agape of metaphysics is something else. It is described as the 'effective work of a plenitude that is prior to erotic lack, or a power of being anterior to the indigence of eros' (BB, 7). In other words, the agape of metaphysics is a mode of transcendence which is a more genuine opening to being as other, not for the sake of the subordination of otherness, but for the sake of relation with what transcends mind in its otherness. For Desmond, as was noted earlier, the notion of the agapeic as anterior is crucial because, he says, eros as pure lack does not make sense. This is surely right. Eros is ambivalent and, as such, it is a dark power. And yet it must be illuminated from elsewhere, since as pure empty lack it is hard to see from where might come the impetus of its transcendence. This is not just a matter of preference or of Desmond's desire to flee the uncomfortable implications of Nietzsche's analysis. It is phenomenologically more sound in the sense that we noted that eros, as motive desire, always suggests something prior to itself from which it is funded. In describing the prior as *mere* power, Nietzsche, in a sense, refuses to think through the meaning of what is revealed in eros.

However, while largely accepting Desmond's analysis, I venture that it might be more accurate not to say that eros cannot be described as pure lack, but to say that eros as pure lack cannot be all there is. The difference is this: we are told that eros is more than just lack; it is also the power of transcending. Yet this power is always described in terms of the plenitude of agape, so in a sense there is nothing more to eros than lack. The situation is simply that this erotic lack is not, and cannot be, all there is in being or in mind.

If we remember again the Platonic myth of the *Symposium* in which eros is the child of *Poros* and *Penia*, we find something similar. The point for Plato was that revealed in eros is lack and also a presentiment of the Good. This idea of the double nature of eros seems to me to be echoed by the dual notions of eros and agape in the thought of William Desmond. These two accounts are similar, I say, rather than the same, and the analogy is not entirely satisfactory for reasons we shall see shortly. The point for both Plato and Desmond, though, seems to be that eros as pure lack cannot constitute an account of the whole. Nor is eros in these terms adequate to what there is. Plato was aware of this from the time of the *Meno*, in which dialogue Socrates is challenged to justify his claim to ignorance. If ignorance is total, says Meno, one could neither look for truth nor recognize it when one found it. This argument is telling, and through it Plato suggests that Socratic ignorance is not total. It is not a mere pretence either, however. There is certainly lack, but ignorance is also marked by an openness to a truth beyond the closed forgetfulness of error. Plato accounts for the 'more beyond lack' here, through the rather fanciful theory of *anamnesis* with regard to mind, and the world of the Forms and the Good with regard to being. In the later dialogues, the Good is the source that fuels the lack of eros, and drives it out of itself. As such, it can be described as god-given madness or intoxication. In William Desmond's work, this role is filled by the notion of the agape of being as what is prior to, and more than, erotic lack.

Insofar as we are empowered as, or given to be, erotic from this anterior agapeic source, it is natural that the human condition be described as one of perpetual striving. Yet we must also, according to Desmond, remain vigilant to the source of this power of transcending in its otherness. To live and think in accordance with this insight is the meaning of faithfulness and the way of truth. The exercise of power is inseparable from the attempt to do justice to the meaning of our own being and being in general. Yet, insofar as this power is given from an agapeic source, it is not self-justifying as it was with Nietzsche. For Nietzsche too, power has an external source, but this was described simply as the monster of energy. In its undifferentiated form, power can only be subordinated to greater power, and so the agonistic becomes Nietzsche's symbol of justice *par excellence*.

For Desmond, by contrast, only the Good is justified (EB, 458), so that power as gift of the agapeic origin is justified only insofar as it essays to do justice to this as the truth of what there is. In other words, power is subordinate to goodness.

Power must be restrained in the face of goodness as other, since the attempt to subordinate what is finally other is the work of injustice. This means that the work of eros is not final. The claim that it is belies, not only the source out of which erotic strength is derived, but also the meaning of eros itself.

However, to return to the analogy between the thought of Plato and William Desmond, I said that this analogy worked only up to a point. At what point does the analogy break down? After all, Plato describes eros as constituted both by lack and by a presentiment of the Good. Furthermore, the Good is the source beyond being, which gives being to be. It is transcendent to the extent that a final, self-completed closure of eros with itself is ruled out. This sounds very close to Desmond's notion of agape. And yet these notions are significantly different.[21] While eros entails a presentiment of the Good, it is the case that, for Plato, the Good is always profoundly absent. Thus there is always a tendency in Plato to place undue weight on the lack of eros. The consequence of this is that the fullness or power of eros is dangerous indeed. It is the dark force in the mind that can be as destructive as it can be enlightening. In the *Symposium*, eros is to a great extent given free rein, but the consequences of this are as bad as they are good.[22] In the *Republic*, eros is present but it must be kept under lock and key for fear of its tyrannical predilections. It is probably in the *Phaedrus* that we find Plato's most balanced treatment of the subject, but even here the struggle to bring eros to heel is immense. It is a divine madness, yes, but it is also the case that it must be tied to the logos of philosophy if its destructive inclinations are to be held in check. In the absence of philosophy, eros will of necessity descend into the rage of an Alcibiades, or, indeed, a Nietzsche. This is why, for Plato, only the philosopher can live the eudaemonic life, since only the philosopher can hope to turn the presentiment of the good in eros into a genuine relation of the soul with the good. Anything other than philosophy is descent.

If for Plato eros involves a presentiment of the absent good, for Desmond the agapeic is not only presentiment but also presence of the good at work in being. This undercuts neither the striving of eros nor its tendency towards tyranny. It is still ambivalent. The difference in the two accounts is that Desmond suggests the possibility of a power of transcending that is open to or for other being, conceived as good. One of the implications of this is that it allows for ways other than philosophy of saying the good; hence his stress on the others of philosophy as ways of articulating the presence of the good. Plato had not subordinated these other ways in the way that, for example, Hegel does, but he subordinates them all the same. It is finally only philosophy that has access to the Good.

The notion of agape as it appears in William Desmond's thought, however, is an attempt to be affirmative of the incarnate good beyond dialectical closure. It is this insight to which metaphysics calls us to be faithful. This is a most difficult path to think and to tread since it claims a relationality within being which resists a final articulation. Insofar as we are erotic beings, this metaxological way challenges us to avoid sliding into Hegelian or Nietzschean responses, the one claiming a final, self-mediated articulation, the other denying the possibility of articulation at all.

This is the challenge to do justice and, as Desmond presents it, it is a humbling challenge, since it is one in which determinations and articulations of being are eminently possible without ever finally issuing in mastery. Thus power is checked at the limits, and a new openness, patience, is called for.

In a certain sense, justice and goodness are inseparable, in that justice is this willingness to care for the good beyond my good. This calls for an almost superhuman vigilance, since the barriers between justice and its opposites are paper-thin, and can be breached, as it were, while we are not looking. In sum, the metaxological asks us to be mindful of the origin, so that what is sought is attentiveness to what is revealed in eros. If we are to follow Desmond in calling this the agapeic, it proves a difficult notion to think. But, if this is so, it is probably because, as pre-eminently present, it is also the easiest of things to take for granted.

Notes

1   Cf., for example, Aristotle's separation of the sciences in *Metaphysics*, E 1.
2   Of course, I acknowledge that there is far more to Aristotle than this. To describe his thought merely in terms of opposition to Plato is to do him a great disservice.
3   Aristotle, *Metaphysics*, A 980a 1 ff., trans. Hugh Lawson-Tancred, London: Penguin, 1998.
4   I use the word 'mindfulness' following Desmond, as it has wider connotations than merely cognition or scientific thinking or the like.
5   Plato, *Symposium*, 203b ff. The translation used here is that of Christopher Gill, Harmondsworth: Penguin, 1999.
6   As a piece of anti-Platonism, this contrasts strongly with Diotima's correction of Socrates in the *Symposium*, where she claims that it is the object desired and not desire itself that is the proper object of love (204c). My claim is that this Nietzschean reversal has a highly significant effect on the meaning of otherness in his thought.
7   Friedrich Nietzsche, *Will To Power*, trans. Walter Kaufman and R.J. Hollingdale, New York: Random House, 1968, p.550.
8   I am sensitive here to the fact that I run the risk of doing an injustice to these anti-metaphysical thinkers by reinterpreting their thought through the lens of metaphysics. However I believe this to be justified insofar as they lack the resources in their own thought to prohibit such an approach.
9   Nietzsche, *Beyond Good and Evil*, trans. M. Faber, Oxford: OUP, 1997, p.69: 'what is done out of love always takes place beyond good and evil'. We are starting to get a sense of what Nietzsche means by goodness, love and justice. With power as the basis of the 'transvaluation of values', it seems difficult to avoid the transmutation of love into its opposite.
10 Again, I must be careful here, since Nietzsche is an opponent of the notion of truth construed in a traditional (or, in his mind, Kantian) sense. Nevertheless it seems to me that alongside his appeal to good beyond good and evil operates an appeal to truth beyond truth and falsity. Therefore the claim is justified.
11 Nietzsche, *The Genealogy of Morality*, ed. K. Ansell-Pearson, Cambridge: CUP, 1994, p.94.
12 Ibid., p.95.
13 Ibid., p.97.

14   Ibid., p.98. Nietzsche claims that the 'ascetic priest', because of his weakness, must not only overcome health but also must guard 'against the envy of health'.

15   Nietzsche, *The Birth of Tragedy*, R. Geuss and R. Speirs, eds, Cambridge: CUP, 1999, p.19. In this passage, Nietzsche says that self-destruction affords a 'mystical sense of Oneness'.

16   *Beyond Good and Evil*, p.154. In fact, Nietzsche claims that the powerful, noble man is the only one who knows anything of reverence.

17   *The Genealogy of Morality*, p.93.

18   I am thinking here of, for example, Plato's classic definition of justice in *Republic* I as 'giving to each according to his due'. The point here is to think of philosophy as the desire to give to being according to *its* due; that is, the attempt to be mindful of being according to its worth.

19   An example might be the claim of John Rawls that the meaning of justice can be discerned through the abstraction of lived experience.

20   According to Desmond, the origin is not *in*determinate but *over*determined.

21   The noun 'agape' never appears in the Platonic corpus. The verb *agapan* appears eighty-three times, but never with any significant strength of meaning.

22   Note that, at 205d, Diotima describes eros as a 'powerful and treacherous love'.

Chapter 12

Plurivocal Eros: A Metaxological Reading of Plato's *Symposium*

Duston Moore

Metaxology and the *Symposium*

William Desmond seeks to explore a type of relating that is distinct from univocal one-dimensionality, deconstructive equivocities and dialectical mediation. He calls it metaxological mindfulness or metaxological intermediation. This is a mindfulness of the porosity of ways of being and the over-determined original. It is a sensitivity to different ways of being: the intimate middle point.

Mataxological mindfulness inculcates a sensitivity to the plurivosity of being. Eschewing the unity of either simple univocity or dialectics while skirting the madness of radical equivocities, metaxological mindfulness genuinely listens to the voices of others. The metaxological is a double mediation irreducible to either self or other. Philosophy must counter its tendency to reformulate the voices of others in its own terms. Stamina is necessary to avoid mediating the others of philosophy and allow the voicing of irreducibly unique ways of being.

It is my contention that readings of Plato's *Symposium* have, with notable exceptions, suffered from a closed dialectical reading wherein all the various voices are understood through the mediation of the speech of Socrates. This is not listening to the voices of the others. Such readings of the *Symposium* reduce this masterpiece of many voices to an overarching conceptual philosophical monologue. The unique perspectives of a physician, two playwrights, a politician and others are either ignored or mediated through Socrates' words.

Taking what Desmond has said about metaxological mindfulness, I have undertaken to read the *Symposium* with an ear, and an appreciation, for each individual voice. Because of space constraints, this essay presents six of the speeches in hasty caricature. Socrates' speech is ignored. This is not because it is unimportant or uninteresting. Rather it is because it is my intention to present the other six speeches, *on their own terms*.

Heroic Death

With a brief reference to Parmenides and a somewhat edited account of a popular genesis story, Phaedrus introduces the equivocal nature of eros into the night's programme. Almost all of the speakers directly criticize Phaedrus' beginning.

However the subsequent speakers deal with topics Phaedrus has introduced. He opens a space for the others to disagree and voice their own opinions.

Eros, for Phaedrus, is the principle 'which ought to guide the whole of life' (Hamilton, 178, c–d).[1] This is a description of the function of eros as distinct from Eros himself. The greatest blessing that a young man can receive is to have a virtuous lover. The young man (the beloved), striving for virtue and nobility, will find that there is something more motivational about an erotic relationship than family ties, public office or wealth. 'I mean the principle which inspires shame at what is disgraceful and ambition for what is noble; without these feelings neither a state nor an individual can accomplish anything great or fine' (ibid., d). Without eros, there would be no sense of shame or virtue and, without this, there would be no noble deeds. Phaedrus is associating eros with the cultivation of noble virtue: a nobility inspired when the beloved is seen, and sees himself, in the eyes of the lover, whose opinion means more to the beloved than life itself.

Phaedrus gives some details about three sets of lovers and their beloveds. In the first example, it is a female lover who willingly gives herself, body and soul, for her husband. Alcestis was the only woman who was willing to die to protect her beloved husband. The second example describes an erotic failure. Orpheus schemes to retrieve his beloved wife from Hades. But this lover loved himself too much, and was disappointed. Not all lovers allow themselves to be so fully possessed by the god as to empty themselves for their beloveds. The third example has a certain priority for Phaedrus. The story involves two famous lovers, Achilles and Patroclus. This time, there is no question of the worthiness of the lover; Patroclus is beyond reproach and possessed completely by love in his devotion to Achilles. This third example circles around the actions of Achilles, the beloved.

Of the three examples of eros, two are successful (one somehow more successful than the other) and one fails. From Phaedrus' examples of the relationship between the lover and the beloved, we can draw the deceitfully simple conclusion that the roles of lover and the beloved are distinct.

Eros brings blessings to the beloved. To have a virtuous older lover is the best that a young man can hope for. The lover is possessed by eros; he may not even know exactly what it is that he desires, only that he needs something. The question for Phaedrus, however, is how eros lures the beloved, given that the beloved is not possessed.

Virtue, good behaviour and courageous deeds are the principles necessary for the lover to sustain the relationship. The lover is both inspiration and example. There is a pedagogical function in the erotic. The beloved can seek to better himself by looking to his lover while the lover, processed by eros, seeks to reconcile something of himself with the object of his desire. For Phaedrus, this seems to mean the suicide of the self for the beloved other. Such suicide is not the same as seeking to better oneself.

Eros possesses the lovers, and any selfishness, indeed any thought of self, leads to an irreconcilable phantasm, as Orpheus found out. The beloved, however, can weigh his options. Achilles employs a certain calculus of fame. He could have left

Troy to return to his homeland. For the beloved, eros is not the final authority, but a guiding principle. Since the beloved is not possessed, he can judge his options and be selective. Or else he can play hard to get and reject his lover's advances out of hand. Accordingly, the beloved is also free to fail to learn anything at all.

It is the lover who gives, while the beloved receives. When Achilles looks to Patroclus, he sees how he, Achilles, ought to act. The gaze of the lover reflects an idealization of the beloved. Eros plays upon a doubling over of the self in a moment of reflection. The lover gives the beloved the possibility of the beloved seeing himself as others would.

Death is Phaedrus' last word about eros. Both the lovers and the beloveds were erotically possessed or inspired to their deaths. The citizens of Athens, like lovers and their beloveds, ought to be united by the lure of eros for the noble and heroic. From the individual citizens of the city, to the whole of society and all groups of men, eros brings out the best and most noble. Hence it is eros that draws all men into a society of mutual affection and respect that is the necessary condition for the existence of the city. Phaedrus claims that an army of lovers of any one city could defeat the whole world. Fear of shame would ensure that all the soldiers acted with the greatest of courage. They may be marching off to certain death, but eros is 'breathing might' into the lover and the beloved; the death of either only intensifies this divine energy.

Prudent Investments

Pausanias' speech is an attempt to direct erotic energies away from the common state of immediate gratification towards a heavenly relationship. The tools he uses in regulating the investment of erotic energy are laws; if one can speak about erotics, one can also control them.

Erotic deeds are themselves neither good nor bad; it is how one loves that bears with it the value of such love: 'It is in the nature of every action to be, in itself, neither right nor wrong ... the outcome depends on the doing, on how each of them is done' (Waterfield, 180e–181a). Pausanias therefore makes a distinction between Common Eros and Heavenly Eros.

As the distinction implies, Common Eros is an unworthy counterpart for Heavenly Eros. Common Eros is the most widespread instance of either aspect of eros. This common erotic is neither spiritual nor permanent. Pausanias dismisses the lure of women as being base, common and undesirable. The same criticism is made of common erotics inspired by immature boys. This desire is without thought, effort or limit. Common Eros runs forth in all directions, from lover to lover, from object to object, from male to female. There is no commitment; there is no focus or goal above the immediate pressure for physical satisfaction. Heavenly Eros 'springs entirely from the male, [and is] far older and consequently free from wantonness' (Hamilton, 181c). Heavenly Eros is consistent because it is both mature and male. Common Eros is inconsistent because of its femininity, or immature character. Common Eros, because it is common, has a certain pre-eminence, insofar as the laws of the city are concerned. The laws of the city recognize that all men are moved by erotic physical desires, and they encourage the relationship between the lover and the beloved to transform what is common, and to invest this energy in a higher, more noble, loving relationship. It is the responsibility of the beloved (empowered by the laws and traditions of the city) to discern the noble or base qualities of his prospective lover. Correspondingly, it is the task of the lover to attempt to love his beloved in an appropriate fashion.

Athenian law is potentially just as permissive as the laws of Sparta, but with an important addition. The Athenian tradition requires that the beloved be thoughtful; that he think independently of his lover; and above all that the eventual gratification of the lover be delayed as long as necessary. It is only the vulgar and unworthy lover who loves only the body of the beloved, and the pleasures it promises. The worthy lover desires more than immediate physical intimacy with the beloved. The laws and traditions of Athens encourage and reward the growth of a heavenly relationship between the lover and the beloved. The primary legal onus of responsibility lies with the beloved, not the lover. The lover must do everything in his power to attract the beloved's attention and affection, and the law of the city protects him from ridicule. The role of the beloved is threefold. Firstly, the beloved must encourage the lover, trying to see him for what he truly is. Secondly, the noble bearing of the beloved will force the lover to act in a noble manner. The beloved's noble resistance to physical satisfaction will force the lover to move beyond the desire for immediate release towards a higher form of eros. Thirdly, the beloved should take the opportunity to learn from his lover. This is, for Pausanias, the vital movement, the transformation as it were, of eros: from Common to Heavenly. While the law treats all *erotes* as common, base and ignoble, it is the purpose of the laws and traditions to assist in the cultivation of Heavenly Eros. It is the articulating power of the law, combined with the consensus brought about by the authority of speech, which directs this longing away from the body towards the soul.

It has been said that it is inexplicable that anyone should respond to desire. The lover is initially nothing more than desire. But in the eyes of the beloved he becomes something more. Different lovers will have different things to offer the beloved. Some lovers will have wealth, others political power. For Pausanias, the difference between Common and Heavenly Eros may be a matter of postponing erotic release. A common beloved may be motivated by wealth or power, while the aim of heavenly erotics is precisely to delay and avoid erotic release.

This delay is far more than foreplay. The energy generated through this suspension of erotic release flows primarily from the lover to the beloved. The longer the beloved refuses to yield, the greater the intensity of the lover's erotic investment. The lover invests time and energy in the relationship while the beloved, simultaneously fending off and leading on the lover, grows in wisdom and virtue. The benefits for the beloved are clear, and help explain why the beloved would show any interest in the lover in the first place. It is not the naked desire of common erotics to which the beloved responds. Rather the beloved is carried beyond himself towards an idealized vision of his own possibilities, known only to the lover.

Why does the lover even bother? Pausanias does not speak about the dividends of such heavenly investments; perhaps he considers the results to be so plainly visible to all the guests that there is no need to mention the obvious. Agathon, Pausanias' own beloved, is both 'spiritually and physically' well developed. No doubt Pausanias feels responsible for Agathon and shares in his accomplishments. It certainly does not hurt that Agathon is strikingly handsome as well. For Pausanias, the result of heavenly erotics is so clear that he does not even need to refer to Agathon by name. The assets accumulated through Heavenly Eros, the return on his erotic investments, are present for all to see, and sitting beside Socrates.

Healthy Balance

Eros is, for Eryximachus, not only a relation between a lover and a beloved, but also a cosmic force. Such abstraction of the idea of eros allows Eryximachus to ignore any recalcitrant erotic equivocities. Any relation outside his totality is dismissible as complications of a particular case. It is enough that Eryximachus can cure the hiccups most of the time.

Eryximachus (as his name suggests) likes to control things. The evening's events started with Eryximachus proposing that they should control the amount they drink, dismiss the flute-girl, and entertain themselves in serious and sober conversation. It was also Eryximachus who suggested that the topic of their conversation be about the god Eros. He even manages to hold things together in the aftermath of Alcibiades' entrance.

Eryximachus assumes that the power to control the movement of bodies, the skill of a craftsman, is coextensive with the widening of the erotic domains. Eryximachus expands the investigation of erotics beyond the trials and triumphs between boyfriends. No longer is eros simply about the possessed lover or the inspired and calculating beloved. The whole of reality is suddenly endued with the potential of the erotic. This sudden expansion of the domain of Eros, like the authority of Eryximachus' tone, comes from the nature of *techne*. There are no parts outside of the whole, and it is the technician alone who can grasp the whole.

Eryximachus does not speculate as to the origins of the god Eros; perhaps such theological speculations are not appropriate to a man of science. Yet, like the speakers before him, Eryximachus believes that Eros is a divinity second to none. Eryximachus sees the hand of Eros in almost every aspect of reality; the rule of Eros applies not only to the love between humans. From the lives of animals, the growth of plants, through the vast range of human endeavours and disciplines, up to the cycle of seasons and the celestial motions, the rule of erotics embraces all there is. Concurrent with this enlargement of Eros's domain, the scope and application of technical knowledge and procedures are simultaneously enlarged and deepened. If medicine is knowledge of eros, and Eros is the all-encompassing deity, it follows that medicine is the most widely applicable human technique capable of providing knowledge of reality.

The unity of eros is evident in music, wherein the discordant elements participate within a harmonious unity. When the physician applies the same principle to the body as the composer does to music, the discordant elements do not disappear. Rather a balance between the opposites is established. In the human body, this balance is synonymous with health. The irreducible elements, held in balance in health, and out of balance in sickness, lead Eryximachus to make a distinction between noble and vulgar erotics. For Eryximachus, the health of the body demands a balance of both. As with eating and drinking, there can be too much of one thing or another.

Such a radical expansion of the domain of Eros comes at a price. While Eryximachus moves through the various technical disciplines that deal with erotics, the figure of the god fades as the scope of the human technical knowledge expands. By the end of his speech, Eryximachus has so inflated the rule of erotics that the god himself is in danger of being unrecognizably dispersed. This seems to be the unavoidable consequence of expanding the technical knowledge of erotics, that Eros himself should slip further away. The danger of Eros dissolving into everything and nothing does not concern Eryximachus. The point of any craft is to gain knowledge of fundamental patterns, as well as the ability to manipulate these patterns. Eryximachus' idea of eros involves more than the successful identification of the primary pattern of eros. Once this pattern is known, the physician seeks to identify ever more general repetitions of the primary patterns.

This multiplication of the erotic is not a baseless hypothesis forced upon the cosmos by a technical control freak. The expansion of the erotic moves through a successive series of domains: each encompassing and affirming the one which precedes it. As the technique is applied along the series of ever more expansive erotic domains, the double criterion which Eryximachus ascribes to eros, that of health and balance, is repeatedly asserted. Health and balance are, for Eryximachus, one and the same. Both qualities are derived from, or dependent upon, the most primordial pattern of existence, that of a concordance of opposites expressed as an attunement.

'The business that we call medicine ... is, in a word, the knowledge of the principles of love at work in the body in regard to repletion and evacuation' (Hamilton, 186c). The general knowledge of eros concerns the movements of filling and emptying. The more specific craft of medicine concerns the same erotic movements of emptying and filling, but as applied to the human body. Thus the power over eros comes from discovering the technique of affecting the balance between seemingly contradictory movements and elements. These sometimes hostile and often opposite elements, full and empty, hot and cold, wet and dry, and the like, are always in danger of becoming lopsided. For the human body, an exaggeration of one side of the pair results in illness. Health is to be found in striking a balance between the two.

Desire for Unity

For Aristophanes, human life is a condition of perpetual desire to obtain an unobtainable objective; there is no cure for eros, for eros is not the cause of desire. The cause is Zeus, whose name stands for those unquestionable forces who or which have made humans the way they are. Eros is simply 'the name for the desire and pursuit of the whole'. He is not the cause of humans' lack of wholeness.

That necessity is inextricably intertwined with eros is a major point of Aristophanes' speech. By explicitly linking parts of the human body with the workings of eros, Aristophanes hopes to stop any talk about eros overcoming the power of necessity. Aristophanes places the locus of the erotic within the body.

The various erotic desires of humans trace their origins back to the initial split of the egg-men. The wholeness, unity and self-sufficiency of the egg-men were split apart. In the process, their immense strength was transformed into a longing for unity of equal intensity. It is in this way that eros enters the world. For eros is nothing more than the desire of humans to recapture, if only for an instant, the primordial unity of the proto-humans from an age long since forgotten. 'It is from this distant epoch, then, that we may date the innate love which human beings feel for one another, the love which restores us to our ancient state by attempting to unite two beings into one and heal the wounds which humanity suffered' (Hamilton, 191d). Thus eros is the reminder of an initial split which has not yet completely healed. This leaves humans as diseased (love-sick) creatures, condemned forever to search for the primordial erotic whole from whence they came. Humans are all sick, erotically charged creatures bearing physical marks (the navel) of their incomplete state.

Aristophanes makes a point that the previous speakers dealt with, yet did not make explicit: the necessity of it all. For Aristophanes, humans have no option but to be erotic creatures. Humans are always and already divided from themselves, and divided from each other. The human condition is, in its essence, incomplete. Thus the search for the perfect partner is the point of departure for these erotic creatures. The work of Eros is to ease the pain of humans' incomplete nature, as best he can.

The promise of eros as a 'return to our original condition' is, in fact, the eroticizing of all that is other to the scarred and fragmented self. The self's necessity of desire is 'canalized' in and through an other or others via the lure of the erotic. Phaedrus noted the energy of eros, Pausanius attempted to transform it, while Eryximachus' balance moderated the discharge of erotic energies. Aristophanes goes a step further. Not only can the necessary discharge of erotic energy be balanced; it can also be canalized or directed. The brute desire of half an egg-man for a singular unity is refracted into a rainbow of erotic promises and lures.

At the same time that eros is opening a space between the self and its others, in no way is the self divested of the erotic. The necessarily lacking human condition anchors the erotic to the very flesh of the self. Aristophanes' account of the 'fall' of the egg-men highlights this aspect of erotic dialectics: the recalcitrance of corporality. By moving the genitals, Zeus provided an outlet for a desire: a desire which, left uncanalized, would kill the creature.

It is the very business or work of life, that of interpersonal relations, which grows out of humans' intrapersonal inability to become whole. This eroticized space that expands out of the fragmented self need not remain affectionate towards simply one object. The object of affection can be suspended and become an undefined variable. In working, humans assign a value to this variable, and canalize the energy of desire. This dialectic of work finds its most noble expression in the achievements of the city. But it is also the city that bears witness to the surd of corporeality's most perverted expressions. No matter how grand the city, at the core of every human there remains an indissoluble necessity. Zeus has assigned the genitals as a default value. But even the erotic function of the genitals is but a substitution for the original object of desire: the state of being whole.

It is more than simple physical pleasure that keeps the lover and the beloved together. Aristophanes does not reject the carnal pleasures out of hand; sexual satisfaction is certainly one element that underlies any relationship. But there is something more than physical gratification. 'It's clear that each of them has some wish in his mind that he can't articulate, instead, like an oracle, he half-grasps what he wants and obscurely hints at it' (Gill, 192c–d). For some, physical pleasure will be the determining factor in their relationships, while, for others, more thoughtful considerations may influence the lover's relationship with the beloved. Whatever the case, they will never be one again.

Empty Beauty

Agathon is a poet, and demands a poet's licence of his audience. If you believe him, the previous speakers were incapable of describing Eros. Agathon makes an ambitious claim; he is going to revise the received theology. Only a poet can attempt such a task: not just any poet, but only the poet who fancies himself on a par with Homer. Being on a par with Homer has more to do with being memorable than with being philosophically convincing. Agathon's speech does not pretend to be philosophically penetrating; he wants to be evocative and convince through images rather than ideas.

Judging by the response that his speech received, Agathon did not misjudge his audience. None of the audience except Socrates was worried about the truth of what Agathon had said; they thought it sounded nice and struck a chord. Even though he explicitly contradicts the four previous speakers on several important points, his speech is greeted with great approval. No-one there expected Agathon to do anything less. Performers will play to their audiences; Agathon said so to Socrates. That one may find it hard to reconcile the soft, supple form of Eros with the sense of justice necessary for governance is beside the point. Agathon makes it all sound so beautiful. Certainly it may be that Agathon's account cannot be reconciled with a philosophical analysis. But when have humans ever expected artistic achievements to be reconciled with anything beyond themselves?

The quarrel between philosophy and poetry is a continuing story. In the case of Agathon's speech, there can be no disagreement over the fact that he is addressing the same topic as the other speakers. Even Socrates, the most prominent philosopher in attendance, admits that Agathon started off well enough by trying to describe Eros himself, not just his functions. Even though poet and philosopher seem to agree, not only about the subject but also about the approach to be taken, there is a profound gap between Agathon's and Socrates' account of eros and erotics.

Despite the differences between philosophical and poetic methodology, it would be inaccurate to say that Agathon's account is incoherent. Agathon is not a master of philosophical dialectics; he is a poet. It is wrong to see the philosophic emptiness of Agathon's speech as a poverty of content. Agathon may be guilty of 'wretched logic', but this is to judge him as something other than he is. His speech is not directed by a single underlying methodological concern. Agathon lets the muses take him where they will, and the power of his speech is not reflected in his consistency, but rather in his ability to impress his audience.

It is impossible to discuss philosophically an overarching erotic dialectic in Agathon's speech, beyond saying that the erotic words of the poet can be a more powerful lure than dry philosophical dialectics. Nonetheless Agathon does not shy away from making explicit statements about the nature of eros. By far the most important claim that Agathon makes is that the link between Necessity and Eros must be severed. Hesiod and Parmenides got this wrong, and Aristophanes makes the same mistake. There is a difference between Eros and Necessity; one ought not to associate the two. Necessity is brutal, hard and fateful. Eros is soft, supple and irresistible. The two are very different. Yet it is easy to see how Hesiod, Parmenides, Aristophanes and the rest got it all confused. From the outside looking in, the role of necessity and the lure of Eros seem much the same. There are no soft options when one is confronted with the hard reality of necessity; one can only go where necessity pushes. So too there is nothing else one can do once Eros has settled in one's heart but follow Eros wherever he leads. Agathon's 'argument thus suffers from an internal contradiction. He believes that Eros can rule the whole by persuasion, but the capacity to persuade is based upon the Necessity that the rule ostensibly overcomes. And the rule is over the whole, but half the kingdom is left to its own devices'.[2] In this, Rosen is correct, but it is hard to imagine that Agathon would care what philosophers think about the internal consistency of his argument. For it may be that Agathon would not find anything very erotic in Rosen's charge of philosophical inconsistency.

Agathon's Eros shakes off the sticky surd of eros through a few well-chosen words: 'Peace among humankind and windless calm at sea, rest for the winds, and sleep for those distressed' (Gill, 197c). There is little agreement among scholars as to what Agathon means, except that whatever he is saying seems to be a bit racy. One analyst of the *Symposium* suggested that this part of Agathon's speech is a joke; that *pono*, *phobo*, *logo* are juxtaposed in a ridiculous way.[3] Perhaps, with Socratic hindsight, line 197e seems funny. Perhaps, to those who heard it on that night in the year 416 BC, it sounded beautiful. Anyway the audience seems to know what Agathon is talking about, even if he has no idea. This is precisely where poets and many philosophers part ways. Philosophers want to be understood as well as to understand. The poets are happy being appreciated. There may have been as many interpretations of what Agathon said as there were people in the room. The important thing is that everyone feels moved by the power of the poet's words; disagreement as to what he meant, although good for the poet's reputation, is a secondary concern.

Carnal Frustrations

Alcibiades' entrance is dramatic to say the least. The orderly, measured pace of the evening is thrown into disarray; Dionysus has entered the building.

Alcibiades' speech is as unique as his entrance. He does not intend to speak about eros as the previous speakers have done. Rather he tells the truth about Socrates, the object of his own erotic attachment. This move from encomium to *epainos* focuses the erotic domain into the skin of one particular object: Socrates. 'It's the [*Symposium*'s] only speech that claims to tell "the truth" in the story of a consuming passion, both sexual and intellectual, for a particular individual.'[4]

Eros is very personal. That is, Eros is only present in particular and special objects. At five points in his speech, Alcibiades turns to Socrates and challenges him to deny the truth of what was just said. No other speaker was so personal about his speech. But Alcibiades is not intimate with the other members of his audience; it is only Socrates to whom he directs his attention. Alcibiades has no time for abstractions (perhaps this is part of his problem); when he talks about eros, it is in relation to one particular body. 'Certain truths about human experience must be learned by living them in their particularity. Nor can this particularity be grasped solely by thought "itself by itself"; it must be apprehended through the cognitive activity of imagination, emotions, even appetitive feelings.'[5]

The refractory erotics which Alcibiades incarnates are an embarrassment, not just to Socrates but also to the whole tradition that has sought total mediation. Alcibiades is a remainder: a surd. Socrates, for all his training and initiation by Diotima, cannot fully mediate all aspects of Eros. Human corporeality can never be fully shaken off, except by shuffling off this mortal coil.

The corporeality of the relationship between Alcibiades and Socrates is stressed from the very moment that Alcibiades inadvertently sits down beside Socrates. Agathon and Socrates had been sitting beside one another. Only when Agathon invites Alcibiades to join them does Alcibiades notice Socrates. 'Good God, what have we here? Socrates? Lying there in wait for me again? How like you to make a sudden appearance just when I least expect to find you! What are you doing here? And why have you taken this place? You ought to be next to Aristophanes or some other actual or would-be buffoon, and instead you've managed to get yourself next to the handsomest person in the room' (Hamilton, 213b–c). Judging from his emotional reaction, Alcibiades is still greatly affected by Socrates' company. Socrates too seems a little unbalanced by Alcibiades' surprise appearance: 'Be ready to protect me, Agathon, for I find that the love of this fellow has become no small burden. From the moment when I first fell in love with him I haven't been able to exchange a glance or a word with a single good-looking person without his falling into a passion of jealousy and envy, which makes him behave outrageously and abuse me and practically lay violent hands on me. See to it that he doesn't commit some excess even here, or if he attempts to do anything violent protect me; I am really quite scared by his mad behaviour and the intensity of his affection' (ibid., c–d).

Socrates' eros for this man is no trifling affair. Both Socrates and Alcibiades are mentally and physically flustered by one another's company. This is an important element of the relationship between lover and beloved: something happens when they are in close physical proximity. The simple physical presence of Alcibiades together with Socrates is enough to excite each of them. There is nothing reflected about what happens; their response to one another is both immediate and uncontrollable. Moreover, whatever the history between them, nothing has broken, or even loosened, the erotic energy that binds them.

Another related facet of eros, demonstrated by Alcibiades, demands that the reader be familiar with events following the evening of the *Symposium*. Eros can fail. Despite being bitten by the erotic lure of philosophy, and despite being tutored by Socrates, Alcibiades fails to realize any of the promise that was so evident, not only to Socrates but to the whole of Athens. The most obvious failure, from Alcibiades' perspective, was his failure to bed Socrates. But there is a further failure, the failure of Alcibiades himself. Alcibiades' frustration and his inability to deal with his erotic entanglements went further than the comic, drunken escapades of the *Symposium*. The castration of the herms and profaning of the Mysteries were only the beginning. In the end, Alcibiades betrayed Athens to Sparta, and contributed directly to the end of the Athenian golden age; all because he could not find a way to express, transform, balance, canalize or mediate the erotic energies that boiled away inside him. Such a man of spectacular promise was an equally spectacular failure.

Was the failure all Alcibiades' doing, or was Socrates partly to blame as well? It is my contention that Alcibiades, both by his presence and in his speech, represents a failure common to all the previous speakers, including Diotima. Hence the failure, as it relates to Alcibiades, is primarily Socrates'. Socrates' speech was philosophically provocative, as the history of philosophy has demonstrated. But assuming that Socrates practised what he preached, Alcibiades' story about his erotic relationship with Socrates casts some serious doubts on how we should appreciate Diotima's speech.

Diotima's teaching was about the move from the physical to something like the idea of beauty. From the corporeality of eros to the sublime transcendence of the beautiful, Diotima's ladder has a particular mediating element of self-restraint. Certainly this was part of Socrates' intention in his telling of Diotima's teaching. Had everything gone according to plan, Aristophanes would have been able to ask Socrates a question or two as he wished. We can imagine what would have followed: Aristophanes would have asked a question, Socrates would have responded with his own question, and shortly Aristophanes would have been reduced to saying things such as 'how right you are Socrates' or 'it seems it cannot be otherwise' or 'quite so'. But things did not go according to plan. More forceful than any argument that Aristophanes could muster, Alcibiades' entrance is a reminder that the physical body cannot be so easily dismissed. Indeed Alcibiades' entrance is most embarrassingly timed as far as Socrates is concerned. Socrates had just finished telling everyone about his belief in the mediation of the erotic from the physical towards absolute beauty, and who should enter but his lover and student, the very physical Alcibiades. Is that not just like the body bringing attention to itself at the most embarrassing and ill-timed of moments? (Recall Aristophanes' hiccup.) Instead of hearing what would have been a most interesting dialogue between Socrates and Aristophanes, everyone gets to see the great Socrates squirm with discomfort while his former student demonstrates, indeed incarnates, the limits of erotic mediation. 'Perhaps we had better pause to wonder at the ground of Diotima's ladder, rather than hurriedly scale it, and for heaven's sake not look down. Plato prevents our thoughtless ascent to a disembodied contemplation of perfect beauty by the violent plunge induced by Alcibiades and the revellers.'[6]

This, then, is the most important aspect of eros brought out by Alcibiades. There is a recalcitrant, irreducible, insoluble element to eros. Try as one might (and almost every speaker tries), the sticky recalcitrance of eros can never be fully mediated. There always remains a surd.

Community not Cacophony

While the plurivocal character of the above reading of the *Symposium* is clear, I shall conclude with several observations as to the metaxological dimension. There are two senses in which the *Symposium* can be read metaxologically. Or, more precisely phrased, there is a sense in which the *Symposium* can be read metaxologically, and another sense in which the *Symposium* is itself metaxological.

In terms of how the *Symposium* can be read metaxologically, the overdetermined between is a necessary mindfulness for an authentically plurivocal conversation. Only by thinking in and through the between of the various opinions can the reader appreciate the richness and subtlety of Plato's notion of eros. Each voice of the *Symposium*'s seven speakers presents an independent opinion of the nature of eros. It is tempting to synthesize these voices into an overarching theory of eros. Plato dares the reader to do so by having Socrates' speech touch on points addressed by the previous speakers. But eros is deceiving, and to follow this suggestion reduces the conversation to a Socratic monologue. Only by adopting metaxological mindfulness, which involves taking each speaker at their word, in their own terms, can one avoid the twin pitfalls of dialectical unity and unintelligible equivocity. For metaxological mindfulness recognizes each voice as independently intelligible yet meaningful; isolated yet within a wider community of meaning.

Indeed each voice is rich in suggestion in its own right. This illustrates the sense in which the *Symposium*, as a text, is metaxological. The text itself is an overdetermined origin of reflection, speculation and discussion. The long tradition of commentary upon the *Symposium* bears witness to the lure of the text. Finite human reason seems inadequate to discuss the text exhaustively. This inexhaustible source of speculation is not an indeterminate mystery tempting speculation; the text remains as it has always been. It is the richness of hints and details that act as an overdetermined origin for subsequent speculation. Yet, while the text offers more thoughts about eros than can be coordinated, the result is not equivocal unintelligibility. The *metaxu* of the *Symposium* creates a community of independent, yet related, meanings. Plato certainly has a favourite voice of the evening; Socrates remains his hero. After all, the other speakers have disappeared or fallen asleep, Socrates leaves Agathon's home, goes about his daily routine, and only falls asleep the following evening: a show of stamina few of us have attempted since our undergraduate years. Taken on their own terms, the voices other than that of Socrates have been, to varying degrees, convincing. And, in point of fact, Socrates had nothing of his own to say about eros. Yet the *Symposium* closes with an affirmation of philosophy in the person of Socrates. Apollodorus is forgotten and the drama ends definitively with Socrates.

This ending is a doubling of comedy and tragedy, failure and triumph. This astonishing drama is a real possibilizing power, in a manner more original than any possible reading or explanation of the text. The *Symposium* remains an inspiring source of creation; more can be thought about the *Symposium* than finite intellect can deal with. This suggests to me ultimate transcendence, as in excess of the immanent transcendences at play in the middle.

Notes

1   I have employed three translations of the *Symposium*. Citations will include the name of the translator and the Stephanus number. The translations of Plato's *Symposium* used are Gill, London: Penguin Books, 1999; Hamilton, London: Penguin Books, 1951; Waterfield, Oxford: OUP, 1998.
2   S. Rosen, *Plato's Symposium*, New Haven: Yale University Press, 1969, p.194.
3   J. Lacan, *Livre VIII Le Transfert*, Paris: Editions du Seuil, 1991, p.132.
4   M. Nussbaum (1979),'The Speech of Alcibiades: A Reading of Plato's *Symposium*', *Philosophy and Literature*, **3**, 134.
5   Ibid., pp.153–4.
6   D. Krell (1972), 'Socrates' Body', *Southern Journal of Philosophy*, **10**, 449.

VII
DESMOND AND GOD

Chapter 13

Maybe Not, Maybe:
William Desmond on God

Richard Kearney

It is an honour to engage once again with my friend, colleague, interlocutor and fellow-Corkman, William Desmond. In a recent piece in the *Irish Theological Quarterly* (**68**, 2003, 99–118),[1] Desmond offered a cogent and challenging account of my notion of divine *posse* as outlined in *The God Who May Be* (2001), a work, let me acknowledge at the outset, that is deeply indebted to Desmond's notion of *metaxu* and metaxology. Desmond's critique was entitled 'Maybe, maybe not: Richard Kearney and God'. His observations, as always, were robust, respectful and thought-provoking. They brought his own ontology of being into direct exchange with my eschatology of possible-being and, as such, set the stage for a veritable *disputatio* (in the best sense of that term!).

In this essay, I would like to respond to some of Desmond's more critical points and thereby endeavour to advance a step further in our continuing dialogue: a dialogue which both welcomes and acknowledges our differences, as well as our deep empathies and correspondences.

One of Desmond's most basic observations on my understanding of divine possibility – from the Greek *dunamis* and the Latin *posse* – is that there is too much eros involved and not enough agape. In other words, while Desmond agrees with me that any deity worthy of its name should be able to inspire, motivate and receive love, there are different *kinds* of loving, and some are more appropriate than others when it comes to God.

But before we get to the question of divine love, the real crux of the matter, let us first address Desmond's comments on divine possibility. Here Desmond argues that we need 'a stronger archeology of possibility to guard against some of the temptations of an eschatology of possibility' (p.108), the latter of which he identifies, quite correctly, with my position in *The God Who May Be*, and earlier still in *Poétique du Possible* (1984). His question here is quite simple and direct: what is it that makes possibility itself possible? What is the original creative possibilizing power that makes all things possible and actual? Is there something that comes before possibility and makes it possible in the first instance? Desmond suggests that there is, and that this something is nothing less than some kind of being. In this sense, Desmond resists the attempts of so many apophatic or postmodern theologians to think of a God without being or beyond being or before being. He stands by metaphysics, while appealing for a more subtle approach to the different kinds and modalities of being. Similarly, he resists the idea of a God of the future which, he believes, is necessarily privileged by the God who may be, for this would be to traduce the time-honoured sense of God as supratemporal and eternal. God cannot be reduced to either the past, present or future. He transcends (*huper*) all such historical determinations.

I would grant a certain validity to Desmond's objections here but would want, straight off, to point out that I speak of divine possibility in terms of an ontoeschatology, following Nicholas of Cusa's idea of *possest* (the converging of *posse* and *esse*). Secondly, I would respond that divine *dunamis* is indeed eternal when it comes to God *in se* (divinity in and of itself), but that when it comes to God *quoad nos* (divinity as it manifests itself to us through human, finite, experience) we can only speak about God, in all modesty, in the limited phenomenological terms of time and history. It is because there is no absolute access to the absolute that we speak of God symbolically, indirectly, hermeneutically, in terms of time and possibility. These are the poetic ideas or concepts that we put upon the divine in our faltering attempts to name and praise it.[2]

I will return to these two points again later, but I want to return briefly to Desmond's outline of six different senses of the possible before proceeding further. This delineation and declension of distinct notions of possibility marks a very significant and welcome contribution to the dialogue between us. I am immensely grateful to Desmond for this painstaking and perspicacious teasing out of the different denotations and connotations of the concept of the possible. Several of these meanings, I must confess, were frequently conflated in my own deliberations on the subject, from *Poétique du Possible* to *The God Who May Be*. The six main definitions offered by Desmond are the following: possibility with respect to (1) origin, (2) creation, (3) coming to be, (4) becoming, (5) self-becoming, and (6) gift beyond self-becoming. He concluded this parsing of the possible thus: 'We need more firm discrimination of the above different senses, to avoid reducing possibility to a too indeterminate and homogenous notion, in the process losing both the distinctiveness of finite possibility, as well as the difference of the divine' (p.113). I could not agree more with Desmond on this point. It is crucial to recognize, in the ultimate eschatological sense of the possible, 'a transcendence more ultimate than human transcendence' (ibid.).

In short, Desmond cautions against any tendency to subject the divine to an anthropological reduction, that is, to render the transcendence of God immanent in history and humanity, without remainder. I share this caution. But I also have some telling differences from Desmond, especially when it comes to the question of divine eros.

Acknowledging that he has no objection to the identification of God with eros 'in a suitably qualified metaphorical, even hyberbolic sense' (p.113), Desmond worries that my notion of divine eros risks ignoring, at times, such critical qualification. In face of this worry, Desmond suggests that we need to discriminate more between different loves just as we needed, above, to discriminate between different kinds of possibility. Central among such different kinds of love/eros he mentions 'the self-affirming, the erotic, the philial, the agapeic' (ibid.).

Again, I agree with this general note of caution but feel that Desmond does not adequately credit the full import of what I am trying to get at when I talk of eschatological eros or divine desire. Desmond goes on to invoke the tried and trusted distinction between (1) *agape* as a love which gives and overflows from a divine superfluity and gratuity, and (2) *eros* which is a striving towards fulfilment from deficiency, towards plenitude from lack, towards sufficiency from insufficiency. Such a distinction has indeed a weighty metaphysical pedigree going back to Plato's *Symposium* and reaching right down to the notion of eros in such modern thinkers as Hegel, Sartre and Lacan. But this seems to miss the basic intent of my distinction, in *The God Who May Be* and elsewhere, between ontological desire (which is just what Plato described, namely the movement from lack to fullness) and eschatological desire (which I define as just the opposite: the inverse move from the more towards the less).[3] Lévinas had already suggested such a reversal of the traditional definition of desire in speaking of divine desire, in *Totality and Infinity*, as an infinite gifting from God to humanity. And when Derrida, following Lévinas, speaks of a divine 'desire beyond desire' in *On the Name*, I think he has something similar in mind. As has Dionysius the Areopagite in *On the Divine Names* when he speaks of Christ as 'eros': a hyperbolic usage practised by other Oriental Fathers of the Church and certain mystics such as John of the Cross. So what I am suggesting when I speak of an eschatological desire which, as gift, goes beyond all forms of ontological desire, as lack, is not something unprecedented. Though it does go beyond the mainstream usage of the term eros in favour of a hermeneutical retrieval of certain neglected or marginalized thinkers. On the basis of this misreading of my notion of divine *desire beyond desire*, Desmond offers this critique:

> with an erotic God we tend to find this: a God that is not truly what it may be in the beginning, but has to become itself, fully realize what it might be, or may be, in a process of becoming or self-becoming, in which it is teleogolically, or eschatologically, more fully itself or complete at the end of the process. (p.114)

And he concludes: 'I think this kind of thinking runs a grave risk of producing counterfeit doubles of God, even if it gives to some the satisfaction of being needed by God' (ibid.).

Now there are a few clarifications I would like to make here. I believe that Desmond, the 'theorist' of discriminations *par excellence*, is here confusing a number of things. First, I suspect that he is confusing (a) the teleological or Hegelian notion of eros as a purely immanent struggle to totalize and fulfil itself in history with (b) the eschatological notion of divine eros as something which comes from before and beyond and after history, inviting humanity to respond to it in history and to bring about the promise of the kingdom in history: this confusion between immanent and transcendent modalities of eros would indeed, as Desmond rightly says, lead to counterfeit idols.[4]

This leads me to what I think is a second confusion: that between (a) divine eros 'in itself' (*per se*), and (b) divine eros 'for us' (*per alio*). If we ignore the divine desire beyond desire it does not cease to desire: to love, give, call, promise, invite. It simply fails to find a human respondent and that is its tragedy, its wound, its crucifixion, its rejection, its failure. It did not just happen on Calvary but happens every instant of every day. God can fail, because God is prepared the take the risk of love, which, like all genuine love, can never be an imposition but only an invitation. For example, if Mary of Nazareth did not have the freedom to say 'yes' or 'no' to divine desire, her impregnation would have been a violation of humanity rather than a salvation. No love, even divine love, can be assymetrical to the point of non-reciprocity, non-response, non-freedom. That is the risk involved in divine eros, a wager of freedom and gratuity which I do not believe is similarly honoured by the notion of divine agape.[5] Even if ignored and unheeded by every living human being, divine eros would remain eternally vigilant, attentive, open, appealing. And that is precisely what gives a sense of urgency and dynamism to God, conceived as eschatological desire and *posse*. It matters to God that God matters to us. And if it did not, then the narratives and testimonies of the Torah, Gospels and lives of the saints are a nonsense.

My own position on this is that divine eros is *in* itself (*per se*) radically infinite, eternal and transcendent; but if we humans refuse the call, remain deaf to the promise, and do not recognize that each time we give a cup of cold water to someone who is thirsting we are giving to Christ and fulfilling, in each such simple instance of giving, the promise of the eternal kingdom, then God can do nothing about it. God does not need us to be God in eternity, but to be God in history. And since we are historical, finite, temporal beings it is normal that we speak of our relation to the divine within the limits of phenomenological experience and hermeneutic understanding. Hence the appropriateness, in my view, of attempts to conceive of the divine gift of creation and salvation in terms of hermeneutic retrievals of terms like desire and possibility, terms which acknowledge that all our thinking must observe finite limits even when it is thinking about the infinite.

This is a lesson made plain by Kant in the *Critique of Pure Reason* and radicalized by contemporary philosophers like Heidegger, Ricoeur and Lévinas. For what all these thinkers share is a critique of the attempts made by speculative metaphysics or ontotheology to wish away our finite phenomenological limits in our presumption to think the infinite itself. All we can do is gesture – hermeneutically, poetically, hyperbolically – towards the infinite and eternal as it is in itself, in its otherness and transcendence, through the mediating lens of our humble human language.

I think Desmond would agree with much of what I am saying here; for example, he fully recognizes that my use of terms like 'divine eros' and 'possibility' is deeply hyperbolic. But in spite of this acknowledgment of my methodological strategies to speak about the unspeakable while respecting its unspeakability, I sense there is a certain impatience in Desmond about my turn towards poetics.[6] Is there not a lingering nostalgia for metaphysical speculation in Desmond's critique of my position? A feeling that greater attention to the absolute origin of being would give a firmer grounding and founding to my thinking about divine desire and possibility? A sense that what we need is a return to an 'agapeic origin ... in

excess of the erotic'? I suspect this is what lies behind his argument that 'A God
that has to become God, must first *be* God to become God, that which has to create
itself, must first be itself to create itself' (p.114). Here again Desmond is
interpreting eros as lack rather than surplus and defining being metaphysically
(relating to what is eternal, infinite, transcendent) rather than phenomenologically
(relating to what is historical, finite, experiential).[7]

This third confusion between the metaphysical and phenomenological
approaches to 'being' is, I suspect, what lies at the root of our disagreement. For
me being is always and only spoken of in a phenomenological sense, which is why
I speak of divine desire in terms of a God-beyond-being seeking to come into
being through the response of humans in history. That for me is the great drama
and mystery of incarnation: the fact that the eternal God calls out to be made flesh,
to enter into the horizons of human relation and response. Why? So that the
kingdom may not just be a kingdom in heaven but on earth. So that the God who
desires and creates and possibilizes (*qua posse*) may also be *ad esse, in esse, per
esse*.

This is what I mean when I speak of divine desire in terms of an 'ontoeschatology'. It is not a repudiation of being, as we find in certain Gnostic and
apophatic movements, but an embrace of being in all its historical contingency,
particularity, *haecceitas*, thisness.[8] If God desires being, and desires to be in
history, in each moment of history from the beginning right down to the end, then
being must be good. It must be good to be. God's desire for us, and God's desire
that we desire God in turn, may thus be understood as the primary affirmation of
being *par excellence*. For, if we desire God's desire, according to God's desire and
in response and co-response to God's desire, then we desire being; the *eschaton* as
being and through being, the coming together of the absolute beginning (before all
temporal beginning) and the absolute end (after all temporal ending) in the
moment of eternity. Epiphany, *Kairos*, *Augenblick*, the Instant – is this not what
Yahweh meant when he said, I was, I am, I will be (Exodus 3:15)? Is it not what
Jesus meant when he said that 'before Abraham was, I am' and that the Kingdom
both is already here *and* is not yet here? And is it not what Paul meant when he
spoke about the kingdom being revealed in the eschatological Instant (*Kairos*)? Or
what Augustine is hinting at in *The Confessions* when he addresses the enigma of
the inscrutability of time by suggesting that it is only in light of the eternal that the
temporal dispersal of the soul (*distentio animae*) into past, present and future can
be reunited in terms of an *intentio animae,* a reorientation and recollection which
requires (as Ricoeur notes in *Time and Narrative I*) a movement beyond
speculative metaphysics to poetics?

My answer to Desmond would be, therefore, that we should try to avoid both
extreme positions – of reducing agape to eros (as he thinks I suggest) or of
reducing eros to agape (as I think he suggests) – and that we should do so by
speaking instead of a very specific modality of eros, agapeic eros, which would be
suitable to God, capturing both the sense of unconditional agape and conditional
dependency on history for this love to be realized as the 'more' (of surplus and
excess) moving towards the 'less' (of human fraility and flesh). Here I think

Desmond and I may find ourselves on common ground again. Certainly such a medial position or mediation would allow us to avoid the tipping of heavenly eros (*eros ouranos*) into Hegel's and Nietzsche's dark and destructive eros (*eros turannos*) which Desmond so rightly warns against. It would also provide us with the basis of a distinction between a number of different kinds of eros, namely, agapeic, philial, romantic, narcissitic, tyrannical, neurotic, and the like. In this light, and with such a hermeneutic retrieval of divine eros in mind, I can fully concur with Desmond when he celebrates a certain 'excess of love that, in exceeding self, can give itself over to a poverty of being to make way for the other as other ... a surplus, supersurplus power that lets be, in order that the good of the other may come to be' (p.115).

By way of conclusion, let me make some further summary comments about certain differences of interpretation in Desmond's reading of possibility and my own. The crux of our potential disagreement here centres on this bold and provocative observation by Desmond: 'A God who needs us to be God would be pitiable. The most difficult and terrifying of the commandments is the first. We secrete idols, even when we call them icons. Maybe the God who may be is another idol. Maybe not' (ibid.). Since the title of Desmond's review essay in the *Irish Theological Quarterly*, 'Maybe, Maybe Not', refers precisely to this passage, it is worth dwelling on its implications in an effort to reach more clarity between us on the matter. Desmond speaks here of the 'risk of idolatry' in my statement, 'God can be God if we enable this to happen.' But what I meant by this is that God can only be God in history, in time, in the flesh, in humanity, if we humans allow this to happen. It was in relation to the eschatology of a kingdom-to-come that I made this claim. So that, when Desmond retorts that, 'God is not the kingdom of God. God is God', I would reply that God is, at least in part, the kingdom of God on earth insofar as God promises, desires and possibilizes this kingdom. Just as when Desmond retorts that 'We are human, God is God', I would reply that God's role as God *per se* does not rule out his role as God-Man *per alio*, *pro nobis*, for us, otherwise there would be no possibility of the intersection of the timeless with time, of word with flesh, no incarnation, no epiphany, no encounter between Abraham and the angels under the tree, no theophany of the burning bush, no redemption, no kingdom of heaven on earth. And that is not something Desmond would want to exclude any more than I do. So, to repeat the point, when Desmond asks: 'God's future being? Conditional on our actions in history? God a being in time then?' I would reply, yes, the divine has a 'future being' in terms of its potential realization and incarnation as a kingdom on earth, and that future being of the divine in historical time does depend, in equal measure, on our actions as well as on God's invitations. We are both in this together. That is the risk God took in creating the world: the risk that the world might reject the eschatological promise of incarnation and redemption in the kingdom. It would have been easier to stay put: to remain safe, sound and secluded in the identity of divine non-being or pre-being or beyond-being. But God wanted more than the sure bet of self-identity. God wanted to be – to be in time and space, human as well as divine. The divine *posse* longed for human *esse*, for history, for flesh, for *haecceitas* and thisness, for the epiphany of the ordinary and the everyday, for the cry in the street (to cite Stephen Dedalus's definition of God in the opening chapter of *Ulysses*). Or, as Lévinas put it, God before creation realized that being alone is not much fun, two are better than one, *'on s'amuse mieux à deux!'*.[9]

So when Desmond claims that, 'there are ways of privileging possibility that end up making no possibility privileged. We risk ending with an indeterminate possibility hard to distinguish from a blank cheque drawn on nothing' (p.115), I would say that this does not apply to 'the God who may be', for such divine *posse* is very definitely privileged according to two main criteria. First, I would invoke the *ethical criterion* that guarantees that all divine possibilities are good (for 'God is all he is able to be', as Nicholas of Cusa notes, and the one thing God is not able to be is evil, if the testimonies of the God of love, justice and peace are to be believed). Second, there is the *eschatological criterion* which privileges only those possibles which are conducive to the realizing of the promise of the kingdom on earth. These are very determinate criteria, supported by the long wisdom traditions, not just of biblical monotheism, but of most world religions, and arguably of most world philosophies also. Divine *posse* is a far cry from the postmodern play of undecidability and indeterminacy as it is from the ineluctable theodicy of Hegel, which I suspect are the two dangers in my position which most worry Desmond – and would worry me too, I might add, if I thought I was prey to them, which I do not. There is no maybe, maybe not here. No cavalier juggling between gods and monsters, good and evil, peace and violence. No shilly-shallying. No soft-shoe shuffle of a thousand hesitations and deflations. The divine *posse* calls for conviction and commitment. Not some non-commital new ageism. Not some postmodern paralysis. And certainly not theodicy in any form!

That said, I do take Desmond's point about the temptation to think of divine *posse* exclusively in terms of the future. God does not just call for a 'deferring or detouring to an always other future to come' (p.116). Agreed: God also calls for remembrance of times past (what are the scriptures, after all, if not narratives of past deeds from the beginning of created time, recounted under the ethical imperative *Zakhor!* – 'Remember'?). And, equally importantly and equiprimordially, God asks for our attention, response, prayer and action *in the present*. The privileging of the future in my phenomenological–hermeneutical analysis of the divine *posse* has arguably been overly influenced by Heidegger's privileging of projection and possibility (*Entwurf* and *Möglichkeit*) in his reading of being as time. And it has also, I suspect, been informed by my formative exposure to the freshness and energy of liberation theology in radically committed thinkers like Moltman, Guttierez and Secundo. It is good and proper that Desmond should seek to redress the balance and request a more equitable apportioning of emphasis to the pastness and presentness of God. This is a lesson which I must confess I have also been learning from my recent readings of Vedantic thinking about the divine, especially through the Christian perspective of the Benedictine interpreters of *Advaita* philosophy, Henri le Saux (Abhishiktananda) and Bede Griffiths.

So on this point about *time* we can, I think, reach consensus, as on the other basic point about bringing eschatology into closer dialogue with ontology. But the difference of 'which eschatology?' and 'which ontology?' does remain a genuine issue of divergence between us, albeit one of emphasis in the last analysis. So let me conclude with some final observations on this difference. When Desmond is compelled to confess 'astonishment' at the thought that we must help God to be God, he is insufficiently attentive once again to the distinction I would make between God-as-God and God in relation to us or God-as-human (Creation–Incarnation–Salvation).[10] To construe God as *posse* rather than *esse* is not to declare that we create God, *à la* Feuerbach, Nietzsche and Sartre, but only to suggest that we create the world jointly with God, helping God to complete the seventh day of creation (the Sabbath), a day left divinely empty so that we would have the freedom and responsibility of an equal and answerable partner in the bringing about of the Kingdom. The Sabbath is a day for God to rest and us to work, not vice versa! This is what the Kabbalists called a divine *zimzum*, a gracious gap in the order of things which invites us into relation, a vacancy yearning for embodiment.

But we might approach this question from a more dramatic and darker angle too. When Etty Hillesum declared, in her final days in a Nazi concentration camp, that 'we must help God to be God', she was not referring to God-as-God (that is, as love, desire, promise, call, creation, healing, spirit – for God is *always and already* all of that). No, she was talking about enabling God to be manifest in the flesh of time and place, of history and humanity. In other words, not God *per se*, but God *per alio*, *pro nobis*, for us. And here we do have a free choice and a vocation to do the will of God by bringing love into the world, by saying yes, amen, to the call of peace and justice. And by acting accordingly, even, and especially, when facing the jaws of death and cruelty, in Dachau, in the Killing Fields of Cambodia, in Rwanda, in Screbernice or wherever it might be. There is no end to our responsibility here. And it is a responsibility that extends from the beginning to the end of time, revisiting us in every instant along the way. So when Desmond asks, 'If God possibilizes us, how can we be said to possibilize God?', my answer would be that, while God possibilizes us in the order of the origin (creation), we possibilize God in the order of the *eschaton* (understood as the coming of the kingdom into history), that is, by helping to make the kingdom that bit more real, more present, more living, in each moment of our lives. As *posse*, God remains, *per se*, both before the beginning and after the end. This is so. Here divine *posse* precedes and transcends both the *possibilitas* of human imagination and the *potentia* of the material world, though it requires both of these finite modes of possibility and potentiality for its infinite Word to be made flesh. But with respect to *esse*, if it is indeed true to say with Desmond that 'we are, because first given to be by God' (p.117), it is equally true to add that God 'is' in the phenomenological order of temporal, historical, incarnational being precisely because we return the gift of being to God. It is we who enable the Word to become flesh, the *posse* to become *esse*. God is 'all that he is able to be' (*possest* in Nicholas of Cusa) to the extent that we say 'yes' to God's 'May I be with you?' If you take away this 'May-I-be?' from God, you take away both God's goodness and humanity's liberty. Not to mention the question of *politesse*! The God who may be has excellent manners. Divine passion has divine patience, as the common etymological roots of these two terms suggest.

Does that mean that God would not be all he is able to be *prior* to all relation to us, to creation, to time and space, to flesh and blood? No, it does not. In that hypothetical situation, God would remain what he is able to be in the order of *posse*, but not of *esse*. For the latter, he needs us.

So is all this a hyperbolic mode of speaking and conceptualizing? Yes. And this is crucial. Desmond is right about this. All my talk of God as desire (*erotics*) and of God as possibility (*dynamics*) belongs to the order of figuration (*poetics*) or, to be more philosophical about it, to the order of a poetic hermeneutics. It is a matter of interpretation, confession, narration. For if God is one, God speaks in many different ways; and these ways are always mediated by human understanding and imagination. There is no immediate access to God. There is no absolute way to the absolute. All ways there are are our ways. God is other than us and this very otherness is guaranteed and known for us only *in relation*.[11] The first and last word in the drama of God and humanity is relation: *Dia-legein*, the gift of one to the other: something which I hope my exchanges with William Desmond will continue to enjoy in the years to come.

Notes

1   All page references in the text are to the Irish Theological Quarterly (ITQ) volume. Desmond's piece is reprinted in a slightly enlarged version in John Manoussakis (ed.), *After God*, New York: Fordham University Press, 2005.

2   See Desmond's formidable analysis of the role of metaphor, symbol, analogy and hyperbole in the 'way of transcendence' in chapter 5 of *Being and the Between*. The chapter, entitled 'Being and the Metaxological', argues that everything we say about the ultimate is figurative in some sense, a sentiment with which I fully concur. Where we mainly disagree, however, is over my privileging of erotic possibility *vis-à-vis* agapeic actuality, especially when it comes to God. My own notion of divine *posse* is outlined in several works, from *Poétique du Possible* (Paris: Beauchesne, 1984) to *The God Who May Be* (Bloomington: Indiana University Press, 2001) and *Strangers, Gods and Monsters* (London and New York: Routledge, 2003). I take my cue here not only from the phenomenological prioritizing of possibility over actuality (Husserl, Heidegger and Derrida) but also from the ancient Pauline and Patristic notions of *dunamis* (see, for example, the Pseudo-Dionysius, *The Divine Names*, 894–6) and from Nicholas of Cusa's much neglected but revolutionary notion of *possest* (see in particular his *Trialogus de Possest* and *On the Summit of Contemplation*).

3   Although Desmond would clearly not want to oppose ontology and eschatology in any absolute sense, his basic point is that, if there is not agapeic fullness in the origin, there is no way to make sense of desire. See Chapter 6 of *Being and the Between*, entitled 'Origin'.

4   Elsewhere Desmond seems to avoid such confusion by pointing to an enigmatic overdeterminate 'purposiveness' beyond all finite or Hegelian teleologies. See, in particular, the concluding chapter of *Being and the Between*, and the penultimate chapter of *Hegel's God*.

5   Desmond appears to favour agapeic love over erotic love, from a metaphysical point
     of view, on account of what he calls its 'overfullness'. See especially Chapter 4
     ('Agapeic Mind') and Chapter 5 ('Agapeic Being') of *Perplexity and Ultimacy*. See
     also here Desmond's distinction between the community of erotic sovereignty and the
     community of agapeic service in chapters 15 and 16 of *Ethics and the Between*.

6   This is not, of course, to deny that Desmond's practice of philosophy is arguably one
     of the most plurivocal and poetic being written today.

7   This view would seem at variance with Desmond's argument elsewhere that there is a
     certain quality of surplus in eros due to its double parentage in Diotima's myth about
     poros (plenty) and *penia* (lack). There is, he admits, a certain 'divine festivity' in eros
     at times. See especially here the final chapter of *Beyond Hegel and Dialectic*. It would
     clearly be wrong to characterize Desmond's entire *œuvre* as some abstract
     metaphysical system. His aim is rather to enact metaphysical mindfulness in fidelity to
     what shows itself in the immanent between, the *mi-lieu* of given being.

8   Desmond too speaks of divine love for the singular as singular, but he construes this,
     once again, more in terms of agapeic than of erotic love. (See BB, 187ff.)

9   For Desmond, letting God be God is a reverence for the surplus of what God is, which
     is not exhausted by, or dependent on, God's being for us.

10   In Chapters 6 and 7 of *Being and the Between*, Desmond distinguishes between
     'origin' and 'creation', arguing that the first relates more to God as God, and the second
     more to God in relation to finite being, and especially human beings.

11   Desmond's metaxalogical thinking is, I believe, an exemplary instance of such a
     philosophy of relation. But there are different *kinds* of relations and this is, once again,
     where the similarities and differences between our two respective positions reside.

VIII
READING WITH DESMOND

Chapter 14

Strangely out of Place: *Phaedrus* 227a–230e

Ian Leask

The *Phaedrus*, as a whole, has four central features: (1) although it starts as a discussion about rhetoric *vis-à-vis* philosophy, the dominant concern is love; (2) it is the site of the famous metaphor or image of well-balanced human existence: the charioteer controlling black and white horses; (3) it is probably the first example of the mature Plato's 'technical' dialectics, involving division and collection according to genus and species;[1] (4) its setting is, unlike any other dialogue, idyllic, dream-like, highly poetic. In this essay, I want to concentrate on the opening section of the *Phaedrus* and to relate some of the detail of this prelude to the four central themes or concerns outlined above. By doing so, I hope to give at least some indication of how this rich segment of philosophical literature serves as an introduction, not just to a solitary dialogue, but to Socratic philosophy as a whole. Throughout I refer to and draw upon central themes and ideas in William Desmond's rich corpus of writing: it is not just that my overall reading comes in and through a 'Desmondian' prism; it is more that the prelude provides a particularly fruitful locus for the application of Desmond's thinking on the nature of the self, of eros and of the desire for wisdom.

I

There are only two characters involved here: Phaedrus and Socrates. We (think we) know Socrates. But who is Phaedrus? (The name means, literally, 'sparkling' and suggests beauty, health and vitality.) Even before we read the dialogue bearing his name, we know something about him from his relatively minor roles in the *Protagoras* and the *Symposium*: he is young[2] and, it would seem, vulnerable to the charms of sophists such as Hippias, the quack-doctor Acumenos, and Acumenos' son Eryximachos (the same Eryximachos who gives the third speech in the *Symposium*). In the *Protagoras*, Phaedrus sits at the feet of Hippias listening to him postulate on astronomy (315c). In the *Symposium*, Phaedrus opens the debate, with the poorest of all the speeches given (178a–180c), and then acts as 'chairman' for the remainder of the dialogue. Crucially, however, Phaedrus is not a long-standing, well-established sophist. He has certainly been wooed and (partially) swayed by sophistry, but he is not irredeemable: his position as 'chairman' of the speechifying in the *Symposium* is already an indication that Phaedrus is not

entirely dogmatic, not a lost cause. We could probably go as far as saying, after
Paul Friedländer, that Phaedrus stands for youth itself, certainly for the youth of
Athens. But more of that anon.

The first textual point we should notice is the significance of the opening
question of the dialogue: 'Phaedrus, my friend, where are you going and where
have you come from [*poi kai pothen*]?' On the face of it, an innocuous enquiry, a
social nicety. Arguably, however, the question has a much deeper (and, we might
say, metaxological) resonance: it is not merely a passing enquiry about what
Phaedrus has been up to earlier that day and what he has in mind for the remainder
of it. It is also, as becomes increasingly apparent, about the very direction of
Phaedrus' life, and the condition of his soul. To date he has been dangerously close
to being won over by sophistry; after this meeting with Socrates, he may choose,
in complete contrast to his life to date, the love of wisdom. At the beginning he is
a fan of an orator (Lysias); by the end, whether or not he becomes a permanent
convert, he shares Socrates' prayers. In other words, far from being empty or
formulaic, this opening question possesses a fundamentally important, existential
dimension. Socrates asks of Phaedrus (and, by extension, of us): what have you
done with your life so far, what are you going to do with the rest of it?[3]

Accordingly, Phaedrus' response to the question is crucial for our understanding
of what is at stake in the dialogue. Where has he been? With the orator (that is, the
sophist) Lysias involved in a *diatribe* – a pass-time, an amusement which wears
time away, or (as the word can also suggest) a waste of time. Significantly the
diatribe in this case has been a *diatribe* against love. Furthermore Phaedrus was
visiting Lysias 'at Epicrates' house, the one Morychus used to have' (227b). The
connotations of these names are important: Epicrates was a renowned rhetorician
and demagogue, Morychus a renowned playwright and glutton.[4] Such is the
unhealthy atmosphere in which Phaedrus has been spending time.

Where is Phaedrus going now? After a day in this unhealthy atmosphere, and
on the subsequent instructions of the quack-doctor Acumenus, Phaedrus is going
'outside the walls': he is leaving the *polis* because Acumenus has told him that it
is better to walk in the country than in the town. Acumenus, Socrates says, is 'quite
right' (*kalos*), but of course, generally speaking, Socrates does not think the
sophists are 'quite right' about anything. So why does he say this? What Socrates
soon discovers (228d) is that Phaedrus is, literally, concealing something: a written
copy of Lysias's speech. Phaedrus is going outside the *polis* – temporarily leaving
the community, that is – to practise rhetoric, to try his hand at reciting one of
Lysias's speeches; this is the motive for 'going outside the walls'. Phaedrus at first
says he is going outside the city walls because it is 'healthy', but his real reason is
to practise precisely that which undermines the health of the community.[5] His real
motive is exposed; so is the value of sophistic advice on 'health'. It seems that the
apparently innocuous remarks about 'leaving the city because it's healthy to do
so', gesture to the way that sophistry is antithetical to the healthy community and,
by further implication, to the Socratic concern with social well-being.

Accordingly, if we jump to the end of the prelude, we find – not surprisingly –
that Phaedrus is not really a guide for Socrates at all; at the least, he cannot guide

Socrates to wisdom. 'I am,' Socrates tells us, 'a lover of learning' (230d) which, of course, is what the sophist is not. 'The people in the city have something to teach me, but the fields and trees won't teach me anything' (ibid.). It is not better to walk in the country when the point is to practise rhetoric, and then to inflict it on the *polis*. Socrates' philosophy is based firmly within the community; it is social, not anti-social. Perhaps this is why Socrates, as Phaedrus notes, never goes beyond the frontiers of Attica, 'or even, as far as I can see, outside the actual walls of the city' (ibid).

II

There is, obviously enough, a curious kind of dialectic at work here, centring around the city and the country (or, rather, around tensions between the two): what goes on inside the *polis*, what goes on outside the *polis*.[6] At one level – and I think Plato's point here is fluid and multi-layered, beyond any single encapsulation – we are being told that sophistry is alien, that it is the 'other' of the civilized, political community (the town, that is). Plato is underlining how sophistry takes shape outside social intercourse but then re-enters the *polis* to make its impact felt. And, in doing so, Plato would seem to subscribe to a bias, or even repression, typical of 'sophisticated' Greek discourse: the self-identity of the citizen defined in contrast to what it is not; the self-satisfaction of the city-dweller only achieved by ensuring that its 'other' (in this case, the 'rough, uncultivated rustic') is suitably caricatured.[7] The Socratic attitude to what is beyond the *polis* (a recurring theme in the prelude) is, apparently, typical of a certain Athenian 'logic of exclusion', ripe for critical deconstruction.[8]

To be sure, the Platonic dialogues are not somehow sacrosanct and 'above' this kind of approach to the political formation and role of 'Identity'. Nonetheless I would urge a certain caution here, because it seems to me that the 'city–country dialectic' in the *Phaedrus* is not at all a straightforward case of 'self-identity formed through differentiating caricature'. There may be an element of this 'logic' to be uncovered. But there is, I think, a more complex constellation here which defies any relatively straightforward reduction, and which shows the fundamental ambiguity of Socrates' position: simultaneously *of* the *polis* and yet *not of* it. As we shall see, the Desmondian notions of 'plurivocity' and '*metaxu*' provide us with important hermeneutical keys here.

Initially, we have to consider the political current Socrates is fighting against: sophistry, the ultimate barbarism, practised and perpetuated right in the heart of the *polis* by Athenian citizens. Socrates' aim is not to legitimize the status quo but to challenge it, to posit the dream of a 'better reality'. We need to remember too that, as Voegelin has noted,[9] the *Phaedrus* was written after Plato had become convinced of the irreparable damage done to Athens, after he had given up on Athens as the possible locus for the ideal state: the ideal Athens could no longer be the 'empirical' Athens, so to speak. Bearing this in mind, we could say that the sophist's movement, his toing and froing, leaving the city to practise rhetoric, re-entering the city to inflict rhetoric, is intended to alert us to the instability and dissolution of the 'empirical' polity. Or, to be more accurate, it is when we consider both the sophist (or would-be sophist) going outside the walls *and* Socrates going outside the walls with him, comparing and contrasting the former with the latter, letting the one throw the other into relief, that we begin to see the wider point being made here. Socrates' own (metaxological) movement outside the city walls becomes a kind of critical (and perhaps mocking) reflection of the sophistic body-politic. How? Because – and here again I follow Voegelin[10] – Socrates is, in a sense, the incarnation of the Idea (the Idea of the Good, no less) and, as such, as an ontological measure, is able to make a double-edged point about 'empirical' Athens: how the Idea of the perfect state has, quite literally, departed the city of Athens, but also how this Idea continues to live on in the 'true' lover of wisdom, Socrates himself. So although (or perhaps because) Socrates prefers the *polis*, his leaving the city can be interpreted as a critique of the city, of 'empirical' Athens, as it was under sophistic domination. Socrates has a deeper social concern than the sophists and yet, precisely because he sees the faults and wrongs of sophistry, he can never be at home in the contemporary *polis* (which is, after all, infected with sophistic *mores*). Socrates, and *a fortiori* any lover of wisdom, is out of place in sophistic society.

Socrates, as Phaedrus would have it here (230d), is 'a very strange person' (Hamilton's translation), 'an amazing and most remarkable person' (Fowler's) or 'an incomprehensible being' (Jowett's). He is *atopotatos*, the superlative of *atopos*, 'being without a place'.[11] The various connotations of the word *atopos* are worth noting (referring to Liddell and Scott's *Greek–English Lexicon*): 1. 'out of place', 'out of the way', 'strange'; 2. 'absurd'; 3. 'unnatural', 'disgusting'. In sophistic society, Socrates is all of these things. Shabby, barefoot and unhygienic, like the caricatured rustic of fifth-century comedy, it is Socrates who is the outsider, the other of empirical Athens, precisely because he embodies the Idea of the perfect state and, *qua* idea, provides the ontological measure of that empirical state.

III

Perhaps, though, we can go further and say that it is not just that the singular figure of Socrates is *atopos* in sophistic society. Perhaps Socrates is saying that, at the deepest level and to an extent regardless of social setting, a part of him is always 'out of place', 'absurd', even 'unnatural'. More than this, though, he is also saying that part of all of us is, in a sense, *atopos*.

Let me expand on this by referring to 229c–230a, the discussion about the mythology connected with the river Illisus. We have already established how close Phaedrus is to the sophists. The sophists, we know, were keen to give 'sacriligious', allegorical, anti-mythological and 'pseudo-scientific' explanations of the old myths; Diogenes Laertius, for example, tells us how various sophists interpreted Homer in such a way that Zeus, Hera and Pallas were 'explained' as symbols of 'physical substances and elemental arrangements'.[12] Now we find Phaedrus trying to get Socrates' line on this, to see whether Socrates agrees.

According to the myth in question, two nymphs were playing by the Illisus: Orithyia, the daughter of one of Athens' legendary founding kings, and Pharmaceia, the nymph of the medicinal waters. Boreas, the 'rude' spirit of the North Wind, had fallen in love with Orithyia, wooed in part by Pharmaceia's narcotic powers. However, he made a poor job of trying to court her (principally because of his breathing difficulties), and eventually, with his growing frustration too much to bear, he seized Orithyia and carried her off. So Phaedrus wants to know whether Socrates accepts all this.

Socrates acknowledges that the 'pundits', that is, *hoi sophoi*,[13] reject the myth, putting the event down to 'natural phenomena': it was simply that the wind blew Orythia onto the rocks; there was no question of Boreas or any other spirit whisking her away. Socrates at first suggests (229c) that it would not be out of place, *atopos*, if he were to do the same as the pundits. But Socrates has no desire to be alongside the sophists. For, as far as Socrates is concerned, once we start with these scientistic explanations, there is (virtually) no end to the process: after Orithyia's abduction, we also need to explain centaurs (half-men, half-horses); the Chimaera (supposed to have a lion's head, a goat's body, and a snake's tail); Pegasus (the horse born from the foam of the sea and the blood of Medusa); the Gorgons (fearsome female monsters with huge teeth and claws, who could cause death by merely looking); and so on. So-called 'rationalists' find themselves overwhelmed by a host of monsters 'as numerous as they are grotesque' (229d); and any sceptic who tries to force plausible explanations on them through the use of 'rustic ingenuity', needs 'plenty of leisure time' (229e).

(To digress for a moment, here. The phrase 'rustic ingenuity' is not insignificant: what Socrates says is that the kind of *sophia* involved in this rationalism is, literally, *agroikos*. The root term, *agros*, is plain enough in its connotations, while *agroikos* itself can mean, in general, 'rustic', and in particular 'boorish, rude, and clown-like' (applied to humans), or 'uncultivated and rough' (applied to fields).[14] Thus, the particular description here underlines what we have already come across: the dissolution of sophistic Athens. We might find it objectionable that someone from outside the city is defined as boorish, rude or clown-like; but we can appreciate, nonetheless, the link with the earlier comments: even if there is a trace of urban bias in all this, the more fundamental point is that, for Plato, sophistic ontology has been *imposed* on the *polis*: it is, he would say, alien, inappropriate and simply wrong. By ideal Socratic standards, it is the sophist who is *atopos*.[15])

But to focus upon the question of demythologizing: Socrates has no time for such a project because he does not yet know himself.[16] For him, 'it seems crazy to worry about these supposed problems when I am still ignorant about my own nature … I study myself, rather than these old myths' (229e–230a). In this context, we should recall Xenophon: he tells us that Socrates, unlike almost every other philosopher of the day, never talked about nature in general (the origin of the cosmos, the patterns of the celestial bodies, or the like); Socrates dismissed this as folly, saying it was wrong to neglect human affairs as long as knowledge of these affairs was incomplete. Natural science had little practical benefit, Socrates felt, and ultimately the secrets of the universe were unfathomable.[17] All of which is highly illuminating in terms of Socrates' response to Phaedrus' question. For the central Socratic point would seem to be that the sophists have got their priorities wrong. Debunking old myths is a waste of time (a *diatribe*). The real question is to know *what we are*, for it is only when we are sure about what we are that we can decide how we should live.[18] As Socrates says in the *First Alcibiades* (129a):[19] 'once we know ourselves, we may learn how to care for ourselves, but otherwise we never shall'. If we do not know what we are, we cannot know what we should do, or how we should act. The truly healthy *polis* depends on this most fundamental ontology. The sophists are looking in the wrong place.

IV

To return to the 'strangeness' of Socrates: Socrates, as he tells us himself, is 'still in ignorance about my own nature' (229e–230a). Is he like Typhon, the fire-breathing monster with a hundred heads (born of the primordial Earth-mother and representing, for the Greeks, a kind of cosmic negation of human civilization, that is, of the city[20])? Or is he a 'gentler and simpler creature', endowed with a good and peaceable nature? What is it that makes him tick: something wild, frightening, 'unnatural and disgusting', or something gentle, humble, kind? Something bestial or something divine? A black horse or a white horse? Dionysus or Apollo?

The answer is, all of these (and more). Part of the self is always, as Desmond would have it, a plurivocity beyond containment, always 'other than self' (DD, 38). But, to get to this answer, a crude, pseudoscientific thinking like that of the sophists is of no use at all. Something 'ingenious and laboured' (229d), forcing 'plausible shapes' onto the strangeness within the self (229e), achieving this by means of a 'rustic ingenuity' – this kind of (univocal) rationalism is not only inappropriate but fundamentally misguided.[21] Merely demythologizing cannot get to the truth of the matter, for the truth is that the dark forces which the sophists would explain away *do* exist in the human soul (or, to use Desmond's term, the 'original self'). Such myths can have a 'reality', inasmuch as they are poetic expressions about the nature of original selfhood; their truth is, so to speak, not dependent on their literal truth. Thus, explaining away the myths of externally existing 'dark forces', showing that there are no absurd and unnatural monsters 'out there', hides from us the real dark forces within us from the beginning; once again, the sophists are confusing knowledge and opinion. And, once more, this means a failure to 'know yourself', and thus, inevitably, a failure to know how to live.[22] Explaining away the non-rational as 'allegory' fails to tackle the reality of the non-rational; without such an engagement, there is little hope for individual and social *eudaimonia*.[23] The point is not to explain away 'psychologically' for, as Desmond has noted, it is precisely the perplexity of the self, as articulated in the *Phaedrus*, that might drive us to philosophize in the first place.[24] Philosophy expresses plurivocity; meanwhile, it is this same plurivocity that 'constitutively energizes' (PU, 34) any genuine philosophical enterprise.

V

We must be careful, however, not to confuse Socrates' recognition of this plurivocity with some kind of 'brute' Hobbesian ontology. According to Socrates' metaxological, plurivocal, view, the self is a *density*, a density within which reason need not be the other of non-reason, and within which the dynamism of the non-rational is deemed essential for philosophical vision. Socrates explicitly recognizes the non-rational element in original selfhood; but his point is not to advocate irrationalism.

To amplify this, we can look to the conclusion of the *Republic* (588c ff), where Socrates constructs his famous model of the human personality. The human being, he says, is

> a bit like one of those composite mythological monsters, such as Chimaera and Scylla and Cerberus and the rest of them, in which different kinds of creature are fused into one overall shape ... So picture a complex, many-headed monster, with the heads of wild and tame beasts all around it, which it can bring forth from itself and change at will ... Now add two other types of creature, one a lion, the other a human. Picture the many-headed monster to be by far the biggest of the three, and the lion the next largest. ... Now combine all the three into one form ... so that this trio has the external appearance of just one of the three, the human, and so that – to someone who is not able to look beneath the surface – there is just a single creature here ...

The conclusion he reaches from this is that we should always refuse to allow the irrational to take control, either in the individual or in the individual writ large, the *polis*. (Allowing such free rein is, he will maintain, the very definition of injustice.) However, what is perhaps too easy to overlook here is what this moral and political injunction presupposes: (a) that Socrates could hardly be more explicit in recognizing the centrality of the non-rational (and even the monstrous) within original selfhood: it is by far the biggest part of us, he says; and (b) that reason must coexist with, rather than seek to deny or even obliterate, this massive, swelling, surging 'other'. Socratic original selfhood is no bloodless intellect, or *cogito*: instead, it is, as Desmond would have it, a necessary plurivocity.

Thus, returning to the issue at hand, we could say that, although the *Phaedrus* is where Plato first unveils his 'advanced' technical dialectics (that method of collection and division which, in a sense, instigates all subsequent logic), although Plato shows a method of reasoning which is far more subtle than any sophistic scientism, even this 'advanced' reason, on its own, is inadequate. Logos is essential but not absolute: the 'just soul' consists of the balanced integration of varied 'elements'. What is more, this balance must itself be expressed through myth. Where the sophists concentrate on demythologizing, Socrates becomes the author of new and 'higher' myths: the human soul as chariot, steered by love, driven by the dark and light horses: the proper integration of all that is within us.

VI

It is this notion of plurivocal 'fusion' that is, I would suggest, the key to understanding Plato's intentions in the *Phaedrus*. For, as a whole, the dialogue shows us that, in the right circumstances or combination, erotic mania is the 'heaven-sent' animation behind any ascent to wisdom (265a):[25] reason needs this charge if it is to be more than mere calculation. More accurately, as Desmond has made plain, there cannot be 'knowing' if there is not, in the first place, *desire* of some sort:

> desire, while obviously not confined to cognition, does flower into knowing, as the articulated self-conscious form of human eros. The desire to know spontaneously breaks forth in our being as the exigence to make sense of the density of being that may initially seem foreign and indifferent to us. This desire reveals itself as an imperative of our being that we can never entirely suppress. (DD, 109)

Desire and the non-rational are central components of philosophy. Desire is far more than 'some vague psychological feeling' (DD, 14): it is philosophy's necessary dynamic. The 'Platonic *metaxu*' is about the *impulse* to philosophize as much as it is about the 'results' of philosophizing (DD, 8).

Bearing in mind the centrality of the erotic impulse, I want to finish by returning to the introduction itself, to consider the one outstanding point: the idyllic, poetic setting. This place where Socrates has been led – sacred to Achelous, the river god, and dedicated to that mad rustic, Pan – this place has, we are told, an enchanting, almost narcotic effect; it is a sensual shrine.[26] Recall Socrates' description:

> By Hera, this is a lovely spot for a rest. The plane tree is tall and spreading, the willow high and shady, in full bloom, filling the air with the finest fragrance. The beautiful spring water cools the feet ... The air is sweet and delicate, throbbing to the very voice of summer – the cicadas chirping; the exquisite grass provides perfect comfort for the head. (230b–c)

What is meant by this panegyric, and why is it Socrates, who had claimed that he would rather be inside the *polis*, who is responsible for it? To approach an answer to this, I suggest that we stay focused on eros, and consider some of the different aspects it displays in the dialogue as a whole: seduction, lust, physical affection, divine love. Once again, Desmond's stress on 'plurivocity' provides our route map.

First, that opening sentence again: what Socrates asks is: *Phaedrus, dear friend, where have you been, where are you going?* So the first words of the dialogue are a statement of Socrates' affection for Phaedrus. He reiterates this at 228d: 'much as I love you'.

Second, the subject-matter of the speech which Lysias has been commissioned to write: against love. Socrates is against being ruled by lust, but he sees its natural extension, non-physical, divine eros, as the highest point for us to reach. After all, the philosopher cannot be against love, for the philosopher is a lover, the lover of wisdom. As far as Socrates is concerned, rhetoric without truth is bad enough, but rhetoric against love is the worst of all. This, I take it, is the point of Socrates' first masked speech 'against' love: it describes lust or 'reprobate rationality' rather than the ideal love of Socrates' second speech.

Third, the importance of the Borean myth: it is no accident that this image of attempted seduction, and then violent abduction, is so central in the opening stages of the dialogue. Nor is it mere coincidence that Socrates and Phaedrus now stand at, or near, the same spot where that mythical abduction took place.

Fourth, the figure of Phaedrus himself: in part a sophist; but still young enough to be wooed by Socratic *philo-sophia*.

Fifth, the fact that the 'new' and advanced method of dialectic, which is revealed later in the dialogue, is applied to love, precisely in order to show its different formations or guises.

Sixth, the fact that Socrates continually stresses the necessary unity of advanced reason and divine madness (the madness of love, that is), the unity of eros and logos.

Bearing in mind this jumble of erotic points, we can say that, for his part, Socrates' own 'animal' passions are surely an element in his attraction to Phaedrus: he is not, as we have seen, in any sense cold or bloodless. But, of course, Socrates is the one person who, if we are to believe Plato, is fully in control of his base passions, and who is able to 'convert' lust into non-physical love: this is essential, he would say, in the love of wisdom. Socrates does not deny his earthy side, but he reins it in, taming its wilder aspects, cultivating its better elements. Phaedrus, in the meantime, may not have physical designs on Socrates, and yet he seeks to seduce him *with rhetoric*, to see if Socrates will succumb to a 'bit of rough', rough thought (*agroikos sophia*), that is. This is why he has 'guided' Socrates to a place of idyllic beauty, a place strongly associated with mythological seduction, a place where one can literally lose oneself and become mesmerized by the cicadas' chirping. This is a place where, as the myth would have it, the nymph of the medicinal waters did so much to attract Boreas to Orythia, an attraction which led, of course, to the violence against Orythia. This divine place has the effect of a drug, a *pharmakon*. It is to be the location for a seduction, a place where Socrates may be fully won over to sophistry.

But, of course, no such seduction takes place: even Socrates' lyrical description of the grove is itself ironically mock-rhetorical.[27] Socrates remains rooted in the Ideal *polis*, a point he makes clear after his panegyric. Socrates will remain the embodiment of the 'ontologically proper' society; he left the 'empirical' *polis* precisely to make an ironic point about the sophists, not to be won over by sophistry. He will resist the charms of all rhetoric which is unattached to reason, unlike Phaedrus himself. He will show the power of rigorous logical thought, unlike all of the sophists. And he will do this in the name of love, unlike the sophist

Lysias, who makes money by writing a speech against love. For all his lyrical description, Socrates remains *atopos*, out of place, a visitor. He remains a stranger to anything that would charm him out of his senses. He resists Phaedrus, but precisely in order to 'save' Phaedrus: his own love for Phaedrus (which, as his dialectical division will later display, is not reducible to lust) is, he hopes, what will see him seduce Phaedrus: not a physical seduction, but a redirection of Phaedrus' soul, away from the love of sophistic rhetoric, towards the love of wisdom, the unity of eros and logos. This, as Friedländer has noted, is what the struggle between sophistry and philosophy is primarily concerned with: it is the struggle for *die Seele der Jugend*, the soul of youth, and it is nowhere better displayed than in this dialogue.[28]

Of course, we cannot be sure that Phaedrus is permanently transformed by this encounter. But, in a sense, this is not really the main point. Perhaps what is more important is that Plato can still bring home to us – when we, as readers, witness the unity of Socrates and Phaedrus in dialogue, and when we study and meditate upon the central themes and concerns here – the perennial power and relevance of that basic, profound, *metaxological*, Socratic question: where are we coming from, and where are we going?

Notes

1 My understanding of the date of composition of the *Phaedrus*, and of the overall chronology of Plato's work, follows Leonard Brandwood, *The Chronology of Plato's Dialogues*, Cambridge: CUP, 1990. The edition used is the Loeb Classical Library edition, but the translations are my own.

2 See *Phaedrus*, 257c, where Socrates calls Phaedrus *neania* – 'young man!', or 267c, where he calls him *pai* – 'boy!' It is possible that Phaedrus would have been older, at the time of the dialogue, than Plato depicts him; for an illuminating discussion of why there might be this deliberate discrepancy, see Martha Nussbaum, '"This Story Isn't True": Poetry, Goodness, and Understanding in Plato's *Phaedrus*', in J. Moravcsik and P. Temko (eds), *Plato on Beauty, Wisdom, and the Arts*, Totowa: Rowman and Littlefield, 1982, pp.79–124, esp. pp.96–7.

3 Cf. John Sallis, *Being and Logos. Reading the Platonic Dialogues*, 3rd edn, Bloomington: Indiana University Press, 1996, pp.105ff.; Ronna Burger, *Plato's Phaedrus: A Defense of a Philosophic Art of Writing*, Alabama: University of Alabama Press, 1980, p.9.

4 See G.J. De Vries, *A Commentary on the Phaedrus of Plato*, Amsterdam: A.M.Hakkert, 1969, pp.34–5; W.H.Thompson, *The Phaedrus of Plato*, London: Wittaker, 1868, pp.2–3.

5 Notice, incidentally, that the Herodicus whom Socrates mentions at 227d is the same figure he criticizes for being another quack-doctor, in the *Republic* (406a–b).

6 For wider consideration of the topology of the *Phaedrus*, see A. Philip (1981), 'Récurrences thématiques et topologie dans le Phèdre de Platon', *Revue de Métaphysique et de Morale*, **86**, 452–76; Ulrich von Wilamowitz-Moellendorff, *Platon*, Berlin: Weidmann, 1920, vol. 1, ch. 13, 'Ein glücklicher Sommertag'; G.R.F. Ferrari, *Listening to the Cicadas*, Cambridge: CUP, 1987, pp.1–36; Charles Griswold,

Self-Knowledge in Plato's Phaedrus, New Haven: Yale University Press, 1986, pp.33–6. For an illustration of the route followed by Phaedrus and Socrates, see L. Robin (1966), 'Notice', *Platon: Oeuvres Complètes*, Tome 4, Paris: Collection des Universités de France, pp.x–xii.

7 For an excellent survey, see Philippe Borgeaud, 'The Rustic', in Jean-Pierre Vernant (ed.), *The Greeks*, trans. Chas. Lambert and Teresa Lavender Fagan, Chicago: University of Chicago Press, 1995, pp.287–98. Considering a range of 'types', from the Cyclops, to Typhon, to Strepsiades, Borgeaud observes (p.297) that, 'The rustic, the primitive, the unsocialized, the bumpkin, the savage, the freak – all these figures haunted and fascinated the imagination of the ancient Greeks.'

8 Cf. Paul Cartledge, *The Greeks. A Portrait of Self and Others*, Oxford: OUP, 1993.

9 Eric Voegelin, *Order and History*, vol. 3, *Plato and Aristotle*, Baton Rouge: Louisiana State University Press, 1957, pp.135–41, esp. p.136.

10 *Order and History*, vol. 3, *Plato and Aristotle*, p.140.

11 We find the same description employed in *Symposium*, 215a, in Alcibiades' portrayal of Socrates.

12 Diogenes Laertius, *Lives*, trans. R.D. Hicks, London: Heinemann, 1925 (Loeb edn), Bii.c.3.s11. Cf. C. Ritter, *Platons Dialog Phaidros*, 2nd edn, Leipzig: Meiner, 1922, p.32, n.15.

13 Cf. W.J. Verdenius (1955), 'Notes on Plato's *Phaedrus*', *Mnemosyne*, **IV** (8), 265–89, esp.268; and Christopher Rowe, *Plato: Phaedrus*, Warminster: Aris & Phillips, 1986, p.139.

14 Cf. Borgeaud, 'The Rustic', pp.291–4.

15 This contrast between how things are and how they should be is explicitly spelt out, later in the dialogue (259e–274b), during the fuller discussion about rhetoric.

16 Cf. Ferrari, *Listening*, pp.9–12. It is this same point that serves as the foundation for Griswold's scrupulous study (*Self-Knowledge*).

17 Xenophon, *Memorabilia and Oeconomicus*, trans. E.C. Marchant, London: Heinemann, 1968 (Loeb edn), 1.1.12–15.

18 See also *Apology*, 20dff.; *Protagoras*, 331c; *Laches*, 187e–188c; *Charmides*, 164d–165b.

19 Whether or not the *First Alcibiades* is an authentic Platonic dialogue, Socrates' point here could hardly be more apposite.

20 Cf. Borgeaud, 'The Rustic', pp.289–90.

21 Cf. Burger, *Plato's Phaedrus*, pp.14–15.

22 Cf. Ferrari, *Listening*, pp.9–12.

23 Cf. Griswold, *Self-Knowledge*, pp.36–44.

24 See BB, 118: Socrates 'equivocates about his own identity. Perplexity at this equivocation, in the form of the following question, drove him to philosophy (*Phaedrus*, 229e–230a): Am I a monster more swollen than Typho, or a creature of a more gentle and divine lot?'

25 Cf. W.J. Verdenius, 'Der Begriff der Mania in Platons *Phaidros*', *Archiv für Geschichte der Philosophie*, **44**, 1962, 132–50.

26 Cf. Philip, 'Récurrences'; E.A. Wyller, '*Phaidros*: Eros und Psyche', *Der Späte Platon*, Hamburg: Meiner, 1970, pp.122–30, esp. p.128; and Kenneth Dorter (1971), 'Imagery and philosophy in Plato's *Phaedrus*', *Journal of the History of Philosophy*, **9**, pp.279–88.

27 Cf. Rowe, *Plato*, p.141.

28 Paul Friedländer, *Platon*, Bd. 3, Berlin: Walter de Gruyter, 1960, p.201.

IX
DESMOND, SCIENCE, THE ARTS
AND THE ENVIRONMENT

Chapter 15

Glissando: Life, Gift and the Between

John Milbank

William Desmond is one of the greatest living thinkers. His work is characterized by a noble simplicity and expansiveness. Unlike most philosophers today, he does not shirk the fundamental and 'obvious' questions, but always tackles them head-on. At the same time, he produces a kind of 'Irish' challenge (at once neoplatonic, Augustinian, Thomistic and post-Hegelian) to Heidegger's attempt to meld philosophy with poetry. A lengthy disquisition on fundamental modes of being will pass seamlessly into a meditation on the flight of a seabird across a Gaelic seashore. And its path is never, for the reader, a diversion …

Since I agree with nearly everything that Desmond has to say, apart from some minor divergencies or hesitancies that are scarcely worth discussing in print, there seems little point in offering a critique of his philosophy. Instead, I prefer to celebrate it by tentatively offering the following essay as an intended application to the topic of 'life' of his 'metaxological' metaphysics of the 'between', which is also, as many passages in his *œuvre* reveal, a metaphysics of 'gift'. In what I hope is an act of tributary *mimesis*, my reflections will veer between natural science, ontology, literature, music and theology.

Evolution and Design

Ever since Darwin, at a popular level, the terms 'creation' and 'evolution' have been set against each other. In this lies little rationale, but we must ask for the rationale behind the constantly re-staged debate. It is, indeed, as if one has a kind of lobster-like double articulation, with superficial hostility between the two pincers, of a single episteme. On the one hand, there is the legacy of post-Newtonian Christian natural theology; on the other hand, there is the explanation of the phenomena of life in terms of the operation of the law of natural selection.[1]

In the first case one has to do with 'creation' only in a bastardized sense. Newton no longer conceived of God as being as such, and as the source of finite being produced from nothing but sharing by various degrees in his infinite, simple *esse*. His God was rather a supremely powerful entity who had shaped, alongside himself, other entities with whom he communicated through a shared dimension dubbed his 'sensorium', manifest to us as an inferred absolute space and absolute time. According to the, as it were, old covenant of the laws of motion, celestial as well as terrestrial bodies travelled in infinite straight lines unless otherwise interrupted, a movement that is perfectly reversible. But according to the, as it were, new covenant of gravity, celestial bodies were regularly bent back from this course to move cyclically in relation to each other. In the case of both 'covenants' one has, on the one hand, an absolutely regularly operating and universal law. On the other hand, one has also the direct presence of God, however precisely conceived, whether in the one case as the absoluteness of space and time, or in the other case as the attractive and repelling force of gravitation. In the latter case, Newton the hermeticist was always in self-conflict with Newton the voluntarist theologian: the latter would have liked to reduce gravitation to mechanism, the former toyed with the notion that God had introduced into reality certain inscrutable and quasi-vital 'active principles'.[2]

This 'designing' God is not the God of classical Catholic theology because his causality operates on the same plane as finite causes, even though it is all-powerful. One can trace the beginnings of such a way of conceiving of divine causality as far back as Bonaventure and Duns Scotus, but it displaced an older and essentially neoplatonic way of looking at things, still holding good for Aquinas, in which the divine cause was a higher 'influence' which 'flowed into' finite levels of causation, entirely shaping them from within, but not 'influencing' them or conditioning them on the same plane of univocal being, as a less metaphorically-rooted meaning of 'influence' tends to imply. Put briefly, the ontological versus ontic difference between primary and secondary causality was lost sight of.[3]

It is still this post-Scotist and Newtonian God who is invoked by advocates of 'creative design' all the way from Paley through to recent evangelical biologists. Just as motion and the planetary system appeared to be organized like clockwork in the Newtonian universe, so likewise Paley saw in organisms far more complex mechanisms whose occurrence could only be explained by the notion of direct and continuous divine causal influence. Similarly, today, biologists like Michael Behe argue that even the most primitive component of a light-sensitive nerve that permits 'seeing' to arise is already so complex that only an extrinsic divine designer will explain its existence.[4] The scandal of 'creationist science' is indeed the idea that God could become an empirical hypothesis, experimentally verifiable, but the scandal is still more theological than it is scientific and, in fact, all the way at least from Newton to Faraday, the main current of natural science was centrally shaped by such scandalous confusion.

In the second case, one has the Darwinian tradition itself. It is, of course, not at all the case that Darwin displaced the ancient monotheistic doctrine of creation with the thesis of evolution by natural selection. To suppose that it is would be to remain within the terms of the bastardized theological assumptions of Paley and the divine design tradition. Yet, within the terms of this tradition, it is possible also to argue that Darwin was in one respect modifying received theology rather than simply standing it on its head. His project shares an important feature in common with the Christian apologetic *The Bridgewater Treatises* (particularly the section by William Whewell) which he indeed cites positively in *The Origin of Species*. For both works, the Paleyite perspective on life is insufficient in terms of its Newtonian analogue. For in the latter case, while absolute space and time and the force of gravity represent the direct divine presence, this is still manifest in a totally regular fashion expressible by comprehensible laws. There appeared to be no biological equivalent to this regular divine governance, so both treatises are interested in compensating for this lack in terms of discovering more regular immanent processes at work in features exhibiting apparent organic design. This included processes leading to the constant creation of new species, such that *both* treatises exhibit a break with the Aristotelian focus upon fixity of species and the search for explanation of variation within species only, in favour of the attempt to account genetically for the variation of species itself. The difference is that, in the case of *The Bridgewater Treatises*, divine design ultimately explains the mutual adaptation of species and environment; while in the case of *The Origin of Species* the immanent law of one-way selective adaptation of species to environment becomes a sufficient *explanans* unto itself.[5]

Nevertheless Darwin, if no doubt for largely expedient reasons, still left open the possibility that he had discovered a 'law of creation'. More decisively, the phrases in which he does so at the end of the *Origin* manifestly echo the design tradition in terms of its conviction that the pain and struggle of natural selection is justified by the beneficial 'good' of later outcomes.[6] A crucial aspect of the latter was theodicist: local and temporary ills were explained as necessary for the emergence of long-term or higher goods – indeed in Paley's case the divine ethics is wholly utilitarian. And for Paley already, long-term or higher goods are conceived in highly ascetic and stoic terms: 'a family containing a dying child is the best school of filial piety', as he joyfully informs us.[7] This same emphasis is consummated by the work of Malthus: the latter is quite misread if we suppose that he thought his gloomy demographic conclusion posed a problem for theology which he then had to solve. To the contrary, it is more as if the dire conclusion is uncritically embraced by a natural theology which thinks of virtue as emerging from a cosmic training in hardship.[8]

Darwin's central move was to extend Malthusian political economy to the economy of life as such. In doing so, he at last completed the Newtonian ambitions of the English design tradition – which one might describe as a bizarre fusion of a rather tame picture of nature on the one hand with the idea of a nature as a 'hard school' of training in order and excellence on the other. On the one hand, watercolours; on the other hand, cross-country runs. For now one had the equivalent of Newtonian motion in a straight line in the form of the *glissando* of constant variation of species. And one also had the equivalent of Newton's law of gravity in terms of the law of the survival of the fittest, as Darwin expressed it after Spencer. This is certainly, nevertheless, an oversimplification: for Darwin variation is still, by and large, a physically imposed alteration of a lingering (Aristotelian) biological and sexual selection, while inheritance of acquired characteristics plays some minor role in mutation. Nevertheless, the twin general model is overwhelmingly the norm: the ceaseless *glissando* along an absolute vital continuum; the emergence of relatively stable biological types interrupting this continuum by virtue of the law of struggle.

To what extent can one say that not just Darwin, but the entire Darwinian tradition remains informed by this Newtonian–Malthusian amalgam? In the case of the latter component, the law of struggle in the face of scarcity, it is not difficult to produce quotations from Richard Dawkins which show that he is essentially a Malthusian: every genetic or phenotypic success will eventually engender a further increased general scarcity to ensure the continuity of refinement produced through competition. Without some continuous dimension of radical shortage rendering terrestrial reality less than infinitely shareable, natural selection could not be the basic process at work.[9]

In the case of the former component, ceaseless chance variation of species, the situation is more complex. Quickly after Darwin came the thermodynamic and probabilistic revolutions in nineteenth-century physics. This could be seen as problematic for Darwinism insofar as it began to move away from the dominant Newtonian paradigm of clearly defined mechanical causation exhibiting a perfectly regular function, towards a looser sense of statistically verified constant conjuncture that might indicate an entire gamut of co-conspiring causal forces at work.[10] On the other hand, critics like Darwin's friend William Herschel had already pointed out that Darwin's selective mechanism could not, like Newtonian law, be deployed to make clear advance predictions, nor be experimentally manipulated – for this reason he described the Darwinian natural norm as 'the law of higgledy-piggledy'.[11] Thus it appeared to many that Darwinianism could be more naturally correlated with the new probabilistic scientific paradigm. However, this immediately suggested that 'natural selection' was something more diverse than originally intended, and perhaps not exclusively focused upon the law of struggle. This has then bequeathed a huge and often suppressed ambiguity to modern biology: insofar as Darwinism remains pure, it belongs to old-fashioned, possibly outmoded, Newtonian science; insofar as it can be correlated with modern physics, it ceases to remain, exactly, Darwinism. (And arguably, the further physics later drifted away from the Newtonian model, the worse this ambiguity has become.)

The new physics in its aspect as thermodynamic also encouraged the idea in biology that the *glissando* of organic variation is not Newtonian mechanical inertia plus Newtonian mechanical rupture, but rather a series tending to *crescendo* or *diminuendo*, to concentration or dispersal. Indeed, the new perspectives in physics offered a greater chance of integration with biology: organisms could be seen as instances of declining energy seeking a temporary refuge in relative equilibrium on the way to final entropy. And when these new perspectives were combined with the newly discovered science of genetics, then Darwin's organic variation could be understood in terms of genetic drift, as random bundles of genes exhibiting collectively certain tendencies measured in terms of statistical probability.

Lack of any understanding of heredity had clearly been a weakness in Darwin's theory. The hypothesis of genes can be seen as shoring it up by providing a precise physical location for organic variation. However, this only helps to confirm the first 'Newtonian' element of *glissando*, it does not necessarily confirm the second 'Newtonian' element, which is the law of survival.

It only unambiguously does so if, as with Richard Dawkins, one seeks to show natural selection at work fundamentally on the genetic level. Yet it is in fact far more likely that natural selection works at every level – genotypic, phenotypic, species-wide – and indeed, contrary to what Dawkins would have the British population believe, the general tendency of genetic theory from its origins until now has actually been to modify orthodox Darwinism. And it is for just this reason that one *can*, I think, claim that mainline Darwinism is Newtonian–Malthusian, and therefore is in a strange collusion with its Christian fundamentalist enemies. For genetic theory suggests, first of all, that the *glissando* of continuous variation is essentially vital rather than mechanically physical; secondly it suggests that this can result in genetic mutations that are not expressed at the phenotypic level and therefore never subject to the tests of natural selection, while further on down the generational line they will of themselves issue in phenotypic alterations. At the macro level of the scale, attention to the properties inherent only in populations, as with the great inter-war Russian–American biologist Theodosius Dobzhansky (incidentally – or not – a devout Russian Orthodox), has long encouraged attention to auto-poetic and internal shifts in animal constitution that are more to do with adaptation to an environment than with struggle for scarce terrain. Indeed, such a perspective has brought to the fore how species actively modify their own environment, and can sometimes modify it in harmony with other species with whom they form a yet larger quasi-grouping. Perception of natural agonism is not of course wrong, but it can be overstressed by too exclusive a preoccupation with the biological individual, rather than the smaller and the greater drifts within which it is swept up.[12]

What is more, one can go beyond Dobzhansky's nominalism which defined a species in terms of a local inter-breeding population. For after all, do we not first of all only *recognize* such a self-generating group because of an inescapable shared likeness?[13] Yet perhaps such recognition only records an 'accidental', not an essential, resemblance between members of a single biological lineage. This would suggest that the basic unit of the processes of evolution and natural selection is the individual. But then the question arises: what makes this individual *biological* in nature? The answer must have to do both with the inner inertial drive to organic self-development, and the drive to reproduce within certain regular parameters. Yet in that case, if one is to evade the most nakedly teleological construal of the biological individual (granting it a kind of 'quasi-intention'), then an entire gene population or sequence, or else an entire population group or sequence, becomes the more likely subject of the evolutionary plot. But if the group assumes priority in this way, then resemblance between individuals reverts from accident to essence, and biological existence must still be construed in metaphysically realist terms.

Accordingly, one must still think of the living individual as in some sense instantiating a formal essence. But this is further to imply that, as for Aristotle, specific form itself (however mysteriously) 'explains' in an ultimate and unsurpassable fashion. Moreover, since the nature of living form is to grow and to reproduce within certain regular, and yet not entirely theoretically delimitable parameters (as gardeners and parents know), then this form is inherently 'teleological' in the sense that its collective nature as internally moving and self-replicating across time (which is 'its own point' – a goal beyond goal) is participated in by individual living organisms, who in this non-intentional sense 'aim towards' their predefined fulfilment and flourishing. For this sort of reason, Etienne Gilson argued that Darwin himself had not really escaped the teleological perspective which defines biology as such.[14] Even Darwinism cannot escape the question as to why there is a 'drive to survival', an expression which sounds just as anthropomorphic as, say, the drive to appear, or to appear as beautiful. One might say, that, of course, nothing is seeking to survive, it is just that certain random mutations turn out, within given equally accidental conditions, to be able to persist. But this still leaves the question of the ontological character of the living unit. Why does a 'single' gene or pool of genes remain single such as to 'underlie' ('substantively') a process of mutation? Still more, why do genes and animals self-replicate over time in an organic way that produces constantly new individual instances of a recognizably 'same' species? These questions mean that one cannot really stop asking exactly what is it that in some sense seeks to survive and to increase, or simply to sustain an inertia beneath variety. Why should there be any tendency in nature consistently to remain rather than endlessly to disintegrate, disseminate and re-form only momentarily? In other words, why is not the *glissando* of continuous variation *far more* absolute than it appears to be? Why are there any consistent living things at all? For if variation were more absolute, if no continuities in growth and reproduction were readily discernible, then there would be no reason whatsoever to speak of 'life' in any sense whatsoever.

But once one has admitted that the drive to survive is teleological, then there is no reason not to suggest that there is equally a biological drive to expand self-manifestation in terms of growth and engendering – an extension of a drive to manifestation which may indeed characterize the individuation of all of physical reality as such.[15]

If, to the contrary, one really seeks to rid biology of all teleology, then, as with Dawkins, one must imply that all of life is epiphenomenal, a mere apparent cover for fully determined chemical and physical processes. Yet no-one has discovered exactly what these processes are that issue in such an upshot, still less, exactly how such processes throw up this sort of an illusion. And arguably it is transcendentally impossible for the latter discovery ever to be made, since the phenomenological experience of a supposed illusion – like that of colour in Locke's philosophy – always occurs in a 'language' that is incommensurable with the language of explanation of what is 'really' going on: nothing within mere mechanical interactions in any way anticipates, or could give rise to, the appearance of a tree anticipating spring, despite the fact that, at least to begin with, one cannot perceive a tree in any other way. Moreover, physics itself has abandoned the notion of all-pervading mechanism and all-pervasive efficient causality by recognizing, at the most fundamental of all levels, spontaneities, elective affinities and obscure tendencies of matter to persist in certain regular patterns. It becomes more plausible to read biological life in terms of an intense manifestation on the surface of a transcendental 'life' that undergirds all of finite reality and is even coterminous with being as such.

Strict Darwinism therefore remains a dubious, unphilosophical and unscientific ideology. It is still ultimately undergirded by exploded Newtonian physics and questionably pessimistic Malthusian demographics and political economy. In both respects, it is secretly a first cousin of its necessary enemy, the divine design hypothesis.

But what does this mean in practice? In either case one has a biological underwriting of the capitalist market system. In the Darwinian case it is true, certainly, that the refusal or minimalization of the inheritance of acquired characteristics does not lend itself as easily to 'social Darwinism' as do vitalist Lamarckian principles.[16] Nor does the inhumanly long timescale in which variation can issue in mutation. Nevertheless, Darwinism underwrites the picture of the struggling individual as the main social unit, of human groups struggling against each other, of eugenic manipulation as improving, along a measurable scale of value – namely survivability – something – namely humanity – which is but an accidental upshot of accidental processes. Left-Darwinians like Dawkins seem to have to project a possible human self-invention without any ontological basis in their scientific conclusions: quite coherently then, everyone knows about Dawkins's selfish gene, but few know about his recommended socially altruistic human being.[17]

It is striking that most, though not all, Christian evangelical opponents of evolution are enthusiastic supporters of the capitalist market. One can suggest that one latent reason for their horror at Darwin is that, in perhaps a very Anglo-Saxon way, it encourages tragic resignation in the face of market competition and not an unambiguous celebration of it as a glorious providential instrument for the training of freedom and independence.[18]

And both Darwinism and divine design envisage a political economy of nature, and for this reason further have in common a reduction of the vital to the mechanical: Dawkins still has a watchmaker, it is just that he is now blind, like the secularized hidden hand of the marketplace.[19] In essence they view animals as complex mechanisms and organic struggles as processes of mechanical action and reaction. Beneath even genetic appearances for Dawkins, as I have already suggested, there presumably lurk chemical and then atomic and sub-atomic ones. Life itself, then, must be an epiphenomenon: we are all always already dead, along with our cats, dogs and geraniums.

But does not the spectacle of the fight between the two fundamentalisms, biological and religious – a fight between first cousins – occlude from view an alternative vitalist way of understanding evolution? Darwin's mechanical reductionism was actually quite politically respectable and, as we have seen, it could readily be given back a theological gloss. In the seventeenth century it is often observable that a vitalist or 'hylozoist' atheism was seen as yet more threatening than the mechanical variety. A machine is implausibly self-constructed and self-operating, unless it is a vitally inspired automaton: but an underlying vital force truly can displace God or at least immanentize him. And this story was repeated in the nineteenth century. Many have argued that Darwin's bias towards design and mechanism was in fact a mode of distancing himself from the evolutionism of political radicals in France like Geoffroi St-Hilaire, for whom there was a kind of forceful (but not strictly 'teleological' he supposed) bias in matter itself towards greater and greater organization and self-awareness favourable to collective organization.

Vitalism and Transcendence

One can then suggest that the modern story of evolution concerns, not just the fate of a Newtonian God and the meaning of a biosphere without God, but also a vitalist and sometimes even semi-mystical conception of the biosphere which has taken many forms. The question of what happens now to a more traditional Catholic notion of God I shall advert to at the end of this chapter.

Quite simply and briefly, the vitalist view makes more sense than does the Darwinian one. To reduce consciousness and life to epiphenomena is not science, but mystification. An adequate ontology has to be able to accommodate the arrival of these emerging realities. A living thing, as Leibniz realized, has parts which, insofar as they are living, reflect to infinity the organization of the whole organism and its infinite relations to all the rest of physical reality: this precisely distinguishes nature (the divine art) from human art, for which the parts of a machine are not in themselves machines as reflecting the organization of the whole. (He also argued that every physical substance, or 'monad', is organic and so infinitely organized.) This infinite referral is the result of a self-sustaining action, an auto-poiesis. Life endlessly engenders life and does not *as* life die, for if death cannot generate life, then the priority of life over death renders it immortal; there is no life without resurrection, as Russian philosophy has often argued.[20] Nor is it born, since it is not caused. More and more, most significant biologists recognize that a vital genetic drift, and even the feedback of random phenotypic alteration, are the major factors in the evolutionary process, with natural selection confined to an ever yet more minor role.[21]

Nor does current biology any longer need to choose between pure chance on the one hand, or divine intervention on the other, in order to explain microcosmically complex phenomena like the eye. Instead, it can appeal to mathematics and to musical theory for the insight that chaos is a phantom mirage: processes can only exist as organized series and patterns, since every 'random' instance already contains patterns discernible for a selective gaze or a repeatable action, and these are the only possible modes of response, even if they are impersonal. What is it that causes selection and why are certain patterns favoured, not just at the organic level but at the sub-organic also? It is very hard to know, but it is at least impossible now not to conceive of ceaseless organic variation as truly a *glissando*, and moreover as one constantly interrupted by mysterious preferential selections which seem to have the force of 'revelations', as they do for the human composer of music when he selects from an infinite myriad of possible combinations.

These sorts of considerations have rightly tended to give a new currency to the thought of Henri Bergson.[22] One could read him as offering a double criticism, both of orthodox scientism and of orthodox theology (or rather as he supposed it to be), which pinpoints their hidden collusion. For Bergson, to suppose that reality is measurable and predictable like Cartesian space is to deny to it any auto-originative dimension and to encourage the deistic hypothesis of an ultimate originator and sustainer. (One can add here that if capitalism is the mechanization and spatialization of social reality – its reduction to statistical outcomes and maximum possible abstract repeatability – then we should not be surprised if a certain sort of deistic or voluntaristic God will always be re-invoked in every neoliberal historical moment ...)

As against this, Bergson reasonably suggested that life and consciousness, since they are upshots in excess of the merely physical, themselves offer a re-manifestation on the surface of the world, of processes at work in its deepest depths. When we gather up our forces to will and to create, we obscurely fuse past, present and future and directly intuit something that, in striving to bring about, we already see. In this fashion we directly experience in temporal *durée* the fundamental work of the *élan vital*. Human art and action are not then an epiphenomenal illusion, but neither are they a sudden alien intrusion upon reality. The consequence of this view, drawn by many of the greatest modernist artists, and perhaps supremely by the Catholic composer Olivier Messiaen and his pupils Iannis Xenakis and Pierre Boulez, is that the artist realizes in free creation also the most revealing experimental work of science.[23]

The priority of the vital over the physical can then be seen as essential to the securing of immanentism, even if this will tend to mean that the *élan vital*, however named, becomes an immanent deity, or even a quasi-transcendent one.

Peter Hallward, in a truly penetrating summary, has shown how most modern French philosophers are in this respect the heirs of Bergson.[24] They tend to identify the absolute as a creative force which consists in a *glissando* of constant variation (or absolute heterogeneity or internal self-differentiation) which is a perpetually non-identical repetition. While, in the case of Gilles Deleuze, this is an immanent absolute that is named variously 'a life' or 'pure composition' or 'the plane of immanence' or 'the abstract machine', the virtuality rather than actuality of this absolute is paralleled in philosophers like Michel Henry or Christian Jambet by the henological or 'beyond being' character of their notion of transcendence. But in either case, one has a resulting dualism in terms of the contrast between a 'good' transcendental creative factor on the one hand and a 'bad' static and representable created element on the other. This dualism is virulent precisely because the virtual creative factor is only actualized or self-realized in terms of the static element which inevitably obfuscates (both in terms of being and of knowing awareness) the very forces which sustain it and always exceed it.[25]

And already, in Bergson himself, the vital impulse does not truly exist apart from its tendency constantly to run into reverse, to look backwards, laying out time as memory and thereby engendering the spatial field that is studied by physics.[26] Picking up on post-thermodynamic notions of evolution, Bergson saw organic life as reverse entropy, temporarily recuperating its diminishing series, although also as that which constantly recuperated the self-renewing ultimate source of being (transcendental 'life') beyond the grasp of physical science as such.

In a similar fashion, Deleuze and Guattari see life as decoding the formally organized circular flows of physical *milieux* and thereby as establishing 'territories'. In their reading of the latter process in the case of animals, they are radically non-Darwinian and learn from both Bergson and the composer Messiaen. A bird singing his song is not primarily defending a territory, according to the chapter 'On the Refrain' in *A Thousand Plateaus,* but is rather continuously establishing it, for territorial animals make more explicit a decoding that removes a haecceity from the organized flux in order to restore and release energy that is endemic to life as such. A territory is for Deleuze and Guattari literally a sacred space established by animal art before it is an assurance of sufficient food and security, since animality *need not* seek these things through a process of individuation: it simply happens to do so, or even in some fashion *chooses* to do so.

Again in keeping with Bergson, the territory is for Deleuze and Guattari already a reaching beyond itself, a deterritorialization precisely because its drawing of a circle in order to contain energy has conjured the power of absolute heterogeneity whose virtual capacity exceeds the circle that it draws in the very process of drawing it. The refrain that the bird sings is equivalently a folding back upon itself of the uninterrupted *glissando* of life in order to establish a theme, and a cry that represents animal identity and wards off the threat of destruction. Yet the territorial refrain can already be expanded into a song of courtship and even into pure variations that have lost sight of all function, as Olivier Messiaen had already concluded.

For Deleuze and Guattari, this same process is simply taken further in human beings: our highest effort is to conjugate forces which send *milieux* and territories spinning into free-play but without disappearing altogether into chaos or invoking the heterogeneous as a new sort of closure. One could say that, for them, this is a new sort of post-human and ecological sociality. It is intended to resist both narrowly defended terrains on the one hand, and entirely abstract universal modes of capture like that of capitalism, on the other. It concerns the 'betweens' of reality and the 'diagonals' that exit from the vertical spatial and horizontal temporal coordinates within which they are inscribed. This is their 'path of flight' – not really one of straightforward escape, but rather of escape both from stifling enclosure and the vacuous loneliness of mere escapism – escape for the sake of escape. Insofar as it aims somehow magically to capture the forces of the cosmos itself it is apparently unlike Derrida's appeal to an 'impossible' donative *différance* which is merely regulative and cannot be in any sense realized. It is also somewhat unlike the usual Marxist injunctions merely to negate the given or await its immanent collapse. It is rather a Spinozistic injunction to individuals already and always to create a positive, joyful conjugation of forces.

In this manner, (Bergsonian or Deleuzian) vitalism seems to combine a sophisticated reading of modern science with a continuing role for metaphysics and an ontological ground for the human pursuit of hopeful social projects.

But is this entirely the case? We saw that the eighteenth- and nineteenth-century

Anglo-Saxon God of intelligent design is a half-immanent God interacting on the same plain with what he influences. From this there results a fundamental dualism of the creative and designing on the one hand and the inert and the designed on the other. This dualism is *not* the result of having a transcendent principle, a transcendent *esse – intellegere – velle* from which finite being is entirely derived in all degrees of its existence, including secondary causality and creaturely freedom. It is rather the result of dividing up the finite world into spheres of influence between a quasi-transcendent principle on the one hand, and sheerly finite causal process, on the other.

But this means that vitalism, by switching to the apparent monism of pure vitalist immanentism, does not get rid of this dualism, but rather augments it by rendering it aporetically virulent. In a hypostasized double negation the fixed and apparent is merely the phenomenal guise for the dynamic and virtual, which nevertheless only 'is' at all through its phenomenal self-occlusion. It is all rather like Thomas Carlyle's deconstructed account of German idealism and romanticism: the phenomenal world is only the 'clothing' of the real ideal world; and yet the examination of human culture reveals that the entire realm of thought is itself but a matter of 'fashionable clothing' or temporarily preferred image and metaphor. Hence by implied analogy the cosmic clothing conceals a null energy which is merely the power to clothe and so to disguise itself.[27]

Any immanentism whatsoever tends to succumb to this model of double disguise, of the real by appearance, but more fundamentally of appearance by the supposed real. In constantly 'uncovering' the illusion of uncovering itself, postmodernism does little more than expound the grammar of such immanentism that it never calls into question. For, to repeat, in any immanentism there is the whole or the director of the whole which is the truly real: for Bergson it is the *élan vital* that is absolutely self-differentiating, with an absoluteness not without *some* kinship with the absolute time of Isaac Newton. But this 'absolute', as with Spinoza's substance, Heidegger's Being, Deleuze's 'a life', Derrida's *différance*, is only 'actual' in another subordinate realm that it ceaselessly erects and dismantles.[28] In Bergson's case this is the realm of space which is all that ordinary cognition ever represents.

Since subordination is involved here, even if the subordinating requires the subordinate in order to be at all (but whenever does it not, one might ask?) then this *schema* involves always not only dualism, but also hierarchy between a higher conditioning power and a lower conditioned reality. One can try, like François Laruelle, to be more avant-garde than all the avant-garde in thinking a purer immanence by constructing and invoking an absolute that exists purely as self-presupposition that is immediately a self-positing without any conditioning of an 'outside'.[29] Yet Laruelle is still led to say that this process itself, in order to attain a thinkable actuality, throws up the spheres of conditioning/conditioned that are conventionally constructed and theorized by both practical life and philosophy, even if these are not supposed to feed back into the ultimate unthinkable nullity that is also everything. Dualism and hierarchy are therefore the secret heart of all immanentisms.

Why should this matter, politically? It matters because immanentist vitalism cannot really think an advance to a better world. Deleuze's intentions were in many ways admirable, but his notion of composition is inherently unstable and contradictory, pulled in two opposite directions at once. To the degree that the path of flight deterritorializes, it also tends to a void nullity or chaos that will either swallow it up or be recruited as an abstract basis for totalizing rule. Inversely, to the degree that, to use the musical example deployed by Deleuze and Guattari, atonality remains rooted in the tonality of territory, it will still affirm local prejudices. That there *needs* to be, ethically and politically, a mean between the concretely local and the merely void and abstract universal is correct, as Deleuze, to his credit, recognizes. And yet his Bergsonian outlook cannot really think this medium.

Why? Because a univocal process of pure self-differentiation is only realized through the very realities that it must also constantly negate: milieux, aggregates and territories. The 'mechanosphere' includes both these things, and to pursue a line of flight is in the end to be resigned to evil as well as good, enclosure as well as freedom, so it is only personal and stoic liberation after all.[30]

Crucial here is a point made by Peter Hallward which supplies a second reason for concern. Absolute heterogeneity is self-generating difference and therefore it is the many insofar as it is one, and the one insofar as it is many, but not in any sense a mediation between the two. It contains no *relation*, and this is not a plea for Hegelianism. Rather, it is a demonstration that even Deleuze's differential metaphysics reduces to an oscillation that is also a coincidence between the one and the many (or the subject and the other) that is actually still the dialectical *failure* to think mediation or 'the between', as William Desmond has argued with respect to Hegel.[31] By contrast, in the spatialized or territorialized level of Deleuze's 'chaosmos' there are apparent relations and representations, but these relations are not originally constitutive, since each spatial reality is ultimately directly engendered by absolute heterogeneity: the acausal deterritorializing force which establishes the real primarily as difference in excess of any preceding continuities of essence. Their harmony is not, indeed, exactly pre-established, but it is constantly re-established by continuous occasional intervention, even if the spatial things do not really occupy any ground independent of such intervention, and even if the intervention is only 'there' in the intervening. Hence Deleuze declares that, while his differential monads are no longer discrete, they remain, in their (Whiteheadian) 'prehending' of each other (non-relationally) 'windowless'.[32]

But without real relations, human beings and all other organisms are reduced to the subservience of a vital flow: their only possibility of salvific self-escape must consist in self-abolition through identification with this vital flux. And if relations themselves cannot mutually constitute something that discloses ultimate reality, then there is no real hope for a social and ecological transformation that acknowledges both individuals and their vital bonds to others, without which they could not live or express any values.

The question here is, if the *glissando* of the vital process is actualized only through 'notes', 'scales' and 'metres', then do we necessarily need to see the latter

as *in any sense at all* interrupting or completing the *glissando* rather than as
serially constituting it? This is the same as to ask, *does* the vital process exist in a
pure heterogeneity that always expresses the same univocal One, or does it rather
consist, as William Desmond has suggested (in a bold attempt to 'dynamize' and
temporalize Thomistic analogy), in endless analogical relations that express
simultaneously identity and difference? In the first case, as with Hegel, one has
only an apparent coincidence of opposites whose constantly renewed *aporia* in
point of fact still respects formal logic. In the second case, one has a more radical
and irreducible coincidence of opposites precisely because there is as much
persisting pleasurable tension as there is reconciliation, a tension that sustains, as
Desmond puts it, the agapeic distance of the other (in its relatively 'univocal'
singularity) within and yet beyond the erotic moment of fusion (which, unlike the
philosophers of difference, he does not moralistically deny). This coincidence of
the genuine *metaxu* can truly only be 'heard' rather than thought, as Desmond
suggests, in poetry or music.[33] And perhaps it can be heard in the most maximally
strained, and so verifying, degree in the most extreme of modern or postmodern
musics, where 'harmony' remains in some extended sense despite all the
disharmony and complexity. Certainly in Messiaen, if not in Xenakis, the
continuous perpetual variation of unpredictable rhythm is not superior to, but is
rather something constantly arriving with, the invocation of a spatial coloration
invoked through sound. This 'synaesthesia' renders his always programmatic
music 'poetic', if one takes poetry to be the instance of the blending of the various
sensory mediums, a blending which, as 'common sense', one can see as giving rise
to language as such and so thought as such. (Here also one has an ineffable
'between', without which, nonetheless, thought would not really operate.)

By contrast with this synaesthetic and metaxological blending of 'organizing'
time and organized space, it is arguable that the continuing downgrading of space
and visibility in modern French thought is still very Cartesian in character.
Bergson had not really felt the force of the new physics, which, in effect, from the
mid-nineteenth century onwards, precisely restored the hermeticism and
neoplatonism that Newton (who was precisely *not* the last of the magicians) had
tried to keep at bay: the primacy of light; the role of descending series; action at a
distance; apparently unmediated harmonization; the coincidence of opposites; the
irreversibility of a time that is not absolute; the multiplicity of finite infinites.
(There are anticipations of most of these things in Robert Grosseteste, Giordano
Bruno and others, as recent research shows, and it is also the case that early
twentieth-century physics was imbued with the spirit of the second wave of
romanticism that mutated into modernism.)[34] By contrast, Bergson still saw
physics as concerned with the precisely measurable, and did not explore the
aporias, given ecstasies and mysterious relationality of space in the same way that
he explored the paradoxes of time. (Perhaps for this reason he not only read,
perhaps validly, Einstein's space–relative time as only spatialized time and not true
durée, but he also failed to read *durée* as itself relative to eminent extension.)[35]

This meant that he did not consider the possibility that the irreducible relational
interfolding of past, present and future is not simply the work of a temporal self-

differentiation, but might equally be the work of a spatial 'laying out' of such moments in a display, such that 'relation' lies not simply 'inside' a thing (G.E. Moore's 'internal relation'), else it would be that thing, or the totality of all things, negating event and contingency, nor simply 'outside' that thing (Moore's 'external relation') in which case it would merely belong to another thing or again to all things (as with Hume, a hero of Deleuze) with the same upshot.[36] For there to be events in time, there must be a spatial 'laying out' of temporal moments, but their mutual ecstasy is not thereby simply abolished, but instead is expressed in a different way in the mystery of the 'between' that is real relationality, neither internal nor external. Temporal ecstasy is the 'erotic' inwardness and savour of mutuality; but spatial mutuality is the 'agapeic' externality and reaching endlessly out towards the ecstatic goal. And each is relative to the other.

The third criticism concerns the question of series and gift, two names for the same thing in the writings of the pagan neoplatonist Proclus.[37] If complexity always falls out as an ordered series, then it is always a rising or a falling, always has a greater or lesser focus or foci. For this reason the usual 'radical' objection to hierarchy as such is the worst naivety, for, ontologically speaking, there is always hierarchy, and equality can only be achieved by the subtle blending of asymmetrical ascendancies. (Most of our current political thought fails to see precisely this.) It is notable that 'hierarchy' was only the name given by Dionysius the Areopagite to the 'series' of the pagan neoplatonists, which always had a mathematical dimension.[38] So I do not altogether complain of Deleuze's immanentist hierarchy – only of its stasis and absolute non-reversibilty. Whereas the neoplatonic series was always psychically ascendable, one can only climb Deleuze's stoic staircase to the end of subjective annihilation. This means, in consequence, that if Deleuze's vital series 'gives', like Plotinus's One, what it does not have (since it is beyond being, which is nonetheless derived from it), namely all the various ontological actualities which he isolates (*milieux*, territories and so forth), it also takes away what it gives, does not allow any return gift of gratitude to the absolute, and finally calls one beyond any generous reciprocity.[39] In this way, the human creative act might, as with Bergson, invoke the absolute, but it cannot as gift invoke an absolute giving and sharing. Yet art is perhaps distinguished from science as gift ... as Iannis Xenakis declared in his thesis defence, *Arts/Sciences – Alloys*, to select is to receive a revelation as if 'by grace'. And to offer a work of art is to offer delight and so a gift 'meritoriously', not just the usefulness of instruction.[40]

The political advantage of vitalism is that the creative human effort is here in tune with, even disclosive of, the ultimate. But the hope for positive social construction demands more than this heroic individualism: it demands that our mutual love, relating and surprising in order to forge new bonds, be also in tune with the ultimate. But supposing that we were to hear the music of Messiaen, whose thoughts about territory and the refrain are invoked at the most pivotal point of *A Thousand Plateaus,* otherwise than he was heard by Deleuze? In his own voluminous but fragmentary writings, the composer constantly tries to fuse the thought of Bergson on time with the thoughts of Aquinas on the relation of time and the cosmos to eternity.[41] He certainly embraces the notion that music is primarily non-identical repetition, continuous variation, and so manifests *durée*, yet he denies that the latter is 'immediately given' to consciousness; instead it is only experienced through all our corporeal and spatial interactions that alone produce continuous rhythm. And even though the latter is the temporal essence of music, sound has a synaesthesic aspect which conjures up for us colours, specific spatial sites and objects of visual contemplation. Hence, for all the abstractness of Messiaen's rhythmic lines, and for all his invoking of the non-narrative dimensions of intensity, timbre, polyrhythm, polydynamics, polyharmony, heteroharmony, and so forth (and arguably he neglects too much the narrative dimension, writing *no* liturgical music!), his music remains situated and   representational. In keeping with this, the step-wise forward movements always simultaneously spread out into a vast and varied simultaneous sonority. As his pupil Pierre Boulez put it, what one should hear through all this is the strange 'diagonal' where harmony and colour blend with rhythm and melody.[42]

But in that case the diagonal is the mediation of the seemingly heterogeneous. It is, in fact, another name for the *metaxu*. And for Deleuze it is this diagonal that is the line of flight. But can his be the true diagonal, the true between, if it veers hopelessly between vertical arboreality and a never fully attained quality of the sheerly rhizomatic? This Deleuzian diagonal is not, indeed, a relation, since it seeks to escape from both traps, but really it can never escape from either, and is stuck in a shuttle. Just because, in order to be a free pure relationality without relation between points, it must escape the vertical and the horizontal, its relationality is fully captured all the time by either pole. Moroever, its diagonality does not *express*, participate in the absolute, since this is the sheer horizontality of the purely virtual ...

In this way immanentism, in refusing a transcendent God, always winds up by deifying an impersonal process and ontologically subordinating those concrete situations within which alone human beings can truly dwell as human.

So Deleuze finally failed to hear Messiaen's diagonal as ultimate, or as on the way to an infinite diagonal. Messiaen's diagonal remains truly a pure relation just because it does not seek to escape its two co-ordinates, and yet is still the 'surplus' to them which alone links them in order to render them elements of a complex, perhaps cosmic, music.

Hence Deleuze misreads the line of flight. It goes just as much upwards with the trees as it burrows along with the roots of the prairie. If it is to escape and yet remain, it must continue to relate and never abandon one pole of this relating for the other. This means that its flight *denies* the ultimacy of any immanent process or any partially immanent Godhead, because this will always consecrate a duality that renders relationality subordinate. To say that the givenness of spatial laws traps us in impersonal fixity and cold terroristic rule is true – but the idea of a one-way, impersonal, temporal gift that gives only itself to itself, traps us just as surely.

Instead, we need to think the vital as relational or metaxological. But in that case there is no controlling power within the finite world, and there is nothing that inscribes a boundary round this world. There is only the sequence and pattern of intertangling diagonals in interaction with pattern-forming processes (horizontally) and open-ended, always developing essences (vertically). Properly to re-constitute this world diagonally is indeed to move along a horizontal path, as when one is ascending an inclined staircase, but it is also to climb upwards, to reach beyond this world altogether. Progress forwards through time is possible because it is simultaneously a reaching to transcendence, not a re-invocation of a primordial impersonal process. We can therefore only reach towards better social relations insofar as we come to understand ourselves as participating in a higher source of relationality that constantly gives itself.

For if relations are to be ultimate within this world, they can only be grounded in relationality. But if this is something finite, then *either* it is a given set of spatial relations which reduces to a totality and is not relation, *or* it is a giving temporal relationality which reduces to the monism of time, and again is not a relation.

No, if relationality or 'the between' is to be ultimate within the world, then the world itself must be purely relation, purely a medium: down to its ground something received, such that it is at bottom a relation to itself as other, a reception of itself as gift which it must then give to itself; this allows that the inner reality of the cosmos is vital, even psychic in Bergson's sense.[43] But it also ensures that the auto-poetic is from the outset also relational, also social, also a response, also involved in giving and receiving. This alone ensures that hierarchic series are gifts and reversible, even the hierarchy of Creator and creation, since by perfect reception and response the human creature, and the cosmos through the human, can be deified.

Within this conception, it does, indeed, remain true, as for Carlyle and as recognized by Shakespeare in *The Tempest*, that finite reality itself is a flimsy garment, a theatre, a dream. But it also ceases to be the case that this dream apparently conceals a 'real' spiritual dreamer, whose supposition in turn conceals the reality *only* of 'concealment', of dreaming. This 'postmodern' scenario was already mooted by the greatest Baroque dramatists, namely Shakespeare and Calderón, but they both also envisaged how it is played out within a Catholic dramaturgy.

For what matters in *The Tempest* within the magical artifice of Prospero's disclosure through fiction (allegorical masques) of the historical truth, and his conjuration of justice, is that both truth and justice must in the end subserve the higher and more voluntary magic of mercy and reconciliation. In this way, even though the cosmos remains a theatrical dream, Prospero can in the end abandon his 'rough magic' because he now sees this dream as upheld by divine mercy and grace. In other words, the 'dream' is real to a finite degree just because it allows some exercise of a non-compromising goodness which seeks a true 'between', or analogical co-dwelling of creatures, human and bestial. So whereas the 'dream' of appearance within immanence is constantly cancelled only to reappear constantly in a shuttle without meaning, the dream that creatively emanates from a transcendent source is granted a certain reality of its own, just to the measure that it is given, and gratefully returns, a certain share of the good. Here, then, a being without the good is 'mere dream' or illusion, but a being with the good is also a good that is (somewhat) actual (rather than being intended, or primarily an imperative, as for Kant, or a pre-ontological subjectively constitutive imperative, as for Lévinas).[44]

It is the same dramatic argument in Calderón's *La Vida es Sueno*.[45] Here the protagonist, Segismund, Prince of Poland, has been imprisoned without any human contact in order to forestall a prophecy that he will rule as a tyrant. His father Basil feels that, in justice, this prophecy should be tested, and has Segismund released, but on the merciful condition that if he should indeed prove tyrannous he will later be told that he has only dreamt that he was for a day a ruler. The prophecy is indeed fulfilled, and Segismund proves in one horrendous day of misgovernment to be both unruly and violent. However, he then himself concludes that whether or not he was dreaming during this interlude is irrelevant: for each of us only dreams what happens to us or what we are, insofar as we are always performing a role (as for Carlyle) and the entire creation is itself a divine artifice in which we play our allotted parts. This means that, for Calderón, beneath the idea of disguise, lies the reality that, if there is *only* disguise then, whatever role we are performing, we are after all only performing ourselves as some mask or another. Thus, in this instance, Segismund only dreams that he is a ruler, but ironically he truly is, by destiny, just this ruler (so that he is, in fact, dreaming who he really is), but then again such a role is purely an artifice, a seeming.

However, Segismund finally repents and is released to become a worthy ruler. It is realized that human beings are not bound to tragic fate, and that the attempt to evade the prophecy itself ensured that Segismund became the inhuman monster that the prophecy foretold. Segismund declares that all that matters, awake or dreaming, is the doing of justice and the granting of mercy, for in this way finitude is granted its true measure of significance, and so of reality, in accordance with the divine intention:

> To act with virtue
> Is what matters, since if this proves true,
> That truth's sufficient reason in itself;
> If not, we win us friends against the time
> When we at last awake.[46]

This is expressed in terms of the absence of any true human life if it is 'without honour', and honour in turn is seen as a preparedness to receive gifts and, still more, liberally to grant them. Thus, within the perspective of transcendence, appearances and temporary states are 'saved' because they are seen as instances of gift which can only be recognized if this founding generosity is taken up and perpetuated.

It follows that, if one allows the seemingly greater dualism of Creator and created, there ensues, paradoxically, no unbridgeable dualism, and no psychically unclimbable stairway. Within immanence one has to choose between the less real appearance of the vertical on the one hand, and the less actual, but more finally real, truth of the horizontal on the other. But if the *metaxu* of diagonal relation is truly ultimate, then there is no duality in this world between appearance and reality or actuality and virtuality, for *all* is now, *more radically than for postmodernism,* ephemeral shadowy image, and yet the shadow can still in itself bear the trace of goodness, and therefore can fully participate in, and not occlude, the real, just insofar as the theatre of shadows becomes also the scene of an enactment of cosmic justice and mercy (towards all creatures, not just human ones).

As for the duality between God and the world: it does not exist in any simple fashion. For in leaving this world for God along the diagonal of Jacob's ladder one only receives back this world with more intensity and more advance towards its *eschaton*. As Maximus the Confessor put it: if the visible things refer always to the invisible, the invisible things refer always back to the visible.[47]

But is not relation abolished in God as the ultimate source? Not according to Catholic understanding. To the contrary it argues (and I am thinking especially of John Scottus Eriugena here) that if God is the one who creates and receives back from the creation its tribute of praise, then he *is* this, as himself outside himself, but also he *is* this, as not merely himself within himself. We are given to ourselves vertically always in the mode of a simultaneous cosmic and social ecstasy towards finite others, because God is in himself both vertical interchange of gift and horizontal absolute continuity. God is at last *entirely* the diagonal medium because the Father is only 'above' the Son in generating the Son, and the process of engenderment is nothing but the Son in his vertical iconicity itself. (For this reason an 'entire' diagonal medium is, in an extraordinary sense, 'univocally analogical', because the Son is a 'perfect' likeness to the Father and univocally at one with him in infinite being, as Eckhart taught.)[48] This diagonal line is infinitely and entirely expressed in the Father–Son absolute substantive relation, but as infinite expression it is also infinitely unexhausted, and like a fractal line winds on, as it were, from two to three and then presumably infinite dimensions in the Holy Spirit, whose substantive relation to Father and Son forms a 'square' on the base of their mutual love.

In the New Testament, the name of the receptive and exchanging Holy Spirit as the ultimate transcendental 'between' is therefore 'gift', but it is also therefore 'life'. For if God is the infinitely sustained exchange of gift, then he is also supremely life, as that which is self-sustaining, self-increasing and self-engendering. And if God supremely gives to the Creation the gift of being, then he must also give to it life since, also in finitude, to be without remainder gift is to be likewise without remainder, yet here by grace of another, perpetually self-renewing.[49]

Therefore the only perfected metaphysics of vitalism must be a Catholic one, a philosophy that is equally a true exegesis of the Gospel.

Notes

1   Even as sophisticated an academic as John Dupré gets this whole area hopelessly wrong, simply because he has no knowledge of the history of theology and the real

nature of its interaction with science. Hence he assumes that 'the argument from design' is the strongest traditional argument for the existence of God, whereas in the most authentic Christian theological tradition (Augustine, Maximus, Aquinas, Cusanus, Pascal) it simply did not figure at all. See John Dupré, 'Human Origins and the Decline of Theism', *Darwin's Legacy: What Evolution Means Today*, Oxford: OUP, 2003.

2   See Simon Oliver, 'Motion according to Aquinas and Newton', *Modern Theology* 17 no. 2 (2001), pp.163–99, and *Divine Motion: Physics and Theology*, London: Routledge, 2005.

3   See Amos Funkenstein, *Theology and the Scientific Imagination: from the Middle Ages to the Seventeenth Century*, Princeton, NJ: Princeton UP, 1986, pp.23–117; Jacob Schmutz, 'La Doctrine Médiévale des Causes et la Théologie de la Nature Pure (XIIIe–XVIIe siècles)', *Revue Thomiste* nos I–II (Jan-June 2001), pp.217–64.

4   Michael J. Behe, *Darwin's Black Box*, New York: Simon and Schuster, 1996.

5   See John Hedley Brooke, *Science and Religion: Some Historical Perspectives*, Cambridge: CUP, 1991, pp.192–226; Anthony Baker, 'Theology and the Crisis in Darwinism', *Modern Theology* 18 (April 2002), pp.183–215.

6   Charles Darwin, *The Origin of Species*, J.W. Burrow ed., Harmondsworth: Penguin, 1979, pp.458–60.

7   Cited by Baker, op. cit.

8   See John Milbank, *Theology and Social Theory: Beyond Secular Reason*, Oxford: Blackwell, 1990, pp.42–5; Baker, op. cit., and Michael Hanby, 'Creation Without Creationism: Toward a Theological Critique of Darwinism', *Communio* 30 (Winter 2003), pp.654–94.

9   See Baker, op. cit. and Hanby, op. cit.

10 For all the following discussion on the probabilistic/thermodynamic revolution and its impact upon biology, see David J. Depew and Bruce H. Weber, *Darwinism Evolving: Systems Dynamics and the Genealogy of Natural Selection*, Cambridge MA: MIT, 1997, pp.167–329.

11 See Hanby, op. cit.

12 Depew and Weber, op. cit., pp.161–497.

13 See Hanby, op. cit. and Marjorie Grene, 'Introduction' to *Dimensions of Darwinism: Themes and Counter-Themes in Twentieth-Century Evolutionary Theory*, Marjorie Grene, ed., Cambridge: CUP, 1983, pp.1–15.

14 Etienne Gilson, *From Darwin to Aristotle and Back Again: A Journey in Final Causality, Species and Evolution*, Notre Dame IN: Notre Dame UP, 1982.

15 See Jacob von Uexküll, *Theoretical Biology*, trans. D.L. Mackinnon, London: Kegan Paul, Trench Teubner and Co., 1926.

16 See Depew and Weber, op. cit., pp.193–217; Peter J. Bowler, *Darwinism*, New York: Twayne, 1993.

17 Richard Dawkins, *The Blind Watchmaker: Why the Evidence of Evolution Reveals a Universe Without Design*, New York: W.W. Norton, 1996. For important critiques of Dawkins and Darwinism, see David Berlinsky, 'The Deniable Darwin', *Commentary* 101 no. 6 (1996), pp.27–8, and Alister McGrath, *Dawkins' God: Genes, Memes and the Meaning of Life*, Oxford: Blackwell, 2005.

18 See Jim Wallis, *God's Politics*, San Francisco: Harper, 2005, for a discussion of the Christian new right by a left-wing evangelical.

19 Richard Dawkins, *The Blind Watchmaker*.

20   See G.W. Leibniz, *Monadology* 64. *Principles of Nature and Grace, Founded on Reason* 4. For the Russian perspective, see Sergius Bulgakov, *Philosophy of Economy: the World as Household*, trans. Catherine Evtuhov, New Haven: Yale UP, 2000.

21   See Depew and Weber, op. cit., pp.479–97.

22   See especially, Henri Bergson, *Creative Evolution*, trans. Arthur Mitchell, New York: Dover, 1998.

23   For ideas on Messiaen and the entire question of musical ontology on which the current chapter is drawing, see Catherine Pickstock, 'Quasi una Sonata: Postmodernism, Religion and Music', *Theology and Music*, Jeremy Begbie, ed., Cambridge: CUP, forthcoming. See also Ian Darbyshire, 'Messiaen and the Representation of the Theological Illusion of Time', and Roberto Fabbi, 'Theological Implications of Restrictions in Messiaen's Compositional Processes', *Messiaen's Language of Mystical Love*, Siglind Bruhn, ed., New York: Garland, 1998, pp.33–55 and 55–84, respectively.

24   Peter Hallward, 'The One or the Other: French Philosophy Today', *Angelaki*, vol. 8, no. 2 (August 2003), pp.1–33.

25   Gilles Deleuze, *Pure Immanence: Essays on a Life*, trans. Anne Boyman, New York: Zone, 2001, pp. 25–35. See esp. p. 31: 'Events or singularities give to the plane all their virtuality, just as the plane of immanence gives virtual events their full reality ... A wound [an instance of the Stoic 'incorporeal'] is incarnated or actualised in a state of things or of life; but it is itself a pure virtuality on the plane of immanence that leads us into a life.'

26   Bergson, *Creative Evolution*, Chapter III, pp.186–272.

27   Thomas Carlyle, *Sartor Resartus: the Life and Times of Herr Teufelsdröckh*, introduced by Alasdair Gray, illustrated by Edmund J. Sullivan, Edinburgh: Canongate, 1987.

28   See Conor Cunningham, *Genealogy of Nihilism*, London: Routledge, 2002.

29   François Laruelle, 'What Can Non-Philosophy Do?', *Angelaki*, vol. 8, no. 2 (August 2003), pp.169–91.

30   Gilles Deleuze and Felix Guattari, *A Thousand Plateaus*, trans. Brian Massumi, London: Athlone, 1987, pp.501–17.

31   William Desmond, *Hegel's God: a Counterfeit Double?,* London: Ashgate, 2003.

32   Gilles Deleuze, *The Fold: Leibniz and the Baroque*, trans. Tom Conley, London: Athlone, 1993, p.81: 'Prehension is naturally open, open onto the world, without having to pass through a window.' See also pp.121–37.

33   In BB, 177–225.

34   See Iain M. Mackenzie, The *'Obscurism' of Light*, Norwich: The Canterbury Press, 1996; Hilary Gatti, *Giordano Bruno and Renaissance Science*, Ithaca: Cornell UP, 1999; James T. Cushing, *Philosophical Concepts in Physics: the Historical Relation Between Philosophy and Scientific Theories*, Cambridge: CUP, 1998; Roger Penrose, *The Road to Reality: A Complete Guide to the Laws of the Universe*, London: Jonathan Cape, 2004.

35   See Henri Bergson, *Duration and Simultaneity: Bergson and the Einsteinian Universe*, trans. Robin Durie, Manchester: Clinamen, 1999.

36   See Gilles Deleuze, *Pure Immanence*, pp.35–53.

37   See, for example, Proclus, *Elements of Theology*, trans. E.R. Dodds, Oxford: OUP, 1963, Propositions 18, 20, 42.

38   Dionysius the Areopagite, *The Complete Works*, trans. Colm Luibhéid, London: SPCK, 1987.

39   For a critique of Plotinus in relation to the gift, see Claude Bruaire, *L' Être et l'Esprit*, Paris: PUF, 1983, pp.95–107.

40   Iannis Xenakis, *Arts/Sciences–Alloys: The Thesis Defence of Iannis Xenakis Before Olivier Messiaen et al.*, trans. Sharon Kanach, New York: Pendragon Press, 1985, pp.27–47 and 61–79; dialogues with Olivier Messiaen and Michel Serres, respectively.

41   Olivier Messiaen, *Traité de Rythme, de Couleur et d'Ornithologie*, vol. I, Paris: Leduc, 1994, esp. pp.7–52.

42   Pierre Boulez, *Notes of an Apprenticeship*, trans. R.Weinstock, New York: Knopf, 1968, pp.231–2, 295–301, 382–3.

43   This is argued by Bruaire, *L'Être et l'Esprit*, pp.51–87 and *passim*.

44   Nevertheless, a Lévinasian thesis of the priority of good over being could be seen as partially confirmed here. See William Shakespeare, *The Tempest*, ed. Anne Barton, Harmondsworth: Penguin, 1996, Act IV, Scene I, 140–58: 'These our actors/As I foretold you, were all spirits, and/Are melted into air, into thin air;/And, like the baseless fabric of this vision,/The cloud-capp'd towers, the gorgeous palaces,/The solemn temples, the great globe itself,/Yea, all which it inherit, shall dissolve,/And, like this insubstantial pageant faded,/Leave not a rack behind'. See also, Act V, Scene I, 40–47 and 10–20.

45   Calderón de la Barca, *Life is a Dream*, trans. Roy Campbell, *The Classic Theatre Vol III: Six Spanish Plays*, Eric Bentley ed., New York: Doubleday, 1959, pp. 407–80, esp. pp. 456, 466, 477.

46   Calderón, *Life is a Dream*, Act III, p.462.

47   Maximus the Confessor, 'The Church's Mystagogy', *Selected Writings*, trans. George C. Berthold, New York: Paulist Press, 1985, Chapter Two, p.189.

48   See Burkhard Mojsisch, *Meister Eckhart: Analogy, Univocity and Unity*, trans. Orrin F. Summerell, Amsterdam/Philadlephia: B.R. Grüner, 2001.

49   Michel Henry has explored this in an indispensable way, despite the fact that his dualism of 'inner' life versus external embodiment and his concomitant claim that 'auto-affection is transcendentally prior to mediation by external sensation' (a conclusion that is importantly disputed by Chrétien) gives a certain quasi-Manichean cast to his exegesis and theological reflections. See Michel Henry, *I Am the Truth: Toward a Philosophy of Christianity*, Stanford CA.: Stanford UP, 2003, and 'Phenomenology of Life' (a useful short summary of his entire philosophy), *Angelaki*, vol. 8, no. 2 (August 2003), pp.97–111.

Chapter 16
All Things Shining:
Desmond's Metaxological Metaphysics
and *The Thin Red Line*

Christopher Ben Simpson

Central to William Desmond's work is insight into a certain basic plurivocity to thought. There is a play and interrelation at various registers within and between thought's voicings – between philosophy and its others. This essay is an attempt at suggesting such a polyphony and intermediation between Desmond's thought and one particular 'other': Terrence Malick's 1998 film, *The Thin Red Line*. It endeavours to bring Desmond's plurivocal philosophy into conversation with the strange voice of this moving picture. It suggests a kind of optics: reading/viewing Malick's cinematic lens through Desmond's philosophical lens(es). We will ask how Desmond's meditations on ultimacy through several metaxological themes can facilitate a kind of 'theological' reading/viewing of Malick's film.

Desmond's Metaxological Metaphysics

The Fourfold Sense of Being

Central to Desmond's philosophy is what he calls the fourfold sense of being. The four principal ways one can think about being are the univocal, the equivocal, the dialectical and the metaxological. The *univocal* (BB, 47–83) stresses simple sameness, unmediated unity between mind and being.[1] For the univocal, all being is intelligible, and all intelligibility is determinate; therefore, all being has determinate intelligibility; to be is to be intelligible (BB, 16). For Desmond, the univocal sense alone does not do justice to 'the *plurivocal nature* of metaphysical thinking' (BB, 17). The *equivocal* stresses unmediated difference between self and other, mind and being: unmediatable plurality (BB, 85–130; PUMT, 119).[2] The *dialectical* achieves sameness through mediating differences; it 'converts the mediation of self and other into two sides of a more embracing and singular process of total self-mediation', thereby achieving 'a kind of dialectical univocity' (PUMT, 120–21).[3] However this system's 'final reduction of the other ways of being mindful to the self-mediation of philosophy's own thought' (PO, 4) is false to a fundamental experience of otherness that Desmond calls 'agapeic astonishment' (BB, 32).

In distinction from, yet in a sense inclusive of, these senses is what Desmond calls the *metaxological*.[4] Building from the Greek *metaxu*, meaning 'between', the metaxological is 'a discourse of the "between"' – a thinking between utter ignorance and total knowledge, poverty and plentitude, frailty and grandeur, infirmity and nobility (PO, 3; BB, 6).[5] In Desmond's scheme, the metaxological sense 'thinks through the intensive truth' that the other senses 'state less profoundly' (BB, 200).[6] This way of thinking takes to heart Aristotle's statement, 'being is said in many ways', and is inclusive of different ways of thinking (PO, 6). It has room for 'the otherness which is never self-produced nor vouched for by the possibility of a categorial intelligibility',[7] and protects 'the excess of being's plenitude that is never mediated by us' (BB, 177).[8] Here one is in 'complex nonreductive community' with being – both a 'being with' and an 'otherness to' – neither reductive (univocal, dialectical) nor dissipative (equivocal) (BB, 177–8). The metaxological 'whole' is a community 'in familial interplay': 'a plurivocal community of voices in interplay ... in their genuine otherness' (PO, 6; PUMT, 122).[9] As such, metaxological thought remains open to the other (BB, 33–4).[10] Desmond describes this 'middle condition of our thought of being' in terms of an 'intimate strangeness', a 'metaphysical mindfulness [that] is aware of difference in itself, as other in thought to being – being with which mind is also intimate' (NDR, 37; BB, 5).[11] Metaxological thought entails a mindful opening of 'mind to being-other', a primal shock or wonder at 'the otherness of being in its givenness' that is the very advent of metaphysical thinking (BB, 8). Desmond calls this shock or wonder 'agapeic astonishment': the seizure, the enthralling, the enrapturing brought about by 'an excess of other-being overflow[ing] towards one', a kind of reversal of perceptual intentionality (BB, 9–11).[12]

Metaxological Metaphysics and Ultimacy

Ingredient of metaxological metaphysics is a certain way of regarding philosophy's relation to other ways of thinking, including religion. A metaxological intermediation between philosophy and religion entails both genuine relation and genuine plurality.[13] Philosophy holds no privileged place; religion must be allowed to speak from itself.

For Desmond, this intermediation yields the common, shared phenomenon of a 'vector of transcendence', an awareness of 'ultimacy'. Inherent to thought's own dynamism, there is a relatedness toward ultimacy (PU, 168). This desire or 'urgency' regarding the ultimate is 'the vector of transcendence that marks being religious', the openness to divine transcendence that is 'at work in any venture of spiritual seriousness' (PU, 182). Beyond mere intentionality, this 'vector of transcendence is already a relation to transcendence, and in a sense not reducible to human self-transcendence' (BB, 5).[14] It is 'an opening to the ultimate other' (PU, 204). There is even a kind of 'excess to the ultimate, and a disproportion between its transcendence and human self-transcendence' (ibid.). Whatever else it might be, the ultimate is irreducibly other. The transcendent other is not a mere function of our self-mediating mindfulness; it intermediates with us as we are open to it. So, in double mediation, one is open to 'the ingression of the ultimate as a superior other that intermediates with the middle out of its own transcendence' (ibid.).

In speaking about that which is ultimately other, the use of metaphor is inescapable (PU, 199).[15] Desmond takes the 'beyond' and 'in the midst' of the 'meta-' in 'metaphor' as 'bespeak[ing] some sense of the beyond in the between' (PU, 209). This speaking is metaxological, between fully identifying the ultimate and utter ignorance thereof. It is 'at the boundary' where no 'finite determinate category will do' (PU, 207). The ultimate is beyond all images, yet we need images to 'articulate our sense of its being' (PO, 113). Metaphor is therefore always suspicious of itself, because it is not itself the ultimate. There are several metaphors that Desmond uses for that which is ultimately other. These metaphors include the absolute original, the agapeic origin, the agapeic absolute, agapeic transcendence and God.

The *absolute original* bespeaks finite being's contingency, that 'its origin is other than itself' (PU, 187). Thus the absolute original points to 'the radical other': 'the ultimate other that always resists thought's claims to absolute self-mediation' (PO, 113, 114).[16]

Agapeic origin refers to an ultimate origination or creation that is a 'giving of being to the other that lets that other-being be as other' (PU, 218). Agapeic origin is 'the ground of a between that is genuinely nonreductive of plurality' (PU, 221). As such, Desmond describes it as 'a dynamic plenitude ... not ... constituted in the end [as with the dialectical], but by already being an origin that is full, overfull in itself' (PU, 207).[17]

Very similar to the agapeic origin is the metaxological *agapeic absolute* that stands in contrast to the dialectical *erotic absolute*. The erotic absolute 'offers a sense of eternity in process of striving to become itself, in process of determining itself fully in the productions of time which are its own self-production' (PU, 215).[18] However, with the agapeic absolute, 'the origin is full in itself, overdetermined in itself, inexhaustible. ... Its origination of the conditional and finite is from the agape of its surplus, its pluperfection' (PU, 216). The agapeic absolute grants 'the otherness of the finite', what Desmond calls 'a gift of ontological freedom' (ibid.). Likewise, *agapeic transcendence* is that which 'goes forth, pours its creative power abroad for the other, for the otherness of creation' (PU, 196).

Desmond attaches these metaphors to the name/word, '*God*'.[19] Insofar as 'God remains other to our thinking in our thinking of God', talk of 'God' is itself a metaphorical intimation of that which is ultimately other (PU, 183). Here one can conclude that the urge to ultimacy, the vector of transcendence and the metaphors for the ultimate constitute the 'theological' horizon of Desmond's metaxological metaphysics. Seeing that the metaphor of 'agapeic origin' seems to be Desmond's preferred metaphor, having a definite meaning relative to certain phenomena and being inclusive of other of his 'agapeic' metaphors, we too will gravitate to it.

Being, Being Religious and Ultimacy: Metaxological Themes

In this section, I will draw out some select metaxological themes to facilitate a kind of 'theological' interpretation of Terrence Malick's *The Thin Red Line*. These various themes congregate around the relations between being, being religious and the ultimate.

The Inherent Goodness of Being

At the heart of much of Desmond's writing is the strange conjecture that being itself is good, that being has inherent value and is (or at least can be) experienced as such.[20] Desmond suggests that 'agapeic astonishment' itself contains, or is, 'the very marvel of being as elementally good' (NDR, 47; BB, 10, 37). As Desmond writes, an 'elemental desire sings in one's blood' intimating 'a certain love of being: being is good and it is good to be' (PO, 296, 300). Desmond expresses this concept of being's goodness metaphorically in terms of what he calls 'golden being'.[21]

Being's value has its root in its agapeic origin. Being's goodness points to something 'other' as its source, its condition for possibility, its ground. Desmond writes: 'A primal original "yes" is spoken: It is good. *It* is good, good for itself. It is as if the Creator, in giving being to the creation also gave it its value for itself' (PU, 226). The experience of the goodness and perfection of being points to its being a gift: being itself is a gift. Again Desmond writes: 'This is the original meaning of the givenness of being: a generosity of being that gives for no reason beyond the goodness of giving being. This, I believe, is the ultimate basis on which also we must think the value of finite being' (PU, 230).[22]

This perception of the goodness and perfection of being has been deadened by the advent of modern 'instrumental mind'. In Desmond's accounting, modern humanity, by dissecting and harnessing the power of nature with science and technology, has 'pushed back the boundary of mystery' (PO, 127). Scientific technology has brought about a 'dedivinized world' in which 'nature is an organization of univocal, impersonal forces' (PO, 121).[23] Being becomes simply there, only valuable relative to its usefulness in human hands.[24] 'This total instrumentalizing', Desmond concludes, 'means nihilism'. It follows: 'If the whole is valueless, then the human being as part of the whole partakes of this basic ontological valuelessness' (PU, 227).

But creation need not be left to be the 'degraded creation' of post-Cartesian mechanism; creation may be 'the gift of agapeic origin, good for itself' (PU, 196). Here Desmond recognizes a certain 'confluence of ethics and metaphysics' (PU, 227). Seeing that the value of being and the value placed on human beings are linked, Desmond asks: 'All said scientifically, does the battered heart, be it rebellious or resigned, stretch out only to a heartless universe?' (PO, 121). Desmond argues that it is incumbent upon us to dig back toward the roots of thought, toward the agapeic astonishment that can yet yield to us 'a new sense of the sacramental earth' (PU, 227). To be fully human, in Desmond's regard, we need to regain this astonishment; being – our vision of being and our being – needs to be transfigured.

Being Transfigured and its Idiot Wisdom

For Desmond, being religious has to do with being aware of, and encountering, a certain 'thereness', an 'It is there', a happening in relation to the goodness of being (PO, 111). Being religious has to do with a 'hierophany' – 'a sensuous show of charged significance' – 'a *poiesis* of being in the form of a show of the sacred' (ibid.). This hierophany 'is not our doing': it is given, coming on its own. This hierophany makes one aware of 'the primordial sacral otherness of being' and demands 'a comportment towards being in which the sense of the holy predominates' (PO, 113). When one encounters an intimation of a profound and awesome otherness in and beyond being, one's awareness of being as such, and one's own being, is transfigured.

The Transfigured Vision of Being

There are moments when we are grasped by an embodied awareness of the goodness of being. These 'acme moments' reveal a significance such that we return to them as touchstones of meaning and substance in our lives. In these moments we touch 'the elemental', gaining 'a refreshed relatedness to being in its otherness' (PO, 270).[25] These moments change one's mindfulness. One becomes aware of the worth of being: one sees its goodness (PU, 156). One smiles, greeting being in its 'benign otherness'.[26] With its changed vision, agapeic mind transfigures what is manifest (PU, 162). One has a 'metaphysical insomnia' and 'sees nothing "ordinary" any more' (PU, 208). Desmond writes:

> A light has flashed momentarily across the middle, and now the day looks dark, and the things one saw in the flash, make one turn to the dark everyday with a new astonishment, with a troubled groping unfamiliarity. Things, too, were briefly other, are still the promise of being other, though sunk again into the invisibility of everyday visibility. (PU, 209)

By agapeic mind's transfigured vision of being, the way is prepared for an awareness of agapeic origin, of the divine (PU, 221).[27] In this, finite being can become 'a conspirator with the sense of mystery, a collaborator pointing to something it fugitively intimates yet also guards in hiddenness' (PO, 137). Through created things, the divine can be approached, if indirectly.[28]

The Self's Transfiguration

The hierophany, the acme moment, does not just change the way one looks at being, it changes one's own way of being: awareness of the goodness of being as ethically transfigurative.[29] One is seized and captivated by 'agapeic astonishment', by the gift of love from other-being to self-being (BB, 10). One's being is a 'being beholden': held, bound, indebted toward community with other-being. Something about the worthiness of being somehow makes us 'feel compelled to make ourselves worthy of it' (BB, 193). One feels called 'to be worthy of worthy being'

(BB, 194). One is inspired to make one's self as bright as one's being.[30] When one participates in this transfiguration, one 'may help midwife the reemergence of sacramental earth ... renew reverence for being; recall a sense of the sacredness of life; reactivate a proper piety of being there' (PO, 158).

One here seeks agapeic being. Desmond explains that 'the mindful taste of the "It is good" arouses in us a call to *live beyond ourselves* the "It is good." ... The gift of agapeic being solicits in us the gift of agapeic being' (PU, 232). Just as being is simply given as good, 'we [too] give because nothing is demanded of us. There is no external coercion. We give, demanding nothing for ourselves. We give ourselves to and for the other' (ibid.). We imitate the agapeic origin by giving out of an 'already full, overfull' abundance (PU, 212). 'Somehow the restless energy of our own being is a charge of the agapeic being, and the charge is that we *be* agapeic' (PU, 243–4).[31]

Idiot Wisdom

This transfigured mindfulness and being makes one privy to a primordial joy, a being pleased prior to thematic or determinate thought, that is almost 'something *childlike*' (an ontological 'peek-a-boo') (BB, 11). Desmond writes: 'A soul is overcome and sings. It sings it knows not why; but an elemental agapeic mindfulness, a motiveless willingness, leaps in the enigmatic goodness of creation. This is an idiot wisdom' (PU, 197). Transfigured mindfulness is an 'idiot wisdom', for it seeks to reach beyond the bounds of certain, determinate intelligibility to speak of the goodness of being and the agapeic origin.[32] One could even say that in agapeic astonishment, the very wellspring of thought, one catches an echo of the first 'yes' – the 'It is good' – 'a kind of idiotic amen to the whole' (PU, 242). One remains open to this astonishment and affirms the goodness of being and its agapeic origin.

The disconcerting 'idiocy' involved in this astonishment and affirmation is regarding the intimate, private (*idios*) nature of the phenomenon of agapeic astonishment, that happens to a singular, particular 'I' (BB, 12). It is initially just a 'given' phenomenon that happens to one without an apparent 'why' (ibid.). The idiot wisdom of agapeic mindfulness also never gets beyond this irreducible (not subsumable in a system) phenomenological givenness; it respects the excessive givenness beyond every determinate science of identification (BB, 186). The final aspect of this 'idiocy' is the coexistence of phenomena revealing the goodness of being and the, perhaps equally phenomenological, reality of evil and death (PU, 241). It is precisely this ambivalence that leads Desmond to consider the next theme.[33]

The Dialectic of Trust and Distrust

Desmond writes that 'the same energy of transcendence that places us in the space of the holy also in time is the womb of our restless questioning' (PO, 156). Thence comes within religion a dialectic of trust and mistrust (PO, 111). All thought and relation to the ultimate, all 'being religious', is 'implicitly mediated' (PO, 112). This dialectic arises out of the duality of our imagination regarding the sacred, and gives rise to a dual piety.

Desmond writes: 'In the gap between the given and the intimated, ontological perplexity excites us into religious imagination' (PO, 114). Between the givenness of being and the intimation of its agapeic origin, we must resort to imagination. The images produced are 'always and essentially double' (PO, 115). They can always be viewed from two perspectives. First, one can see this imagination as 'the flight of sheer fantasy ... creating pictures that are incredible, unbelievable pictures with no coincidence with actuality' (ibid.). Here the image is the product of fantasy, and 'fantasy projects illusions, nonexistent things, figments, nothings' (ibid.). Second, one can see 'imagination as more than constructing fantastical nothings but as a power that draws from the well of being, as articulated in the original energy of the self itself': 'the ability to body forth powers of being that otherwise remain nameless' (PO, 115, 116). With this second option, 'given being (the finite, the immanent) *is* the image of the sacred in the sense of its heirophany or manifestation. The sacred as original (in itself) remains still elusive and mysterious' (PO, 116). So the image, if it is to claim to refer to the ultimate other, must maintain a metaxological doubleness, 'holding trust and distrust together in order never to close out otherness' (PO, 139). For 'an image is an image of some other. ... It is neither identical with its original, nor absolutely different, it necessarily both reveals and conceals' (PO, 138).[34]

As was intimated, relative to the double image there is the 'dialectic', 'struggle', 'tension', between two metaphysical postures: those of trust and mistrust, suspicion and faith (PO, 122). Desmond identifies the central expression of this dialectic relative to the problem of evil: 'perhaps *the* stumbling block to religious trust, the place of radical rupture to our spontaneous intimacy with sacred otherness' (PO, 123). In the intermediation between Leibniz's *Theodicy* and Voltaire's *Candide* we see 'our double need: both to dream the absolute dream that is God and to debunk that same dream' (PO, 124). Because of 'the precariousness of our finitude in the middle', and the concomitant possibilities of suffering and death, there arises a condition of metaphysical mistrust in tension with any affirmation of the good (PO, 123). There is a tension between the idealist, who 'points us beyond to a hidden heaven', and the realist, who 'reminds us with sweet glee that life is hell' (PO, 122). Desmond suggests that to be genuinely religious one must navigate and negotiate between the extremes of untempered idealism and cynical realism. Unmoored idealism, a fully blind trust, can yield flights of fancy.[35] Yet an unbalanced 'realism', an equally indiscriminating suspicion, can lead to an equal if opposite error. Suspicion must itself be seen as possibly suspect, and thus not absolute. In the metaphysical mistrust arising out of a sense of finitude one can come to deny this very 'finitude of our intermediate being by wilfully seeking to overreach all otherness. [Here] we overstep the boundary of our due lot' (PO, 124). Thus Desmond remarks that 'realists are right in the recognition of distrust, but wrong if they fail to fight it' (PO, 123). Religious respect for 'sacral otherness' both demands and fuels this metaxological dialectic of trust and mistrust (PO, 122).

Following the dialectic of trust and mistrust is a double piety, a dual mode of relating to these two metaphysical postures. Piety, as a response to the 'overpowering otherness of being', manifests itself as both negative and positive, as sacred terror and ontological gratitude (PO, 125). Desmond contends that terror is where we first clearly encounter otherness. He writes: 'Religious terror first makes us human. This is the first piety, the first respect. The world articulated by a difference, an otherness we cannot comprehend' (PO, 126). This terror finds its focus in the otherness and absurdity of suffering and, ultimately, in death. 'Death,' Desmond observes, 'brings us our greatest terror, our undefeated dread' (PO, 127).

But terror is not the whole story. There is, Desmond writes, 'another kind of singing' (ibid.). Just as in the face of suffering 'everything has become tainted with suspicion', so does life remain saturated with wonder at the goodness of being: it is still good to be (PO, 125). We have an 'ontological gratitude for being as such' (PO, 128).[36] We humans are innately 'religious' in the sense of our awareness of, and participation in, a *religio* – a binding together, a connectedness – 'a metaxological link with powers of being more ultimate than ourselves' (ibid.). Gratitude is a piety born 'in praise of the powers that vitalize and beautify and perfect creation' (ibid.). It is aware of the way 'being showers its bounty on us. It bestows us with power, beauty, fertile springs, full harvests, the dawn song of a blackbird. Its gifts seem too much, unmerited by us, a motiveless benevolence' (ibid.). We are ontologically grateful.

Because of the double image and the double piety arising out of the dialectic of trust and mistrust, there can result a certain feeling of schizophrenia. On account of this, many eventually tend to 'doubt the reality of the spirit' and become 'not very different from the ordinary atheist' (PO, 130). Not willing to live in the paradoxical struggle of the metaxological middle, they give in to mistrust and collapse the tension of the dialectic. How can one do otherwise? How does one cultivate trust and gratitude toward the agapeic origin of inherently good being in the presence of evil and death?

Death, Ultimacy and Posthumous Mind

In strong tension with the phenomenon of the goodness of being is the phenomenon of death: 'violating … smothering … assailing … consuming … hollowing … souring … devouring … tormenting … torturing … mocking'. 'Death,' Desmond observes, 'is the cold word that undoes every word' (PU, 164). The shadow of loss and death puts a question mark over all talk about the goodness of being. 'The transfigurative power of agapeic mind', the consent of 'true goodwill to being' seems impossible (PU, 163). Our finitude, our being-towards-death, keeps us from consenting to the goodness of being. Of what use is goodness in the face of death? Desmond asks: 'What purification would be necessary for us to be restored to ontological consent? Would we not have to die?' (ibid.). He continues:

Why this idiot wisdom? Why any desire still to speak of the goodness of creation? I came upon a dead small bird on the causeway near Inchydoney. Still whole. I picked it up. Blood in its eye. Delicate beauty. So perfect. Its life gone. Never again. Cold and perfect still. I looked at the estuary, tide ebbed. Other birds, so various, oyster catchers, herons, gannets, gulls. ... The quiet stunning beauty of the world. The world is perfect. Yet there is death. Blood in the eye of beauty. I turned to the grey, darkening clouds over the hills. And the beauty of the world was menacing, menaced. *How can one see this perfection, in death, beyond death? Does mindfulness itself have to go into death, to see if it can consent, beyond death?* (PU, 164, italics mine)

Desmond identifies this mindfulness that seeks consent to the goodness of being beyond death as the 'agapeic love of posthumous mind' (PU, 164).

'Posthumous mind' is a kind of thought experiment, 'the metaphysical imagination of being dead', whereby one can be helped to bring to mind the experience of agapeic astonishment (PO, 280).[37] It is, as Desmond writes, 'a thinking from the future when we are dead, about the ontological worth of the present, imagined beyond death as our past' (PO, 278). Because of our immersion in the present (read Heidegger's everydayness), we have become numb to what is closest to us – to being itself in all its plenitude and worth.[38] Posthumous mind is a way to try to look at being-other without ulterior motive (BB, 37). With the thought of being already dead, I can imagine the good of being beyond its good for me, a mindfulness 'not subsumed into instrumentalized mind' (BB, 37; PO, 278).[39] Being-beyond-death can reveal being as other than equipment.

Desmond contends that looking at being beyond life and death one only sees the good in being – which is agapeic mind, the 'love of being in its intrinsic good' (BB, 37). The hinge of the thought experiment follows: 'If being would so appear from beyond, is it not *now* so from within, as we live it, though now we cannot see it so?' (ibid.). It is thus that posthumous mind can reawaken agapeic astonishment; one's 'looking on life as if dead' is a 'rummaging through time for what made it good' (BB, 192; PO, 280). Thus can one be aided in seeing being's worth beyond our present immersion, toward renewing the 'astonishment at the elemental fact of being at all' (BB, 192).[40]

Malick's *The Thin Red Line*

Turning to Terrence Malick's 1998 epic, *The Thin Red Line*, it is helpful first to sketch its various narrative elements. Regarding *setting*, *The Thin Red Line* ostensibly takes place in the pivotal World War II battle between American and Japanese forces over the strategic Pacific island of Guadalcanal. The more immediate settings vary from native village to bamboo forests, to tall grassy hills, to chaotic, violent battle. The film has several principal *characters*, all American GIs, predominantly members of Charlie Company. If there is a main character of this film (and I think there is) it is Witt, a simple, compassionate, mystical private from Kentucky. For the purposes of this essay, there is also Witt's counterpart, the character of First Sergeant Welsh, a cynical, disillusioned pragmatist who keeps the company running smoothly.

The *plot*, the structure of the narrative of the film (nearly three hours in length), can be seen as operative on several different levels. There is the level of the story of the battle itself: the Americans coming upon the island and their defeat of the Japanese forces. There is also the level of the story of Charlie Company: the disembarkation, the landing, the march inland, the battle to take the hill, r&r, the near escape of the company from advancing Japanese forces, the departure.[41] There is the level of the stories of the individual soldiers, particularly (for us) Witt's progression to deeper agapeic being in the midst of the war. Finally there is the level of the stories of the relationships between various characters, particularly (for us) the relationship, the continuing conversation, that takes place between Witt and Welsh.

Perhaps the major element that comes to the fore in *The Thin Red Line* is that of *tone*. One can speak of the tone in terms of an interweaving of several modes of engagement. There is that of a normal third-person, objective observer, watching the action play itself out. There is the mode of a kind of first-person present participation – of feeling oneself in the midst of the film, in the beautiful landscape or in the tense madness of battle (as being engrossed in an artwork). Finally there is, at least potentially, a mode of second-person engagement: there is a theological, hierophany-laden dimension that invites one into relationship with the ultimate. These modes are effected by the masterful synergy of cinematography, editing and musical score. Along with these multiple modes there is a lack of any one static narrative voice. There is a multiple *narration*, through the use of voice-overs, of different characters' inner thoughts, and through the camera's contemporaneously acting as the vision of the disembodied spirit of a given character at a given time.

A Metaxological Interpretation of *The Thin Red Line*

We now turn to a series of metaxological meditations on various elements of *The Thin Red Line*, utilizing the particular themes explicated above (in the second part of our essay) to aid us toward a 'theological' interpretation of the film.

The Inherent Goodness of Being

There are several elements of the film that can be read as signifying the strange goodness of being that hearkens toward ultimacy. First and most explicitly, there are numerous voice-overs that bespeak agapeic origin. For example, early on in the film there is the monologue: 'Who are you that lives in all these many forms? ... the source of all that is going to be born ... You give calm of spirit ... the contented heart'. Many, if not all, of the voice-overs in the film are prayers of sorts, addressing the ultimacy behind experienced phenomena.

Second, the element of tone, particularly that effected by the cinematography and the use of light, reflects Desmond's idea of the inherent goodness of being. Throughout the picture, there is a recurring type of shot that strongly figures in the tone of the work. Time and again, the camera is pointed up or pans upward toward the sky. Repeatedly one is shown a canopy of trees with sunlight shining through, sometimes through a mist or smoke, effecting a cascade of translucent rays of light – one does not just see things lit up; one sees light – as if the goodness of being is shining through. Repeatedly one is shown the serene blue sky, with occasional snow-white clouds drifting along. Even in the central battle scene, the battle for the hill, the shots are commonly from the soldiers' perspective, looking *up* the hill or *up*, out of their positions lying in the tall grasses, toward the blue sky. Even here, the visual composition of that which is captured in the shots moves one's eye upward. The shots of the hill are all shots of the horizon. For a large part of the movie, the soldiers are moving through the tall grasses, a myriad of fragile vertical lines. The sun bathes this film; it is a war movie almost entirely shot in daylight. The light that fills this sometimes very dark film gives it a tone such that one becomes aware of golden being hearkening toward agapeic origin.

Third, the goodness of being can be seen as displayed in the numerous scenes of natural beauty. In the scene of the soldiers' disembarking for the island, for the battle, there is sunlight sparkling on the water, the deep blue-green and translucent waves, the white surf, the still silhouette of the hills of the approaching tropical island. There are, liberally sprinkled throughout the picture, close-up shots of various tropical plants and exotic animals. Even the grassy hill, the place of the great battle, is a beautiful sight. The breeze stirs in the tall green grasses as it does in the leaves of the trees and, as with the ray of light through the mist, one can see what is in itself invisible: beings betray glimpses of being, and being is good.

On the other side, *The Thin Red Line* tempers the goodness of being in nature's beauty with instrumental mind and the destructiveness of modern technological warfare. The first time people are killed in the movie is a shock. Two soldiers are sent ahead up the hill, walking through the same peaceful tall grasses; we see them from the perspective of the rest of the troop behind them; two single shots ring out; small distant bursts of blood; they both drop and disappear into the sea of grass rippling in the breeze. One is left with the juxtaposition of the calm, pastoral beauty (goodness) of nature, and the terror of instrumental technology whose purpose is to reach across great distances and kill with precision. After this scene, there is a quiet pause in the serene landscape, then the soldiers charge up, and the war-machine thunders to life – the air is filled with flying metal, smoke and blood.

The hill, manifestly beautiful and good in itself, is a thing to be seized, 'taken' as a means to a military end, an object for instrumental mind. As the character Welsh says, 'Property. The whole thing's about fuckin' property.'[42] Even human beings have worth only relative to their usefulness as instruments for achieving certain ends. His only answer to a request: 'Only time to worry 'bout a soldier's when he stops bitchin'.'

In Desmond's accounting, modern humanity, by dissecting and harnessing the power of nature with science and technology, has 'pushed back the boundary of mystery' (PO, 127). Here in war is both an exemplar and an exception, both the apex and the possible breach of instrumental mind. Seeing the terribly destructive power of technology, the 'good' of instrumental mind can break down, starkly unveiling the nihilism inherent in it, revealing the 'outside', the limits of instrumental mind. I think of the shell-shocked soldier (earlier earnestly leading other soldiers in prayer), the last left alive in his unit, tearing up grass and dirt and throwing it into the air, saying, 'That's us! That's us!' – the same character who has to find his dog tags to remember his name. But war can also give one the perspective to see beyond instrumental mind toward astonishment, seeing being as good. Here I think of the powerful remorse and repentance of the American soldier hugging himself and crying in the rain, who had earlier cruelly extracted and collected gold-filled teeth from dead and dying Japanese soldiers. The 'gold', the inherent worth, of these humans grasping him, demanding, judging him.

Being Transfigured and its Idiot Wisdom

In *The Thin Red Line*, the character of Witt can be seen as exemplary of the transfigured vision of being and the transfigured self. Regarding the transfigured vision of being, the change of mindfulness that makes one aware of the worth of being, Witt seems to have undergone something like this at the beginning of the film while he is AWOL. On the island with the natives, Witt seems to be affected by their immediate community with nature and being.[43] The natural beauty of the island and the goodness of the people seem to serve as a kind of hierophany – an acme moment. He glimpses through them a 'primal sacral otherness' in being (PO, 113). A depiction of this closeness to the goodness of being can be seen in the recurring shot of the native children swimming underwater in bright blue. Witt watches the natives, smiling. He plays with the children. He too swims, smiling at the sky. At the end of this opening section on the island, there is a scene of the native people in procession to worship, singing a hymn whose melody had formed the theme for much of the scoring for this first section. This hymn, as a musical theme (a *leitmotif*), is a recurring symbol of the agapeic origin shining through the goodness of being. The music that underlies the natives' lives, hearkening to the goodness of being, comes to the fore and becomes clear in the context of worship, of thinking and thanking the agapeic origin of being and goodness. This ecstatic acme (AWOL) moment, Witt recalls throughout the film: it is, as Desmond writes, one of those moments that 'occur to be mindfully recalled or sung' (PO, 268).[44] Referring to this opening section, Witt later confesses: 'I seen another world.'

For Witt, this experience of being's transfiguration can be seen to be ethically transfigurative as well. His consistent compassion displays his agapeic being, that he is a 'golden soul' who 'catches brightness in its being' (PO, 267). In the earlier part of the battle, Witt is a stretcher bearer, caring for the wounded, tenderly pouring water onto a soldier's head to refresh him, to comfort him. Witt's voice-over muses, 'maybe everybody got one big soul'. Later, Witt is with Sgt Keck, helping him to die with a sense of meaning and comforting him in the face of the cruel absurdity of his, Keck's, accidentally pulling the pin of a grenade that fatally wounds him. Later in the film, when Witt comes upon another native village, he is visibly hurt when a native child backs away from him in fear as he holds out his hand in friendship. His voice-over: 'We were a family. ... How'd we lose the good that was given us? What's keepin' us from reachin' out ... touchin' the glory?'

Even after Witt is dead, his voice is heard over shots of the soldiers (seeing through Witt's posthumous eyes), departing from the island at the end of the film: 'Who were you that I lived with? Walked with? The brother, the friend …'.

Witt's compassion, his agapeic being, is powerfully evident in his actions toward the captured, wounded, and even dead Japanese soldiers. While the other soldiers are mocking and abusing the enemy prisoners, Witt offers a captured Japanese officer a stick of gum. Between shots of soldiers killing the Japanese in their camp, there is a poignant scene of Witt kneeling down with his arm around a wounded Japanese soldier, looking into his agonized eyes with sad sympathy, holding him up, holding his hand. Even when he comes upon a dead Japanese soldier almost completely buried in dirt, he looks at the face of the dead man and hears his posthumous voice(-over).

Witt's final scenes are a striking picture of agapeic being: the form of the self-sacrificing hero. When two obviously terrified young soldiers are ordered to scout out a dangerous enemy position, Witt insistently volunteers to go with them. Later, with one of the young soldiers severely wounded, and the other almost paralysed with fear at the approaching mass of the enemy, he sends the latter soldier (Fife) back to report to the company, while he stays behind with the wounded man. As the enemy advances towards them, Witt leads off the enemy so that the wounded soldier can live to escape down the river. Witt, surrounded by the enemy in a clearing, is shot and killed. The scene cuts immediately to smoky beams of light through the canopy of trees – the agapeic origin shining through being – then in a flashback, Witt is underwater, swimming with the native children, a bright blue glow.

Finally, there are times when Witt's childlike joy in his private experiences of the goodness of being betrays what Desmond calls an 'idiot wisdom'. One scene has Witt playing with water: enjoying the fall of water on a big tropical plant and standing in a waterfall accompanied by a flashback to the village from the beginning of the film, with the hymn theme in the background. In the face of the evil and death that pervade this film, particularly before Welsh's practical, if not pragmatic, or downright cynical wisdom, this behaviour seems idiotic indeed. Witt's reply: 'We can't all be smart.' This leads naturally to our next theme.

The Dialectic of Trust and Distrust

In *The Thin Red Line*, the series of dialogues between Witt and Welsh can be seen as representative of the dialectic of trust and distrust, suspicion and faith, the two metaphysical postures which are ingredients of one's being genuinely religious. There are four of these brief dialogues, in which Witt and Welsh are alone together, interacting, spaced fairly evenly throughout the film.[45] Witt can be seen as embodying the dialectical pole of metaphysical trust in a goodness pointing beyond to an agapeic origin ('I seen another world'). Welsh can be seen as representing the dialectical pole of metaphysical mistrust arising from the precariousness of human finitude ('In this world a man, himself, is nothin'. And there ain't no world but this one'). While Witt is the idealist who 'points us beyond to a hidden heaven', Welsh is the realist, who 'reminds us with sweet glee that life is hell' (PO, 122). Relative to these two metaphysical postures, Witt and Welsh can also be seen as representing Desmond's double piety. While Witt seems to have an abiding sense of ontological gratitude for the evident goodness of being, Welsh is all too aware of the 'first respect' before the destructive force of the world, and is concerned with simply pragmatically getting on, surviving, keeping from dying ('We're livin' in a world that's blowin' itself to hell as fast as everybody can arrange it. A situation like that ... all a man can do is shut his eyes and let nothin' touch him, look out for himself').

On the surface one can fruitfully see Witt and Welsh as a picture of Desmond's dialectic of trust and mistrust. But on a deeper level one can see Witt as the one tending toward balance, maintaining the tension, while Welsh can be seen as representing the one who leaves the tension. Witt always sees the goodness of being in the midst of (if not, indeed, through, as is discussed below) suffering and death. His affirmation of the goodness of being and its agapeic origin is rarely direct, usually in the form of questioning ('Sometimes I think it was just my imagination ...'. 'Who are you?'). Welsh is the realist who fails to fight mistrust (PO, 123). He gives up and gives in to mistrust and scepticism, collapsing the tension of the dialectic. He tells Witt: 'You seen things I never will.' Welsh is closed to the possibility of a greater goodness.

Death, Ultimacy and Posthumous Mind

We turn now to the way the themes of death and posthumous mind can be seen in this film. Desmond's tension, between the goodness of being and ultimacy on one side, and death on the other, is present throughout the film. This can be seen in several exemplary instances. Early on in the picture there is a scene in which a terrified young soldier is babbling on before disembarking for the island. He concludes: 'The only things that are permanent are dyin' and the Lord.' Later, there is a shot of the face of a Japanese corpse, all but completely buried in the dirt. A voice-over, apparently of the dead man, asks Witt: 'Do you think your suffering will be less because you love goodness?' In another scene, of Americans taking an enemy camp, killing the unarmed, there is another voice-over: 'This great evil ... where'd it come from? ... who's doin' this? ... who's killin' us? ... is this darkness in you too?' But perhaps, again, the strongest intimation of this tension is in the tone, rather the dual tones, of the goodness of being (as described above) and the ugliness of cruelty, violence and arbitrary death. One is continually reminded of the proximity of death. This is effectively done in the several shots in which you can see and hear bullets flying by the camera. The battle contains many scenes of masses of men running and being shot or blown up, seemingly at random. One thinks of Sgt Keck's meaningless death, accidentally pulling the pin of one of his grenades.[46] The 'thin red line' that divides the sane and the mad likewise holds the goodness of being and the meaninglessness of death in close proximity.

Regarding Desmond's strange concept of posthumous mind, an early sequence in the film so powerfully lends itself to interpretation in these terms that it deserves a rich description. Pte Witt is AWOL on a tropical island. He sees the native mothers with their babies, and he remembers his own mother's dying: 'I asked her if she was afraid. She just shook her head. I was afraid to touch the death I seen in her. Couldn't find anything beautiful or uplifting about her goin' back to God. Heard people talk about immortality, but I ain't seen it.'

Then there is a scene with his mother on her deathbed. There is a little girl in a white dress, his mother's spirit, who hugs Witt, smiling – fully appreciating the good that he is. Then the camera pans up past a ticking clock on the wall to a blue sky where the ceiling should be (toward ultimacy, eternity). Then the scene shifts back to Witt sitting on the shore looking at a lone empty boat. Witt's voice-over: 'I wondered how it'd be when I died . ... I just hope I can meet it the same way she did. With the same calm. Cuz that's where it's hidden, the immortality I didn't see.' Then there is a shot of native children looking for things on the beach. Then a shot of a native child sitting with his cupped hands full of what looks like pebbles, but on closer examination are tiny moving shells – little hermit crabs – living rocks. The vision of immortality, the ultimacy behind the goodness of being, that makes rocks alive, is hidden beyond death. Witt shortly afterwards (in his first dialectical dialogue with Welsh) affirms: 'I seen another world.' He has seen another world where things and people have value, through this posthumous mind.

In the later part of the film, there is a scene of a native village, another picture of posthumous mind. As opposed to the corpses violently strewn about, littering the rest of the movie, there is set up a ceremonial burial shrine where numerous bones and skulls of the departed are carefully and reverently placed. The remains of the dead are reverently hallowed because, through the natives' posthumous mindfulness, the bones signify an experience of the beyond, of ultimacy.

Finally another instance of posthumous mind can be seen in Witt's several interactions with the dead and dying. He, a stretcher bearer, is sympathetic toward their pain, yet he is serene, even smiling as he looks in their dying eyes. It is as if he allows his sympathy for them in their suffering to continue after their death. He smiles because, in his sympathy with the departed, he sees through their eyes to goodness, the golden being that is in excess of the anxiety of being-towards-death. Like the experience of sitting at a deathbed or a grave (like Welsh at Witt's grave later on), one's awareness of the departing/departed as a person like oneself, and seeing them die, gives one the opportunity, in death's near proximity, to engage in an awareness of posthumous mind: an awareness of value and ultimacy beyond death.

The film closes with a shot of the rippling waves, the wake of Charlie Company's ship departing Guadalcanal. The posthumous Witt addresses the agapeic origin, thanking, one last time: 'Oh my soul, let me be in you now. Look out through my eyes. Look at the things you made. All things shining.'

Notes

1   William Desmond, 'Perplexity and Ultimacy: Metaphysical Thoughts from the Middle', in N. Georgopoulos, and Michael Heim (eds), *Being Human in the Ultimate:*

Studies in the Thought of John M. Anderson, Atlanta: Rodopi, 1995, p.118. Hereafter 'PUMT' in parenthetical notes.

2   The equivocal turns on the same hinge as the univocal; ultimately we cannot know anything determinately, therefore there is no thoroughgoing intelligibility, no meaningful talk about 'being' – indeterminacy reigns. It emphasizes a sheer plurality of beings that resists unification, such that any community of mind and being is sceptically called into question (BB, 20–21).

3   The dialectical sense surpasses and reconciles the equivocal and univocal (BB, 131–75). The dialectical mediates opposition in an absolutely self-determining thinking that subsumes all transcendence in immanence (BB, 30). It instates a new 'faith in the logic of determinacy' to overcome all sceptical oppositions (BB, 31).

4   This is first systematically spelled out his *Desire, Dialectic, and Otherness*.

5   Metaxological metaphysics is presented as a thinking that is *metaxu* ('between'), *meta* ('in the midst of') and *meta* ('beyond') things, and is, as such, a 'complex realistic fidelity' (BB, 44).

6   The metaxological affirms the univocal's stress on determinate thinking as far as it goes, but holds out for something more complex and open. It takes up the equivocal's sense of the ambiguity, rupture and breakdown inherent to finitude. It affirms the dialectical's search for mediated wholeness, while adding on openness to ultimate excess and plurality (BB, 201).

7   William Desmond (2000), 'Neither Deconstruction nor Reconstruction: Metaphysics and the Intimate Strangeness of Being', *International Philosophical Quarterly*, **40**, March, p.47. Hereafter, 'NDR' in parenthetical notes.

8   Desmond describes the metaxological as a pluralized intermediation, a double mediation, that grants the possibility of 'irreducible otherness' (PUMT, 121–2). So it is true to the very origins of thought, in wonder at the uncomprehended: the inexhaustible mysteries of thinking itself, and of the other (BB, 35).

9   Being in this community entails a kind of 'metaphysical perplexity': 'a *tense togetherness* of being at a loss *and* finding oneself at home with being' (BB, 6). Here is displayed the 'intimate strangeness' of being, 'that being reveals a certain kind of ontological community' (NDR, 49).

10   It is an '*open* dialectic': 'an open wholeness that is midway between completed totality and sheerly indefinite incompletenesss' (PO, 5).

11   Desmond writes: 'Being is strange because it has an otherness, indeed marvel, of which we are not the conceptual masters; it is also intimate, in that … we are participants in what we think about' (NDR, 37). 'We are given to be in the intimate strangeness of being – always. Astonishment before this is the beginning of mindfulness' (NDR, 47).

12   Particularly illuminating is the relation between the dialectical and metaxological senses. The dialectical and the metaxological are both kinds of *mediation*. The dialectical achieves unity through self-mediation, while the metaxological aims toward an irreducibly plural community by way of intermediation, or what Desmond calls 'dual' or 'double' mediation: inclusive of, but going beyond, mere self-mediation. He speaks of philosophy's 'dual exigency': the first exigency, to attend to its own form of mindfulness (self-mediation); the second exigency, to be open to other ways of thinking and being (intermediation) (PO, 6). While the dialectical attends to the first, often to the neglect of the second, the metaxological seeks to be faithful to this dual exigency, holding the two sides together in tension. With the metaxological there is a double transcendence, a double mediation: the other toward the self (in the opening

givenness) and the self toward the other (the 'vector of transcendence') (BB, 11). Here there is an 'excess of mindfulness' and an 'excess of being in its otherness', converging in the middle (BB, 13). Desmond writes of Hegel's dialectical middle: 'in the end I think it undercuts the difference between the ultimate in its transcendence and our own self-transcendence' (PU, 204). So Desmond holds out for a metaxological middle, 'to preserve the double mediation' (PU, 204).

Desmond coordinates the dialectical and the metaxological in terms of what he calls *agapeic and erotic mind*. Eros signifies a lack seeking completion and comprehension, while agape signifies an excess that is mindful of the excess of otherness in being (BB, 7). Desmond places erotic mindfulness as the engine behind the dialectical, and that of agapeic mind behind the metaxological (BB, 8; PU, 105). Erotic mind is 'a relativity of mind to what is other to self, but a relatvity that subsumes what is other into the self-relativity of the mind seeking its own self-satisfaction and self-certainty' (PU, 105). It seeks 'mediated self-possession, self-possession mediated through the other' (PU, 113). Agapeic mind is 'a mode of mindfulness in which thinking is for the sake of the other, thinking for the sake of what is other to thought itself'; it is the mind's self-transcendence, the 'release of thinking from itself towards the other as other' (PU, 104). Agapeic mind 'includes a disquiet about every ... self-satisfaction, a perplexity before the other it cannot include in its own conceptual schema, a loss of self-certainty, and at best a trust that its motion towards the other calls for a faithfulness beyond guarantees' (PU, 105).

Agapeic mind and the metaxological sense of being operate with an open sense of the 'whole' that allows for genuine otherness to self. So 'thought as metaxological is a self-mediating openness to otherness', an intermediation; as such 'it may sometimes find itself breaking on forms of otherness it cannot completely master in terms of its mediating categories' (PO, 7). This intermediation cannot be reduced to self-mediation: 'this "between" grants certain forms of otherness as irreducible' (PO, 4). Thus metaxological metaphysics is never complete; if it is mindful of its agapeic astonishment, it is always opened, ever renewed (BB, 15). As such, metaxological metaphysics is a 'plurivocal philosophy', a thinking 'not reductive of all the voices of meaning to one overriding logical voice' (PU, 6). It welcomes the coming of the other; it is an 'active patience', a 'watching', a 'vigilance', an 'expectation', a 'solicitation' (PU, 122). Desmond writes: 'The community of being sings, sings silently. ... Agapeic mind tries to be attuned to the voices of otherness' (PU, 123).

While we are on this topic, it seems that what Lévinas calls 'metaphysics', allowing for the other as other, can be seen to correspond with Desmond's agapeic mind and the metaxological. What Lévinas calls 'ontology', as subordinating the other to the same, can be seen to correspond to Desmond's erotic mind and the dialectical (PU, 229).

13 Desmond describes this as being between the 'Wittgensteinian' and 'Hegelian' options (PO, 1). For the Wittgensteinian option, philosophy is one among many discrete language games (PO, 2). For the Hegelian option (not necessarily Hegel's own position), philosophy is 'the crowning mode of mind', and while religion (along with art) exhibits absolute content, only philosophy has absolute form (ibid.). Religion and art are finally subordinate to philosophy. While the Hegelian option dialectically reduces plurality to a 'totalizing wholeness', the Wittgensteinian option leaves a 'discontinuous plurality' (PO, 3). Desmond seeks a path between excessive unification and excessive pluralization toward 'a different balance of sameness and otherness, unity and plurality, human wholeness and variousness' (ibid.).

14 Desmond states elsewhere: 'The urgency of ultimacy reveals the self-transcending of human desire, as a restless intentional infinitude in search of actual infinitude in otherness itself' (PO, 111). See DD, chs 7–8.

15 Desmond uses 'metaphor' in *Perplexity and Ultimacy* in a more general sense than he does in *Being and the Between*, where metaphor is one of several ways of speaking 'at the boundary', such as analogy, symbol and hyperbole (BB, 207–22).

16 See DD, ch. 8.

17 Desmond observes that Hegel's dialectic has no room for 'the affirmative otherness and transcendence of ultimacy, as an indeterminate *plenitude*, never to be made absolutely determinate by our categories': a fullness at the beginning, not at the end (PU, 208).

18 Thus 'the absoluteness of the absolute only comes at the end of a process of self-realization; and to get to this end, the dunamis of the absolute has to realize itself in and through the finite and conditional' (PU, 216).

19 'God is the absolute origin' (PU, 187); 'Only God *is* agapeic transcendence' (PU, 195).

20 Desmond writes: 'Could it be that what is deepest, sleeping and most hidden in us is an affirmation of being beyond rupture?' (PO, 297).

21 He writes that 'gold is metaphorical of the presence of being itself in its welcoming yet resistant inexhaustibility' (PO, 262). Golden being speaks to an 'openness to being's plenitude', a signal of 'the intrinsic worth' and 'perfection' of being (PO, 261–2).

22 Interestingly, Desmond describes the idea of God's giving for nothing as 'a kind of agapeic nihilism', insofar as being's goodness is not tied to a teleology but is simply and mysteriously inherent (PU, 231).

23 Here science and technology are functions of 'the will to univocity of instrumental mind' which achieves an 'objectification of being that turns the metaxological into a univocal "It"' (PO, 121). 'In their objectifying will to reduce the ambiguity of metaxological being to mere equivocity and thence to manipulable univocity, scientistic and technicist minds have produced a disenchanted earth' (PO, 158).

24 As Desmond states: 'Neutralized of any intrinsic value, being is made a means to an end, namely, to serve our desire, flattened into something that only is for us' (PU, 226). Desmond, echoing the later Heidegger, observes that this way of thinking is so common that few in the modern age are troubled by such a 'disenchanted earth'. Indeed, 'instead of trembling with grief at the vanishing of the god we have become blandly, even chirpily at ease with desolation. We are having a nice day, though the sun is black and the moon and stars are blotted out' (PO, 158).

25 Desmond writes: 'The physical world itself in its elemental being-there precipitates the acme moment, the moment of releasing wholeness full of compacted significance' (PO, 268). These moments 'occur to be mindfully recalled or sung' (ibid.).

26 Desmond considers the smile to be 'a living song of the elemental ... one of our metaphysical marks' (PO, 272). He goes on to say that 'it is our being to smile, especially when another welcomes us ... . The smile is a salutation of being, an elemental greeting of benign otherness' (PO, 272–3).

27 With agapeic mind's vision of the goodness of being, 'one is open to being remade as a way wherein transcendence may come to manifestness' (PU, 156).

28 'In the finite we divine the infinite' (PO, 138).

29 'We look at being as good, and sometimes being looks to us as good' (PU, 163).

30 Desmond writes affirmatively of Plato's conception of good persons being 'golden souls ... imitating, partaking of Goodness itself' (PO, 267). He continues: 'As the Sun radiates over things and casts its glow, the Good itself throws a golden mantle over the

entire universe, on beauty and the ugly alike. ... The good self, as it were, catches brightness in its being' (ibid.).

31   In places, Desmond writes of how 'being agapeic' is 'almost an impossibility for us' (PU, 229). 'We must choose. Consent or refuse' (PU, 164). But perhaps we cannot break through to consent; perhaps 'we must be aided to the deeper willingness from some other source' (PU, 164–5). This seems to be an opening for the operation of grace in coming to be transfigured.

32   Desmond writes: 'At the limit thought opens to an unlimit and stutters into deeper speech' (PO, 138).

33   Desmond tells of how the Irish use the phrase, *duine le Dia*, meaning 'a person of God; naming the simple-minded, the idiot' (PO, 272). There is an interesting parallel with Desmond's discussion of the mystic as one who reaches beyond (?) being to experience the ultimate origin, God. Before God, who is not a finite object, the mystic teaches us that 'we must deconstruct the representations, or rather use them as a ladder that crumbles as we climb it, to a space of divine emptiness beyond all representing' (PO, 142). Here 'a certain silence, a certain reserve is best' (PO, 141). In this 'space', the mystic has 'a positively saturated sense of the unsurpassable mystery of Godhead' (PO, 142).

34   This, for Desmond, brings up the problem of naming the other. It seems that 'by directly naming the divine we objectify it, turn it into a finite object, turn it into something it is not. ... The name leaves God's otherness out' (PO, 135). Yet without some name the divine tends to dissolve, to disappear (even words like 'divine' and 'God' are names). So it seems we are stuck between a rock and a hard place. 'We have to name otherness in a way that names our failure to name otherness' (ibid.). Thus 'the name must be metaxological: a non-reductive "identity" that intermediates with, that is, *lets be, while intimately relating to*, the sacred other as other' (ibid.). So any 'proper' naming of God operates between the suspicious atheistic dismissal of the religious as projection/fantasy, and the univocal claim to direct, complete knowledge of God (PO, 136).

35   Desmond describes of how 'idealism becomes saccharine when it fails to offer a lodging for the realistic principle' (PO, 122).

36   In Heidegger's terms, a thinking (*denken*) that is a thanking (*danken*).

37   Desmond tells how the Irish call death, *slí na fírinne,* 'the way of truth' (PO, 278).

38   Desmond: 'the present in its plenitude is lost to us; we love it; we do not see it; we are too close to it; it lives us' (PO, 280). Being is an 'otherness only visible from distance. The elemental is normally lived in and almost impossible to think' (PO, 280).

39   Posthumous mind 'would seek ... the justified values of being that are incarnate in the present. Nor would it have any ulterior motive, since it would be beyond the fear of death and hence be metaphysically honest in a way that instrumental reason can rarely be (instrumental reason is driven by the fear of death)' (PO, 278). This 'radical honesty serves nothing but praise of the worth of being, truly worthy being. This elemental honesty is simply being mindful as thought singing its other' (ibid.).

40   Desmond asks: 'What kind of eyes are those that look on life from this death? Such eyes are *double*' (PO, 279). They see loss, but more deeply they see 'what is worthy to be praised and perpetuated'. They are 'eyes in search of the occasion of greeting, when one can thank, and renew a community of being with the elemental things that charged one's being there with its sense of intrinsic worth' (PO, 280).

41   Gavin Smith (1999), *The Thin Red Line, Film Comment,* **35,** January/February, p.10.

42   This instrumental mind-set is exemplified by the character, Tall. Lt Col. Tall is at the distant command post, talking on the radio with Capt. Staros, who is in the midst of the battle in which his men are being massacred. Tall, the power- and position-fixated careerist, looking from a distance speaks of the battle as 'beautifully executed ... magnificent ... brilliant', while Capt. Staros is crouched down in the midst of deafening artillery, dying men and soldiers going mad with shock and terror. The same Tall later engages Staros, asking him to calculate how many lives victory is worth – the same Tall who neglects to ship up water for his men because he is so preoccupied with their taking the hill.

43   Desmond writes how 'originally the divine is immediately, powerfully there, and there arises no question that all being finds its origin and end therein' (PO, 156).

44   Another one of such acme moments that Witt recalls in a flashback when he is in the brig is a memory of standing on hay bales as a child with his father, the wind blowing around them.

45   *First dialogue*: Welsh is reprimanding Witt in the brig for being AWOL. Welsh kicks Witt out of Charlie Company. Witt, obviously pained to leave, tells Welsh: 'I can take anythin you dish out. I'm twict the man you are.' The tone is adversarial. A little later Welsh proclaims: 'In this world a man, himself, is nothin'. And there ain't no world but this one.' Witt replies: 'You're wrong there ... I seen another world. Sometimes I think it was just my imagination ... .' Welsh: 'Well, then you seen things I never will.' He continues: 'We're livin' in a world that's blowin' itself to hell as fast as everybody can arrange it. A situation like that ... all a man can do is shut his eyes and let nothin' touch him, look out for himself.' Welsh concludes: 'I might be the best friend you ever had, you don't even know it.' After Welsh leaves, another soldier in the brig comments to Witt: 'He hates you worse than poison.' Witt replies: 'I never felt he hated me ... I don't hate him.'

     Second dialogue: They are in a field on the evening before the final assault on the hill. Welsh: 'I feel sorry for you kid.' Witt: 'Yeah?' Welsh: 'Yeah, a little. ... This army's gonna kill ya. If you're smart, you'll take care of yourself, there's nothing you can do for anybody else. We're just runnin' into a burnin' house where nobody can be saved.' Witt just looks at him. Welsh: 'What difference you think you can make? ... one single man in all this madness. ... If you die it's gonna be for nothin'. There's not some other world out there where everything's gonna be okay. ... There's just this one, just this rock.' As Welsh is speaking, Witt faintly smiles. When he has finished speaking, Witt looks up. It cuts to a shot of the blue evening sky, a silhouette of a palm tree flowing in the wind, the moon.

     Third dialogue: They are in an abandoned house on r&r. Witt walks in; Welsh is lounging, darkly brooding. Welsh: 'Who are you makin' trouble for today?' Witt: 'What d'ya mean?' Welsh: 'Well, isn't that what you like to do? Turn left when they say go right? Why are you such a troublemaker, Witt?' Witt walks around the house: 'Lonely house. ... You ever get lonely?' Welsh: 'Only around people.' Standing, he addresses Witt sincerely: 'You still believin' in the beautiful light are ya? How do you do that? You're a magician to me.' Witt: 'I still see a spark in you.' Cut to Welsh walking in a field and among some soldiers at evening. Witt's voice-over: 'One man looks at a dyin' bird and thinks there's nothin' but unanswered pain ... that death's got the final word ... it's laughin' at him.' Cut to Witt lying in the grass asleep. The voice-over continues: 'Another man sees that same bird ... feels the glory ... feels somethin' smilin' through it.' [Desmond's bird – 'Blood in the eye of beauty' (PU, 164).] Cut to Welsh stamping out a campfire.

Fourth dialogue: Welsh is alone at Witt's makeshift grave in the jungle, visibly saddened: 'Where's your spark now?'

46   Another possibly interesting place to see this tension is the structure of the film as a whole. On the largest scale, the film exhibits an *inclusio* (or perhaps even a sonata form). In the first voice-over in the film there is described a 'war at the heart of nature' in which 'land contend[s] with the sea'. The overall structure of the film is from sea (approaching the island) to land (the battle for the island) to sea (leaving after costly victory). There are two strong signals of the agapeic that appear in the movie that are associated with the sea: the islanders' processional hymn and the underwater shot of the native children swimming, both of which appear at the beginning and the end of the film, in proximity to the disembarkation and the departure (both on the sea). I would suggest that the sea can be seen as representing the goodness of being, the agapeic, while the land can be seen as representing death, where people die. This can be seen as an inversion of sorts. The agapeic good is not in the heights, the hill (the hill as holy place; Greek myths of ascent toward the good/true/absolute forms); the hill ends up being where 'knowledge', in the form of military technology, brings terror, death and madness. It is the sea (classically the place of chaos and death) that is the place of the agapeic other. Here is a warning that one must keep one's metaphors fluid.

Chapter 17

Towards a Metaxological Ethics of Architecture

John Hymers

Our current architectural practices are damaging to the spontaneous environment. Heavy reliance on highly processed and new materials tends toward a wasteful use of energy, a waste compounded by the shipping of these materials over great distances through the use of fossil-fuel transportation. The architect Christopher Day reports that 50 per cent of all waste stems from building construction.[1] Extensive employment of materials composed of toxic substances (such as paints, plastics or adhesives) harms both the environment and humans. Volumes have been written on the constructed environment's negative impact on the spontaneous environment, an impact I suspect that many people simply sense even without recourse to scientific literature. A movement, generally termed 'green architecture', has unsurprisingly sprung up within architecture to address this impact, and attempts to build in what it calls an environmentally responsible manner. I am concerned in this essay with broadening the ontological horizon of this movement so that it may provide a more satisfactory ethics.

I take some guidance from the Canadian architect Jorge-Dietram Ostrowski, who has correctly sensed that a term like 'green architecture' is not quite sufficient, because it still takes itself as architectural. To him, architecture means concern with 'arches and aesthetics', and not the environment.[2] Architecture, in his reading, is a practice concerned with efficient means alone. For this reason he proposes a new term, 'ecotecture', embracing the ethical interaction between the constructed environment and the spontaneous environment, and between the constructed environment and the human being that green architecture advocates, but which also shifts the connotation of the concept appreciably away from technology. I accept Ostrowski's distinction; concern with arches will never ethically improve the constructed environment. But I go on to ask: is Ostrowski's own project anything more than a concern with arches, that is, with technology? I ask this, not to call into question his project, nor to tell him how to build. I simply wish to investigate whether his and similar positions can escape unscathed the equivocities that the univocally technological approach generates.

To this end, I begin with a discussion of Ostrowski's concept of ecotecture, showing it to be a technological approach, and I suggest that, were it to be ontologically grounded, it would be a meaningful expression of architectural concern for the spontaneous environment and the human person. Leaving a discussion of this ontological ground to the final section of the essay, I then show that the technological approach of Ostrowski's ecotecture trades in problems and solutions, and therefore in mastery. This leads to a discussion of anthropocentrism, which has a weak and a strong sense. The strong sense is that of technological mastery, and the weak sense is trivial but unavoidable: whatever humans do is, insofar as humans do it, anthropocentric. This, however, wins us the position that architecture is not always anthropocentric in the strong sense. Modern architecture functions as my example of strong anthropocentrism, and Greek and medieval architecture for weak anthropocentrism. I then term weakly anthropocentric architecture ecstatic architecture, that is, architecture which leads humanity out from mere concern with itself. This in turn leads to a possibility of a well-grounded concern with the spontaneous environment. Following William Desmond, I inscribe this concern within a metaxological framework, wherein humanity and the spontaneous environment are intimately related without being sublated by each other, or by a third. I end by claiming that ecotecture must embrace this metaxological community in order to distinguish itself fully from what it considers to be mere architecture: that is, concern with technique alone.

The Ecotecture of Ostrowski

Ostrowski begins by offering us his 'Ecotecture Equation': 'Building + Lifestyle + Site + Transportation = Environmental Success', an equation also mirrored in his prose with the grammatical structures of predication and conjunction replacing the mathematical symbols: 'Ecotecture design is grounded on natural dynamics, healthy materials, biological principles, human ergonomics, cultural respect and compassionate understanding for the planet and all living creatures.'[3] This equation attempts to bear the theoretical weight of the paper, since it is the 'key to the entire exercise'.[4] Thus we should approach Ostrowski's criteria for ecotecture with close attention. And the first thing we should ask is, why these categories?

In other words, what links Ostrowski's concerns together, and what makes them specifically ecotectural? Most architecture embodies these considerations in one way or another, and hence one could suspect that perhaps Ostrowski's vision of architecture is a straw man. What contemporary architecture, for instance, would claim to be unergonomic? But, for the sake of argument, let us accept architecture as not sharing in Ostrowski's list of criteria. In this case, the specificity of the ecotecturality lies, one must imagine, in its being the explicit programme of an architecture which is self-consciously concerned with the environment, with the *oikos*. And when we look to his article, we find a further list of activities undertaken and materials used in order to build his house; his proof-of-concept for ecotecture is a detailed checklist of very ontic (and hence ultimately arbitrary) considerations that suggests, *inter alia*, recycling old refrigerator fans and the specific thickness of glass for energy conservation. But whether ecotecture must be a purely technical and inductive pursuit is precisely the question. For, if ecotecture is a technical pursuit, then how does it differ from architecture, except as a neologism?

This list attempts to flesh out the distinction between ecotecture and architecture. But no list could ever fully do justice to the unending chain of relations which constitutes the environment, whether spontaneous or constructed. Simply put, the introduction of technological patches potentially generates a non-ending row of equivocities. When I build with 'environmentally friendly' materials, I have no guarantee that, technically speaking, I remain environmentally friendly. What if I use asbestos insulation, at one point the cutting edge? What if I buy energy-efficient windows shipped from overseas? Does my heating efficiency offset the embodied energy these windows pick up from their shipping? The frailty of ontic, or ad hoc, ecology can be comical: in the USA, Representative Joe Knollenberg (R-Michigan) has authored federal legislation (H.R. 623) designed to repeal the Energy Policy and Conservation Act of 1992, which requires toilets to use a maximum of 1.6 gallons of water, largely because his constituents are fed up with flushing their toilets twice. What is missing here is an ontological understanding of the matter at stake. And, without an ontological understanding, we constantly run the risk that we are acting within the wrong paradigm, one in which humanity is seen as intruding upon nature. Thus, rather than criticize Ostrowski, I wish to offer an ontological ground to his efforts, so that the holism at which his project aims may be fulfilled.

We must consider ecotecture (and architecture) ontologically, rather than technologically, because architecture is not just a question of piling bricks upon each other, any more than ecotecture is merely in line with Ostrowski's suggestion of efficiently combining heating with cooking (an ancient idea, by the way). Architecture has always had an effect on the human in its totality: for instance, people spontaneously lower their voices when they enter churches, museums, courts of law and unfamiliar places. Tradition or respect does not explain this; from where did the tradition or respect arise? The explanation lies in the fact that architecture is a meaningful and/or practical delimitation and articulation of space. As either meaningful or practical or both, it springs from the mind of the human, and reflects, even if silently, a world view. Ultimately the world view itself is a reflection of a particular grasp of ontology. To *be in* is first to *be*. Hence we order ourselves toward the world in accordance with our conception of existence, through ontology (loosely defined). Since Descartes the regnant ontology has been technological, wherein *on* (being) has been replaced by *techne* (making). However we should not be too quick and lay all the blame at Descartes's feet; he himself warns us, 'It seems strange to me that so many people should investigate with such diligence the virtues of plants, the motions of the stars, the transmutations of metals, and the objects of similar disciplines, while hardly anyone gives a thought to good sense – to universal wisdom.'[5]

But since Descartes did, as we shall see, define the modern conception of the subject in such a decisive and influential fashion, I will treat him here unfairly as a trope for the modern malaise. Descartes's subject is the isolated and independent subject *par excellence*.

Technology: Problems and Solutions

If we continue to apply technological solutions to the questions which our architectural 'intervention' into nature poses, we shall consider these questions not as questions *per se*, but as problems. As problems, we have something which can be solved, at least in principle. Solving is a mastery, an *owning*, as it were, because in solving we triumph. The history of architecture and engineering is full of examples of this mere mastery: forests and landscape levelled to attain materials, swamps filled in to straighten roads and to create more land, larger and larger landfills created to meet the refuse needs of a vastly expanded industrial, productive and consumptive base, and so on. We see problems as something external to us, and the proof of this is simply that we can solve them: in solving them they go away. But what is integral can never go away; to treat the questions which architecture raises as problems is to externalize our relation with the spontaneous environment. Thus when architecture shows us that we must have an ethical concern with the environment, whether spontaneous or constructed, we must approach this as a question, or rather as a mystery,[6] and not as a problem.

Of course the working-out of the question may have a technical expression, but this expression may not be taken in abstraction, because in abstraction it is emptied of much of its content. For instance, a question could be, 'How is this building going to cut down on its use of non-renewable energy?' In abstraction, by only considering the technical aspect, I *could* solve this by turning to solar energy (notice the contingency of 'could'). Then the problem goes away. But the question should still remain. A historical example will help here: when Feuerbach suggested that the Holy Family was merely the alienation of the terrestrial family, Marx took him to task for not asking what it is about the human family that allows for such an alienation.[7] This is the approach I am here suggesting: not explanation, but rather reflection. We ought not to alienate the situation through a technological projection, but instead analyse it and hopefully remove the need for the projection. I should ask: why do I need energy in the first place? Do I need that TV, that radio, that computer and other such things? And even if I do, can I not apply my own energy in a better manner, perhaps in a charitable fashion, or by being active within my community? Religious people have always seen in possessions a distraction from the divine. Perhaps in our postmodern age we should rekindle this understanding of distraction. I do not mean to rename the divine as Gaia or humanity or something else, but simply to point out that often technical fixes obscure the deeper issue. Another example will help: the failed-engineer-turned-bureaucrat Adolf Eichmann wanted to convey as many bodies as quickly as possible through his extermination chambers. He set himself a *quota*. Focusing on the technical fix allowed him to ignore the real issue: why was he gassing and burning people? Or why was he treating persons as units? This is an extreme example, but it shows clearly that to solve a problem is to put us at a remove from the mystery, and to absolve ourselves from complicity in it.

Technical solutions tend simply to reiterate a mistaken view, the view that created the present predicament in which we find ourselves. I trust nobody would argue against our industrial paradigm's having caused a fair amount of damage to our planet, and to ourselves. Whether it is possible to industrialize without harmfully affecting nature is not my concern here. But it is a large mistake to turn to technology to redress this damage. Instead we need a fundamentally changed view of our relation with the spontaneous environment, one in which we do not set ourselves over and above nature as *homo technicus*, but rather one within which we recognize our co-dependency with nature. 'Because it is holistic,' says Peter Buchanan, 'green architecture is concerned with synthesis. It neither ignores nor externalizes any factors or problems.'[8] And this is not to say that our ingenuity is a negligible aspect of humanity. As Buchanan goes on to say, 'This does not contradict the rational so much as reveal dimensions that it tends to overlook, especially ... the relationship between nature and human nature.'[9] I am arguing that human rationality, represented here by technology, may not take centre stage. We must become more open and less hubristic.

Since we do meet problems in architecture, we must solve them. But these problem sets shift: earlier the question of how to place a dome on a square base fired up the architectural imagination, and later the objective of reducing the bulk of their buildings drove architects. Now the spontaneous environment has arisen as the great concern. But just as the dome and bulk are particular, and thus arbitrary, considerations, so too is the question concerning the spontaneous environment, in its present form. The similarity among these three is shown by the technical answers to these questions: pendentives for domes, flying buttresses and later I-beams and ferro-concrete to reduce bulk, and now, it seems, R-17 windows for energy conservation. In fact, a whole industry has sprung up around the needs of ecotecture.

But architecture usually swallows up any arbitrariness. It either finds the reason behind a seemingly arbitrary concern and integrates it into something approaching essentiality (for instance, glazed windows), or allows it a brief flourishing, and then consigns it to the fate of passing trends (such as the Neoclassical/Romantic ruins garden, or the Gothic triforium). The contradictions inherent in abstract positions collapse around themselves as readily as an arch that has but one abstract *voussoir*. Martin Pawley, for instance, seems to take great joy in relating how fleeting an impact the OPEC energy crisis of the early 1970s had on architecture, even though at one point the resultant conservationist architecture was the *cause célèbre*.[10] If the spontaneous environment is a valid concern for architecture, it must also be a necessary concern. We must then search for the ground of the necessity of this concern.

Strong and Weak Anthropomorphism

I propose that this concern is found in the conception of human *being*. This proposition does not necessarily lead to a strong anthropocentric position, which Warwick Fox defines as being informative or substantial anthropocentrism, a viewpoint which allows no escape from concern with the human being.[11] Strong anthropocentrism sees humanity as at the centre, whereas weak anthropocentrism sees humanity as in the midst. Strong anthropocentrism is an attempt either to univocalize nature in our image, or to condemn nature to an equivocal status in which it is other (*in sich*), but its meaning becomes human (*für uns*). Instead we must embrace what Desmond calls the metaxological community: being which is not understood in a reduction either in the direction of the one or the many; neither in the direction of the subject nor the community; and neither in the direction of humanity nor of spontaneous nature. The metaxological is a plural and open dialectical *inter*mediation which preserves all the terms of its mediation, thus it avoids Hegel's tendency to overwhelm idiotic singularity with an all-encompassing rational universality. As the *logos* (discourse) of the *metaxu* (between), the metaxological guards against the strong sense of anthropocentrism, as Warwick Fox defines anthropocentrism[12] by maintaining that we are in the midst and not at the centre.

Yet the ethics of the constructed environment does have a much more anthropocentric element than does the ethics of the spontaneous environment. That this is so may hardly seem to need saying. While it has become contentious to claim that the spontaneous environment exists to serve humanity (which instrumental environmental ethical theories in general hold), it is manifestly true that the *constructed* environment exists to serve humanity. The constructed environment is special, in that it is a human construction, for humanity. Architecture is profoundly anthropocentric in its goal to house humanity, and to give humanity space for its various expressions (commerce, worship, play, entertainment, education, and so on). This necessarily anthropocentric moment of architecture often overwhelms it, and results in buildings, and ideologies, which do nothing but reflect humanity back to itself in the starkest possible relief. This is the architecture of strong anthropocentrism.

Strongly Anthropocentric Architecture and Modernity

Before I discuss a metaxological view of being and ethics, I wish first to develop a picture of the types of architecture which must drive us to abandon our present instrumentalist point of view through their strongly anthropocentric, and paradoxically anti-humanistic, vision. Milan's Central Station, Toronto's CN Tower, Le Corbusier's unbuilt but influential 'Contemporary City for Three Million Inhabitants': these examples all embody anthropomorphic hubris – in fact, they scream it; their disproportionate size alone stifles human being, and they fall neatly in line with Albert Speer's later characterizing of his own architecture as the architecture of domination and submission.[13] But hubris is not necessarily the hallmark of anthropocentric architecture (nor is size a hallmark of hubris – see Boullée's sublime designs); usually the anthropocentric is much more subtle. I wish to focus on this subtle version first.

We find perhaps the most insidious vision of anthropocentrism in North American suburbia. Here we come across Descartes's ontology in its most domestic form. The vernacular architecture of suburban North America is, of course, the single family home, offset from the pavement and street by a longish driveway, and plonked down right in the middle of the lot, so as to guarantee maximum distance between front doors of neighbours. Its fenced-off lot contains further barricades disguised as greenery, which has been selected and planted with the help of that modern agricultural scientist, the landscape designer. This tiny castle is moated only by a general lack of knowledge of who populates, with the help of the bank, the neighbouring kingdom. Neighbours are less than merely accidental in suburbia; they are thoroughly interchangeable. This explains the phenomenon of Neighbourhood Watch, which has replaced neighbourly concern. Neighbourhood Watch is often coordinated by the police, and is instructed to report suspicious activity – say, an unfamiliar car parked in front of a vacationing family's house – and to pass on warnings gathered by the police. The interchangeability of neighbours also explains the garage sale: nobody knows to whom they should give that old pair of rollerskates or that unused fondue set, because suburbanites often do not know who many of their neighbours are. The solution is to turn one's front driveway into a modern *agora* and invoke Hermes. Most social interaction in the suburb is, of course, carried out by the children, suburbia often being seen as where one moves once one wants children, and where one stays until one is ready to move into a condominium. Hence the age bracket of the suburb is fairly homogenous; almost nobody dies of old age living in suburbia. Though perhaps this description is exaggerated, its central point is not: the suburban home is not part of a community, but is rather a node where the orbits of the inhabiting monadic family cross.

Modern architecture also emphasizes the isolation of the subject in a metaphoric fashion. It does so by emphasizing the break from the past; the past is something over and done with. As Descartes empties himself of his past in order to discover his being, so modern architecture takes the form of manifestos, movements and protests against the past. The past was dirty, exclaims Le Corbusier in his *Towards a New Architecture*, let us build a hygienic society with clean buildings![14] Loos prefigured this call in his 'Ornament und Verbrechen':

You see, this points out the greatness of our time: that it is not in the position to issue in new ornaments. We have overcome the ornament; we are through wrestling with our ornamentlessness. You see, the time is near; the fulfilment awaits us. Soon the city streets will gleam like white walls, like Zion, the holy city, the capital city of heaven! Then shall fulfilment arrive.[15]

White is the colour of purity, of cleanliness, the modern colour, and the opposite of the clerical black: hence the scientist's white robe. The only utility of ornaments seems to be dust collection; Buchanan reports that the fourth largest industry in Sweden is cleaning buildings.[16] The modern expression of the uniqueness of the subject, then, is the *sui generis* nature of its project; independent of the past, it gives us new forms and new interpretations of the functions of buildings, which are offered as modern. Hence, even when the moderns silently borrow an ancient form, say the Greek *pilotis*, they reinscribe it into the modern dialect of reduction to function: the columnation is basically reduced to a perimeter of poles. This is done successfully, I think, in Le Corbusier's Villa Savoye, or Mies van der Rohe's Seagram Building, but unsuccessfully in Le Corbusier's later Unité d'Habitation in Marseilles. Or, rather than to speak of reinscription, perhaps it is better to say that the modernized ancient fragment is limited to its functional nature. This is an especially pregnant example, as the *pilotis* describes the dividing line between mundane and sacred space in the Greek temple.

Martin Pawley's recent book, *Terminal Architecture*, brings such functionalization to its logical conclusion. Pawley radicalizes Loos to the extent that *any* aesthetic appreciation of a building is misguided if not simply wrong. Loos thought that ornamentation was wrong in that it allows a building to lie, as it were, to dissimulate itself and pretend to be what it is not. Let the materials speak for themselves, Loos said. Eschewing his theoretical call for white walls, his few buildings were stunningly beautiful through judicious choice of materials, but lacking any ornamentation (the Viennese have since 'corrected' Loos's buildings). Pawley thinks that the proscription on ornaments must be extended to any 'art-historical appreciation' of architecture.[17] Architecture, for Pawley, is no aesthetic endeavour, and has no reason to be; anything beyond mere functionality is a waste of resources. Hence one of the few praises you will ever hear sung to superstores and automated factories – both examples of what he calls 'big-shed architecture' – you will find in Pawley. For this modern architecture is seen as 'Terminal 2' architecture, that is, where people, or products, or information, or whatever, intertwine and are processed.[18] Again these are nodes wherein orbits intersect. This architecture concerns itself with the most efficient way of accommodating as many intersecting orbits as is cost-effective, and with the concomitant exchange of goods, services or information. We even see this in suburban architecture, the more so now that 'home theatres' and the Internet allow the monadic family direct access to the information of the entertainment and infotainment corporations. Modern architecture, Pawley says, 'presented our century with a culture of buildings that identified them as instruments instead of monuments'.[19]

And here in Pawley we see modern architecture explicitly as the technical fix to determinate problems. Of course, this approach did not originate in Pawley, who is rather one of its most recent troubadours. For instance, Le Corbusier's unbuilt 'Contemporary City for Three Million Inhabitants' approaches mass housing from this perspective of the 'problem'. Problem: how to house efficiently a large number of people? Answer: by building four huge tower blocks on a massive pediment. Problem: how to keep the unsightliness and noise of mass transit at bay? Answer: under the pediment, multi-layer highways channel traffic out of sight. Problem: how to soften the soulless nature of a large mass of concrete? Answer: verdure is supplied on top of the pediment by a massive planting of grass and trees. Yet each of these solutions leads to more problems which, in fact, remain unsolved in his plan.

First, the uniform nature of the apartment blocks housing three million people is dehumanizing alone; notice that Le Corbusier refers to them in their functional nature: they are inhabitants, and are thus defined in terms of their functional relation to the architecture. Second, this hiding of the highways obscures a deeper fact: the apartment block complex is basically an island, and its inhabitants are thus enslaved to this highway for any escape from the concrete and the controlled landscape. Although one could make this claim about any city, a quick inspection of Le Corbusier's plan shows that this city has none of the variety and interest of a normal, more organic, city. Third, the break that the greenery provides from the constructed environment is only present in the summer and spring, and its lack of any wildness would definitely provide a poor substitute for spontaneous nature.[20] This thoroughly constructed environment does not so much interact with the spontaneous environment as obliterate it, or at least mask it completely.

That modernity would go in this direction is more astounding than is usually thought. As William Desmond points out in *Philosophy and Its Others*, Modernity, as the New Time (*Neuzeit*), 'was to be a renewal, renaissance of our naturalness, in distinction to Medieval supernaturalism. But the modern self does not find itself as at home with nature as expected, and tries to secure its own being by technological will-to-power over its otherness' (PO, 275).

Modernity was born itself, at least in part, from a reaction to the medieval focus on the other world; as a decidedly this-sided project, modernity was to relate us to nature, and not to the supernatural. But instead of reconnecting us with nature, it placed us in opposition to it, so that nature becomes an 'other'. As an other, humanity is in confrontation with nature. Descartes is famed, for instance, for calling us to be masters and possessors of nature, and for claiming that animals were mere automatons. Why did modernity go in this direction? This is too complicated a question for such an essay as this, but Descartes's subject points us toward the answer. The self is seen as something abstracted from that which is not the self. In other words, the self is isolated, as I showed above. If I am only myself, then I am not you; I am also not that tree, nor this building, or the like. In a move typical of modernity, the separated individual finds its separation projected onto the species. Hence humanity is separate from nature. Since humanity is taken to be autonomous and nature taken to be law-governed, it only follows that free humanity takes possession of law-bound nature, and the best way to do so is to take possession of the laws of nature. Hence the atomic subject of Descartes discovers the power of the atom and builds the atomic bomb. Has this remove from the supernatural got us any closer to nature than, say, the tribes which Frazer describes as trying to enrich the generative power of their land through the addition of their own semen?[21] These acts of imitative magic, though supernatural from the point of view of modern science, certainly illustrate a mind which is connected closely with nature. The mind which holds that there is a relation between human sexuality and natural regeneration certainly does not set itself over and against nature.

Modernity's tendency toward isolation simply reiterates Descartes's discrete subject, the *cogito*, pure self-identity. That is, the individual is found only when the mind is emptied of all externality; in this scheme, to follow a Hegelian critique, thinking is identical to negation or doubt; that which I doubt is not me, and *that* I actually do doubt, well, that *is* me: *cogito ergo sum*, which is better expressed as *dubito ergo sum*, according to Feuerbach.[22] I *am* my doubting, my negating of that which I am not. But this has a corollary: if I am found in abstracting all content away, and if that means that all that is left is that I doubt, that I think, then all I am is my thinking, but this thinking has no content beyond its not being anything else. It is empty, contentless, purely formal, or simply pure.

Hence the Cartesian self, in being simply itself, is indeterminate, abstract and empty. This, rather surprisingly, allows for a shift from the autonomous individual to the unit of society. Everyone is an individual. Even though the individual is defined as not being anyone else, this means that everyone is not anyone else. Everyone then has the same constitution as everyone else, and thus there are no real differences between people. Everybody is isolated because everyone is isomorphic, but this isolation is what they all have in common, a conclusion readily embraced by our modern ontology of production. Here we see equivocity invoked by univocity.

The works of the High Moderns (such as Gropius, Mies van der Rohe and Le Corbusier) also highlight this latter sense of the individual. Instead of merely strengthening the modern subject as an isolated subject, they also sublate this isolated subject into a more universal subject, commensurate with the new forms of production. Le Corbusier's *Towards a New Architecture* is explicit about wanting to bring the world of architecture to the same level as the world of industry; in fact, the world of industry is to provide the new language for architecture. For this reason he designed his intriguing Citrohan House, the name consciously evoking the Citroën, whose 1922 model gave the house its shape.[23] For this reason, he compares the Parthenon with the form of a car. And for this reason too, Gropius wrote that the aerial viewpoint was the principal point of view of modernity, an idea he extended into a joke by forming his Bauhaus building vaguely into the shape of a propeller, for the benefit of test pilots from the neighbouring Junker's aircraft factory, who could see it from the air.[24] Charles Jencks's definition of modern architecture well captures this technological and generic bent: 'Thus we might define Modern architecture as the *universal, international style stemming from the facts of new constructional means, adequate to a new industrial society, and having as its goal the transformation of society, both in its taste and social make-up.*'[25]

The factory, the production line, the staff of an office or business – these become the new paradigm of the subject wherein the subject is seen as an instance of personnel. Hence the factory shift, or the office cubicle.[26] This conclusion is guaranteed by the abstract definition of self which Descartes promulgated: I=I, the ultimate isomorphism.[27]

Why do I seem here to be reiterating a fairly common and cynical view of modernity? Because the hubris of modernity seems constantly to pull us back into its orbit. And we see this quite clearly in the suggestion of Ostrowski that technology is to redress our overtaxing of nature. But we landed ourselves in our present ecological malaise precisely through technology, or better, through our hubristic belief that the human situation relies on technology alone. I question whether it is sufficient to claim that we now have *better* and *less invasive* technology. This belief is the self-affirmation of the strongest possible anthropocentrism, and reeks unbearably of hubris.

Ecstatic Architecture

While architecture is *per se* anthropological in its construction and aims, it does not follow that it must stem from strongly anthropocentric views. We are not the first age to realize this. If we put aside any thought of religion as human projection (whether Euhemeristic, Humean, Feuerbachian, Freudian or the like), we can accept that the Greeks saw their temples as excised space; space outside of the human, and thus outside of the profane. This is Heidegger's reading of the Greek temple, to be sure, and it is intimately tied to his influential ontology of elusive being. Regardless of whether or not his ontology is fruitful, I believe that his reading of the Greek temple is instructive, since it points us toward an ecstatic architecture. The temple is sacred – cut off, excised – from the human world by the presence of the god;[28] the god fills the space of the constructed walls with a non-human content. In this sense, the temple is not at all constructed according to an anthropocentric programmeme: it is to let the god *be*, and not to reflect the human back to itself directly. (But perhaps indirectly, as it shows humanity has the ability to let itself come into contact with that which is other, without subsuming it to itself.) To this extent, Vitruvius tells us that temples to Jupiter, a sky god, were to have openings in the ceiling, while Venus was to be housed within the delicate Corinthian order.[29]

The example of the Greek temple is, however, problematic, since Vitruvius tells us that the columns are representations of men and women (Doric and Ionic, respectively) and that the orders of the buildings in general are thought of as expressing the respective genders of their columnations.[30] Nevertheless I maintain that these anthropomorphic forms are sublated by the presence of the god enclosed within it.

We do not have this same problem in Abbot Suger's conception of St-Denis in Paris, since Gothic orders are non-gendered. Panofsky's influential translation of Suger's works informs us that Suger's drive toward curtain-like and diaphanous walls was an attempt to overcome the human (and all too Norman) drive toward security, in the direction of letting light be.[31] This architecture of light finds its apotheosis in Paris's Sainte Chapelle. Light here symbolizes God, and the architecture of light was to allow contemplation of the beauty of the divine and thus to be lost in the divinity; it was an attempt at a profoundly ecstatic architecture – ecstatic in the sense that it attempts to lead the human being out of itself and into something larger and more inclusive. Again this is hardly anthropocentric in the strong sense.

These buildings *are* anthropocentric in the weak sense, that they were built by humans and are for the worship of God by humans, or that they are human monuments to the gods. But the substance of these buildings is non-human; or they are not anthropocentric in the strong sense, wherein we focus on the latter half of the word: they are not centred around humanity, but around a more inclusive presence, regardless of either the object of reverence or the contentious ontological status of this presence. They are historical and constructed expressions of humanity's desire to transcend itself. These buildings also reflect a concept of the individual, not trapped in an abstract view of its discrete particularity, but intertwined within a larger community. Neither the Greek temple nor St-Denis was conceived as a private chapel, reflecting the importance of a discrete self communing with itself. Neither was conceived according to the same concept of the subject to which the monadic dwellings, which *infest* our suburbs like so many caterpillars, subscribe – *cocooning* indeed![32]

I have indicated above that ecstatic architecture does not directly reflect a concept of humanity back to itself: it is not the photographic negative to the plate of humanity. As ecstatic, it leads humanity out of itself. But I also indicated that it reflects humanity indirectly, by showing that humanity can also let entities be what they are; that humanity does not with necessity make an idol of itself in everything that it sees or makes. This indicates a very specific concept of humanity: the human as metaxological.

Metaxological Being

'If the land belongs to you,' asks Desmond, 'but you do not belong to the land, can you make a real home there, an abode?'(PO, 277). Desmond thus implicitly asks us to avoid the Conservationist position. Conservationism is basically a technological position of what Desmond calls the instrumentalist mind. This is made explicit by ecologists such as Warwick Fox, who convincingly shows that conservationism employs a 'mini-max' strategy in which we minimize our intervention into nature but still maximize the results of our intervention;[33] this is still the instrumentalist mind at work. Regardless of its intentions, such a position still sees the earth as something external and *merely* exploitable, something with no intrinsic value; such a position sees the earth as some*thing*, a thing among other things.

Conservationism is a futural approach which is intended to ensure a constant supply of exploitable resources. Some conceptions of green architecture fit into this mould; the title of Robert and Brenda Vale's *Green Architecture: Design for a Sustainable Future* alone points this out. But Desmond calls us to a 'posthumous mindfulness' (PO, 278), which is a metaphysical therapy intended to help us recognize the inherent goodness of being beyond the subjectivistic and instrumentalist standpoints. That is, if I imagine myself to be dead, I have stripped my thought of any relation to my needs or wants, and can then think about the inherent goodness of being, independent of subjective and instrumentalist desires. This does not remove the concrete subject from the picture. I am still consciously thinking the goodness of being; I have not removed myself to the view from nowhere and become a worldless I, which is Thomas Nagel's thoroughly modern position.[34] By thinking myself dead, I merely think myself as dead to my desires.

I can then be open to what being extends in its indeterminate plenitude and goodness, without subsuming it to my own desires.

But suppose we transfer this posthumous mind to the question of the inherent value of both the spontaneous and the constructed environment, and think the inherent goodness in them? Then we could investigate their status without those nostalgic or conservationist viewpoints which taint much of our relation with the environment. For, finally, we would be addressing the environment, not as our object, but as something of inherent value. And also we would not be in opposition to it, for the briefest contemplation would reveal that we both spring from, and give shape to, the environment. This reveals itself as a metaxological relationship in which neither term is subsumed in the other, but in which both terms exist in intimate relation.

This may sound like Hegel who, for instance, shows with great dexterity that there is no me without you, no positive without negative, no parent without child, and so on. However each of these is subsumed into a larger whole, which is eventually swallowed up by the Idea. The metaxological is not in search of this larger rational totality; instead of rational logic it offers idiot wisdom (*idios*, intimate). This is the wisdom to see that, though beings are intimately related and give themselves to each other, this giving is not a swallowing or determining. But at the same time it is the recognition of a prior unity. These givings are part of a larger giving, one which gives freedom in freedom, which gives absolution from the total determination of the source, a source which gives from its infinitely overdetermined, and thus indeterminable, being. This is the wisdom that rejoices in the idea *that* there is being, *that* the mind was given at all. *That* being is, that is the excess; it is the non-answer to Heidegger's unanswerable question, borrowed verbatim from Leibniz, of why there is being rather than nothing; in place of an answer only: *that*. The *that* is excessive precisely because it exceeds our ability to think it; it is the *nihil* in *creatio ex nihilo*.

Let us remove this from its metaphysical setting and apply it to the environment. If we think of nature in terms of idiot wisdom, nature ceases to be other, and becomes instead a source that gives from out of an indeterminable plenitude. The instrumentalist framework is synonymous with 'ontological nihilism' (BB, 508ff.), a nihilism which is particularly silent. This is not the nihilism that preaches the death of values, morals, society or God; nor is it the political nihilism of Dostoevsky's *Crime and Punishment*; nor is it the caricature of nihilism of the Coen brothers' *Big Lebowsky*. This is a nihilism which is simply blind to any intrinsic value in being; whatever value there may be is super-added by humanity (ibid.). This nihilism sees humanity as the creator of *all* value, and is thus thoroughly instrumentalist. The wonder directed at the thereness of being, which is not subsumable to concepts, is thus simply ignored. As such, nature is taken as a valueless aggregate of forces and materials present in order to be given extrinsic value by humanity, instead of being a system of inherent order (BB, 510). By atomizing both ourselves and nature, we lose the *ordo naturalis*, and with it the idea of final causality, covering this completely with an expanded efficient causality.

Conclusion: Ecotecture Must Follow a Metaxological Ontology

To address the questions posed by the relation of the constructed environment with the spontaneous environment through technology, through efficient causality, is to miss the very point of the questions. Such 'green architecture', even if we call it 'ecotecture', misses its vocation by issuing checklists. Toilets that use no water and convert human waste into *useful* fertilizer are laudable inventions indeed, but to turn to them as a response to the ecological crisis is a short-sighted appeal to technology. It does not change our fundamental approach to nature, merely its scope. It is by no means obvious that the scope of our intervention needs changing. However it is obvious that the explicit understanding of our relationship with the spontaneous environment needs changing. Loos realized this when he admonished architects: 'think not about the roof, but rather about the rain and the snow'.[35] In this perspective the roof becomes part of the environment. Hence this change must be a complete repudiation of the concept of intervention.

As long as we are concerned with *syntagmata* such as 'environmental impact' and 'intervention', we remain within a framework which alienates us from nature: we become one of two poles, and nature the other. However metaxology calls us to understand our relation with nature as co-dependent, but also to understand that neither humanity nor nature is exhausted in this co-dependence, precisely because neither can come under exhaustive determination. To recognize this is to recognize that we are not apart *from* nature, but neither merely a part *of* nature. Just as a child does not intervene in its family, humanity does not intervene in nature. But when we see the environment as inherently valueless, our relation *is seen* as one of intervention. And, as if burlesquing *esse est percipi*, it then becomes intervention. This is the position of the hubristic technological human being.

If ecotecture is to be a sufficiently important force in architectural reform, it must reflect our metaxological being. It must call us to dwell amidst, and give us buildings which embody this call. It must answer Loos's imperative: *wohnen lernen!*[36] It must use technology, but not be technological. The technology it uses must not be aimed at fixing our relationship with nature, but must instead be a reflection of our relation with nature, which too has its efficient aspect. And since our relation with nature is not external but intimate, our technology must not treat nature merely as a means. If the environment is inherently good, then it must *also* be treated as an end in itself. To treat the earth as a means to an end is not necessarily wrong; we rightly treat people as means to various ends every day, for example, as students treat their teachers as a means.

The technologist position, however, treats the being of the earth as a means; the metaxological recognizes that in the between things must get done, but that the meaning of things does not lie in their acquiescence to this goal. Ecotecture can only distance itself from architecture by forswearing the overwhelming technological approach of what it considers architecture. Ecotecture is not about numbers. It is about dwelling amidst, about dwelling metaxologically.

Notes

1   Christopher Day, 'Ethical Building in the Everyday Environment: a Multilayer Approach to Building and Place Design', in Warwick Fox, ed., *Ethics and the Built Environment*, London: Routledge, 2000, pp.127–38 (p.127). See also Robert and Brenda Vale, *Green Architecture: Design for a Sustainable Future*, London: Thames and Hudson, 1991; and Peter Buchanan (1990), 'Green Architecture', *The Architectural Review*, **123**, pp.37–8. These works all contain ready catalogues of such damage to the spontaneous environment.
2   Jorg-Dietram Ostrowski, 'Ecotecture: the Language for Ecological Homes', *Environmental Design + Construction*, 25 January 2001 (<http://www.edcmag.com/ edc/cda/articleinformation/coverstory/bnpcoverstoryitem/0,4118,19439,00.html.>). Latest access, 16 March 2003. Also in print: Jorg-Dietram Ostrowski (1998), 'Ecotecture: the Language for Ecological Homes', *Environmental Design and Construction*, September/October, pp.20–30. Only the Internet version accessed.
3   Ostrowski, op. cit.
4   Ostrowski, op. cit.
5   René Descartes, 'Rules for the Direction of Mind', in John Cottingham, Robert Stoothoff and Dugald Murdoch, eds and trans., *The Philosophical Writings of Descartes*, 3 vols, Cambridge: CUP, 1985, vol. 1, pp.7–78 (rule 1).
6   Gabriel Marcel, 'On the Ontological Mystery', in *The Philosophy of Existentialism*, trans. Manya Harari, New York: Citadel Press, 1991, pp.9–46. A problem is a question which we take as external, and a mystery is a question which involves us intimately: 'A mystery is a problem which encroaches upon its own data, invading them, as it were, and thereby transcending itself as a simple problem' (p.19).
7   Karl Marx, 'Theses on Feuerbach', *Karl Marx–Frederick Engels: Collected Works*, trans. not given, 47 vols, London: Lawrence and Wishart, 1976, vol. 5 (1845–47), pp.3–5 (thesis 4).
8   Buchanan, 'Green architecture', p.38.
9   Ibid.
10 Martin Pawley (1990), 'Backfire: Exogenous Shock', *The Architectural Review*, **123**, 94–7 (p.97).
11 Warwick Fox, *Towards a Transparent Ecology*, Boston and London: Shambhala, 1990, pp.20ff.
12 Fox, *Towards a Transparent Ecology*, loc. cit.
13 Albert Speer, *Architecture: 1932–1942*, ed. and trans. Léon Krier, Brussels: Archives d'Architecture Moderne (1985), p.213. In fact, Speer's aesthetic seems to have survived, *mutatis mutandis*, in the North American fixation on the domed stadium. Compare the *Meisterstück* of his *Grosser Platz*, his Great Dome, with any domed stadium.
14 Le Corbusier (Charles-Edouard Jeanneret), *Towards a New Architecture*, trans. F. Etchells, London: The Architectural Press, 1976 (rpt of 1946 edn), *passim*.
15 Adolf Loos, 'Ornament und Verbrechen', in *Trotzdem*, ed. Adolf Opel, Vienna: Georg Prachner Verlag, 1982 (rpt of 1931 edn), pp.78–88.
16 Buchanan, 'Green architecture', p.38.
17 Martin Pawley, *Terminal Architecture*, London: Reaktion Books, 1998, pp.93ff.
18 Pawley's definitions of Terminal architectures are based on an acknowledged, and to my mind acceptable, equivocation: while Terminal 2 architecture is nodal architecture, Terminal 1 architecture is architecture that has come to an end, that is, is terminated.

Terminal 1 architecture is any architecture with pretensions to being 'art-historical' (ibid. pp.7ff.).

19 Ibid., p.113.

20 See Marvin Trachtenberg and Isabelle Hyman, *Architecture*, New York: Harry N. Abrams, 1986. I am indebted to their discussion of this project (p.531).

21 James Frazer, *The Golden Bough*, abridged edn, Hertfordshire, UK: Wordsworth Editions, 1993, p.136.

22 Ludwig Feuerbach, *Geschichte der Neueren Philosophie von Bacon von Verulam bis Benedikt Spinoza*, in Werner Schuffenhauer and Wolfgang Harich, eds, *Gesammelte Werke*, 19 vols, Berlin: Akademie-Verlag, 1969–1990, vol.2, p.260.

23 Trachtenberg and Hyman, *Architecture*, p.524.

24 Ibid.

25 Charles Jencks, *What is Postmodernism?*, London: Academy Editions, 1986, p.28 (emphasis in original).

26 This is not *per se* a modern idea; medieval monks too had their own cubicles (*cellulae*) and shifts (*horae canonicae*). But the difference lies in the direction of the sublation: in the Middle Ages this sublation was self-understood as being in the direction of a universality, a more inclusive presence. In modernity, the sublation tends in the direction of an aggregate or sum, which is in keeping with the overwhelming stress on the economic. In this sense, it is almost better not to speak of sublation but of cancellation and replacement.

27 We are here within the movement of Hegel's dialectic of the one and the many; in formal terms, this dialectic says that that which rends asunder also unifies. We can find a succinct treatment of this dialectic in G.W.F. Hegel, *The Encyclopaedia: Logic. Part I of the Encyclopaedia of the Philosophical Sciences*, trans. T.F. Geraets, W.A. Suchting and H.S. Harris, Indianapolis and Cambridge: Hackett Publishing Company, 1991, pp.97–8.

28 Martin Heidegger, 'The Origin of the Work of Art', in D.F. Krell, ed., *Basic Writings*, trans. Albert Hofstadter, 2nd rev. edn, New York: HarperCollins, 1993, pp.143–212 (pp.167ff.).

29 Vitruvius (Marcus Vitruvius Pollio), *The Ten Books on Architecture*, trans. Morris Hicky Morgan, New York: Dover, 1960 (rpt. of 1914 Harvard University Press edn), Book 1, 2:5.

30 Vitruvius, Book 4, 1: 6–7.

31 Current work on a critical edition of Suger's works strongly suggests that Panofsky's interpretation, in his *Gothic Architecture and Scholasticism*, New York: Meridian Books, 1957, is simply wrong, and is the result of a Hegelian desire to see the material as a manifestation of the ideal. The idea that Suger was not lost in Neoplatonic emanation theology is, to put it bluntly, shocking, and actually calls for a complete rereading of the standard presentation of the development of Gothic architecture. However I would maintain that Suger's liturgical view of St-Denis still qualifies it as ecstatic architecture. See Andreas Speer, 'Art as Liturgy: Abbot Suger of St-Denis and the Question of Medieval Aesthetics', in *Roma, Magistra Mundi. Itirneraria Culturae Medievalis. Mélanges Offerts au Père L.E. Boyle à l'Occasion de son 75e Anniversaire*, Louvain-la-Neuve: Textes et Etudes du Moyen Age, 1998, pp.855–75.

32 I would add that Christopher Day's modern work deserves to be called ecstatic architecture. His core vision – community involvement, natural materials, buildings as healing the soul – certainly embodies an attempt at liberating the concentrated self without overwhelming it in collectivism. And this architecture clearly demonstrates an

ethical awareness of the environment; his ethics is all the more fruitful as it stems from a true *ethos*, the community. See his wonderful book, *Places of the Soul. Architecture and Environmental Design as a Healing Art*, 1999, London: HarperCollins.

33 Fox, *Towards a Transparent Ecology*, pp.208ff.

34 Nagel tells us, incredibly, 'an objective standpoint is created by leaving a more subjective, individual, or even just human perspective behind', as if the objective standpoint were not a human perspective in the first place. See Thomas Nagel, *The View from Nowhere*, Oxford: OUP, 1986, p.7.

35 Adolf Loos, 'Regeln für den, der in den bergen [*sic*]' baut, in *Trotzdem*, pp.120–21 (p.120). Considering it to be ornament, Loos does not follow here the German orthography of capitalized nouns.

36 See: Adolf Loos, 'Wohnen Lernen!', in *Trotzdem*, pp.165–9.

Chapter 18

Towards a Metaxological Hermeneutics of Plants and Animals

Peter Scheers

While it is not the case that William Desmond has developed a systematic philosophy of plants and animals, his metaxological project does contain numerous insights, often by way of poetic articulation, implying and supporting a nonconstructionist (and nonreductive) reading of the vegetal and animal world. His fertile efforts deserve no less than comprehensive environmental consideration. Needless to say, this is not something to be undertaken in the context of a short essay; I will focus only on a metaxological appreciation of plants and animals – the possibility of human interpretation of natural otherness beyond constructionism (and beyond reductionism and productionism) – and the development of a theory of bionarration. My reading of human interpretation will make use of Desmond's theory of benevolent interpretation. My reading of plants and animals will focus on a thematic appreciation of vegetal and animal life stories in line with the spirit of metaxological interpretative benevolence (including its sense of benign anthropomorphism). The issue of a non-human life story, as we will see, allows us to articulate meaning and value beyond humanity. This is what a metaxological approach, in the style of Desmond, exactly wishes to accomplish.[1]

The Benevolent Interpreter

The problematics of human interpretation of natural otherness directly concerns the issue of animal being. Our possibilities and ways of interpretation strongly, if not fully, determine our dealings with animals. According to constructionism we cannot reach otherness in its otherness. Human interpretations are fictional constructions we make up for the sake of our own advantage. We cannot go beyond, so we are told. Desmond offers a powerful hermeneutic alternative opening up a benign sense of interpretation in which otherness can be authentically received. He explicitly argues against Rorty (AO, 280).

Constructionists such as Rorty see the human interpreting self as an entity enclosed in its own interpretative productions, grounded as these are in purely instrumentalist concerns (survival, gratification). The constructionist sense of interpretation remains captured by what Desmond characterizes as erotic mind. The life of interpretation is fully controlled by the effort to subsume what is other into the self-relativity of the mind seeking its own self-satisfaction (PU, 105). Rorty suggests, for example, that our interpretation of a giraffe as a distinct object, distinguished from what surrounds it, finds its source only in our human activity of hunting.[2] If we had other activities and desires, we would perhaps not come to such a conception of a giraffe as an independent object. Constructionism extrapolates the vitalist and instrumentalist role of interpretation to all levels of human interpretation. There is no way to discern better and worse interpretations with an eye on respecting otherness in its own way of being. In the context of serving survival (and aesthetic gratification) one interpretation becomes as good as another. Otherness itself is not able to influence the quality of our interpretations. And the interpreting self will always remain captured by a self-serving erotic mind. Interpretation becomes a kind of dense fog through which we can reach nothing, through which nothing can reach us. And the interpretative fog is produced by our stubborn and often unconscious schemes.

Desmond proposes a serious alternative to constructionism. His proposal can be defined as a theory of benevolent interpretation. One finds the figure of the benevolent interpreter in the context of other philosophies, but Desmond has developed one of the more impressive contemporary contributions to a benign sense of interpretation. Based on certain interpretative possibilities, finding their source in an intermediation not fully controlled by self or otherness, human selves are capable of noninstrumental hermeneutic generosity. Desmond refers to an agapeic hermeneutics, organized according to the following principle:

> Seek the strength in the other, the point of ripeness, or if not that, seek the promise of ripeness in the other. And if one seeks the good in the other, do not define this good simply in terms of its congruence with oneself; let this promise of the good of the other emerge; welcome and make way for its emergence for itself. (PU, 124–5)

Hermeneutic generosity implies benevolence within the interpreting self as well as authentic interpretative possibilities of meeting the other in its otherness. We need to clarify these two implications. I will start with the second issue.

Desmond depicts a self situated in a middle with other things. We are things amongst things. In the middle space we have a plurality of centres of active being. This play of positive plurality leads to a sense of intermediation allowing both sides (interpreting self and otherness) 'to flower out of themselves and so to meet in the middle that neither defines completely by itself and in which neither is completely determinative of the other' (DD, 115). The process of interpretation is not a matter of an interpreter subjectively controlling everything while the object remains mute. Exclusive subjectivism (such as constructionism) is not a valid option. It is also not the case that reality completely determines the interpretative reception while the human self and its mediating capacities have no say. Exclusive objectivism (such as empiricism), too, is not an option. Intermediation, according to metaxology, is 'not a relation in which the knower overreaches the other, stamping his own space on the knowing process as a whole, not a question of the other imprinting its configuration on the knower' (ibid.). The fact that otherness has itself an active voice within the hermeneutic field of intermediation turns interpretation into something other than a solipsistic adventure. There is no absolute erotic sovereignty. The privilege of self-mediation cannot be sustained. Intermediation 'shapes the *inter* such that it can never be closed by either side alone, or even by both sides together, for the very *inter* is kept open just by the openness of the participants in this community' (BB, 451). I believe Desmond's approach hits an important issue setting the destiny of human interpretation on another, more productive track.

One manner in which otherness reaches us and shocks us out of self-enclosure is through our aesthetic, fleshed way of being. Our fleshed humanness is not self-enclosed but immediately brings us in touch with things (PO, 65). In our organic, sensual dimension we experience, in an elemental and pre-reflective way, the immediate givenness of aesthetic being of otherness in its singular thereness (*idios*). The senses, as such, are the flesh of agapeic mind, since they are in fact developed with the purpose of sensing otherness (PU, 110). The bodily self is often ignored in hermeneutic literature. One reads about intellectual selves involved in reading literature. But Desmond shows that our openness toward otherness already begins on an organic pre-intellectual level, a level which needs to be taken into account in a full hermeneutics. Through the senses we are 'surges of the energy of being responsive to the being of otherness as it touches us in the flesh' (PO, 65). Our aesthetic way of being, situated in bodily context, leads to a celebration of other-being coming towards us while there is also a process of receiving:

> The other as other seizes us, and offers itself to our minding, but we then go towards it out of our seizure. This seizure puts us in the hold of other-being; it puts us in its thrall, enthralling us. This is a receptivity that is both ruptured and enrapt. One is captivated, as if something in the sight of the other falls upon us, showers itself upon us, and we fall in love with it. (BB, 10)

The aesthetic moment contradicts the constructionist focus on instrumental reception. For Desmond, there is a preconceptual and non-erotic experience of being pleased with being, with the fact that beings are, with the fact that otherness astonishes us. Already on this level, one could say, beings outside us talk back to us and proclaim their presence. This has nothing to do with a pragmatist appropriation. There is an idiotic innocence in aesthetic presencing and in the human aesthetic reception of otherness. Humans, to be sure, are also involved with other types of reception of otherness which could eventually ignore or betray the initial experience of openness, but a cardinal point in metaxological hermeneutics is that we should as humans continue to recapture astonishment and intimacy with being and beings in their idiotic particularity. A child lives in the aesthetic rapport more spontaneously and immediately, but in all stages of life we should (re-)experience the aesthetic envelopment of value (EB, 22). Such a continuation will help later, more articulated interpretative activities to remain guided by the aesthetic surplus of otherness.

There are other ways in which experience of otherness co-directs human interpretation. Things are stubborn. As determinative happenings of the power of being they possess a recalcitrant thereness. They have a nature that follows its own way, even against our will to determine otherness (BB, 300). There is order in nature and in things beyond us. This order is not a fiction, otherwise there would be no supporting earth in which humans can survive and interpret. We are ourselves products of this order, and of this 'poetic' process of nature naturing. This order, and the inherent structure of things, offers a strong presence of otherness beyond our constructive devices. As Desmond underlines:

> Beyond human order, the real exhibits order that is not our own making. We see it in the wandering of the planets, which do not wander at all. We greet it in the cyclic recurrence of nature's seasons. We silently live our homage to it with every rising of the sun and every setting. We meet it when a seed sprouts, reaching down into the dark earth for roots, stretching out for growth, up into the bright air. (PO, 228)

This sense of non-human determinate structure permits the formulation of a hermeneutic principle of resistance. Our preconceptions and interpretations in fact find themselves confronted by resistances beyond our personal control. Think even of the experience of otherness implied in our own bodies. Indeed, as Desmond remarks, let a person get a stomach cramp and it will become clear to him or her that there is something beyond 'creative subjectivity' (ibid.). Realities beyond our interpretations are out there. These are the intelligible bonds that hold diversities together and that command or ask for respect. Precisely through their stubborn presence, resistances teach us a benign lesson. Resistance causes interpretation to be under constraint. It is not a free play. Each negative experience of resistance narrows and thereby controls the positive direction that can be taken. Constructionism can be expected to insist that our experience of resistances, too, is a matter of fictional construction: we pick out whatever we want and we invent signs of direction and resistance along the way. The interpreting self is pictured as being unable to learn from its interpretational confrontations. It is unable to learn because otherness is portrayed as a silent victim that will never scream out against wrong interpretation. With Desmond, however, we can come to understand how resistances do manage to break through our personal scenarios and do come to direct our interpretations.

Constructionism is in one sense based on the assumption that there is a radical gap between humans and non-human otherness. And once the absolute gap is accepted, human interpretation of the non-human is of course destined to go wrong. Others such as plants and animals are so different from us that our attempts to make sense of them are bound to fail. Desmond points out that such a gap is not exactly there. Metaxological hermeneutics brings into play a hermeneutic principle of similarity, based upon an even more basic principle of shared earthliness. Humans, animals and plants belong to one and the same planet. We are all creatures of the earth. Things are expressions of a process of nature naturing.

Many of our interpretations are focused on forms of otherness that came to be in the earthly process. In numerous instances we can observe similarities between ourselves and others (other humans, other organisms, other aspects of being). How are we to explain these similarities? Should we automatically assume that such similarities are constructionist figments of our mind? For Desmond there is a community of mind and its essential other, being. He refers to an ontological affinity between the 'I am' of selfhood and the 'it is' of real otherness (DD, 139). For example, we share certain organic capabilities and needs with other organisms. It is rather foolish to deny the validity of these interpretatively constituted observations of similarity: 'The human self, even in its distinctiveness, need not be in estrangement from the rest of creation. A profound kinship with things is engraved on us' (PO, 163). The fact that we are indeed fellow-voyagers with other creatures suggests that the categories of human mind may sometimes be deeply appropriate to the order of being.

The interplay of the principles of similarity and resistance shows that human interpretation is more than a matter of closure and constructionist fiction without a sense of otherness. This surplus beyond closure makes it valid to assume there are more and less healthy ways of functioning within the hermeneutical circle. We are not the measure of the truth of things. We are not fully locked up in interpretative schemes. There is movement and evolution in interpretation. Estimation in terms of better and worse can be applied to interpretations which more and less appropriately deal with combined experiences of similarity and resistance.

The capacity to interpret otherness beyond constructionism does not as such imply that we shall actually undertake fair and benign interpretations of otherness. There is openness, but we can always decide to close our eyes and to indulge ourselves in erotic mind as much as possible. We may not care for the other, and deny its value. Desmond offers a further elaboration on the benevolent state of human interpreters in terms of agapeic mind. This is the second implication we need to discuss.

Agapeic minding involves a believing and trusting in the inherent value of the other (EB, 355). This introduces a *full* conception of benevolent interpretation.[3] Such a conception is nowadays not an evident proposal. Constructionism has become widely accepted and, more often than not, embodies a theory of vicious interpretation. One finds here a disposition opposite to benevolent disposition. Interpreters are determined by a will to power. And one expects in others only processes of manipulation. The figure of the aggressive interpreter surfaces. This figure, itself the product of an aggressive approach to hermeneutic consciousness, is bound never to expect goodness in others. The other as other cannot be appreciated but is to be suspected, not respected. We should anticipate imperfection, not perfection. Desmond turns the tide again, and proposes a new version of the benevolent interpreter versus a constructionism of suspicion.

In intermediation, as sketched in Desmond, we come to understand that we are not alone, that otherness has a role to play, that there is something beyond our control. Another point that may make us more humble (and therefore more generous) is the fact that we are ourselves defined in a web of intermediating relativity with others in a community of being. We are involved, not only in self-mediation, but also in dialogue with otherness: 'We are what we are, not only through ourselves and our own activity, but also through our relatedness to others' (PU, 56). We are not everything, and we do not ourselves completely produce our own being. We are products of an original process, we are participants in the gift of being. The necessary togetherness and immersion of human selves in a community of being and beings may bring us to a state of mind beyond the privilege of self-determination without a sense of the other's goodness.

Also, in the aesthetic presence of creation we experience the elemental worthiness, the goodness of being and beings beyond ourselves. Desmond endorses a precognitive experience of value and goodness. The following quotation offers a good illustration of this:

> Think of being enveloped by a perfume of the good – the presence of an other so overcomes one that one is as if thrown into a swoon of longing. If one lacks such moments, has one lived? The sun is shining, there is a gentle breeze, the light falls over things with serene luminosity, and one wonders if one is just a step away from a secret paradise, and the consenting 'it is good'. (EB, 52, footnote 1)

Such experience confirms goodness beyond the human self. The fundamental fact that there is a reality, that there is an earth, that there are beings, is good. The gift of being is itself the first good of being. As Desmond notes: 'The good of being is not for the sake of anything in particular; to be is to be good; the good of being is to be, and to be is good' (BB, 505). To be sure, the celebration of being as good can always be doubted if one intellectually wishes to do so, but the critic's own explicit effort of being unavoidably testifies to another truth, namely that it is good that we are. It is good that there are plants, animals, rivers, mountains, and numerous other integrities of being. According to Desmond the idea that goodness is but a human construction imposed on worthless being only results in an unfruitful axiological anemia. In the end this will destroy our own value:

> For if the creation is valueless in itself then the human being as a participant in creation is also ontologically valueless, so likewise his human construction is also ultimately valueless. Every effort to construct values out of himself will be subject to the same deeper, primitive, ultimate valuelessness. Human values collapse ultimately into nothing, if there is not a ground of value in the integrity of being itself. (BB, 509)

The benevolent interpreter accepts the universality of non-human goodness. The worthiness of otherness subsequently installs the challenge to attempt to respect and articulate its original meaning. What is good in itself should be recognized, not subordinated.

What we need, so Desmond makes clear, is 'an active respect of the other, a courtesy to its being, an engagement with otherness that is not dominating' (PO, 105). This is agapeic minding. The benevolent interpreter is characterized by goodwill. This goodwill is part of our ethical experience: 'Our being ethical is exactly the struggle to widen the yes to being that is particularized in our self-insistence to all otherness' (PO, 173). While it is true that human beings are on the one hand the most self-insistent beings, we are on the other hand blessed with 'the most expansive openness to being beyond self, the greatest promise of agape of being relative to other' (BB, 518). Human interpreters have interpretative and moral capacities opening up opportunities beyond constructionism and erotic sovereignty. We can, in fact, become the 'promise of knowing alertness to all otherness' (PO, 222).

One important disposition within agapeic minding, besides humility and generosity, is patience. What matters is a longer staying with being and beings. In being patient to the other we are receptive to what comes to one out of the externality of the other. Desmond describes the patience of agapeic mind as a 'state of high alert that has nothing insistent about it', as 'a strange mix of patient readiness and active mind' (PO, 122). In such patience we become interested in the elemental, idiotic thereness of otherness. Desmond realizes the complexity of this elemental condition of human spirit. He understands that humans can never completely embody agapeic mindfulness: this state of mind will to some extent remain an ideal (PU, 119). One qualification is, of course, that human beings also have to use things in the world. We need to eat and survive. This unavoidably implies an existential role for erotic mind. But it is important for humans also to appreciate the surplus of agapeic mind and its possibilities beyond the framework of self-determination and self-concern.

I believe Desmond's sense of interpretative benevolence and agapeic mind embodies a stubborn project, namely to discover original meaning and value wherever it may be found. An authentic benevolent interpreter will want to receive as much significance as possible: it is for him or her a cause for joy not to be alone with value and intelligibility.

This benevolent stubbornness can be applied to the non-human world of plants and animals. Benevolent interpretation, in a metaxological setting, opens up the possibility of interpreting living nature in certain ways. There is, in fact, a moral urgency to do so. The way one talks about varieties of vegetal and animal otherness deeply influences the moral/immoral character of one's action towards these varieties. The denial of meaning gives free play to destruction or transformation of otherness. Once 'meaning' is acknowledged (not our sense of meaning, but meaning beyond us) it suddenly becomes much more difficult (albeit not impossible) not to turn toward a moral reception of non-human otherness.

Human Interpretation of Plants and Animals

On the basis of Desmond's theory of benevolent interpretation it is possible, with an eye on interpreting plants and animals as entities of original meaning and value, to set aside the workings of radical anthropomorphism, reductionism and productionism.

It is obvious that there are forms of anthropomorphic projectionism which one ought to avoid in a benign interpretation of vegetal and animal otherness. One popular form that comes to mind is projectionism in the style of Walt Disney. In cartoons we find trees and animals that speak. Certain theorists, however, consider every human interpretation and articulation of animal being as invalid human projections. A Desmondian perspective on the hermeneutical principles of difference, similarity and shared earthliness allows us to counter this view. True, there are many things we should avoid in our attempt to interpret nature. The naïve projectionist humanization of nature does not properly honour non-human otherness. But why would certain other human terms and interpretations be equally invalid to apply to animals and even plants? If a profound kinship with things is indeed engraved upon us, we ought not to resist the attempt to develop a subtle language in which to speak about the way of being of living nature. Metaxology confirms the possibility of such an approach. This is specifically backed up by Desmond's sense of a more refined anthropomorphism based upon a community between us and nature (BB, 424). The application of human words, combined with a sense of poetic refinement and terminological adaptation, is not automatically misdirected. The point is to sift out better articulations. The application of certain human metaphors, for example, may lead to 'a going of mind towards an original that cannot be exhaustively included in one univocal language' (BB, 101–2). According to Desmond, metaphors are vectors of transcendence and relatedness to otherness. Obviously, it is not a matter of uncomplicated application. Our anthropomorphic language certainly has to 'fight any temptation to think that the otherness of being is merely the mirror in which we recognize ourselves' (BB, 424). We need a benevolent anthropomorphic language focused on 'metaphors with the power to decenter us towards the otherness of nature' (ibid.). This otherness plays itself a role in the formation of our interpretations and articulations.

Think of a bat. We cannot directly enter the way of being of bats, but we can manage, if we wish, to become aware of how a bat flies, moves and eats. It provides us with an expressive testimony of its power to be. It is, and it is in a particular manner. Bats, and other animals, are 'immediacies of intelligibility which are self-mediating in their own right, and not just as a product of human mediation' (PO, 345). The otherness of bats, as it plays a role in intermediation between us and them, may guide the particular process of applying metaphors and concepts in a certain, transformed manner. We use human words and look with human eyes, but we know that what we see is not human. Experience of resistance will introduce the recognition of difference, often the recognition of difference in dimensions of being which in a more general sense are similar (bats and humans share eating as functional response, but their way of eating is of course not identical to ours). A benign and subtle anthropomorphism can, at least to some extent, arrive at an understanding of the non-human. We can understand something of the function of nutrition in plants. This is not something foreign to us. Of course, one should not ignore the fact that we shall never totally capture the singular thereness of animals and plants. Nonetheless, a process of better and worse interpretation of animal and vegetal particularities can be set up.

The metaxological version of anthropomorphism, especially in its affinities with the language of art (as an alternative to the univocalizing strategies of scientism, technics and mathematics), is interested in a nonreductive and nonproductionist celebration of animals and plants. For Galileo only a univocal mathematical reading of the book of nature makes sense. Without mathematics one would wander around in a dark labyrinth. For Desmond, however, there is singing outside calculation (PO, 103). The language of the aesthetic (including the language of metaphors) is unavoidable if we wish to understand something of nature as a process of becoming and of natural entities as idiotic singularities possessing their own worthiness.

A univocalizing, reductive interpretation of animals and plants automatically opens the gate for a productionist domination of nature. We are confronted with 'the flattening of the earth into a resource for our serviceable disposability' (AO, 253). In fact, productionism and reductionism install each other. Attempting to produce security and control in a fragile world in which we are placed in a posture of helplessness, we develop a univocal, often reductive interpretation of things. And nature without original meaning and value beyond mechanicism or *mathesis* justifies our urge to absorb nature into human history by way of industrialization and violent appropriation. The modern city has, so its seems, come to fulfil the dream of a technopolis: complete self-mediation in an entirely man-made environment (PO, 275). The city is a complex technological network where almost all that is has become a sign of human presence. Natural otherness is a regressing reality for most city-dwellers. To turn the tide of ecological crisis and violent appropriation and reduction of nature it will be important to install interpretations of plants and animals addressing the richness and original goodness and meaning of entities and processes beyond humanity.

The Question of Bionarration

Desmond himself has developed different 'poetic' sketches which attempt to appreciate the otherness of plants and animals.[4] However I have opted for a more independent approach. I shall seek to apply the metaphor of life story – a metaphor through which humans are accustomed to celebrate their own value, meaning and dignity – in a certain way to the world of plants and animals. I will clarify, thus, the problematics of bionarration. There is no theory of vegetal and animal life stories to be found in Desmond, but I believe that the hermeneutic possibility of bionarration (the application of life story in the natural world of plants and animals) is strongly in line with the spirit of his work; it is in line with the task of the benevolent interpreter to articulate meaning and value beyond humanity, it is in line with the metaxological review of anthropomorphism, and it is in line with Desmond's own way of applying certain human metaphors to nature. Concerning this last point one may especially refer to Desmond's application of 'community' – a human term often limited to the way of being of humans – to natural being.[5]

Numerous studies underline the deep connection between life story and humanity in the context of different academic disciplines such as psychology, history, literature, religion, law, and so forth. Narrative is everywhere in human existence. Human beings live with the complex perfective miracle of narrative signification, a miracle defining us in a most profound way. One may wonder whether something like life story could be of any relevance to the way of being of plants and animals. Many will be inclined to deny a connection of this kind and see humans as the only heroes of narrative being. However I think we should take up the challenge of formulating a sense of bionarration addressing the particular existence of plants and animals. Of course, if life story is somehow present in the vegetal and animal world, it cannot be identical with human storied existence. Nature does not speak in words and sentences. Only humans have the capacity to tell stories and can explicitly connect past, present and future. We must therefore discover, if possible at all, original qualities in terms of which non-human living nature can be properly comprehended in terms of life story. Let us begin with the realm of plants.

Plants do not narrate or interpret narratives themselves. They live a mindless, unconscious way of being. They are inactively intelligent. However this may still allow another kind of connection with the idea of a life story. Vegetary life has a beginning, a middle and an end. Things happen with and to plants. For example, confronted with an oak we sense a texture of histories. A storm may threaten the oak's existence, rain provides renewed opportunities, insects may make its life difficult.[6] A tree is in this way a history of progress and decay, a history exactly to be articulated in a narrative form. Vegetal history deserves to be told in the form of a story of a certain kind. To address the inherent dramatic nature of the existence of plants, narrative articulative means are necessary. The plant cannot tell its own story but other entities, namely human beings, can. We tell stories about our own lives and about the lives of other humans precisely because story is a proper, and in a sense the only proper, instrument by which to capture our own existential dramatic history. I believe the same narrative necessity is present when dealing with plants.

Not everyone will agree with this claim. Plants remain where they are, passive and immobile. Is the lack of mobility in plants not a sign of non-dramatic being, of a being without a history that deserves to be told? To sense the dramatism of plants it is fruitful to become aware of the different rhythms of being of plants and humans. We live with a rapid rhythm of time, but the time in which plants develop and exist is often situated on another scale. This scale is part of vegetal singularity. In nature shows we are sometimes confronted with an accelerated film about trees or flowers. We observe in a few minutes how a tree develops, what happens to it, how it recovers or fades away. This artificial acceleration makes much more visible the historical and dramatic texture of a tree. More directly and intensely, we observe growth, blossoming, development, recovery and decay. These observations support the idea of a vegetal effort to be one that invites articulation in terms of a life story that takes, or has taken, place.

This is all the more true because there are possible futures for a plant. The next moment or event may influence its chance to remain alive. These events cannot be completely predicted, even if plants as such have more predictable lives than humans or animals. Histories are processes that may evolve in different ways, owing to obstacles, sudden events and contingency. Each species is organized in response to regularities and contingencies of earthly being. This also introduces the element of suspense. Plants are organically directed toward survival, but things can go wrong. There is the presence of danger. Ultimately danger is deadly danger. Vegetal stories in this sense, like the stories of animals, are death stories. What is alive will die, and what can die is embedded in a narrative, a history characterized by suspense.

One other, very essential point allowing us to apply the metaphor of life story to the being of plants concerns the inherent good and value of plants: the fact that plants, themselves, are axiological entities. There are many things that matter to plants, even if plants cannot mentally conceive their own values. In line with this some things within the world are contributively important or valuable to a plant (water, minerals, earth, sun). Other things are contrary or neutral. Vegetal beings are values for themselves because, once given to be, they maintain their integrity and strive to perpetuate themselves (BB, 513). A plant preserves its life as a good. It is obvious that a plant cannot itself apprehend the good, but in our human interpretation of plants we can arrive at the idea of a vegetal axiology (on the basis of a hermeneutics of similarity). We know for ourselves what it means to be an effort to be. Precisely this dimension of value deepens the connection between the vegetal realm and narrative being. The narrative dimension as we know it best (namely in the context of human reality) is itself defined by essential reference to values and ends. Narratological studies (in the style of Greimas, Bremond and Genette) bring to light the fundamental axiological structure of human narratives. A 'hero', for example, is defined as striving to obtain certain things and to avoid others. Without such values, situated in time and space, there would be no dramatic history and there would be no striving deserving to be told. Since only living organisms, including plants, are axiologically structured, and since narrative expression is concerned with values, we can propose the idea of a vitalist narrative. Story, in one way or another, is a metaxologically adequate form by which to offer expression to the histories of living creatures. 'Bios' of this kind form a history deserving narrative articulation.

Narrative (vegetal) vitalism offers a first supplement to narrative humanism. Once the process of narrative vegetal appreciation has started, we should take care to make the reading of plants more adequate, always at a distance from reduction and uncontrolled projection. One of the complexities is to allow similarity its positive role (the resemblance between plants and humans as historical efforts-to-be), while also allowing the otherness of plants to remain in place. Plants are original versions of narrative being which cannot be fully captured in a hermeneutics of similarity. Vegetal narrative is not human narrative. However this should not prevent us from applying the concept of narrative being in its most basic interpretation to the world of plants, trees and flowers. Plants do not tell stories, do not have capacities of planning and self-reflection, and do not know themselves as narrative beings, but humans can and should read plants in a narrative manner. I think this is a conclusion quite continuous with the metaxological framework of Desmond. The idea of plant narrative has a place in a benign anthropomorphism in which human metaphors and terms are applied, with care, to the non-human world. The narrative view of plants, even while it remains to be seen how one could more concretely develop a narrative language proper to the way of being of plants, portrays non-human lives of meaning and value beyond radical and self-centered humanism.

What about the realm of animal being?

Our earlier findings concerning plants remain valid. Animals, too, are efforts to be, involved in axiological self-insistence and response to their surroundings. Of course, the histories and life stories of animals are far more complex than those of plants. They provide us with more intense opportunities for narrative interpretation. Vital narrative being is much more dramatically available in animals. Animals not only develop through time but are involved, much more visibly than plants, in differentiated forms of mutualism and antagonism. Animals move, fight, run away, look for partners, and protect their offspring. There is a complex life of action and interaction in animals. According to narratological theory the negative and positive relational dimension holds a central position in life stories on the human level. We live with friends and enemies, with helpers and antagonists. The actional and interactional complexities which we may observe in the animal world provide us with ample opportunity (in combination with issues such as development, axiology and suspense) to grant a sense of life story to animals.

Another fundamental narrative element emerges in the animal world, namely the dimension of animal interpretation and *semiosis*.[7] Human lives are in large part guided and controlled by the ways in which we are involved in signification, communication and interpretation. How could we even move around and make contact with our human others if not without interpretation and signs? The fact that human existence deserves to be told in the form of a life story (itself an eminent interpretative and semiotic undertaking) has much to do with our ways of interpretation and communication. The fact that we can consider animals as interpreters provides us with an interesting similarity with our own life stories. Animals live in *Umwelten* (subjective environments), based upon species-specific interpretation of aspects of being.[8] The world experience of a fly is drastically different from that of a bat or a scorpion. Animal environments are constituted as an interplay of things noticed and things acted upon. The same 'object' may constitute a different reality for different species. A table for humans is a thing to lie under for dogs. Specific interpretation defines the histories, and hence the life stories, of animal kinds. Interpretation, so it seems, is one cardinal expression of the animal effort to be. Interpretation matters to an entity which, in interpretation, expresses its concerns and interests. In combination with interpretation, animals are also involved in explicit *semiosis*, that is, in the production and reception of signs. In higher animals there are the more structured and explicit communications and signs, but *semiosis* comes in different shades and varieties. Think, for example, of the communication to others of one's territory in the form of chemical *semiosis* (urine). Think also, for example, of the ways that hares communicate to a fox that hunting them further has no meaning, by way of posing in a certain way (thereby communicating to the fox that he has been spotted in time). Interpretation and *semiosis* offer complex content to the idea of animal life stories.

Obviously there are numerous animal kinds. The interplay of similarity and difference will have to be played out differently with respect to different species. The application of life story, as part of a benign anthropomorphism, will mean something else when dealing with the history of a tick. The plot used to describe the life of a tick, capable of waiting in a tree for years until a mammal passes by, is likely to involve and excite humans much less than plots applied to the lives of dolphins or horses. However, hermeneutic generosity ought to bring us to acknowledge the originality and authentic perfection of the life story even of a tick. In their own functional context, animal competences and experiences are valuable, not as poor imitations of human performance, but as original ways of being. Even if animal desire will always be more pointillistic and circular than the desires of the human ape given to excess, in their own settings animals are masters; sometimes they master things better than humans. As Desmond points out:

> Many other animals outdo us in the range of sensuous attunement of eye or ear or nose. They sense a presence, where we feel nothing but the vacant wind; they see a prowler haunting the darkness which for us is only black night; they scent the coming of the thunder clap, while we balm heedlessly in the sleepy sun. Biologically they are on the alert, while we just picnic. (PO, 72)

The application of life story to animals (and animals) can help us to come to the realization that we, humans, are not islands of meaning in a desert of nothingness. Somewhere between the radical denial of narrative beyond humanity, and a too simple application of human narrative to the non-human, lies a fragile interpretative middle in which a basic scheme of natural life story can, and should, be articulated. One may, and many will, continue to doubt the relevance of human terms, such as narrative, for the interpretation of living nature. Ultimately one may end up without any conceptual means to say something about the non-human. But one should not forget that not speaking about nature by way of a creative and subtle anthropomorphism will lead us to ignore its original qualities. Then the languages of reduction and productionism will rule (as they in fact do now).

Conclusion

In this essay I wished to underline and clarify the role of Desmond's work for the development of a hermeneutics of plants and animals. As an alternative to constructionism he proposes an original theory of the benevolent interpreter, a theory which can subsequently be used in an assessment of the problematics of anthropomorphism. Countering the language of reduction and the human productionist drive, benevolent interpreters as depicted in Desmond find themselves confronted by the challenge to interpret and articulate nature's meaning by way of appropriate metaphors and concepts. The duty not to be silent is an urgent moral task in any environmental hermeneutics. Desmond makes this point particularly clear. We need benevolent interpreters who continue to bring up the issue of natural meaning and value in a variety of ways. I have attempted to address this need by way of a narrative treatment of plants and animals. The application of life story is meant to constitute one productive response directly inspired by the agapeic spirit of Desmond's comprehensive metaxological project.

Notes

1   To be sure, Desmond has not himself developed a reading of plants and animals in terms of life story. However, I consider such a reading an adequate application of metaxological interpretative benevolence. One inspirational model to use in this matter is Desmond's understanding of nature in terms of community. See BB, 417–61.
2   Richard Rorty, *Philosophy and Social Hope*, Harmondsworth: Penguin, 1999, p.xxvi.
3   On the idea of benevolent interpretation as developed in the hermeneutical tradition, see W. Künne, *Intentionalität und Verstehen*, Frankfurt am Main: Suhrkamp, 1990, pp.212–36.
4   See, for example, Desmond's words on swallows and on the heliotropic flower in BB, 318–19.
5   See reference in note 1.
6   W. Schapp, *In Geschichten Verstrickt*, Wiesbaden: Heyman, 1976.
7   The application of 'interpretation' and '*semiosis*' in the animal world is itself based upon a benign anthropomorphism. The application of 'interpretation' and '*semiosis*' in the world of plants remains a more difficult issue.
8   J. von Uexküll, *Kompositionslehre der Natur*, Frankfurt am Main: Ullstein, 1980.

A Bibliography of
William Desmond's Works

Books

Art and the Absolute: A Study of Hegel's Aesthetics, State University of New York Press, 1986.

Art, Origins, Otherness: Between Art and Philosophy, State University of New York Press, 2003.

Being and the Between, State University of New York Press, 1995; winner of the Prix Cardinal Mercier, 1995, for a work in metaphysics; winner of the J.N. Findlay award of the Metaphysical Society of America for the best book in metaphysics, 1994–5; Chinese and French translations in progress.

Being and Dialectic, edited with Joseph Grange, State University of New York Press, 2000.

Being Between: A Condition of (Irish) Thought?, to be published in the monograph series of the Centre for Irish Studies, National University of Ireland, Galway.

Beyond Conflict and Reduction: The Interplay of Philosophy, Science and Religion (editor), Louvain University Press, 2001.

Beyond Hegel and Dialectic: Speculation, Cult and Comedy, State University of New York Press, 1992.

Desire, Dialectic and Otherness: An Essay on Origins, Yale University Press, 1987.

Ethical Perspectives, **5** (4), guest editor for a special issue 'On Autonomy', 1998.

Ethics and the Between, State University of New York Press, 2001; Chinese translation in progress.

God and the Between, Blackwell, 2007.

Godsdienst/Filosofisch Bekeken, edited with Ignace Verhack and Paul Cortois, Pelckmans Uitgever, Belgium, 2003.

Hegel and His Critics: Philosophy in the Aftermath of Hegel (editor), State University of New York Press, 1989.

Hegel's God: A Counterfeit Double?, Ashgate, 2003.

Het tragische en het komische, Amsterdam: Boom, 1998 (translation of essays from *Beyond Hegel and Dialectic* and *Perplexity and Ultimacy*).

Is There a Sabbath for Thought? Between Religion and Philosophy, Series in Contemporary Continental Thought, John Caputo, General Editor, Fordham University Press, 2005.

Perplexity and Ultimacy: Metaphysical Thoughts from the Middle, State University of New York Press, 1995.

Philosophy and its Others: Ways of Being and Mind, State University of New York
Press, 1990; Portuguese translation by José Carlos Aquiar de Souza, *A Filosofia
e Seus Outros: Modos do Ser e do Pensar*, São Paulo, Brasil: Edicoes Loyola,
2000; Chinese translation in progress.

Philosophy and Religion in German Idealism, edited with Paul Cruysberghs and
Ernst Otto-Onnasch, Kluwer Publishing, 2004.

Translation and introduction to L. Heyde's *The Weight of Finitude: Concerning the
Philosophical Question of God*, State University of New York Press, 1999.

Articles

'Collingwood, Imagination and Epistemology', *Philosophical Studies* (Ireland),
XXIV, 1976, 82–103.

'Hegel, Art and Imitation', *Clio*, **7** (2), 1978, 303–13.

'Memory and Metaphysics', *Seminar*, **3**, 1979, 21–31.

'Hegel, Philosophy and Worship', *Cithara*, **19** (1), 1979, 3–20.

'Plato's Philosophical Art and the Identification of the Sophist', *Filosofia Oggi*, **11**
(4), 1979, 393–403.

'*Phronesis* and the Categorical Imperative', *Philosophical Studies* (Ireland),
XXVII, 1980, 7–15.

'St. Augustine's *Confessions*: On Desire, Conversion and Reflection', *Irish
Theological Quarterly*, **47** (1), 1980, 24–33.

'Hegel, History and Philosophical Contemporaneity', *Filosofia Oggi*, **4** (2), 1981,
211–26.

'The Child in Nietzsche's Menagerie', *Seminar*, **5**, 1981, 40–44.

'Hegel and the Problem of Religious Representation', *Philosophical Studies*
(Ireland), **XXX**, 1984, 9–22.

'Hegel, Art and History', Chapter 8, *History and System*, R.L. Perkins (ed.), SUNY
Press, 1984, 173–84.

'Art, Philosophy and Concreteness in Hegel', *The Owl of Minerva*, Spring, 1985,
131–46.

'Hegel, Dialectic and Deconstruction', *Philosophy and Rhetoric*, **18** (4), 1985,
244–63. Reprinted in *Nineteenth-Century Literature Criticism*, vol. 151,
R. Whittaker (ed.), Gale, 2005, 271–80.

'Hermeneutics and Hegel's Aesthetics', *The Irish Journal of Philosophy*, **2**, 1985,
94–104.

'Art as "Aesthetic" and "Religious" in Hegel', *Hegel's Philosophy of Spirit*, Peter
Stillmann (ed.), SUNY Press, 1986, 170–96.

'Schopenhauer, Art and the Dark Origin', *Schopenhauer*, Eric von der Luft (ed.),
Edwin Mellen Press, 1988, 101–22.

'Philosophy and Failure', *The Journal of Speculative Philosophy*, **II** (4), 1988,
288–305.

'God, Kearney and Contemporary European Philosophy', *The Irish Theological
Quarterly*, **54**, 1988, 237–42.

'Hegel, Legal Status and Otherness', *The Cardozo Law Review*, **10**, 5–6, 1989, 1713–26.

'Can Philosophy Laugh at Itself? On Hegel and Aristophanes', *The Owl of Minerva*, **20** (2), Spring 1989, 131–49.

'Art, Origins, Otherness: Hegel and Aesthetic Self-Mediation', *Philosophy and Art*, Dan Dahlstrom (ed.), Catholic University of America Press, 1991, 209–34.

'Being Between', *Clio*, **20** (4), 1991, 305–31.

'In Reply', *Clio*, **20** (4), 1991, 393–422.

'Evil and Dialectic', *New Perspectives in Hegel's Philosophy of Religion*, David Kolb (ed.), SUNY Press, 1992, 159–82.

'Being at a Loss: Reflections on Philosophy and the Tragic', *Tragedy and Philosophy*, Nenos Georgopoulos (ed.), Macmillan, 1993, 154–86.

'Thinking on the Double: the Equivocities of Dialectic', special jubilee edition of the *Owl of Minerva*, **25** (2), Spring 1994, 221–34, with other essays by past Presidents of the Hegel Society of America.

'Philosophies of Religion: Jaspers, Marcel, Lévinas', *Routledge History of Philosophy: Contemporary Continental Thought*, Richard Kearney (ed.), Routledge, 1994, 131–74. Reprinted in *Emmanuel Lévinas: Critical Assessments of Leading Philosophers*, *III*, Claire Katz (ed.) with Lara Trout, Routledge, 2005, 80–120.

'Perplexity and Ultimacy: Metaphysical Thoughts from the Middle', *Being Human in the Ultimate*, Michael Heim and Nenos Georgopoulos (eds), 1995, 101–33.

'Between Finitude and Infinity: Hegelian Reason and the Pascalian Heart', Presidential Address for the Hegel Society of America, October 1992, published in *Hegel on the Modern World*, Ardis Collins (ed.), SUNY Press, 1995, 1–28; also in *The Journal of Speculative Philosophy*, **IX** (2), 1995, 83–110.

'Creativity and the *Dunamis*', *The Philosophy of Paul Weiss: Library of Living Philosophers*, L. Hahn (ed.), 1995, 543–57.

'The *Mathesis* of Nature, the *Poeisis* of Naturing', *Journal of Dharma*, **XX** (4), October–December 1995, 321–33.

'Being, Dialectic and Determination: On the Sources of Metaphysical Thinking', Presidential Address for the Metaphysical Society of America, published in *The Review of Metaphysics*, **48**, June, 1995, 731–69.

'Rethinking the Origin: Hegel and Nietzsche', *Hegel, History and Interpretation*, Shaun Gallagher (ed.), SUNY Press, 1997, 71–94.

'Kant and the Terror of Genius: Between Enlightenment and Romanticism', *Kant's Aesthetics*, Herman Parret (ed.), de Gruyter, 1998, 594–614.

'The Solitudes of Philosophy', *Loneliness*, Lee Rouner (ed.), University of Notre Dame Press, 1998, 63–78.

Reprint of 'Thinking on the Double: The Equivocities of Dialectic', *The International Library of Classical Essays in the History of Philosophy, HEGEL, Volume II*, David Lamb (ed.), Ashgate, 1998, 171–84.

Reprint of 'Hermeneutics and Hegel's Aesthetics', *The International Library of Classical Essays in the History of Philosophy, HEGEL, Volume II*, David Lamb (ed.), Ashgate, 1998, 335–45.

Reprint of 'Hegel and the Problem of Religious Representation', *The International Library of Classical Essays in the History of Philosophy, HEGEL, Volume II*, David Lamb (ed.), Ashgate, 1998, 405–18.

'Philosophical Audacity – Shestov's Piety', *Lev Shestov Journal*, **Winter** (2), 1998, 45–80.

'Serviceable Disposability and the Blandness of the Good', *Ethical Perspectives*, **5** (2), 1998, 136–43.

'Dream Monologues of Autonomy', *Ethical Perspectives*, **5** (4), 1998, 305–21.

'*Autonomia Turranos*: On Some Dialectical Equivocities of Self-determination', *Ethical Perspectives*, **5** (4), 1998, 233–52.

Interview with Richard Eldridge, *Ethical Perspectives*, **5** (4), 1998, 285–304.

'Dream Monologues of Autonomy', *Ethical Perspectives*, **5** (4), 1998, 305–21.

'Freedom Beyond Autonomy', *Freedom in Contemporary Culture*, University of Lublin Press, 1999, 163–74.

'God, Ethos, Ways', *International Journal of the Philosophy of Religion*, **45**, 1999, 13–30; also published in *God and Argument/Dieu et argumentation*, William Sweet (ed.), University of Ottawa Press, 1999, 65–83.

'Caesar with the Soul of Christ: Nietzsche's Highest Impossibility', *Tijdschrift voor Filosofie*, **61**, 1999, 27–61.

'Gothic Hegel', *The Owl of Minerva*, **30** (2), Spring, 1999, 237–52.

'Hyperbolic Thoughts: On Creation and Nothing', *Framing a Vision of the World: Essays in Philosophy, Science and Religion*, Santiago Sia and Andre Cloots (eds), Louvain University Press, 1999, 23–43.

'Over Gott en het Transcendentale Ego', *Reflectie en Fundering – Studies van het Centrum voor Duits Idealisme*, 1999, 79–85.

'Chinese Philosophy and the Problems of Modernity – A Reply', *Contemporary Chinese Thought*, Summer, 1999, 75–80.

'Art and the Impossible Burden of Transcendence: On the End of Art and the Task of Metaphysics', *Hegel-Jahrbuch*, 2000, 75–91.

'Art and the Absolute Revisited: The Neglect of Hegel's Aesthetics', *Hegel's Aesthetics*, William Maker (ed.), SUNY Press, 2000, 1–12.

'Philosophy of Religion', *The Examined Life*, Stanley Rosen (ed.), Random House, 2000, 105–23.

'God beyond the Whole: Between Shestov and Solov'ëv', *Vladimir Solov'ëv: Reconciler and Polemicist*, Selected Papers of the International Solov'ëv Conference, University of Nijmegen, September, 1998, Wil van den Bercken *et al.* (eds), Peeters, 2000, 185–210.

'On the Betrayals of Reverence', *Irish Theological Quarterly*, **65** (3), 2000, 211–30; also in *Beyond Conflict and Reduction: Between Philosophy, Science and Religion*, W. Desmond, J. Steffen and K. Decoster (eds), Leuven University Press, 2001, 175–98. Selected proceedings of the International Conference on The Interplay of Philosophy, Science and Religion, Leuven, November, 1998.

'Neither Deconstruction nor Reconstruction: Metaphysics and the Intimate Strangeness of Being', *International Philosophical Quarterly*, March, 2000, 37–49.

'On Obedience and Conscience', *Studies van het Centrum voor Duits Idealisme*, II, 2000, 53–6.

'Murdering Sleep: Shestov and *Macbeth*', Ramona Fotiade (ed.), *The Tragic Discourse: Shestov and Fondane's Existential Thought* (Peter Lang, 2006), 67–78.

'Enemies', *Tijdschrift voor Filosofie*, **63**, 2001, 127–51; also in *Yearbook of the Irish Philosophical Society*, Thomas A.F. Kelly (ed.), 22–37.

'Exceeding the Measure: On Ethics and the Between', *Ethical Perspectives*, **8** (4), 2001, 319–331.

'Response to Ignace Verhack', *Ethical Perspectives*, **8** (4), 2001, 250–53.

'Response to Garrett Barden', *Ethical Perspectives*, **8** (4), 2001, 268–71.

'Response to Cyril O'Regan', *Ethical Perspectives*, **8** (4), 2001, 303–6.

'Response to Arnold Burms', *Ethical Perspectives*, **8** (4), 2001, 313–18.

'Sticky Evil: On *Macbeth* and the Karma of the Equivocal', *God, Literature and Process Thought*, Darren Middleton (ed.), Ashgate, 2002, 133–55.

'On the Secret Sources of Strengthening: Philosophical Reflections on Courage', *Courage*, Barbara Darling-Smith (ed.), University of Notre Dame Press, 2002, 11–29.

'Surplus Immediacy and the Defect(ion) of Hegel's Concept', *Philosophy and Culture: Essays in Honor of Donald Phillip Verene*, Glenn Alexander Magee (ed.), Charlottesville, Virginia: Philosophy Documentation Center, 2002, 107–27.

'Religious Imagination and the Counterfeit Doubles of God', *Louvain Studies*, Fall, 2002, 280–305.

'A Second Primavera: Cavell, German Philosophy and Romanticism', *Stanley Cavell*, R. Eldridge (ed.), Cambridge University Press, 2003, 143–71.

'Maybe, Maybe Not: Richard Kearney and God', *Irish Theological Quarterly*, **68** (2), 2003, 99–118.

'Het intiem-universele: tussen religie en filosofie', *Godsdienst/Filosofisch Bekeken*, W. Desmond *et al.* (eds), Pelckmans, 2003, 71–87.

'Exceeding Virtue: Aquinas and the Beatitudes', Aquinas Lecture, Maynooth, 2003, to be published in the next volume of the collected lectures.

'Religion and the Poverty of Philosophy', *Philosophy and Religion in German Idealism*, W. Desmond *et al.* (eds), Kluwer, 2004, 139–70.

'Tyranny and the Recess of Friendship', *Amor Amicitiae: On the Love that is Friendship*, Thomas Kelly and Philipp Rosemann (eds), Peeters, 2004, 99–125.

'*Paidea*: Anachronism or Necessity?', *Educating for Democracy: Paideia in an Age of Uncertainty*, Alan Olson *et al.* (eds), Rowan and Littlefield, 2004, 11–24.

'The Need of Finesse: The Information Society and the Sources of Ethical Formation', *Ethics and Values in a Digital Age*, Report of the Information Society Commision, Department of the Taoiseach, Government of Ireland, December 2004, 24–39.

'Autonomy, Loyalty and Civic Education', *Civic Education and Culture*, Bradley, C.S. Watson (ed.), ISI Books, 2005, 15–28.

'Neither Servility nor Sovereignty: Between Politics and Metaphysics', *Theology and the Political*, C. Davis, J. Milbank and S. Zizek (eds), Duke University Press, 2005, 153–82.

'Consecrated Thought: Between the Priest and the Philosopher', *Louvain Studies*, **30** (2005), 92–106.

'Is there Metaphysics after Critique?', *International Philosophical Quarterly*, **45** (2), June 2005, 221–41.

'Consecrated Love: A Philosophical Reflection on Marriage', *INTAMS Review*, **II**, Spring 2005, 4–17.

'Hegel's God, Transcendence and the Counterfeit Double', *The Owl of Minerva*, **36** (2), Spring/Summer 2005, 91–110.

'Response to De Nys', *The Owl of Minerva*, **36** (2), Spring/Summer 2005, 165–74.

'Response to Houlgate', *The Owl of Minerva*, **36** (2), Spring/Summer 2005, 175–88.

'Response to Hodgson', *The Owl of Minerva*, **36** (2), Spring/Summer 2005, 189–200.

'Doing Justice and the Practice of Philosophy', American Catholic Philosophical Association, *Proceedings of the ACPA*, 2005, **79**, 41–59.

'Pluralism, Truthfulness and the Patience of Being', *Health and Human Flourishing: Religion, Medicine and Moral Anthropology*, Carol R. Taylor and Roberto Dell'Oro (eds), Georgetown University Press, 2006, ch. 3.

Reviews and Review Articles

William Barrett, *The Illusion of Technique*; *Independent Journal of Philosophy*, **III**, 1979, 148–9.

Ralph S. Walker, *Kant: The Arguments of the Philosophers*; *Philosophical Studies* (Ireland), **XXVII**, 1979, 364–9.

Simone Weil, *Lectures on Philosophy*; *Philosophical Studies* (Ireland), **XXVII**, 1980, 387–8.

Warren E. Steinkraus and Kenneth L. Schmitz, *Art and Logic in Hegel's Philosophy*; *The Owl of Minerva*, **12** (4), June 1981, 7–9.

Erazim Kohak, *Idea and Experience*; *Philosophical Studies* (Ireland), **XXVIII**, 1981, 362–7.

William Dray, *Perspectives on History*; *Philosophical Studies* (Ireland), **XXVIII**, 1981, 367–9.

The Philosophers' Annual, Vol. II; *Philosophical Studies* (Ireland), **XXVIII**, 1981, 369–70.

Stanley Rosen, *The Limits of Analysis*; *Philosophical Studies* (Ireland), **XXIX**, 1982–3, 318–22.

Carl Vaught, *The Quest for Wholeness*; *Philosophical Studies* (Ireland), **XXIX**, 1982–3, 322–6.

Agnes Heller, *A Theory of History*; *Philosophical Studies* (Ireland), **XXIX**, 1982–3, 326–8.

D.D. Raphael, *Moral Philosophy*; *Philosophical Studies* (Ireland), **XXIX**, 1982–3, 317–8.

James Yerkes, *Hegel's Christology*; *Bulletin of the Hegel Society of Great Britain*, **8**, Autumn/Winter 1983, 25–7.

Peter Singer, *Hegel*; *Philosophical Studies* (Ireland), **XXX**, 1984, 334–5.

Piotr Hoffman, *The Anatomy of Idealism*; *Philosophical Studies* (Ireland), **XXX**, 1984, 335–8.

Richard Carter, *Descartes' Medical Philosophy*; *Phenomenological Inquiry*, **9**, 1985, 118–21.

Richard Kearney, *Dialogues with Contemporary Thinkers*; *Review of Metaphysics*, September 1985, 160–62.

Brian Martine, *Individuals and Individuality*; *Review of Metaphysics*, March 1986, 572–4.

Werner Marx, *Schelling*; *Review of Metaphysics*, June 1986, 778–9.

Richard Kearney, *The Irish Mind*; *Philosophical Studies* (Ireland), **XXXI**, 1986–7, 374–80.

Charles Hartshorne, *The Divine Relativity*; *Philosophical Studies* (Ireland), **XXXI**, 1986–7, 475–7.

Clark Butler and Christine Seiler, *Hegel's Letters*; *The Owl of Minerva*, Spring 1986, 204–8.

F.C. McGrath, *The Sensible Spirit*; *Bulletin of the Hegel Society of Great Britain*, **14**, Autumn/Winter 1986, 49–52.

Stephen Bunjay, *Beauty and Truth*; *Journal of the History of Philosophy*, April 1987, 307–9.

Alan White, *Absolute Knowledge*; *Review of Metaphysics*, September 1987, 170–71.

H.G. Gadamer, *The Relevance of the Beautiful*; *Review of Metaphysics*, December 1987, 386–9.

Piotr Hoffman, *Doubt, Time, Violence*; *Canadian Philosophical Review*, **12** (12), December 1987, 497–8.

Werner Marx, *Hegel's Phenomenology of Spirit*; *Review of Metaphysics*, June 1989, 845–7.

Trudy Govier, *God, the Devil and the Perfect Pizza*, and Donald Palmer, *Looking at Teaching*; *Teaching Philosophy*, **13** (3), September 1990, 306–8.

S.A. Grave, *Conscience in Newman's Thought*; *Review of Metaphysics*, June 1991, 883–4.

Donald Stoll, *Philosophy and the Community of Speech*; *Philosophy and Rhetoric*, **24** (3), 1991, 267–70.

Andrew Bowie, *Aesthetics and Subjectivity*; *International Studies in Philosophy*, **XXIV** (2), 1992, 125–6.

Andrew Shanks, *Hegel's Political Theology*; The Owl of Minerva, **24** (2), Spring 1993, 207-8.

Pierre Bourdieu, *The Political Ontology of Martin Heidegger*; International Journal of Philosophical Studies, **2**, 1992, 147–8.

Giacomo Rinaldi, *A History and Interpretation of Hegel's Logic*; International Journal of Philosophical Studies, 1993, 381–3.

Merold Westphal, *Suspicion and Faith*; International Philosophical Quarterly, **XXXIV** (4), December, 1994, 511–12.

Joseph Dunne, *Back to the Rough Ground*; The Review of Metaphysics, March, 1995, 654–5.

Louis Dupré, *Passage to Modernity*; American Catholic Philosophical Quarterly, **LXX**, Winter 1996, 298–300.

Leszek Kolakowski, *God Owes us Nothing*; Modern Theology, **12** (4), October, 1996, 489–91.

Harvie Ferguson, *Melancholy and the Critique of Modernity*; Tijdschrift voor Filosofie, **58** (4), December 1996, 765–8.

Richard Kearney, *Poetics of Modernity*; Tijdschrift voor Filosofie, **58** (4), December 1996, 785–6.

Gilian Rose, *Mourning Becomes the Law*; Modern Theology, **13** (4), October 1997, 539–41.

Richard Winfield, *Systematic Aesthetics*; Clio, **26** (3), 1997, 384–90.

Joseph Grange, *Nature*; Tijdschrift voor Filosofie, June 1998, 407.

Robert Nozick, *Socratic Puzzles*; Tijdschrift voor Filosofie, June 1998, 418.

Maria Antonaccio and William Schweiker (eds), *Iris Murdoch and the Search for Human Goodness*; The Journal of Religion, October 1998, **78** (4), 648–9.

Catherine Pickstock, *After Writing*; Modern Theology, January 1999, **15** (1), 99–100.

D. MacGregor, *Hegel and Marx after the Fall of Communism*; Tijdschrift voor Filosofie, **61**, 1999, 381–2.

S. Barnett (ed.), *Hegel after Derrida*; Tijdschrift voor Filosofie, **61**, 1999, 382–3.

Edward Pols, *Mind Regained*; Tijdschrift voor Filosofie, **61**, 1999, 394–6.

Jerome Schneewind, *The Invention of Autonomy*; Tijdschrift voor Filosofie, **61**, 1999, 398–400.

Thomas Carlson, *Indiscretion: Finitude and the Naming of God*; Modern Theology, **16** (2), 244–7.

Melvin Woody, *Freedom's Embrace*; International Philosophical Journal, **8** (1), 143–5.

C. Janaway (ed.), *Willing and Nothingness*; Tijdschrift voor Filosofie, **61** (4), December 1999, 802–5.

James Marsh, *Critique, Action and Liberation* and *Process, Praxis and Transcendence*; Tijdschrift voor Filosofie, **61** (4), 820–25.

S. Rosen, *Metaphysics in Ordinary Language*; Tijdschrift voor Filosofie, **62** (1), 156–60.

A. Wood, *Kant's Ethical Thought*; *Tijdschrift voor Filosofie*, **62** (4), 758–9.

J. Llewelyn, *The HypoCritical Imagination: Between Kant and Lévinas*; *Tijdschrift voor Filosofie*, **62** (4), 759–61.

Merold Westphal (ed.), *Christianity and Postmodernism*; *Tijdschrift voor Filosofie*, **63** (1), 2001, 183–5.

Terry Pinkard, *Hegel: A Biography*; *Tijdschrift voor Filosofie*, **63** (2), 414–16.

Robert Wood, *Placing Aesthetics*; *Tijdschrift voor Filosofie*, **63** (2), 432–4.

I. Lévinas, *Entre Nous*; *Ethical Perspectives*, **8**, 2001, 65–6.

Alan Badiou, *Ethics: An Essay on the Understanding of Evil; Ethical Perspectives*, **8** (2), 2001, 130–31.

James W. Felt, *Coming to Be: Toward a Thomistic-Whiteheadian Metaphysics of Becoming*; *Tijdschrift voor Filosofie*, **64** (3), 2002, 602–4.

Cyril O'Regan, *Gnostic Return in Modernity* and Cyril O'Regan, *Gnostic Apocalypse: Jacob Boehme's Haunted Narrative*; *Tijdschrift voor Filosofie*, **64** (3), 2002, 607–11.

Eero Tarasti, *Existential Semiotics*; *International Philosophical Quarterly*, **42** (4), December 2002, 547–9.

Charles Taylor, *A Catholic Modernity*; *Modern Theology*, **19** (1), January 2003, 141–3.

Joseph Bracken, *The One in the Many*; *Tijdschrift voor Filosofie*, **66** (1), 2004, 168–70.

Stephen Holland, *Bioethics: A Philosophical Introduction*; *Ethical Perspectives*, 11, 2004, 205–6.

Michael Mack, *German Idealism and the Jew*; *The Journal of Religion*, **84** (4), October 2004, 660–61.

Donald Verene, *Knowledge of Things Human and Divine: Vico's New Science and Finnegan's Wake*; *Journal of the History of Philosophy*, **43** (3), July 2005, 362–3.

Discussion of Desmond's Work

The journal *CLIO*, **20** (4), Summer 1991, 'Willian Desmond: Beyond Hegel? – Discussion and Response', is devoted to the discussion of Desmond's work. It includes a preface by the editor, Clarke Butler, essays by Merold Westphal, Brian Martine, and Stephen Houlgate, an essay in intellectual autobiography by Desmond, and an essay in reply to commentary and criticism.

Ethical Perspectives, **8** (4), (2001), was devoted to discussions of *Ethics and the Between*, with articles by Cyril O'Regan, Ignace Verhack, Arnold Burms, and Garrett Barden, with Desmond's responses, as well as an essay.

The Owl of Minerva, Spring 2005, Journal of the Hegel Society of America, special edition dedicated to essays discussing *Hegel's God*. Contains William Desmond, 'Hegel's God, Transcendence and the Counterfeit Double', as well as responses to critics; also Martin De Nys ('Conceiving Divine

Transcendence'), Peter Hodgson ('Hegel's God: Counterfeit or Real?'), and Stephen Houlgate ('Hegel, Desmond and the Problem of God's Transcendence').

Other Publications

Between 1980 and 1987 Desmond also published a regular weekly column on issues in philosophy in the Tuesday magazine of the *Cork Examiner* for a less specialized audience. Over 200 pieces appeared.

Index

Abelard, Peter 68
'absolute originals' 126, 241
achronicity 76
'acme moments' 243
'actual infinitude' 126–7
'adolescent freedom' 141–3
aesthetics 73–4, 83, 281, 287
agape and agapeic thinking 5–8, 102, 108,
    126, 129–30, 151–3, 157–9, 170–73,
    191–5, 239–45, 280–85
d'Alembert, Jean le Rond 82
alterity 3, 104–5
analogy, doctrine of 68
animals, human interpretation of 285–92
anthropocentrism 262, 265–72, 285–91
Aquinas, Thomas 16, 55, 68, 102, 107,
    113, 218, 230–31; *see also* Thomism
'archaeology' 129, 134
architecture 8, 261–74
Aristophanes 75, 100–103, 181–6
Aristotle and Aristotelianism 3, 16, 28, 33,
    55, 57, 97, 100, 102, 163, 165,
    219–21, 240
Arnold, Matthew 153
Athenian law 178
Augustine, St 8, 68, 70, 80–81, 107–20,
    125–7, 130–34, 195
Averoës 68
Avicenna 113
Ayer, AJ 108

Bacon, Francis 71, 75–84
Badiou, Alain 108
bats 286
Behe, Michael 218
benevolent interpretation, theory of
    279–85, 291
Bergson, Henri 224–32
Berkely, George 3–4
'between', meanings of 6, 14–16
bionarration 287–8

Bonaventure, St 218
Boulez, Pierre 225, 231
Bradley, FH 41
Bridgewater Treatises 218–19
Bruno, Giordano 79, 229
Buchanan, Peter 265
Burke, Edmund 157

Calderón de la Barca, Pedro   232–3
Carlyle, Thomas 227, 232–3
Catholic Church 1, 24, 30–31
charity 157–9
Christianty and Christian tradition 6, 44–6,
    80, 114, 120
Cicero 80, 84
'cinematic' approach to philosophy 63
'conceptual persona' 62
conic sections 152–6
conservationism 272–3, 279–85
conversion, religious 130–34
Copernicus, Nicolaus 155
Cork Examiner 30
creation
    as distinct from evolution 217–18
    story of 45, 109–12, 130–31, 198
creative design 218
curiosity 78, 117

Darwin, Charles (and Darwinism) 218–23
Dasein 4–5, 69
Dawkins, Richard 220–23
Day, Christopher 261
deconstruction 95, 101–3
Deleuze, Gilles 19, 55, 61–3, 108, 225–31
Denken 100
Derrida, Jacques 53, 57, 95, 99–104, 193,
    226–7
Descartes, René 4, 18, 21, 23, 46, 62, 67,
    70, 75–80, 83–4, 100, 108, 119–20,
    263, 266–70
Desmond, William